Framing the Mahābhārata

Other Works by the Author

Boots, Hooves, and Wheels: And the Social Dynamics behind South Asian Warfare

Framing the Mahābhārata

Against the Evolution of Early South Asian Society

Saikat K. Bose

Vij Books India Pvt Ltd
New Delhi (India)

Published by

Vij Books India Pvt Ltd
(Publishers, Distributors & Importers)
2/19, Ansari Road
Delhi – 110 002
Phones: 91-11-43596460, 91-11-47340674
Fax: 91-11-47340674
e-mail: vijbooks@rediffmail.com

ISBN: 978-93-86457-56-1 (Paperback)

ISBN: 978-93-86457-57-8 (ebook)

The views expressed in the book are of the author alone, and do not represent views or opinions of the Indian Army, the publishers, or any other institution in any manner whatsoever.

To my Father

Contents

Preface ix

Acknowledgment xiii

Pronunciation Guide xv

Abbreviations xvi

List of Maps and Figures

Map 1: Migratory Corridors and Zones of Conflict xvii

Map 2: Places and Polities in the Mahābhārata xviii

Map 3: The Indo–Gangetic Divide xix

Map 4: Sites Traditionally Associated with the Battle xx

Figure 5: Anatomy of the Vipatha Chariot xxi

Introduction 1

Chapter 1 Format, Structure and Growth of the Epic 16

Chapter 2 The Backdrop of the Proto-Indo–Iranian Migrations 32

Chapter 3 Imperial Assimilation by the Bharata 68

Chapter 4 Formation of the Kuru–Pañcāla Moiety 112

Chapter 5 The Pāṇḍu and the Yadu 145

Chapter 6	The Armies, and Nature of Combat	190
Chapter 7	Reconstructing the Battle	230
Chapter 8	The Fallout	269
Epilogue		312
Bibliography		315
Index		351

Preface

I do three things in *Framing the Mahabharata*. The first is, I try to inspect the nature, content and structure of the epic, hoping to identify who the groups, peoples, and individuals involved in the war, and what their reasons to go to war, were. I thus try to see what each of these groups or individuals hoped to win or stood to lose, and how each defined winning and losing. Assuming I get this correct, I then seek to understand how they fought, aiming at a reconstruction of the course of battle.

Next, I examine the consequences of the war, aiming to understand how the war impacted evolution of South Asian society. Surveying several disciplines—history and ethnology, military science and technology, sociology and economics, comparative mythology and religion—I build on insights of several experts (and respectfully deconstruct those of several others) to construct a model of early Indo–European and Indo–Iranian folk movement. It is against this backdrop that evolution in lifestyles, social norms, warfighting procedures, and the numerous correlations between these aspects, are framed. For instance, an aspect that most poignantly illustrates the evolution is the emergence, growth, culmination, and obsolescence of war-chariotry.

The third thing I attempt in this work is to place the epic story, its associated compendia of narrative material, and narrative traditions of South Asia, against the backdrop of evolving socioeconomics and religious consciousness over the more-than-a-millennium gap between the war and the appearance of the first acknowledged extant version of the epic. This helps not only understand the classical forms of current South Asian religious thought, but also the societal forces that gave the epic its shape and timbre, making it what it is today.

The war, which is the epic's centrepiece, occurred among peoples at the cusp of the Bronze and Iron Ages, and situated at different points of view in a very dynamic milieu. This milieu had resulted from semi-nomadic and pastoral social forms coming to terms with forms that were at various stages of being sedentary, agrarian, and urbanized. Thus, tales and battle-lays kept *evolving*, taking on hues, colours, and purposes, often becoming rather unrepresentative of reality. Also, the epic acquired endless tales nested into tales, often with no relation to the plot, and for a variety of purposes not all related to the narration of the battle-story. In the process, individuals, groups and events got covered with hyperbole, engendered by evolving social consciousnesses and agendas. This naturally led to many apparent exaggerations, misrepresentations and inconsistencies, which makes it difficult to take every event in the epic at face value.

The renascence of mythology, seen in books on myth, religion and epic flooding bookshelves in Indian, Europe, Africa and the Americas, has had a social cost. Where older generations had grown up with *personal* ideas of epic or mythic landscapes, characters and events, younger generations today, under audio-visual assault of television, movies, animations, video and computer games, harbour corporatized and homogenized ideas of these things. In other words, others having done their imagination for them, power of imagination of the growing generations is stifled. In such a situation, it is easy to promote the epics as vivid costume dramas, often sponsoring sanitised but inaccurate, and anachronistic, ideas.

The above discussion shows that, just as it would be impractical to accept everything at face value, discarding the epic in its entirety as ahistorical would be akin to throwing the baby out with the bath-water. I say this because much of the exaggerations do portray socioeconomic backdrop of the epic—if nothing, they represent what people that wrote, edited, modified and used the epic, thought and felt about their past, present, and future.

What I do here is to seek a mean. I deal with events and characters *not as historically accurate facts, but as concepts*, after stripping them of hyperbole and agglomerated layers. Indeed, these were concepts, and very much live at that time, their resolution impacting the community in several crucial ways. For instance, whether Karṇa or Aśvatthāmā were indeed chiefs of nomad tribes of the Northwest or not, *there were* nomad chiefs of the Northwest who impacted the dynamics of the Indo–Gangetic plains in the way represented in the stories of the epic Karṇa or Aśvatthāmā.

Likewise, I treat the Yadu as a conglomeration of pastoral groups jostling for control over the southern end of the Indo–Gangetic Divide, at that time in the throes of changing social formats represented by Kaṅsa's attempt to subvert the matrilineal succession and Krishna's leading away the Vṛṣṇi, a more rugged, nomadic sept of the Yadu. In other words, whether these personae, families and tribes were real or not is not important—what is important is that such occurrences and traditions were real, have been noted in many parts of the world, and might not have been improbable in this part of the world, too.

It is these aims that I try to achieve, hoping at the end of the steps outlined above, to create a base model for early South Asian society which can be built upon. I also hope that this work will contribute towards restoration of part of the lost imagination.

Acknowledgment

This book seems to have taken shape on its own, while I worked on my earlier book and also indulged myself in the reading of comparative mythology. Thus, all persons who I thanked for my first work I thank again. As I thank innumerable others who have helped me specifically in this venture. Acknowledging the influence of those who built up in me, on the one hand, love for the epic and mythology, and on the other, a love for rational investigation, I want to thank the older generations of the nation, and specifically my parents.

I want to thank that splendid brotherhood, my battalion, which I spent some of my happiest years with. My friends Prateeksha and Sukanya have, as always, been great helps in the shaping of my ideas, giving the ideas their forms, and helping me put them on paper sensibly. I can never thank Brigadier Hardeep Narang enough for his kindness in giving me unrestrained access to his wondrous library of military images, a master's work in itself. I specifically want to remember Gajinder, Ratan, Arjun and Anil, for making sure I had the leisure to work on the project without having to think too much of other things. Brigadier PK Vij has always been a guide who was there, encouraging me and letting me know I could count upon him.

Pronunciation Guide

IAST is used for Sanskrit and affiliated words. Other words have been represented by a sound approximation.

Element	***Pronounced like ...***
a	*'u' in but.*
ā	*'a' in cart.*
ai	*'i' in gripe.*
au	*'ow' as in clown, but shorter.*
c	*'ch' in chap.*
d	*Close to 'th' in then.*
ḍ	*A heavy, reflexive 'd', heavier than in den.*
e	*'ai' in pain.*
ḥ	*Aspirated 'gh', in ugh.*
i	*'i' in pin.*
ī	*'ee' in preen.*
n	*'n' in den.*
ṇ	*A heavy n, merging with the reflexive*
ñ	*'n' in ranch.*
ṅ	*'n' in junk.*
ṛ	*'wri' in wring.*
s	*'s' in sip.*
ś	*Sharp 'sh', in ship.*
ṣ	*A heavy, reflexive 'shh'; in some regional dialects it tends towards kh.*
t	*Soft 't'.*
ṭ	*Hard, reflexive 't'.*
u	*'u' in put.*
ū	*'oo' in boot.*
'ch', 'jh', 'th', 'dh', 'ṭh' and 'ḍh'	*All aspirated versions of the first character.*

Abbreviations

BMAC	Bactria–Margiana Archaeological Complex
BORI	The Bhandarkar Research Institute, Pune.
BOTK	Battle of Ten Kings.
BRW	Black and Red Ware
IA	Indo–Aryans
IE	Indo–Europeans
IIr	Indo–Iranian.
Ir	Iranian.
IVC	Indus Valley Civilization.
NBPW	Northern Black Polished Ware
NWFP	North–West Frontier Province.
OCP	Ochre Coloured Pottery
PGW	Painted Grey Ware
PIE	Proto-Indo–European.

Abbreviated/ shortened forms of names of texts, like *Ait.Br* for the *Aitereya Brahmana*, appears in the Bibliography. Journal names have been left un-shortened.

MAP 1: MIGRATORY CORRIDORS AND ZONES OF CONFLICT

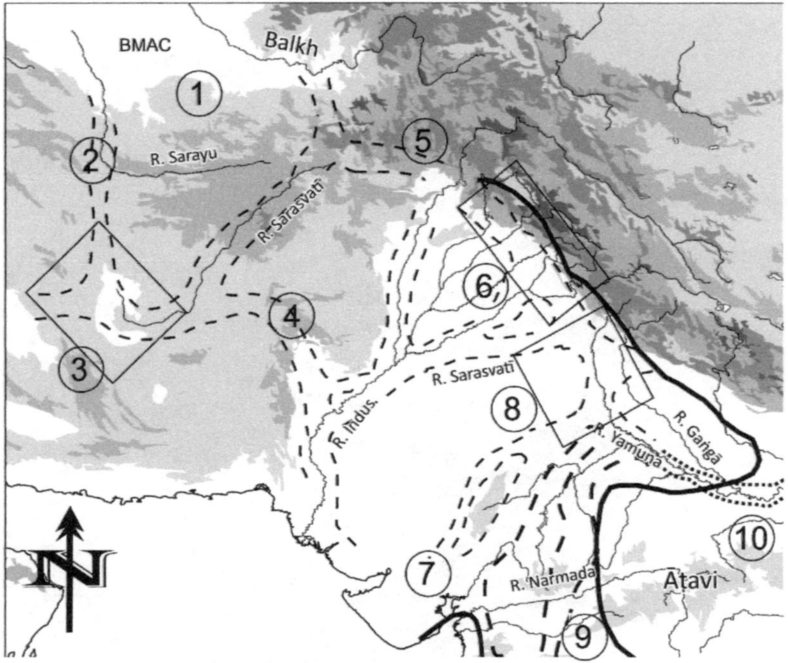

Pastoral Corridors

Amphibious Corridors

1. Early Zone of Early Conflict
2. Sarayu Corridor
3. Congregation - Hamun / Dasht-e-Margow flats
4. Bolan route
5. Khyber - Gomal route
6. Uttarāpatha and the *Daśarājña*
7. Aparānta
8. Kurukṣetra, and the zone of conflict
9. Dakṣiṇāpatha
10. Prācya

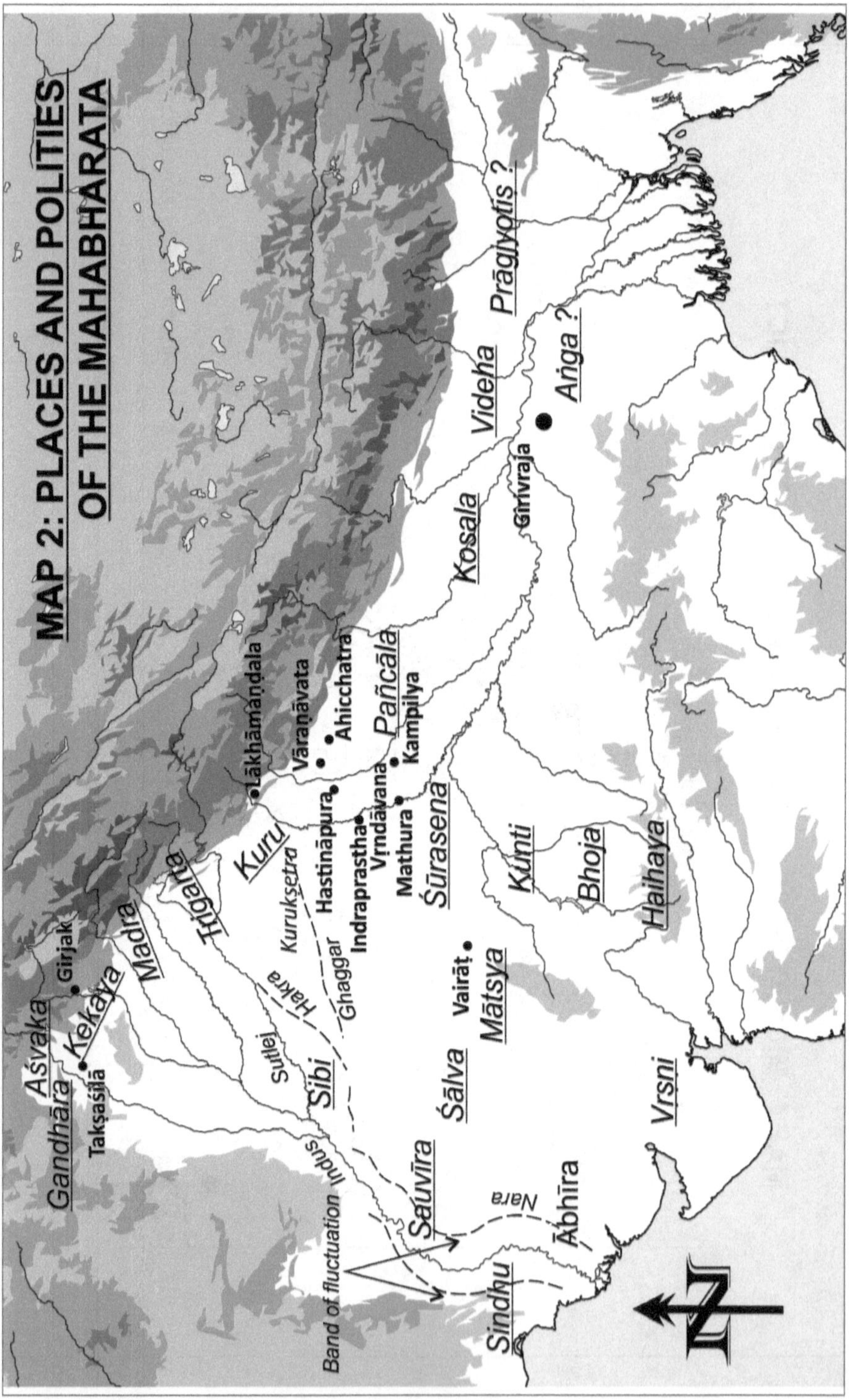
MAP 2: PLACES AND POLITIES
OF THE MAHABHARATA
Gandhāra
Aśvaka
Takṣaśilā
Kekaya
Girjak
Madra
Trigarta
Kuru
Kurukṣetra
Lākhāmaṇḍala
Vāraṇāvata
Ahicchatra
Hastināpura
Indraprastha
Vṛndāvana
Mathura
Kampilya
Pañcāla
Śūrasena
Kosala
Videha
Prāgjyotis ?
Girivraja
Aṅga ?
Sutlej
Hakra
Ghaggar
Śibi
Indus
Sauvīra
Śālva
Vairāṭ
Mātsya
Kunti
Bhoja
Haihaya
Vrsni
Ābhīra
Nara
Band of fluctuation
Sindhu
N

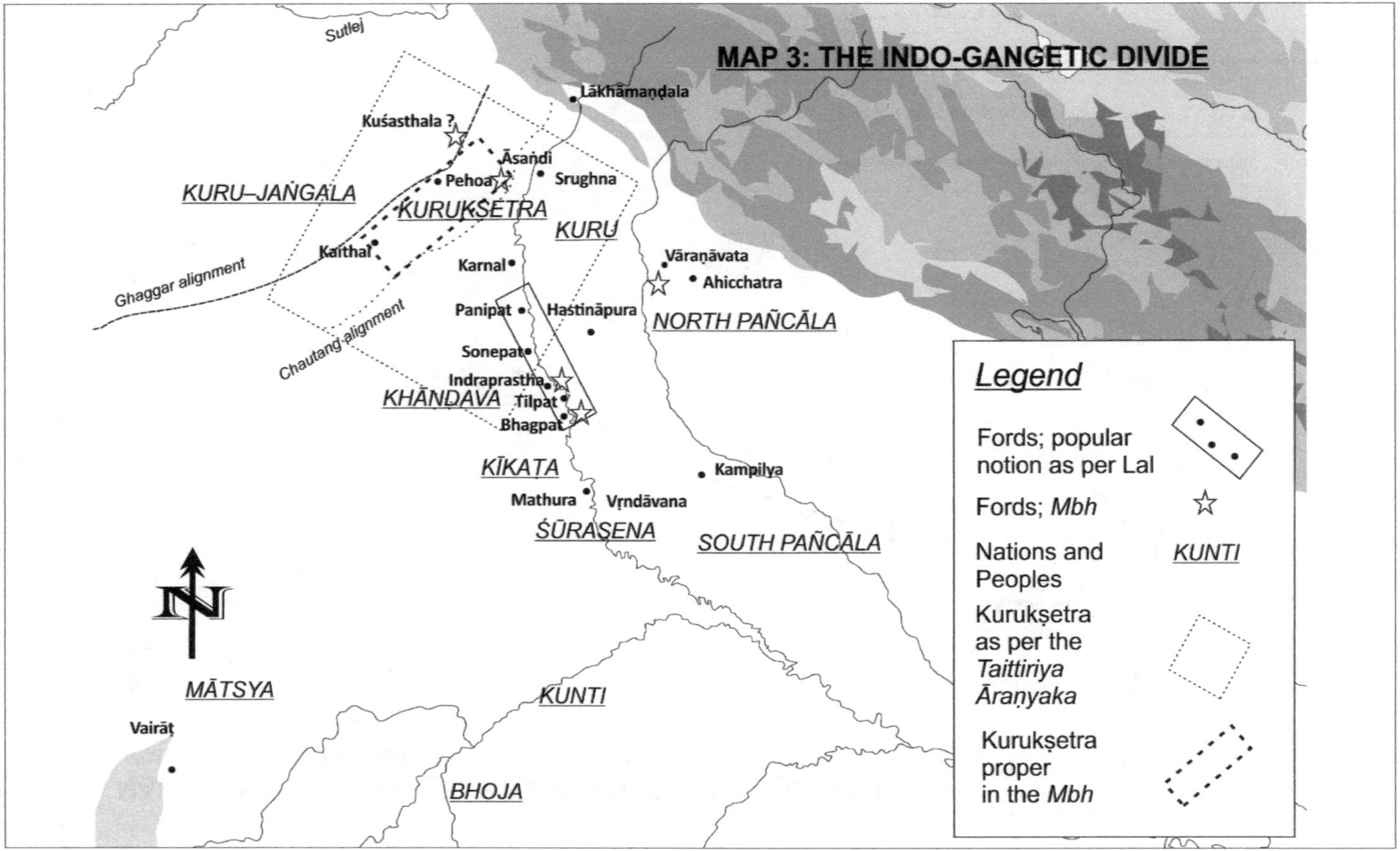
MAP 3: THE INDO-GANGETIC DIVIDE
Sutlej
Lākhāmaṇḍala
Kuśasthala ?
Āsandi
Pehoa
Srughna
KURU–JAṄGALA
KURUKṢETRA
KURU
Kaithal
Karnal
Vāraṇāvata
Ahicchatra
Ghaggar alignment
Panipat
Hastināpura
NORTH PAÑCĀLA
Chautang alignment
Sonepat
Indraprastha
KHĀṆḌAVA
Tilpat
Bhagpat
KĪKAṬA
Kampilya
Mathura
Vṛndāvana
ŚŪRASENA
SOUTH PAÑCĀLA
MĀTSYA
KUNTI
Vairāṭ
BHOJA
Legend
Fords; popular notion as per Lal
Fords; Mbh
Nations and Peoples
KUNTI
Kurukṣetra as per the Taittiriya Āraṇyaka
Kurukṣetra proper in the Mbh

MAP 4: SITES TRADITIONALLY ASSOCIATED WITH THE BATTLE and Rough Reconstruction

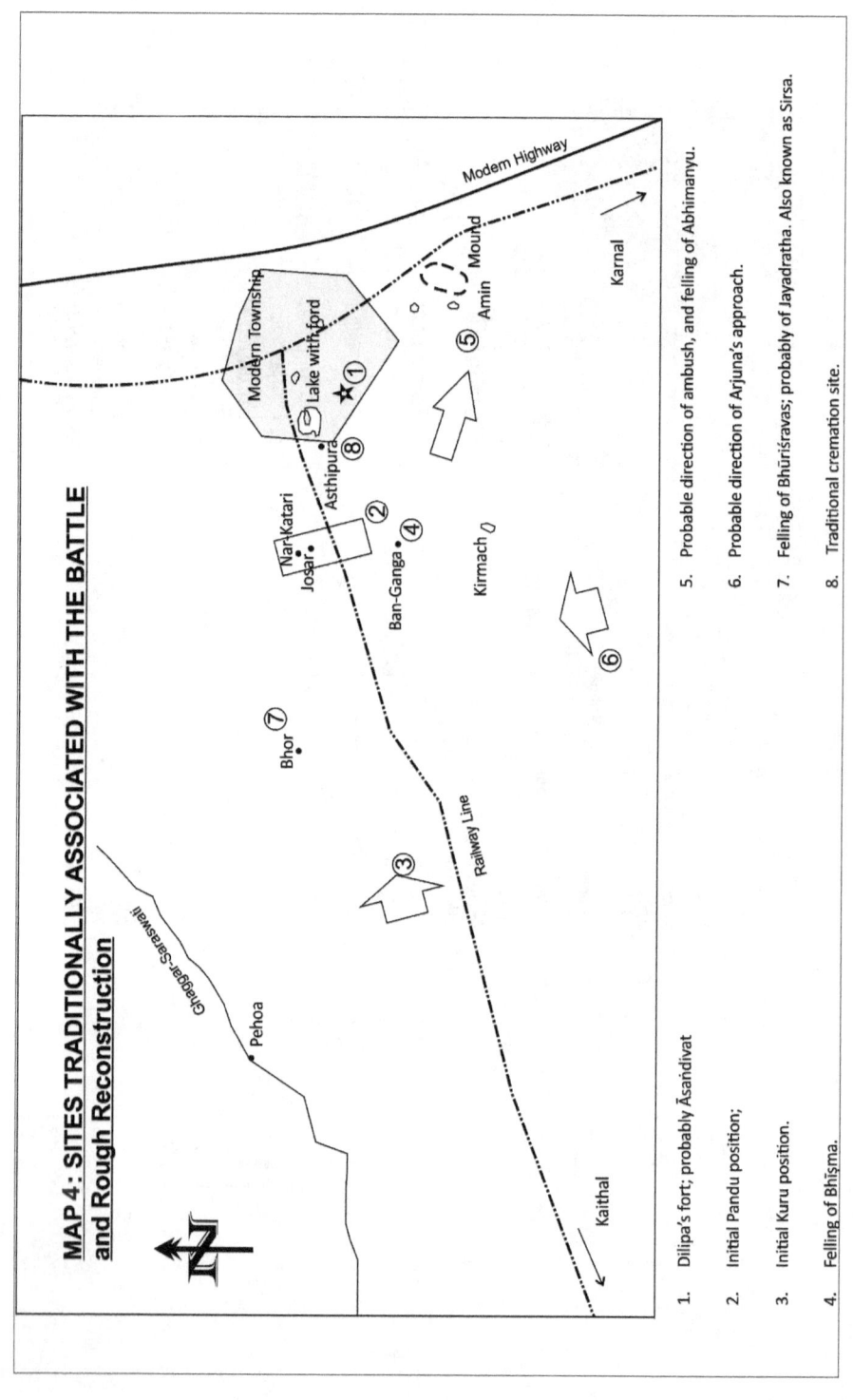

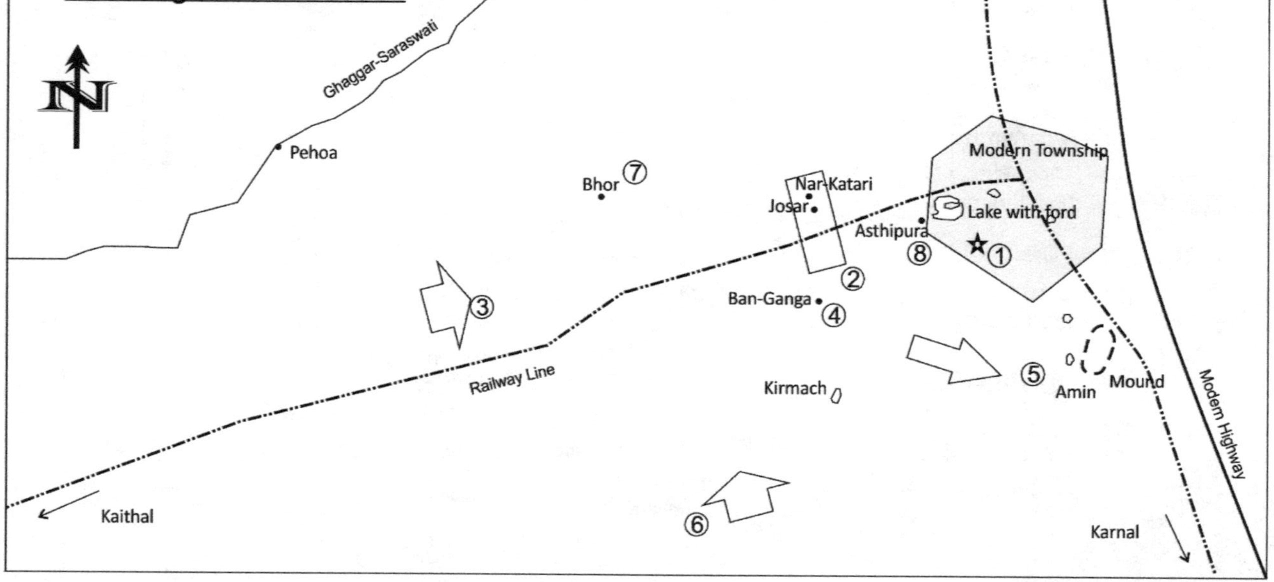

1. Dilipa's fort; probably Āsandivat
2. Initial Pandu position;
3. Initial Kuru position.
4. Felling of Bhīṣma.
5. Probable direction of ambush, and felling of Abhimanyu.
6. Probable direction of Arjuna's approach.
7. Felling of Bhūriśravas; probably of Jayadratha. Also known as Sirsa.
8. Traditional cremation site.

Figure 5 **ANATOMY OF THE *VIPATHA* CHARIOT**

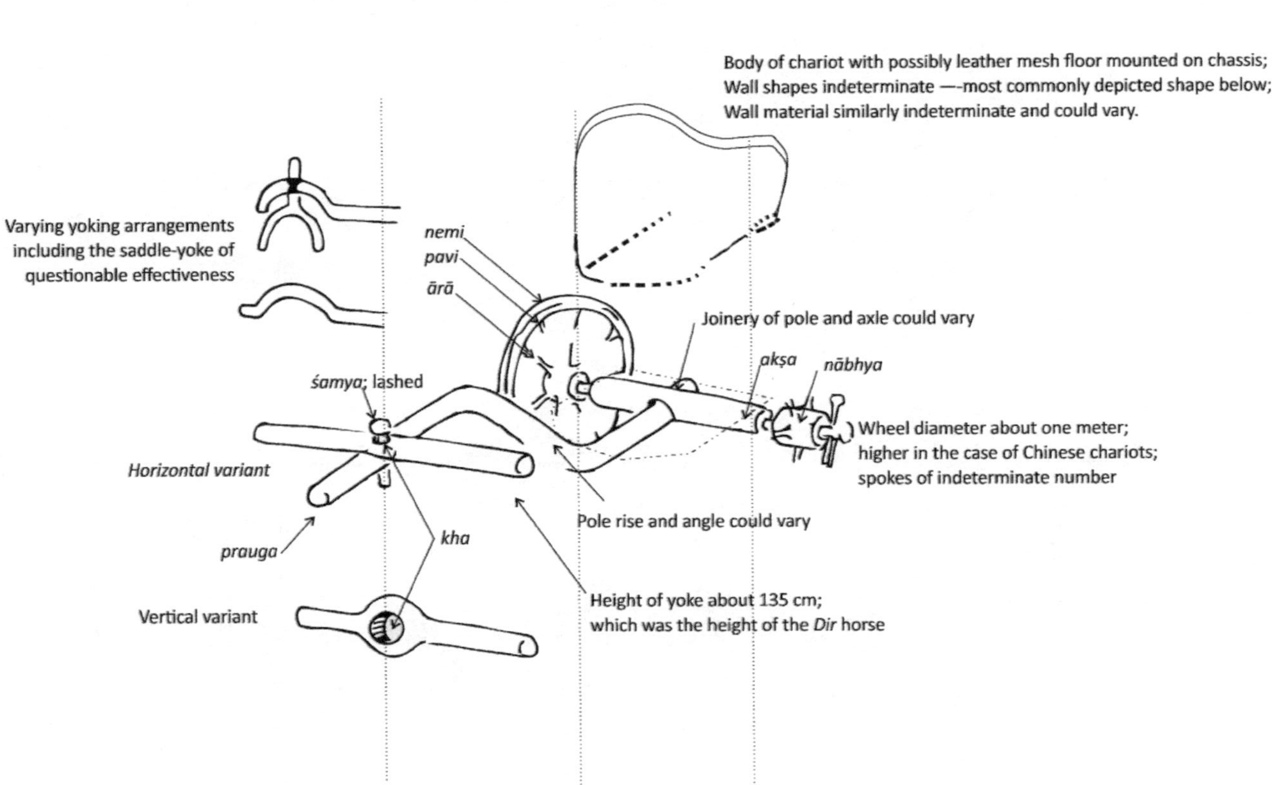
Body of chariot with possibly leather mesh floor mounted on chassis;
Wall shapes indeterminate —-most commonly depicted shape below;
Wall material similarly indeterminate and could vary.
Varying yoking arrangements including the saddle-yoke of questionable effectiveness
nemi
pavi
ārā
Joinery of pole and axle could vary
akṣa
nābhya
Wheel diameter about one meter; higher in the case of Chinese chariots; spokes of indeterminate number
śamya; lashed
Horizontal variant
prauga
kha
Pole rise and angle could vary
Vertical variant
Height of yoke about 135 cm; which was the height of the Dir horse

Introduction

"The nucleus, however, is a story"

—Edward Washburn Hopkins[1]

The two Indian epics, the *Ramayana* and the *Mahabharata*, have captured South Asian imagination on such a continental scale that they are today the cornerstones of Hindu morality. Of the two, the *Ramayana* is a compactly knit story with the dual theme of a palace intrigue leading to an exile and a war during that exile. On the other hand, the *Mahabharata*, which is the longer of the two, is a gigantic compendium of story, drama, homily and allegory, one for each moral dilemma, all woven into the plot in the frame-in-tale style so much so that the larger part of its text has little or nothing to do with its plot. This epic also features almost all South Asian communities in some context or the other, and all ethnic groups claim themselves represented in it somehow or the other. In fact, so overwhelming has been its social and moral import that the epic has been considered a *Fifth Veda*.

Now, though the centrepiece of the *Mahabharata* is a cataclysmic war, the epic has been studied more at religious, philosophical, and sociological and less at military levels. Further, most studies ignore its stratigraphy[2] and are thus anachronistic, speculative rather than analytical, and at times quite unable to construct a cohesive picture of period society and warfare. In fact, so profound the social and moral impact of the epic has been, and so speculative the conclusions of its studies, that the very historicity of the epic has been doubted, and it seen as a gigantic exercise in didacticism. A

1 E. Washburn Hopkins, *The Great Epic of India: Character and Origin of the Mahabharata*, Delhi, Motilal Banarasidass, 1993 (first published 1901), p. 363.

2 Hopkins, *Great Epic*, p. 383. Elsewhere, Arjuna's horses are compared to Uccaiśravas of Indra, but whereas they are white, Indra's were tawny.

small example of the anachronisms in the epic is provided here. Arjuna, who is somewhere fair and somewhere dark, is said in *Mbh* IV: 43.1–6, where he is still a young man, to have been carrying his *Gāṇḍīva* bow for 65 years already!

Thoughts on the Historicity of the *Mahabharata*

Two extremes mark studies of the epic—one that takes everything at face value and offers explanations relying on philosophy and speculation, at times bordering on sophistry,[3] and another that sceptically rejects everything as spurious, illogical, and exaggerated. Of the latter category are scholars like D.C. Sircar, who rejected the epic's historicity altogether, and others, like Maggi Lidchi-Grassi, to whom the epic is nothing but an allegory of natural and atmospheric phenomena.[4] The doubts of the latter set of scholars are reinforced by the apparent silence of Vedic literature on the epic's war—the Vedas do mention some epic names like Parīkṣit, Janamejaya, Śāntanu, Devāpi, Krishna, or Dhṛtarāṣṭra, but do so in contexts that are different and the names may not denote epic namesakes at all. For instance, while Dhṛtarāṣṭra is the Kuru king in the epic whose successor Janamejaya conducts a snake–sacrifice (*sarpasattra*) to *exterminate* snakes, in Vedic literature the duo appears as priest-officiants, the *Brāhmaṇa* and the *adhvaryu*, in a *sarpasattra* conducted by the *snakes themselves* to become more powerful. Elsewhere, Dhṛtarāṣṭra Airāvata is *ancestor* of the snakes.[5]

However, this *argumentum ex silentio* is not convincing—the *Ṛgveda* does not mention salt, but salt is found everywhere in the Punjab.[6] Also, a Kurukṣetra war is mentioned in the *Upaniṣad*s, and the *Chandogya Upaniṣad* mentions one Devakīputra Kṛṣṇa who may be identical with the epic Krishna—statesman, philosopher, and son of Devakī.[7] Further, it is doubtful if an imaginary, moralistic nature–tale could have become as

3 See Hopkins, *Great Epic*, p. v.

4 See Maggi Lidchi-Grassi's novel, *The Great Golden Sacrifice of the Mahabharata*, 2 vols., Vol 1: The Battle of Kurukshetra, New Delhi, Roli Books, 1986.

5 *Pañcaviṁśati Brāhmaṇa* (*PB*), 25, 15; *Baudhāyana Śrautasūtra*, (*BŚS*), trans., Sparreboom, 1983, 17, 18.

6 A.A. Macdonell, *History of Sanskrit Literature*, Delhi, Motilal Banarasidass, 1990 (first published 1900), p. 127.

7 *Chandogya Upaniṣad* (*Ch.U*), 4.17.9, and Hopkins, *Great Epic*, p. 385.

popular as the epic has always been, a popularity quite unlike the artificial and scholarly popularity of the *Arthaśāstra* which was a result of 19th century European scholarship.

The indignation stirred up by such outright rejection of the epic's historicity[8] was to some extent mollified by Sankalia and others who suggest that the epic's core event was historical, a '*small tribal skirmish*' over a *family feud*, which was later blown out of proportion. This core some scholars have identified with the *Dāśarājña*, or *Battle of the Ten Kings* (hereafter BOTK), a Vedic battle between an alliance of ten chiefs against the Bharata tribe.[9] Curious resemblances can indeed be detected between these two legendary wars. The tribes of the *Pañcajana* (Five-folk)—the Pūru, Yadu, Anu, Druhyu and Turvaśu—, and the mountain tribes of the Alīna, Bhalāna, Pakhta, Darada and Śivi, together form the 'ten' adversaries of the Bharata. In the *Mahabharata*, they are closely replicated in the alliance led by the Kuru, themselves the political successors of the Pūru, all of which tribes are based on the same places as the BOTK allies.

Also, the Pandu (sons of Pāṇdu) who challenge the Kuru, and their Pañcāla allies, are closely associated with the Bharata. In the BOTK, the Bharata chief Sudās was aided by Indra, the Maruts, the Aśvins, Varuṇa, and Agni, and their priest–preceptor was Vaśiṣṭha. In the *Mahabharata*, the Pandu are often referred to as Bharata, their leader Yudhiṣṭhira fits the character of the 'sage king' Sudās,[10] while his brothers Arjuna, Bhīma, and the twins Nakula and Sahadeva are sons of Indra, wind god Pavan associated with the Maruts, and the Aśvin twins, respectively. Further, their counsel Krishna is Nārāyaṇa, dark lord of the waters and thereby Varuṇa, lord of the cosmic darkness, while Yudhiṣṭhira and Sudās are equated with Yama and Agni[11]—in one *ṚV* hymn Vaśiṣṭha addresses Sudās[12] as *Agni Vaiśvānara*, i.e. *fire, universal man*, or *world ruler* while elsewhere Agni is

8 For a summary of contemporaneous objections, see P.L. Bhargava, 'A Fresh Appraisal of the Historicity of Indian Epics', *Annals of the BORI*, vol. 63, no. 1/4, 1982, pp. 15–28.

9 S.S.N. Murthy, 'The Questionable Historicity of the Mahabharata', *Electronic Journal of Vedic Studies (EJVS)*, vol. 10, no. 5, 2003, pp. 1–15.

10 *ṚV*, X: 133.

11 Murthy, 'Questionable Historicity', also *Mbh*, I: 193,382; V: 36,75; V: 48,111; V: 50,122; or VI: 85,209.

12 *ṚV*, VII: 6. 5–7.

referred to as *Agnibhārata.*[13] Finally, Kṛṣṇadvaipāyana Vyāsa, 'composer' of the *Mahabharata*, Pandu sympathiser, and even biological progenitor of both Kuru and Pandu, is descended from Vaśiṣṭha. In addition, many Bharata names like Sṛñjaya or Tṛtsu reappear as clans and septs of the Pañcāla.

And yet, the epic characters are distinct and *descended* from characters of the BOTK. There is no reason why a *new set of characters* would have been used to replace those in the old story, and it is doubtful that a tale based on imaginary characters could capture continental imagination. Further, Devāpī, composer of *ṛc* 98 of *maṇḍala* (Book) X of the *Ṛgveda*, is a great–great–great uncle of the Pandu. The Book X of the Vedas, which is markedly different from the other Vedic books and has modern linguistic traits[14] (see later), was composed shortly *after the BOTK*. It can thus be said that the Pandu follow several generations *after* the BOTK.

One possible reason for a transfer of identity, suggested also by Hopkins, is that real people from a later time associated themselves with an old war and lineage in order to derive legitimacy. While this theory cannot be disregarded, it is also plainly evident that the epic core area was historically, sociologically, and militarily very significant and saw several crucial battles in the last several thousand years, being in military parlance the *Key Battle Area* for the Indo–Gangetic Divide (hereafter Divide). There would thus be nothing unusual if one more battle, that of the *Mahabharata*, had been fought here. In fact, as the position of Devāpī *vis-à-vis* the Pandu indicates, the centre of Aryan activity, the Chenab–Ravi region which was the setting of the BOTK, had shifted to the Indo–Gangetic Divide, the setting of the epic, in the few generations between these two wars.

It is thus difficult to reject the historicity of the battle, just as it is to reject the historicity of its participants, aspects that will be inspected at length later. It is pertinent to mention that while the Kuru *are* mentioned in Vedic literature, the Pandu also, even though not mentioned, do have a strong presence in literary and oral traditions, showing that both were real

13 *ṚV*, IV: 25.4.

14 Michael Witzel, 'Substrate Languages in Old Indo-Aryan (Ṛgvedic, Middle and Late Vedic)', *EJVS*, vol. 5, no. 1, 1999, pp. 1–67.

peoples, and not mere shadows of the participants of the BOTK.[15] It is also pertinent to mention here that there appears in the Vedas another, as yet unstudied war, involving twenty kings.[16]

Dating and Situating the Epic

Some schools, especially those that take every statement in the epic at face value, have used complex astronomical and astrological calculations to date the battle to the 4th millennium B.C., the year 3102 B.C. being especially popular with them. The fallacies and contradictions in this approach have been summarised by Yardi and need not be repeated here.[17] Comparison of epic and Purānic genealogies on the other hand yield a more plausible peg of *c.*1000 B.C.[18]; some epic characters feature in the latest layers of the *Ṛgveda* which closed around this time—Asīta and his son Devala, who composed *ṚV*, IX: 5–24, are contemporaries of the Pandu[19]—, use of iron weapons is hesitatingly observed in the war, and the battle has been considered so cataclysmic and its effects so disturbing that it is said to have ushered in the lamented and decadent Age of *Kali*, i.e. the Iron Age, which commenced at about this time.[20]

Indeed, increasing availability of iron at the turn of the 1st millennium could have triggered an agrarian colonization of the Gangetic plain, whose

15 Though the Vedas are silent on the Pandu, Raychaudhuri has shown that the Pandu are not a strange people unknown in the Vedas. H.C. Raychaudhuri, *Political History of Ancient India*, Calcutta, University of Calcutta, 1938, pp. 34–35.

16 *ṚV*, I: 53.9, of Savya Pājra refers to Suśravas fighting the *Battle of 20 Kings*; in *ṚV*, I: 54.6 this battle is referred to in close connection with the fight between Tūrvayāśa and Āyu, two of the constituents of the 'ten kings'.

17 M.R. Yardi, *The Mahābhārata: Its Genesis and Growth*, Poona, BORI, 1986, pp. 138–144. Also see Upinder Singh (ed.), *Delhi: Ancient History*, New Delhi, Social Science Press, 2006, for a résumé of the theories on the dating of the epic.

18 Rajesh Kochhar, *The Vedic People: their History and Geography*, Delhi, Orient Blackswan, 2009, pp. 49–57, brackets the date between 1000 B.C. and 850 B.C.

19 V.B. Athavale, 'The Movements of the Pandavas', *Annals of the BORI*, vol. 29, 1948, pp. 85–95.

20 David Christian, *Inner Eurasia from Prehistory to the Mongol Empire*, vol. 1 of series 'A History of Central Asia and Mongolia', Massachusetts, Blackwell, 1998, *passim*, has shown how pastoral societies were especially susceptible to the pressures and attractions of a settled society. Also, nomad protectors patronizing oases become immobilized and thus vulnerable. In other words, all nomad groups *underwent their own versions of the Age of Kali.*

great primeval forests (*mahāvanas*) could only be cleared by the iron axe and whose heavy alluvial soil could only be turned by the iron ploughshare. Indo–Aryan tribes, which had been gravitating to the Divide and infesting the pastoral corridors radiating from it, could now enter the Gangetic plains, though no major rush of population is supported by archaeological evidence. In the epic, the Pandu clear a settlement by *burning*, a suboptimal, Bronze Age procedure suited only to scrub country (even where it left fire–hardened stakes in the ground that could be extremely difficult to prise out). Reckoning the *Kali* Age—miscegenation, sedentization, and xenophobia, all concomitants of agrarian colonization—from immediately after the war indicates that the *Mahabharata* occurred at the cusp of the ages when iron was superseding bronze as the primary metal of civilization.[21]

Historicity of the Epic

The Kurukṣetra of the epic is traditionally identified with the district of that name in the modern state of Haryana, while the two major epic cities, Hastināpura and Indraprastha, are identified with Meerut and Delhi. However, the daily traffic attested in the epic between the cities and the battlefield does not conform to such identification, Delhi and Meerut being significantly distant from modern Kurukshetra. This has led to suggestions of other locales for the war, largely to the west. For instance, Kocchar is of the opinion that the epic Gomati is the Gomal, Hastināpura the city of Astakenoi/ Hastinayana near Pekeulotis/ Puṣkalāvati mentioned by Paṇini and Greek chroniclers, and the Swat VI culture at the base of the Khyber the scene of jostling that was the *Mahabharata*.[22]

Though consistent on the whole with the locales of the Gandhāra, Madra, Kekaya, Uttara–Kuru, and Uttara–Madra peoples who feature so prominently in the epic, and though two later-day Pūru kings contemporary of Alexander were actually found in this region, Kochhar's argument has several inconsistencies. For instance, it identifies Gandhāra with Qandahar though it is a known fact that Qandahar got its name from *Alexandria* or

21 H.A. Phadke, 'Kurukshetra: A Historical Reconstruction', *Quarterly Review of Historical Studies*, Calcutta, vol. 23, no. 1, 1983–84, p. 23.; H.A. Phadke, 'Date of Bharata War', in S.P. Gupta and S. K. Ramachandran (eds.), *Mahabharata: Myth and Reality, Differing Views*, Delhi, Agam Prakashan, 1976, and also H.A. Phadke, Press Notes, September 20, 1975, 'The Indian Express', October, 28, 1975. The date given here is 1200–1000 B.C.

22 Rajesh Kochhar, *Vedic People*, pp. 215–219.

Iskandariya. Further, this shift in locale *west* of the BOTK, even though the *Mahabharata* was generations *after* it, is questionable as overall movement of the tribes was towards the south and east. A far better approach would be to question the authenticity of the two 'capitals' *vis-à-vis* the terrain of the battle, questions that shall be returned to later.

On the whole, it appears that the *Mahabharata* was situated at crucial junctions in time and space—the cusp between the Bronze and Iron Ages, and the Divide between the arid north and west and humid east—which made a naturally volatile backdrop. It was not therefore unnatural for the war to be real. In the last century, two world wars were fought almost within the same generation between remarkably similar alliances, the second one largely over the unfinished business of the first. No one would however argue that WWII is nothing but a dramatized retelling of WWI. It is thus too early to conclude that the *Mahabharata* was a retelling of the BOTK, and it is more reasonable to assume that tribes who first fought the BOTK drifted towards the Divide, where they clashed again over burning questions engendered by unresolved issues of the older battle.

We also see that the protagonists of the epic have been put through a catharsis—they do unwarranted things first and then are absolved of blame by a set of justifications. As no playwright would have taken the trouble of first painting the characters of his didactic play in 'negative' hues and then whitewashing them, it is more reasonable to conclude that the characters were *real*, but because they did things that fell out of acceptability due to changing values and morality, they had to be whitewashed.

The working hypothesis that we arrive at here is that the war was real, fought across terrain traditionally associated with it, and over a principle of general appeal for so many peoples to have participated in it. It may have been a 'minor tribal skirmish' because in that age wars usually were *minor* and *tribal*, and took the sub-military form of *skirmish*; it must be noted that out of innumerable such minor skirmishes only this one captured a continent's imagination. Further, reckoning the *Kali* from the *Mahabharata* war shows that the battle was independent of the BOTK, else it would have been reckoned from that war, upsetting all traditional timelines.

Socioeconomic Backdrop of the Epic

As the terrain along the *Uttarāpatha*, i.e. the migration–cum–trade avenue from the hills west of Peshawar to the Indo–Gangetic Divide, did not permit undiluted pastoralism, immigrating nomads were increasingly influenced by agrarian cultures that had reasserted themselves after the passing of the mature Harappan civilization and forced to adapt to various degrees of agro–pastoralism. The adoption of agriculture is seen in the incorporation of the Dravidian word for plough, *ḷāṅgaḷa*, into Aryan vocabulary. However, the component of agriculture was weak, and though the ox was used, the yoke is nowhere mentioned till later; Piggott was of the opinion that the plough was tied with traces to the *horns*, in an obviously suboptimal manner.[23]

The immigrants were also influenced by regional socio–political and religious forces. Their egalitarian, open-status societies were influenced by formats like chiefdom and kingdom, as seen in the gradual supplanting of the *rājanya*, the Vedic tribal elite, by the increasingly feudal and landed *Kṣatriya*.[24] Further, their animistic, shamanistic religion, centring on fire-oblation, veneration of the elements, negotiation with and propitiation of diverse spirits peopling the departments of nature, and worship of ancestors,[25] all characteristic of the oldest layers of the Vedas (though scholars have been reluctant to acknowledge it, considering the *shamanistic* references peripheral or vestigial), morphed into a sacrificial religion including ritual *soma*-pressing wherein the free-lancing *shaman* was gradually supplanted by regimented priests and officiants. Other societal formats, like the *vrātya* rite of passage and matrilineal succession, also fell out of use as destabilising to a sedentising, agrarian society.[26]

---

23 Stuart Piggott, *Prehistoric India to 1000 B.C.*, Middlesex, Penguin Books, 1950, p. 265.

24 In the *ṚV*, *kṣatra* appears at *ṚV*, I: 24.11; II: 136.1–3; IV: 17.1; V: 62.6 and *Kṣatriya* appears *ṚV*, IV: 12.3; 42.1; V: 69.1; VII: 64.2; VIII: 25.8.

25 Human and animal sacrifices would have played a role in their religion, as they did in all Eurasian religions. The Scythians made human and animal sacrifices to Ares, who was represented by an iron sword.

26 Suppression of matrilineal practices was important as they could be cited to upset the established order. For instance, Edward III staked a claim to the throne of France through the female line, his mother being sister of Charles IV, stating that only a male could hold it; in contrast the French claimant, Philip VI, could claim the throne only through a junior paternal line. The purpose of Edward III of course was to 'try a great

While the rudimentary forms of the new features are discernible in Book X of the *Ṛgveda*, reckoned from shortly after the BOTK, they are found in more finished form, largely symptomatic of later Hinduism, in the elaborate, formalised, formulaic, and liturgical texts of the *Brāhmaṇa*s and *Kalpasūtra*s that appeared in this period. For example, the once-simple fire oblation—the *sattra*—elaborated into the spectacular *yajña* of the *Śrauta-sūtra*, going on to become the *end rather than the means*. From a magical procedure of transferring oblations to the gods through fire, it became a thing in itself with the *status of god*, its performance being essential to keep the world going. A class of priest–officiants, deriving their exalted status from expertise in super-complex sacrificial procedures, replaced the *shaman*. The *mantra*, or magical formulae coded in the manuals that they specialised in intoning flawlessly, gave the period its other name, the *Mantra* age.

The traditional terrain of the *Mahabharata*—lake–studded Kurukṣetra and riverine Pañcāla astride the Yamuna–Ganga *doābā*—are intimately associated with these developments. It is acclaimed as the ideal ground for sacrifice, a statement with political implications as sacrificing was a royal prerogative. In fact, the dominating or pioneering role of the Kuru–Pañcāla in development of the sacrificial religion is indicated in the sacrificial manuals instructing priests to address the patron of the sacrifice as 'O Kuru' or 'O Pāñcāla'.

Against the backdrop of these socioeconomic and religious developments, the fifty or so discernible Indo–Aryan (IA) tribes are seen to consolidating into a fewer *janapada*s (principalities) on the Indo–Gangetic plains. Lists of *janapada*s appearing in later texts include more and more eastern ones, indicating a gradual eastward expansion. These *janapada*s are later consolidated into sixteen super–principalities or *ṣoḍaṣa-mahājanapada*s, most of which are on the Gangetic plains. Alongside this colonization, the sacrificial religion extended eastwards. The *Śatapatha Brāhmaṇa* story of the king Videgha Māthava *advancing eastwards with fire* across the River Sadānīra (or Sarayu, then eastern limit of Aryandom)[27] is often assumed to be the story of the *colonization*

---

adventure and to see what would come of it'. See Hillair Belloc, *Creçy*, British Battles, London, Stephen Swift, 1912, p. 25.

27 *Śatapatha Brāhmaṇa (ŚB)*, trans. Julius Eggeling, Netlancers, (first published 1882), 2014, i.4.1.14ff. This view is subscribed to by Bhargava also; see P.L. Bhargava, 'A

of the Ganga basin.[28] It is unlikely to be so, as the primeval forests on these plains were impermeable to fire; it is rather the account of spread of *mantra* orthopraxy and *śrauta* ritualism to the east, fire here being the *sacrificial fire*.[29]

The new religion was accompanied or rivalled by other changes—feudalism, a concomitant political philosophy based on chivalry and conservative social morality, popular cults based on extreme devotion to selected deities, and a tendency towards asceticism. All these changes are reflected in the stratigraphy of the *Mahabharata*. The Pandu clear scrublands by burning but iron weapons appear in the context of the war, albeit hesitatingly. The *dyūta* list of countries, from the earliest layers of the epic but in a later episode, shows familiarity with only north-western regions, but the *digvijaya* list, a later addition to an earlier episode, is familiar with eastern places which had since been accessed. Epic characters are seen performing Vedic sacrifices in their original forms, while the oldest layers are ignorant of *sūtra* literature but later layers mention great *yajña*s like the *rājasūya*. Epic characters behave in certain ways, and are then absolved with not-so-convincing justifications, reflecting a tightening social morality.

The seeds of the devotional cults of Śaivism and Vaishnavism are seen stirring at the time of the core events of the epic. The *sāṅkhya*-based philosophy of the *Bhagavad–Gītā* establishes Vishnu–Krishna as godhead in an open church that encouraged worship through the simple means of offering flowers and water, obviously a reaction against the great Vedic sacrifices which could ruin the richest of men. Much of these changes took place in *janapada*s ruled by cadet lineages that had supplanted the old ones *annihilated by the war*, under the leadership of the Kuru–Pañcāla political combine which was a *product of the war*. Not surprisingly, the war drew so many peoples, and the epic became so popular that it was granted the status of a *Veda* in the Age of *Kali* that the war had precipitated.

Fresh Appraisal of the Historicity of Indian Epics', p. 16.

28 Even by D. D. Kosambi, 'The Autochthonous Element in the Mahabharata', *Journal of the American Oriental Society*, vol. 84, Baltimore, 1964, pp. 31–44.

29 See Witzel, 'On the localisation of Vedic texts and schools', in G. Pollet (ed.) *India and the Ancient world: history, trade and culture before A.D. 650,* P.H.L. Eggermont Jubilee Volume, Leuven, 1987, pp. 173–213. For an overview of the spread of the Vedic religion and orthopraxy, see S. W. Jamison and M. Witzel, *Vedic Hinduism*, 1992, available at www.people.fas.harvard.edu/~witzel/vedica.pdf, last checked 17 April 15.

Nature of the Battle

As said earlier, despite its key role in the epic, the war or battle has itself been inadequately studied. Of the few efforts made, the successes of Sensharma,[30] Bakshi,[31] and Sandhu do not match the efforts they invested, their contributions lying mainly in collating data and references from the epic and other period literature. Singh,[32] Chakravarti[33] and others have reconstructed a fair picture of South Asian military environment in the early 1st millennium, but the picture is from *after* the epic battle.[34]

It is argued here that the course and nature of the epic battle is as important to understanding the role of the epic in the formation of early South Asian society as are the various philosophical and social clues embedded in it. The most visible aspects of this battle are that it was fought over eighteen days, diurnal battles ceased at sundown, chariots and archery had crucial roles bordering on the spectacular, and combat was marked by high chivalric content with warriors fighting to the accompaniment of hot words of philosophical and didactic import and blatant, self-congratulatory boasts.[35] Unlike in the *Iliad*, another major chariot epic from half-way across the world, *Mahabharata* warriors seldom dismount to fight, the few dismounted combats occurring only when their chariots are smashed. Also, while cavalry action is rare and elephants are mentioned but unconvincingly, vast infantry formations appear, forming arrays, acting as arrow-fodder for enemy heroes, cheering own heroes in victory, and bearing the consequences of their defeat. There is no case of chosen champions fighting duels to settle the outcome, unlike in the *Iliad*, except Yudhiṣṭhira's challenge to Duryodhana to fight one of the Pandava in a mace duel at the end of the battle, the prize for which would

30 P. Sensharma, *Kurukshetra War: A Military Study*, Ganganagar and Calcutta, 1975.

31 G.D. Bakshi, *Mahabharata: A Military Analysis*, New Delhi, Lancer International, 1990.

32 S.D. Singh, *Ancient Indian Warfare, with Special Reference to the Vedic Period*, New Delhi, Motilal Banarasidass, 1989.

33 P.C. Chakravarti, *The Art of War in Ancient India*, New Delhi, L.P.P., 2004.

34 See S.P. Gupta and K.S. Ramachandran, 'Mahābhārata: Myth and Reality', in Upinder Singh (ed.), *Delhi: Ancient History*, pp. 77–118 for the debate on the issue.

35 Boasting marks both epics. One warrior in the Ramayana even announces '*even without boasting I shall slay thee, behold my prowess*', *Rmn*, VI: 67.15.

be the victory; this however was in an entirely different context, and at once earned the reproach of Krishna.

Also unlike the *Iliad*, there is no minute-to-minute divine intervention unless the acts of Krishna, who was not deified yet, are counted. Divine influence was only in the form of weapons and charms dispensed to specific heroes *before* the battle, and gods do little more than watch heroes in action, applauding them at times. Only in a late and interpolated episode the terrifying figure of the mother goddess appears to some warriors and, on being pacified, grants them a weapon.

There are some difficult aspects in the narrative. The first is the *vyūha*, gigantic battle array of all arms, are too sketchily and formatically described to permit reconstruction, and have little bearing on the subsequent course of combat. Another is that supreme commanders on either side, selected by common consent and anointed with Vedic rites,[36] do little more than select the day's array and set the example by fighting. They have little control over course of action, all tactical decisions being taken by leaders of the two aggrieved parties, Yudhiṣṭhira and Duryodhana. Also, despite pretensions, chivalric injunctions are violated with impunity while intelligence of opponents' plans seems to be always available to one another. Finally, the arrangement of the battle in eighteen days appears too formal and schematic, as the days evidently merge with one another after the first thirteen days.

So startling are some of these inconsistencies—the travesty made of chivalry especially by the Pandu and the undercurrent of their castigation, the feting of the Kuru by the gods and their apparent betrayal by their top men—that it has been suggested that it were the hapless Kuru, beleaguered by unsupportive kinsmen, who were the original tragic heroes of the epic, and that the roles were reversed only later. However, comparing epic stratigraphy with the evolution of social morality indicates that whatever the Pandu did during the war was perfectly acceptable at their time, becoming *unacceptable* only later and requiring didactic justifications lest they be cited as precedence. *The characters are neither heroes nor villains, but people behaving just as their circumstances expected of, or required, compelled, or impelled them.*

36 Use of such hoary rites also shows that the battle was not fought long after the closure of the Vedic Age.

The volume of violence, indicated by casual, uncritical readings of the epic, seems immense, and far beyond what societies of that age could generate or support. In this context, Sankalia's phrase, that the battle was a *minor, tribal skirmish,* is a good framework of enquiry as all three words are significant. It addresses the volume of violence, i.e. whether it was a minor or major, social pattern of the violence, i.e. whether it was fought on tribal, kingly, or statal lines, and manner of applying violence, i.e. whether in the form of skirmish, raid, or a general onslaught. We know that pre-state societies endlessly simmered in conflict, over honour, woman, revenge, sacrificial victim, and so on, the violence never quite erupting above the so-called *military horizon* as defined by scholars like Hoebel or Turney–High.[37] Quarrels over the Pandu queen Draupadī, the many vendettas—Pandu's against the Kuru, Vṛṣṇis' against the Śūrasena, Pañcālas' against Drona, Śikhaṇḍi's against Bhīṣma—, endless contests between warriors, and quest for personal distinction, suggest that even the *Mahabharata* war was below the military horizon, and of the Hobbesian category.

However, while endemic strife may have featured in hunter–gatherer lore, the fact that this one war was elevated to epic proportions shows that it was fought over principles of crucial importance, some of which, like control of fords and settlement of territory, are in reality discernible. Further, participants are able to deploy regulars, engage mercenaries, mobilise militias, field *vrātya*s, and enlist levies; they can forge coalitions, form multi-generation policies, and plan and execute tactical operations. The above, which imply command and control forms and military authority, imply political structures more evolved than those that indulged in endemic contests. The very continuance of combat after first contact shows social cohesion and discipline, motives higher than private vendetta, and social mechanism to sustain battle over days, all the above quite at variance from early societies that were incapable of sustained policies.[38] Thus, despite some of the features of endemic warfare, the battle of the *Mahabharata,* as also the BOTK, satisfy conditions of being above the *Military Horizon,* the apparent confusion arising only because *participants* were at varying

37 H.H. Turney–High, *Primitive War: Its Practice and Concepts*, Columbia, SC: University of South Carolina Press, 1949.

38 For how tribally organized armies functioned above or below the so-called *Military Horizon*, see Tacitus, *Complete Works of Tacitus*: Germania, ed. Alfred John Church, William Jackson Brodribb, Lisa Cerrato, New York, Random House, repr., 1942, p. 275 (Chapter 7). Also see *Iliad*, II.362, for tribal warfare.

levels of transformation from tribe to state. And yet, as we shall see, the massive infantry formations mentioned in the epic are anachronisms.

The Thesis Statement, Research Techniques, and Organization

The book argues that there is enough reason to suppose that the *Mahabharata* was distinct from the BOTK, was actually fought in early 1st millennium B.C., and over terrain traditionally associated with it. It further shows that it was fought between peoples undergoing disturbing social evolution, and later morality added loads of extraneous material, giving the epic its didactic character. With little hope of ever encountering physical evidence of the war—the geographical and social peculiarities of South Asia make it impossible for artefacts to survive—it uses a qualitative, interdisciplinary approach, combining close reading of the epic with comparison of its internal evidence with other period sources like the Vedic corpus, and historical, geographical and geological, botanical and hydrological, and cultural and traditional data from secondary and tertiary sources. This is to enquire if the principle of great import, that drove so many nations to war, was not the question of transformation of traditional, pastoral lifestyles under the influence of iron-based sedentary agriculture at the cusp of the Chalcolithic and Iron Ages. Against the backdrop of this social and technological quandary, it seeks to reconstruct the nature and course of the showdown.

Organization

This book has eight chapters, *Chapter 1* dealing with format, structure, and evolution of the epic in order to bracket the date of its core events and understand the narrative tradition that caused it to expand later. *Chapter 2* traces migration of pastoralists across Eurasia, and into South Asia, inspecting the archaeological evidence of the passages through modern Afghanistan and across the Indus Valley, i.e. the *Uttarāpatha* and its laterals. *Chapter 3* inspects socio–cultural evolution of migrating tribes along the fords of the northern Indus plains and across the Punjab rivers, and the divisive and assimilative trends that led to the BOTK. In addition to discerning the instabilities that precipitated the epic war, the chapter also inspects the idea of horse and chariot in early warfare and religious practices of steppe people, and how the idea migrated to South Asia in a modified form.

Chapter 4 evaluates the results of the BOTK, which interacts with further migration to form the Kuru–Pañcāla moiety astride the Divide, with the Kuru and their more pastoral allies along the *Uttarāpatha* and the agrarian, sedentised Pañcāla groups east of the Divide. *Chapter 5* studies how newer belligerent and pastoral groups, represented by the Pandu and Vṛṣṇi, challenge the Kuru and other occupiers of the Divide, and ally with the Pañcāla against them. It also inspects the Pandu's search for political legitimacy, their ouster in an ancient political procedure represented by the dice game, and their return to nomad status after a brief phase of sedentization, which led to the gathering of the opponents for war.

Chapters 6 and *7* inspect the nature and composition of armies with the aim of reconstructing the progress of the 'eighteen' days of battle, developing the horse and chariot theme *vis-à-vis* the influence of South Asian ecology to understand turn-of-the-millennium warfare. *Chapter 8* puts it all in perspective, analysing the situation after the war to reveal why the war was considered so cataclysmic and world-shaking, so much so that the most decadent age of *Kali* is reckoned from it.[39]

Lack of common datum, unlike the (supposed) year of nascence of Jesus in the west, makes treatment of time in Indian history very nebulous; added to this is the characteristic indifference to passage of time, only to be expected of a people traditionally immersed in thoughts of rebirth, recycling, and endless repetition of the ages. The epic treats time as casually as any other Indian literary work, evaluating it in relative terms—as not one of the exact values is known, it is a wonder how some scholars have managed to actually arrive at specific dates like 3102 B.C. as the date of the outbreak of the war.[40] This book has preferred to be modest on the issue and treat time in terms of generations and seasons than in actual terms.

39 Some works reckon the *Age of Kali* from the date of the passing of Krishna many years after the war, but that is a result of the pious horror at the prospect of Krishna living in the age of *Kali*.

40 P.V. Holay. 'The Year of the Kaurava–Pāṇḍava War', in Ajay Mitra Shastri (ed.), *Mahābhārata: The End of an Era (Yugānta)*, New Delhi, Aryan, 2004, pp. 58–89.

CHAPTER 1:

Format, Structure and Growth of the Epic

The Epic, its Structure and Contents

The *Mahabharata*, as we know it today, is arranged in 18 *parvans* or volumes of unequal length, and also includes almost independent texts like the *Bhagavad Gītā* and *Harivaṅśa*, and tales like those of *Rāma*, *Ṛṣyaśṛṅga*, or *Nala*. The broad structure of the epic, and its outline story, is presented in this section. It must be noted that names of the *parvans* are often different between recensions and editions from various parts of South Asia. For example, *Bhīṣma-parvan* in some is *Bhīṣma-vadha-parvan* in others.

Book I: *Ādi-parvan* or *Book of the Beginning*, with sub-*parvans* 1–19, starts with telling how the bard Ugraśravas *Sautī* narrates to the *ṛṣis* at Naimiṣāraṇya an improved version of the epic narrated by Vaiśampāyana at Janamejaya's *sarpasattra*. It also gives the history and genealogies of the Bharata protagonists and the priestly clan of Bhṛgu, and recounts the birth and early lives of the protagonists wherein the Pandu (sons of Pāṇḍu, or the *Pāṇḍavas*) suffer much humiliation at the hands of the Kuru (*Kauravas*). It includes the attempted assassination of the Pandu by the Kuru by burning them in the lac palace, and their polyandrous marriage with the Pāñcāla princess Draupadī.

Book II: *Sabhā-parvan* or the *Book of the Assembly Hall*, sub-*parvans* 20–28, tells how the Pandu, who had been reluctantly permitted to settle in the scrubland of Khāṇḍava-prastha south of

Kurukṣetra, clear it by burning, flushing out the demon Maya who erects their palace and the court of Indraprastha in return for his life. The *parvan* also describes the *rājasūya* or the Pandu imperial quest, and the dice game with the Kuru that leads to their 'exile' for twelve years, to be followed by one year of living incognito.

Book III: ***Vana-parvan*, *Āraṇyaka-parvan*** or ***Araṇya-parvan***, the *Book of the Forest*, in its sub-*parvan*s 29–44, deal with the twelve years of exile in the forest (*araṇya*), and the adventures there in. It contains a large amount of interpolated tales and legends.

Book IV: ***Virāṭ-parvan*** or the *Book of Virāṭ*, sub-*parvans* 45–48, tells of the year spent incognito at the court of the Mātsya ruler Virāṭ, as required by the terms of the exile.

Book V: ***Udyoga Parva*** or the *Book of the Endeavour*, sub-*parvan*s 49–59, has the run-up to battle and the diplomatic initiatives that were taken prior to it.

Book VI: ***Bhīṣma-parvan*** or ***Bhīṣma-vadha-parvan***, or the *Book of Bhīṣma*, sub-*parvan*s 60–64, is the opening book of the war and deals with the first ten days' battle wherein the Kuru are commanded by Bhīṣma till his incapacitation. It includes the *Bhagavad Gītā*.

Book VII: ***Droṇa-parvan*** or the *Book of Drona*, sub-*parvan*s 65–72, deals with the next four days of battle under the command of Droṇa. It has much important action, and sees the fall of many of the greatest warriors on either side.

Book VIII: ***Karṇa-parvan*** or the *Book of Karṇa* is a short book with only the sub-*parvan* 73, which deals with the brief period of battle under the command of Karṇa till he is killed.

Book IX: ***Śalya-parvan*** or the *Book of Śalya*, sub-*parvan*s 74–77, is almost the last day of battle when Śalya is commander, telling how the Kuru prince Duryodhana is felled in a duel of maces by Bhīma. It also deals with the pilgrimage of Baldeva (Rāma) along the Sarasvatī, which is very significant.

Book X: ***Sauptika-parvan***, the *Book of Sleeping Warriors*, sub-*parvan*s 78–80, sees the last major action of the epic wherein the three surviving Kuru warriors raid the Pandu camp at night and kill many of the remaining warriors.

Book XI: ***Strī-parvan***, the *Book of the Widows*, sub-*parvan*s 81–85, has the lament of the widows of both sides, who visit the scene of carnage after it was over.

Book XII: ***Śānti-parvan*** or the *Book of Peace*, sub-*parvan*s 86–88, has the anointing of Yudhiṣṭhira as the new Kuru king and his instructions from the immobilised Bhīṣma on political economy. Though just three sub–*parvan*s, it is the longest and most didactic volume of the epic.

Book XIII: ***Anuśāsana-parvan*** or the *Book of the Instructions*, sub-*parvan*s 89–90, continues with Bhīṣma's instructions to Yudhiṣṭhira.

Book XIV: ***Aśvamedhika-parvan*** or the *Book of the Horse Sacrifice*, sub-*parvan*s 91–92, describes the *Aśvamedha* by the victorious Pandu. This book also contains the *Anugītā* episode.

Book XV: ***Āśramavāsika-parvan*** or the *Book of Retirees*, sub-*parvan*s 93–95, tells of the retirement of the older generations to the forests and their eventual deaths.

Book XVI: ***Mauṣala-parvan*** or the *Book of the Clubs*, sub-*parvan* 96, wherein the Yadu people scatter as a result of infighting (curiously, with *mauṣala*s or clubs) at a picnic.

Book XVII: ***Mahāprasthānika-parvan*** or the *Book of the Great Departure*, sub-*parvan* 97. In this volume, the Pandu leave the country on foot to ascend the Himalayas; each of the brothers and their wife drop dead one by one except Yudhiṣṭhira.

Book XVIII: ***Svargārohaṇa-parvan*** or the *Book of the Ascent*, sub-*parvan* 98, has Yudhiṣṭhira finally reaching heaven in his corporeal form, and several didactic events thereafter.

The ***Harivaṁśa*** or *Genealogy of Hari*, sub-*parvan*s 99–100, as also the ***Bhaviṣyat***, are *khila*s or *addenda*; the former fills in more data on the life of Krishna, especially on his childhood which is not covered in the eighteen books.

The Evolution of the Epic

The compendium of eighteen *parvan*s with 100 sub–*parvan*s is a massive *hundred thousand verses* long, the verse usually being the *catuṣpada* or quartet. The mass was not composed in its entirety at one time but displays stratification. Internal evidence indicates two versions—the full length *Maha–Bhārata* (*mahā* being great—*magna*) which includes appended stories (*upa-ākhyāna*s), and the *Bhārata*, which shorn of the *upākhyāna*s, is only 24,000 verses long.[1] The epic also is said to have been first recited by the sage–bard Vaiśampāyana at Janmejaya's *sarpasattra*; later, other bards, like Lomaharṣaṇa the *Sūta* and his son Ugraśravas *Sautī*,[2] worked on it, *Sautī*'s version being presented at Naimiṣāraṇya. In addition, there are indications that a nuclear 8,800–versed version, called *Jayaḥ*, composed by Vyāsa, had once existed.[3]

There are other evidences of accretion of the epic. Vedic literature does not mention the epic but does mention some of its characters; it is also aware of an *itihāsa* ('it so happened')[4] by which probably the *Jayaḥ* was meant. This shows that the period of the epic was the end of the Vedic age. And yet, the epic is aware of Vedic and Upaniṣadic schools that did not come into existence till many centuries afterwards.[5] Also, it mentions

1 The stanza:
Caturviṅśatisahāsṛṅ cakre bharatasaṅhitām /
upākhyānir vinā tāvad bharataṅ procyate budhair

has been interpreted variously as, one, the *Bharata* was only 24,000 verses long, shorn of the *upākhyāna*s, and two, that the *Mahābharata* was expunged of the *upākhyāna*s, leaving the *Bharata*. The two meanings only invert the sequence of composition but do not deny *two versions*, which is attested in the later *Āśvalāyana Gṛhyasūtra*.

2 The *Bharata* had 24,000 *śloka*s and the Mahabharata, 82,000, the latter figure according to the count given in the *adhyāya 2 of the Ādiparvan*. The contribution of *Sūta* is not in the form of a full-fledged epic but only that of isolated episodes like the *Āstikaparvan*.

3 *jayonāmetihāso'yam śrotavyovijigīṣuṇā*, in *Mbh* (KMG), I: 62.20, is 'this history is called *Jaya*. It should be heard by those desirous of victory'. Also, *jayo nāmetihāso'yam śrotavyo jayamichhatā*, *Mbh* (KMG), XVIII: 5.46, 'This history is known by the name of Jaya. It should be heard by everyone desirous of victory'. This *Jaya* is supposed to be 8,800 verses long. Also see *Mbh* (KMG), V: 136, 18.

4 *Atharvaveda Saṅhitā*, (*AV*), trans. R.T.H. Griffith, Banaras, Lazarus, 1895, XV: 6.11–12.

5 M. Witzel, 'Ṛgvedic History: Poets, Chieftains and Polities', in G. Erdosy (ed.), *The Indo–Aryans of Ancient South Asia: Language, Material Culture, and Ethnicity*', Walter de Gruyter, Berlin and New York, 1995, pp. 307–352.

the Kṣudraka–Mālava, a political combine that came into being not before Greek rule,[6] and *forecasts* that Śaka and Yona[7] will rule the *Kali* Age,[8] who were known in India not much earlier than the 3rd century B.C.

That the epic remained open for yet more centuries is seen in its mention of the Hara-Hūṇa and implicit reference to the *Uttara Ramayana*, whereas the Huns appeared in South Asia only in the second century and the *Uttara Ramayana* was not composed till several centuries A.D.[9] While Paṇini and the *Aśvlāyana Gṛhyasūtra*, dated to the latter half of the 1st millennium B.C., mention both *Bhārata* and the *Mahābhārata*, indicating two extant versions, the Greek chronicler Dio Chrysostom, *c.* 40–120 A.D., mentions an Indian *Iliad* of 100,000 verses. Finally, copper-plates of Śarvanātha, 533–534 A.D., found at Khoh in Satna District, Madhya Pradesh, describe the epic as *śatasahasrī saṅhitā*, i.e. 'collection of 100,000 verses'.[10] It is thus reasonable to conclude that from an early *Jayaḥ* spawned two versions by late 1st millennium B.C., of which only the larger version survived by mid-1st millennium A.D., the smaller one having fallen out of use. By this time, the epic was no more *itihāsa* but a didactic composition.

Extraneous Material and Inconsistencies in the Epic

Strict rules of transmission, called the *padapāṭha*, had ensured that the *Ṛgveda* remained consistent from Assam to Kerala. There was however no such arrangement for the epic, and bards and minstrels added to and edited it freely, interpolating masses of material between sections or nesting them up to several levels in the *frame-in-tale* style, introduced with the help of certain stock phrases.[11] The additions and modifications,

6 *Mbh*, II: 52.15.

7 See also Raychaudhuri, *Political History*, pp. 3–6.

8 *Mbh*, III: 188.35.

9 It refers to the *Rāma Śūdraghātin* episode, see Hopkins, *Great Epic*, p. 72

10 John F. Fleet, *Corpus Inscriptionum Indicarum: Inscriptions of the Early Guptas*, vol. 3, Calcutta, Central Publications Branch, 1888, pp. 111–12. Six copperplate inscriptions found near Jabalpur in Central India belonging to the Uccakalpa feudatories of the Kaḷacuris dated from the 420s to 460s mention the *Mahabharata* as *śatasāhasri-saṅhitā* or *Thousand-Versed*. Also see Kochar, *Vedic People*, p.27.

11 *Idam yad sṛṇuyadvṛtam*, *Mbh*, III: 46.62, or '*now you listen to this*'; *tatrā tasyādbhūtam karma sṛṇu tvam*, *Mbh*, III: 214.7, or '*now you listen to this wondrous act of his*'; *purā kṛtayuge rājan*, *Mbh*, IX: 40.3, '*once upon a time a king …*'

reconciled from time to time, are of three categories—that providing background information of characters and events, that offering moral advice, didactic lessons, and justifications of certain disturbing episodes, and that which is entirely unrelated to the plot, like the copious Bhārgava legends. In addition, the epic 'copied itself'—many episodes occur at multiple places,[12] often in divergent or contradicting forms.

The inconsistencies in the narrative led scholars, like Hopkins, to remark that '[t]*ale is added to tale, doctrine to doctrine, without much regard to the effect produced by the juxtaposition*'.[13] Several inconsistencies are directly related to the war. In the mace duel between Bhīma and Duryodhana, Bhima wins by the foul move of hitting Duryodhana on the thigh, a move suggested by Krishna himself. As Duryodhana lay writhing on the ground, Baladeva appears on the scene, berates Krishna for having used foul means, and departs. Immediately afterwards, Krishna turns on Yudhiṣṭhira and berates him for having supported the act, whereas it was he that had suggested it in the first place; Yudhiṣṭhira, who had earlier been reluctant, now finds himself justifying the act! Krishna himself concedes later that there was indeed no other way in which Duryodhana could have been felled. The anomaly, including the appearance of Baladeva, is an obvious insert in order to showcase Krishna as the pious hypocrite—*dharmacchala*.

The epic also spawned many versions and sub-versions of which, while the *Kashmir Recension* has been judged the most stable, the *Southern Recension* is quite different from the *Northern*. There are also vulgate editions. The Bhandarkar Oriental Research Institute (BORI), Pune, undertook the onerous task of formalising the many versions and identifying the original—over painstaking decades of consulting, selecting from, and rejecting, materials from up to twelve hundred different manuscripts from all over South and Southeast Asia, it offered the *Critical Edition* in September 1966.[14] However, the *Critical Edition* has been criticized by many; the spearhead of this effort, V.S. Sukthankar, himself considered the didactic material, dropped largely on grounds of

12 Hopkins, *Great Epic*, pp. 1–2.

13 Hopkins, *Great Epic*, pp. 370.

14 *The Mahabharata: Text as Constituted in its Critical Edition*, Bombay, BORI, 1971.

late inclusion, as part of the one and the same whole.[15] For instance, to Sukthankar the dropping of Draupadī's celebrated prayer to Krishna when she was being molested by Duḥśāsana was unwarranted.

Getting at the Roots

Hopkins had concluded after comparing differences in compositional styles that the epic could not have been created by a single person. Others, like Holtzmann,[16] Hopkins,[17] or von Schroeder,[18] tried to exfoliate the epic to get at its core but have admitted that their results are incomplete. Even the *Critical Edition* does not claim to be the *ur–Bharata*, i.e. the original *Bharata*. M.R. Yardi, intimately associated with the *Critical Edition*, took the approach of subjecting variations in compositional style to statistical analysis and segregating the redactions. Denying, in agreement with Hopkins or Brockington, that the *Jayaḥ* was a distinct redaction and arguing that it was only a generic *class* of heroic poetry,[19] Yardi claimed to have distilled Vaiśampāyana's *Bharata*, which to him was the oldest redaction.[20]

There are inconsistencies in Yardi's statistical method. For instance, though it could remove the fantastic nativity tales of all the other characters, it could not expunge the equally if not more fabulous nativity of Vyāsa. Mehendale has raised several objections to the statistical approach of

15 V.S. Sukthankar, *On the Meaning of the Mahābhārata*, Bombay, Asiatic Society, 1957, p. 85–6.

16 Adolf Holtzman, *Das Mahabharata und seine Theile*, 4 vols., Kiel, Osnabrück Biblio, 1892, p.5.

17 E.W. Hopkins, 'The Social and Military Position of the Ruling Caste in Ancient India as Represented by the Sanskrit Epic', *Journal of American Oriental Society*, vol. 13, 1889, pp. 57–376; especially pp. 67–8; E.W. Hopkins, 'The Bharata and the Great Bharata', *American Journal of Philology*, vol. 19, 1898, pp. 1–24; Hopkins, *Great Epic*, chapter 11 *et passim*.

18 Leopold von Schroeder, *Indiens Literatur und Cultur*, Leipzig, 1887, pp. 459ff.

19 M.R. Yardi, *Mahābhārata*, pp. v–vi. See also J.L. Brockington, *The Sanskrit Epics*, part 2, vol. 12, Leiden, Brill, 1998, p. 21; Brockington says that the term *Jaya* was a misreading of the *Bharata* itself.

20 M.R. Yardi, *The Mahābhārata*. Based on statistical analysis of the tendency to use different types of words, syllables or rhyming techniques, Yardi identified several styles which he has called the A, Alpha, B, Beta, and C Styles, which he has then attributed to Vaiśampāyana, Sūta, and Sautī, and the eponymous Harivaṅśakāra and Parvansaṅgrahakāra, respectively.

Yardi, arguing that compositional styles could vary for many reasons, only one of which was that different authors were composing the texts.[21] Nevertheless, Yardi, who insists on the validity of his methodology,[22] does give us something to go by, but only as long as we are careful not to apply the different compositional styles to specific redactors *personally*. It will be more fruitful to consider that instead of three or four redactors, additions and editions were made by a continuum of redactors and users whose styles and philosophies were marked by ambiguous bands, and which were *formally compiled and edited* at certain specific times. The above approach requires a case-to-case comparison to determine logically what period or redaction a particular passage could belong to.

This can be explained with an example.

The *Mahabharata* contains the names of a total of 300 nations, tribes, or regions. Those that appear in the *dyūta* list (their rulers visit the victor's court bearing tributes after the *rājasūya*) are largely from north and west of the Divide, while those that were attacked during the Pandu *digvijaya*, i.e. the conquest of the quarters part of the *rājasūya* episode and thus earlier to the *dyūta*, were largely from the east and south, including a Yavana city on an eastern river, obviously a Greek or Roman trading port. Why are the latter nations and peoples absent in the *dyūta*, a later episode than the *digvijaya*? Obviously because the *digvijaya* list was composed after the *dyūta* list, by when geographical awareness had advanced further to the east and the south.[23] It also shows that the *digvijaya* episode had been interpolated into the *rājasūya*.

The risk in this approach is to conclude that only the *ur-Mahabharata*—the *Jayaḥ* or the *Bhārata*—is the sole authentic document, and reject all additions as spurious, ignoring the possibility that much authentic data may

---

21 M.A. Mehendale, 'Book Review: Yardi's The Mahābhārata, its Genesis and Growth—A Statistical Study', *Annals of the BORI*, vol. 69, no. 1/4, 1988, pp. 349–355.

22 M.R. Yardi, 'My Studies on the Mahābhārata: A Clarification', *Annals of the BORI*, vol. 70, no. 1/4, 1989, pp. 235–241.

23 For another demonstration of the expanding geographical knowledge, this time with the help of separate lists of Pandu peregrination and pilgrimage during their exile, see T.S. Shejwalkar, 'The Mahābhārata Data for Aryan Expansion in India I', *Bulletin of the Deccan College Research Institute*, vol. 5, Sukthankar Memorial Volume, 1943–44, pp. 201–219.

have survived independently and then included only in later redaction.[24] This calls for an inspection of South Asian narrative and literary traditions.

Narrative Traditions and the Dynamics of Accretion

Before the advent of books and television, storytelling was a specialised art and had its own science and theory, etiquette and propriety, and style and purpose. There were specialists in its different genres. For instance, origin–legend and genealogy were the specialization of *vaitālika* in the ancient and *bhāṭa* in medieval India, who like the West African *griot* were venerated as preservers and transmitters of heritage. Closely associated with them were panegyrists and laudators, like the post-Vedic *sūta* or *māgadha*[25] and later day *cāraṇa*, who sang of their patrons' valour and generosity.[26] Now, *cāraṇa*s and *bhāṭa*s were fighting–minstrels, appearing together as *bhāṭa–cāra* or *cāra–bhāṭa*;[27] principally they were similar to the *sūta*, where *sūta* was also chariot builder and charioteer, who accompanied his lord in war and was thereby in the best position to sing of battles. There were other classes, like the ancient *kuśīlava*s or rhapsodists, of the medieval *bardāi* who rhapsodised the *rāso*s—heroic ballad and genealogy rolled into one. The present epic, the oldest manuscript of which comes from no earlier than the Kushan period,[28] was determined by the manner in which these and other specialists in preservation and narration used it.

As per the *Gṛhyasutra*s, rhapsodists performed to the seven-stringed lyre or *saptatantrī vīṇā*; whether they used other props like the painted screen—the *paṭa* or *phar*—used by later troubadours and *bardāi*s is not known. Rhapsodising narrators would repeat passages from time to time to recapitulate what had gone before and enable latecomers to catch up—such repetition was the equivalent of turning back pages of a book or rewinding

24 Hopkins has admirably illustrated this with the help of the *Ramayana*, much of which material for instance is older than the *Mahabharata* though they were included and versified later. See Hopkins, *Great Epic*, pp. 58–84.

25 *ŚB*, xiii.4.3.3.5; of these classes, the *māgadha*s were of lesser social status, and only supposed to sing the praise of the king when the latter entered court.

26 *Bhāṭa* and *cārana* play important roles in verifying genealogies in Rajput marriage negotiations.

27 Śrīharṣa, *Naiśadhīya Carita*, I: 32, '*pade pade santi bhaṭa-raṇodbhaṭa*'.

28 Dieter Schlingloff, 'The Oldest Extant Parvan–List of the Mahābhārata', *Journal of the American Oriental Society*, vol. 89, no. 2, April–Jun 1969, pp. 334–338.

a cassette tape. Also, reciting from memory required performers to be on a kind of mental autopilot, recalling and preparing the next passage while still full swing in the current one. Thus, mechanical phrases which could be uttered without thinking, like stock descriptions of cities, forests, battles, meeting respectable people, babble of crowds, punctuate the narratives, allowing time to recollect the next passage. These techniques account for the numberless repetitions and the endless clichéd passages to the point of distraction.

Apart from the rhapsodies which were sung for entertainment at courts and fairs, formal narrations were made by a class of priestly gentlemen known as *vācaka*, who spoke not sang, neither dramatizing nor rhapsodising but reading selected passages (complete recitations could take months) from the texts while comfortably seated.[29] There were several purposes behind such narration—at one time, like young European knights listening to the exploits of Greek or Scandinavian heroes from the *Iliad* and the *Heimskringla* and discussing their actions thereafter as a form of rudimentary military education, *Yajurvedin* or *Kṣatriya*[30] youngsters received education in military science and morality from the epic stories. With time, the purpose of the epic changed from a war–book to a means to teach of the destructiveness of ambition; to Warder, the aim of listening to the epic was to experience the '*calmed state arising from the renunciation of destructive worldly ambition*'.[31] It was in this form, i.e. the *itihāsa* which included *ākhyāna* and *purāṇa*, that the *vācaka* used the epic—prosaic, terse, and abrupt like the *Brāhmaṇa*s, and with none of the aesthetics of *kāvya* or poetry.[32] To Hopkins, the epic was the result of the fusion of these two genres—formal reading with rhapsodic rendering,[33] the terse passages with verse-filling epithets provided by the

29 Hopkins, *Great Epic*, pp. 363–364.

30 Hopkins, *Great Epic*, p. 368.

31 A.K. Warder, 'Classical Literature', in A.L. Basham (ed.), *A Cultural History of India*, Oxford University Press, 1975, p. 171.

32 Which in addition to the *āgama* (religious scripture) and *śāstras* (scholarly treatise), were the main genres of Post–Vedic traditional literature. See A.K. Warder, 'Classical Literature', pp. 170–96.

33 Hopkins, *Great Epic*, p. 367. '*The story and lay are equally old. Their union was rendered possible as soon as the lay, formerly sung, was dissociated from music and repeated as a heroic tale of antiquity. This union was the foundation of the present epic.*'

formal *itihāsa*, and the florid passages adorned with figures of speech and profuse with metres contributed by the *kāvya*-style rhapsody developed after the 5th century B.C.

In the age before cinema and television, storytelling was an extremely popular art, an entire street in Peshawar being named *Kūcā Kissa-Kh*ʷāni or *Storytellers' Street*, a street that is supposedly strewn with nails to make people sit down to remove them from their shoes and get drawn in to hearing a story! Rules and protocols governed not only formal narration of stories but also tales of travellers huddled around inn and camp fires—a teller was to stick to the correct version, he was not to be interrupted, and he was to finish the story, be it over several nights. At the same time, narrators improvised and embellished to enable audiences to relate better, often adding background information which served the same purpose as footnotes or appendices do in modern text. Thus, stories were living and growing organisms, and naturally tended to diversify and take on local hues. Different versions of the same story have been found on the Deccan, along the *Uttarāpatha*, or in Bokhara and Isfahan—the fact that a particular story had been *told* in a certain way at some gathering also *lent authenticity* to that version.

There were efforts to maintain homogeneity—at times, under initiative of kings or scholars, stories were edited, undesirable additions expunged, suitable ones legitimised, and contradictions reconciled, giving rise to the various redactions. The conclave at Naimiṣāraṇya convened by Śauṇaka, which was so important to the formalization of the epic as well as the Vedas, was probably one such initiative.

Further accretions occurred when the epic, once an elitist preserve,[34] lost its exclusivity and obtained great appeal among a laity increasingly denied access to Vedic and sacred literature, if only because they no more understood their language. Naturally, the plebianised epic now became a vehicle for public instruction in morality, so much so that it was acknowledged as the *fifth* Veda. This explains the volumes of morale precepts and didactic passages that are part of the epic. Episodes were tweaked, and characters made to commit blunders or ask inane questions and then get helplessly lectured. The *Śāntiparvan* makes Yudhiṣṭhira listen

34 Through its genesis and evolution, the epic always had an elitist character, telling little of common men, peasants, soldiers, even charioteers and junior knights, and everything about the great lords and chiefs.

attentively to lessons in political economy which were irrelevant to his socio–political milieu. However, use of the *Mahabharata* as a vehicle of morality to propagate a righteous and reserved code of conduct posed a difficulty—the excesses and abandon of its older, brutal, and violent age made its protagonists appear 'guilty' of unsavory acts and in need of being 'whitewashed' lest these acts were cited as precedents by the unscrupulous. Where whitewashing was not possible without adversely affecting narrative structure, individuals were absolved by giving it out that the acts were 'divinely inspired' and thus beyond the judgment of man. This is the reason behind a common misconception, first presented by Schroeder, that the Pandu were originally negative characters who were recast as heroes.

Finally, we come to the third great body of extraneous material—volumes of unrelated material like the *Śakuntalopākhyāna*, *Rāmopākhyāna*, or *Nalopākhyāna*, that were fitted into the epic under various guises and pretexts. This had been done for their preservation, as everyone knew that the epic was too popular to be lost and no one was very fastidious about what was to be included and what not. Also included were tales and legends of communities nowhere associated with the epic's plot but added merely for the 'snob value' of being *al–qitabi*. Finally, there are the copious Bhṛgu legends, added for no apparent reason other than flattering the Bhṛgu priests who had become very powerful, and who in fact controlled the growth of not only the epic but also much of the religious lore.

Changes occurred even after the epic was committed to writing, for reasons ranging from substitution of similar looking letters, '*as if the copyist spoke the word to himself while copying, but mispronounced it,*' errors in assimilation or comprehension, shortening of words, drafting errors, erroneous editing, i.e. the copyist feeling something was wrong and 'correcting' it, replacing a 'senseless' word with a familiar word, and so on. The dynamics of amendment to written documents has been demonstrated with the help of the Bible by Bart D. Ehrman,[35] who has shown that the story of Jesus as a real person had been fleshed out no earlier than between the 8th to 12th centuries.

35 Bart D. Ehrman, *Misquoting Jesus: The Story Behind Who Changed the Bible and Why*, Harper San Francisco, 2005.

Situating the Accretions

Vaiśampāyana's *Bharata*, which is the first acknowledged redaction of the epic, seems to have been presented at the *sarpasattra* of Janamejaya;[36] in other words, it was composed at the victor's court and could not have been but sympathetic to it. Generations later, the epic was formalised by Ugraśravas at Naimiṣāraṇya, at a congregation of Bhṛgu sages under the elderly Śaunaka; it was probably here that the Bhṛgu legends were added, no doubt to flatter him, creating a corpus sympathetic to the Pandu and the Bhṛgu. However, Ugraśravas says that he was merely repeating what he had learnt from Lomaharṣaṇa, who he calls father; this shows that there were other redactions between the two.

Now, while a *Pandu* epic is attested in references in Patañjali,[37] Sañjaya, companion and counsel of the blind Kuru chief Dhṛtarāṣṭra, had also given a running commentary of the battle he could supposedly witness by television or telepathy. Now, this Sañjaya, portrayed in later redactions as a conscientious noble with Pandu sympathies who upbraids Dhṛtarāṣṭra on his failure to check his sons' adventurisms, was really *sārathi* or charioteer of Dhṛtarāṣṭra, thus *sūta*, which at once puts him in the position of narrator of the battle–song. Perhaps his composition contained the *Kuru* point of view. In the light of the above it is premature to discard the *Jayaḥ*—albeit its highly ambiguous indications, the *Jayaḥ* has an independent tradition according to which Kṛṣṇadvaipāyana Vyāsa took three years to compile its five *saṁhitās*, which he then transmitted to his five pupils. Among the pupils, all of whom created their own *saṁhitās*, were his son Śuka, and also Vaiśampayana.[38] The small nucleus of 2000 *triṣṭubha* metres (most of the epic is in the *anuṣṭhubha* metre), identified as the core of the epic by M.C. Smith,[39] may or may not have been the *Jayaḥ*. We will return to this question after inspecting and comparing with

---

36 Raychaudhuri, *Political History*, p. 33; also, *Mbh*, XVIII: 5.34.

37 *asidvitīyo'nuśas-ara Pāṇḍavam*, Patanjali, *Mahābhāṣya.*This is one of the very few versions known by the name of the Pandu; the epic is known by the name of the Bharata everywhere. Also see Subodh Kapoor (ed.), *An Introduction to Epic Philosophy*, 6 vols., Cosmo Publications, New Delhi, 2004, vol. 5, p. 1406. Another example of a tradition explicitly related with the Pandu is the *Pandavani* folk theatre of Chattisgarh.

38 *Mbh*, I: 56.32 and 57.74–75.

39 M.C. Smith, *The Warrior Code of India's Sacred Song*, New York, 1992.

the *Mahabharata* another great battle–epic from across the world—the *Iliad.*

The Story of Ilium

The *Iliad* of Homer only covers part of the story of Ilium or Troy, i.e. from the anger of Achilles which makes him hold back from fighting, to his killing of Hector and the latter's funeral. It does provide some preceding matter in flashback, narrative, and background information, but to piece together the full story one must consult other works, the closest of which is Homer's *Odyssey*, story of Odysseus' eventful return from Troy which recounts many episodes in flashback. Other materials are the *Aenid*, which details the sack of Troy and the supposed emigration of a batch of Trojans to what became Rome, the six *Epic Cycle poems* which deal with different parts of the story, and many other Aegean poems, ballads, and mythological themes, not all Hellenic, which refer to episodes of the war or provide background information on it. Had the 1st millennium Greeks thrown all the material into one macro-poem, added any and every tale and legend of human or divine characters they found, thrown in the extracts and conclusions of all schools of philosophy then appearing in the Aegean, and added for good measure all strands of evolving morality and religion, using one or the other heroes as dummies, they would have had a chaotic *Mega-Iliad* on their hands.

Yet, it would be unwise to reject all this material as spurious, as it would be to seek the *ur–Iliad* of an original Homer and reject all layers added by subsequent 'Homers' as inauthentic. Undoubtedly, the various contingents of the many island nations that fought at Troy would have taken back their tales, which they sang of in their castles and at their banquets. While some of this material may have been collected and compiled into an enlarged *Iliad*, the rest could have survived independently in myth, legend, tale, or ballad, which may have then found their way into other compositions, or even in the *Iliad* itself, at a later time. Thus, all accretional or parallel material must not be blindly rejected because they could contain much of what had been left out earlier, and also diverse perspectives of immense value.

It is reasonable to test a similar model for the *Mahabharata*. Warrior nations returned from Kurukṣetra with their experiences and claims to fame, which their charioteer–bards composed into ballads and drinking–songs for troubadours to sing at their courts and banquets. It is perfectly normal for all these diverse material to have been compiled, by someone like Sañjaya or the eponymous Vyāsa (whose name simply meant *redactor, expander, one who spans*), and perhaps also recast into a common metre to aid memory.[40] This contradictory and amorphous mass of heroic poetry, probably called *Jayaḥ*, could have then been used as base for development by bards and panegyrists, not personal retainers of kings but compilers seeking a larger canvas and audience; recasting, expanding, editing, and teasing into shape, they could have created early versions as Vaiśampāyana's *Bharata.*

Also, tradition associated with the *Jayaḥ* suggests that Vaiśampāyana was the possessor of one of its five *saṁhitās*; thus, there remained four other versions which contained authentic material, and which may have entered the corpus in later redaction or spawned variant recensions. The situation can be illustrated with a contemporary example. The story of the *First Afghan War* had always been told in a certain way, from the English point of view based on English sources, but this does not render Dalrymple's *Return of the King: the Battle for Afghanistan*,[41] which uses Persian and Dari material that had always been known to and used by Afghan writers[42] but seldom used by mainstream scholars, spurious. These materials, written in styles ranging from livid Asian to florid court Persian, reveals entirely new perspectives of the events, for instance the tensions that rift Afghan forces and the intrigues that still kept them patched together.

Thus, we see that neither compositional style nor early or late inclusion is conclusive indicator of authenticity. For instance, only Krishna of Dvārakā appears in the earliest redactions identified by Hopkins or Yardi, while Krishna of Mathura appears only in later layers or in the appendix

40 The earliest material is in the *chanda* or metre called *Triṣṭubha*, while the largest part is in the *Anuṣṭubha.* It was important to cast the material in a similar, if not the same, metre because the entire corpus was transmitted by rote.

41 W. Dalrymple, *Return of the King: The Battle for Afghanistan*, Bloomsbury, 2013, pp. 495–502.

42 Like Munshi Abdul Karim's *Muharaba Kabul wa Kandahar*, Maulana Hamid Kashmiri's heroic poem *Akbarnama* (The History of Wazir Akbar Khan), Mohammad Gholam Kohistani Ghulami's *Jangnama* or History of the War, and Shah Shuja's autobiography *Waqi'at-i-Shah Shuja.*

Harivaṅśa. This does not authorise the discarding of Krishna of Mathura as spurious—a Devakīputra Krishna in later Vedic texts, especially the *Chandogya Upaniṣad*, may be identical of Krishna of Mathura, son of Devakī. As shall be seen later, the life of Krishna at Mathura meshes well with his subsequent career at Dvārāvati or Dvārakā, though the descriptions of its fortress are later additions. In a similar vein, the failure of the *Rāma Śūdraghātin* episode from appearing in the older *Ramopākhyāna* section in the *Mahabharata* but only in the late *Uttara Ramayana* does not render it spurious. It does not appear in the *Rāmopākhyāna*, which was nested into the *Mahabharata* as a tale told to Yudhiṣṭhira by Mārkanḍeya of one who was more unfortunate than him or his wife Draupadī, because it is irrelevant there, and may have had an independent existence till it was incorporated into the newly added *Uttara Ramayana*.

The Upshot

A workable timeline can be derived from the above. We have already seen that the epic events took place at the turn of the millennium, which was also the close of the Vedic age. As per Hopkins, lays and songs of these events were preserved till 400 B.C. when they were recast by Puranic diaskeuasts into epic form. Between 400 and 200 B.C., this epic acquired the passages casting Krishna as a demigod (though not with divine supremacy), and later, by 100–200 A.D., it acquired its didactic mass and also recast Krishna as all-god. By 400 A.D., the books were rearranged, the first book added, the *Śāntiparvan* enlarged the *Anuśāsanaparvan* separated; there were occasional amplifications thereafter. M.C. Smith traced how the epic transformed from its original *Kṣatriyadharma*—sanctity of alliances, preoccupation with keeping one's social obligations, maintaining clan spirit (*kula-dharma*), and following the Ṛgvedic ideals of truth and keeping one's oath, which are prominent in the early sections of the *Gītā*—and, alongside Krishnaism, acquired Brahminical material and concerns till it finally became a popular lore and a vehicle for mass morality.

Can we thus say that the *Mahabharata* is not primary evidence of the war, but only secondary evidence of indifferent value?

CHAPTER 2

The Backdrop of the Proto-Indo–Iranian Migrations

Racial or Communal Memories

The current age is marked by an ongoing revisionism aimed at recasting the Indus Valley Civilization, the IVC, as a *Sindhu–Sarasvatī* civilization, centred on the Sarasvatī identified with the Ghaggar–Hakra relic channel, rather than the Indus itself, and establishing its identity with the Vedic culture. The obvious intention of these efforts is to shift the IVC to within the political boundaries of modern India, and 'prove' that this was the zone of typification of the 'Aryan race' from where the latter spread across the world.[1] There are difficulties with this line of reasoning. While it is true that more IVC sites have been found along the Ghaggar–Hakra in modern Haryana, Rajasthan, and Multan than on the Indus itself, this is because desiccated conditions along the former channel forced early abandonment of the sites which then got sealed. On the other hand, the Indus was under continuous occupation, and the sites here were naturally overwritten. Further, most sites on the Ghaggar–Hakra lie *on the*

1 While there is no intention of joining this contentious debate here, as there are enough participants to whom it is best left, it must be said that not all proponents of the Out-of-India (OOI) theory are regional nationalists trying to re-appropriate history; Kazanas, for instance. See N. Kazanas, 'The Ṛgveda and Indoeuropeans', *Annals of the BORI*, vol. 80, 1999, pp. 15–42, and N. Kazanas, 'The Ṛgveda and Harappa', in A. Agrawal (ed.), *Vedic-Harappan Relationship*, Delhi, Voice of India, 2005,whose serious arguments have been considered, and to a large extent countered, by E. Bryant, *The Quest of the Origins of Vedic Culture: The Indo–Aryan Invasion Debate*, Oxford, 2001, and E. Bryant, "'Somewhere in Asia' and No More" Response to 'Indigenous Indo–Aryans and the Ṛgveda by N. Kazanas', *Journal of Indo–European Studies*, vol. 30, 2002, pp. 136–48.

flood plains of the rivers, indicating that the river was not too powerful or mighty, making its identification with the mighty Sarasvatī of the Vedas, supposed heartland of the Aryans, suspect.

Given that no life–form, animal or vegetal, ever originated in South Asia, folks implied by the term Aryan cannot but have entered it from outside like everyone else. More specifically, movement of migrants, infiltrators, and invaders from the Afghan mountains to the plains has been an ever-present reality of South Asia—Pakistan closed the Durand Line against the *Powendah* caravans in 1962, yet more Afghans come to Peshawar than Pakistanis go to Kabul even today. There is no reason why only the Aryan movement would have been the other way.[2] Elst himself, one of the most prominent proponents of the *Out–of–India* front, acknowledges an 'invasion' far in antiquity that had brought the Aryans *into India* first, but assures that it was at a time *so remote that it need not concern us*[!][3]

However, what is really intriguing in the case of the Aryans is that whereas most immigrant groups have preserved memory of extraneous origin—the Iranians claim their original homeland, *Airiiyanam Vaejo*, lies somewhere to their northeast—there is apparently little recollection of immigration among the bearers of the Aryan heritage today, a near–complete lack of reference in Vedic textual material, and little surviving steppe material culture in South Asia.[4] The situation is compounded by the substitution of burial by cremation, which has destroyed volumes of what could have been valuable anthropological data.

Absence of references to immigration in the Vedas is understandable. The Vedas are not history but religious and liturgical compendia, arranged in an anachronistic schema whose criteria for inclusion and exclusion is unknown today. No coherent mythology directly emerges[5] from it as does

2 The Gypsies, who have been convincingly demonstrated as having moved out of South Asia, are possibly remnants of long distance *Banjara* trading caravans that could not return.

3 Konrad Elst, *Update on the Aryan Invasion Debate*, Delhi, Aditya Prakashan, 1999, p. 172.

4 C.C. Lamberg–Karlovsky, 'Language and Archaeology: The Indo–Iranians', *Current Anthropology*, vol. 43, 2002, pp. 63–88, especially p. 74.

5 Louis Renou, *Religions of Ancient India*, [Jordan Lectures, 1951], Athlone, University of London, 1953, p. 12.

from Scandinavian texts, because the *ṛk*s or hymns—poems, incantations, and praise, including secular poems and even shamanistic self-praise or *ātmastuti*[6]—refer to gods in an ambiguous manner, often using veiled and oblique references, and at times using similar phrases for different gods. They allude, hint, remark, and pun, often incidentally and casually and at times in a veiled manner, more often than they make direct references to a context that is unknown to us but presumably was better known to their original users.

Further, in keeping with the Asiatic tradition of esoterism, the Vedic material mixes the sacred with the profane. Louis Renou has drawn our attention to the Middle Age *vakrokti* or twisted speech, a trend so acute in Asia that the highly spiritual poetry of Omar Khayyam was at one time discarded as erotica. Renou thought that the *ṛk*s were results of poetic contests between *ṛṣi* clans over composing hymns with veiled meaning but according to strict rules of form. In fact, the texts acknowledge that comprehension must cease at a point and the gods only *felt* indirectly—*parokṣa-kāma hi devāḥ*[7]—providing great scope for a speculative and esoteric religion. It is thus not very useful looking for a comprehensive story of migration in the Vedas.

Nevertheless, the Vedas yield much indirect evidence of an extraneous origin. Its society is pastoral, in contrast to the city-based and agrarian IVC, and is fascinated with cattle and horse, grassland and migration, and cart and camp. The *ṛk*s talk of using ruins (*armāḥ*) for navigation, temporary homes and permanent graves, and cultivation of *godhūma* and *yava* (wheat and barley) but not rice, even though rice had been known at Mehrgarh and the Indus since at least the 7th millennium B.C. These features, entirely at variance from what is discernible in the IVC, cannot but have originated in the pastoral world of the steppes. And yet, failure of communal memory to preserve it in oral traditions is understandable. Nomad migrations were seldom conscious, point-to-point marches—nomads peregrinated through the year between two or more pastures, like the Turcoman *qishlaq* and *yailaq* winter and summer pastures, along fixed circuits with several staging places. While these circuits could remain

6 Witzel is prepared to acknowledge little *shaman* element in the Veda, but I implore him to consider the fact that the *Ṛgveda* was compiled among a society at that time moving away from shamanism and which therefore suppressed all overtly shamanic elements.

7 Renou, *Religions of Ancient India*, p. 16.

stable over generations, they could shift in response to socio–political or ecological stimuli, at times imperceptibly. Due to the nomad taboo against using place-names when they are *at any place* (in order not to offend the resident spirit of that place) and reserving their use when they were far away,[8] and the universal migrants' habit of carrying toponyms along with them, the near imperceptible shifts are difficult to detect in verbal records.

Only when circuits were interrupted abruptly—a group prevented from undertaking the next stage, halted, dispersed, forced to change route, or adopt different arrangements like transhumance—might references enter communal memory. Also, lapses in memory could at times be deliberate. Huns in Europe appear to have preserved little memory of their north Chinese origin, perhaps a deliberate attempt to forget their defeat at Barkhol at Chinese hands. And finally, it is natural for a people obsessed with cyclic ages and rebirth to not bother with chronology of temporal events.

Evidence of Migrations in the *Ṛgveda*

And yet, when read between the lines, the Vedic texts do provide several pointers to migrations. Witzel, in adding flesh to Vedic history as have Kulke and Rothermund,[9] detects a shift in the core area of the Vedic people through incidental references in the *Ṛgveda*. Large parts of the *Ṛgveda*, especially Books II, VI, and VIII, display strong Iranic connections. Groups like the *Dṛbhīka*,[10] *Uśij*,[11] and *Balhīka* of Book II resemble the IIr *Derbikes*, *Usig*, and *Bāxdi*. Book VI mentions *Parśu* (Persian) and *Pakhta* (Pakhtun?), calls Abhyāvartin Cayamāna a *Pārthava* (Parthian), and has many Iranic terms like *Arśāsana* and *Anarśani*. Book

8 For instance, the Mongols have no fixed *K'unlun* Mountains unlike in the atlases. For them, the *K'unlun* are ever–present, mythical mountain *somewhere out there*. Mongols give one place many names, and many places one name, and refrain from mentioning the place by its real name *when they are there* out of respect for the *Gajar-un-ejen*, i.e. the resident spirit or *genii locii*. Also, nomad–like, they do not like to be identified with one place, till the later banner organization cut this up. See Owen Lattimore, *Mongol Journeys*, Varanasi, Pilgrim, repr., 2006, pp. 183–87 and 239.

9 H. Kulke and D. Rothermund, *A History of India*, New York, 1986.

10 *ṚV*, II: 14.3.

11 *ṚV*, II: 21.5.

VIII refers to western mountains, camels,[12] Parśu,[13] *mathra* horses,[14] and wool, sheep, and dogs,[15] and also mentions several tribes that are unknown to other books, showing that its locale was different.

Books II and VI refer to relocations—Indra *brought the Yadu and Turvaśu from far away,*[16]*across many waters;*[17] he *carried the Turvīti and Vayya across the rivers,*[18] the *Sindhu was crossed,*[19] the *Uśija cross the waters,*[20] and so on. Bongard–Levin[21] has postulated that the Vedic word *rip* is a recollection of the Rhipaean (Ural) mountains, while it has been argued elsewhere that the river-name *Rasā* in the Vedas and *Jaiminīya Brāhmaṇa* corresponds to the (mythical) Iranian **Rasā/ Raŋhā/ Rahā*, i.e. Greek *Rhā* or Volga. Taken together, these references suggest association with what are today eastern Iran and Afghanistan, and even more western regions, and also migration through mountainous country *via narrow passages*. We shall also see references to defeating of mountain chiefs on the way.

Mapping the *ṚV*

To Kochhar, the Vedic core area was a restrictive zone around the Hamun or Dasht-e-Margow region in south-western Afghanistan, and the post–Vedic *Ramayana* and *Mahabharata* situated on lower and upper Indus plains respectively. He thus unwittingly introduced a contradiction. There is no denying that the Hamun region was an important staging area in the migrations, but it is incorrect to suppose that a migrant people would have stayed at one place for so many generations, especially when

12 *ṚV*, VIII: 5.37–39; 46.21,31.

13 *ṚV*, VIII: 6.46.

14 *ṚV*, VIII: 46.23.

15 *ṚV*, VIII: 56.3.

16 *ṚV*, VI: 45.1.

17 *ṚV*, VI: 20.12; 30,17; also,*ṚV*, I: 174.9

18 *ṚV*, II: 12.13, IV: 19.6. The Vayya and Turvīti were identical with Yadu and Turvaśu, and were the names of the same people in the dialect of a different group.

19 *ṚV*, II: 15.6.

20 *ṚV*, II: 21.5.

21 See the discussion on the question of *Rip* in M. Witzel, 'Autochthonous Aryans? The Evidence from Old Indian and Iranian Texts', *EJVS*, vol. 7, no. 3, 2001, pp.1–115. Witzel has since then distanced himself from the identity.

the migration was not in the form of one wave but a continuous stream. Witzel has more reasonably traced the Vedic arena in a wide swathe from western Afghanistan to the Indo–Gangetic Divide, to understand which it is important to be familiar with the structure of the Vedic corpus.

The Vedas are arranged anachronistically into ten *maṇḍala*s or Books, most of which are specific to 'priestly clans'. Within them, the material is arranged by deity, metre, and length, in that order. The above is most applicable to Books II to VII, which are called family books because they are specific to clans of *ṛṣi*s, clan implying not only genetic decent but also spiritual adoption. Books I, and VIII to X are slightly different. While *ṛk*s 51–191 of Book I are by nine different clans, they are still arranged by deity, metre, and length; the first 50 hymns, also arranged in the same manner, are not specific to any clan. This is a curious case of the 'miscellaneous section' appearing at the beginning rather than the end of a corpus. Book VIII is the work of two clans, hymns 1–66 by the Kaṇva and the rest the Angira, but it is far less fastidious in subsequent arrangement by deity, length, or metre. Book IX has only the *Soma* hymns, apparently culled out from the other books and compiled when the *Soma* cult grew in prominence. Evidently, Book VIII was once the last book in the corpus, but that position today belongs to Book X, which appears to have started as an appendix, which is aware of the other books, and whose language is more modern than those of the other books though it contains older material as well.

The reason for such an anachronistic arrangement was probably to create a catalogue–index for users to refer to and select hymns, which were never to be written down but preserved orally with an elaborate memorization technique called the *padapāṭha*. In fact, so effective has been this technique that not only the index but each *ṛk* has been consistent across South Asia from the time of their compilation,[22] though the same

22 All manuscripts, the oldest of which is no older than the 11th century, are generally inferior to orally transmitted versions. The oldest MSS, kept in Nepal (National Archives), are said to have been written *c.* 1040 A.D., which agrees with Albiruni's testimony that his contacts in the Panjab and Kashmir informed him at a time shortly before this (*c.* 1030 A.D.) that the Kashmiri Vasukra had written down the Veda and composed a commentary. See Edward C. Sachau, *Albiruni's India*, London, 1888, 1:126. Some MSS may have been written slightly earlier, such as the *Paippaldda Saṁhitā* or the Upaniṣad collection, extracted by Safikara from Vedic texts a few hundred years earlier.

cannot be vouchsafed between their composition and compilation. The consistency prompted Witzel to call the *ṛk*s as *tape-recordings* of the ancient performances.[23]

Scholars have tried to arrange the corpus chronologically by inspecting style and context. While Arnold, in his *Vedic Metre*, used philological and etymological comparison to arrange the hymns into five periods,[24] most others, like Witzel, have preferred three stages of development.[25] Witzel postulates an *Early Ṛgvedic* stage from 1700–1500 B.C., to which belongs Books IV (Vāmadeva), Book V (Atrī), and Book VI (Bhāradvāja), and the early hymns of Book II (Gṛtsamāda) that refer to the Yadu–Turvaśa or Anu–Druhyu.[26] This material shows familiarity with western mountains and rivers of Afghanistan, where the rivers Sarayu, Sarasvatī, Yavyavatī, and Krumu are the equivalents of the Iranian or Afghan *Horayu* or Herat, *Horax$_v$aiti* or Helmand (the Greeks called this *Erymanthus*), Zhob, and Kurram respectively. It is also familiar with the Punjab rivers and the Yamuna and Ganga, though Kocchar suggests that these names here denote tributaries of the Helmand.[27] Significantly, the rich tin and copper deposits along these rivers made them suitable for occupation in the Bronze Age.

Witzel's *Middle (*or *Main) Ṛgvedic stage*, 1500–1350 B.C., has Books III (Viśvāmitra) and VII (Vaśiṣṭha), hymns 1–66 of Book VIII (Kaṇva) and the miscellaneous hymns 51–191 of Book I. This material focuses on the Pūru–Bharata moiety; Book III is familiar with the Punjab and Kurukṣetra and has Viśvāmitra arriving on the swollen Beas with the

---

23 I would introduce a layman's objection here—the hymns as they are recorded and rendered today cannot be called tape-recordings, because despite everything else, accents of the users have changed.

24 See E.V. Arnold, *The Vedic Metre in its Historical Development*, Cambridge, Cambridge University Press, 1905.

25 M. Witzel, 'Early Indian History: Linguistic and Textual Parameters', in G. Erdosy (ed.), The Indo–Aryans of Ancient South Asia, 1985, pp. 85–125. Also see A. B. Keith, 'The Age of the Rigveda', in E.J. Rapson (ed.), *The Cambridge History of India*, vol. 1, Ancient India, Cambridge, Cambridge Univ. Press, pp. 77–113.

26 Witzel, 'Substrate Languages', p. 3 and 'Ṛgvedic History', pp. 188–271.

27 Kochhar, *Vedic People*, pp. 120–2, *Rmn*, Ayodhya, 65.5 where Bharata crossed the confluence of the two rivers; *Mbh*, III: 84.38, 88.176,201 mentions the confluence and a lake named *Gaṅgāhārda*. This is the origin of the myth of the confluence at Allahabad, where the Ganga and the Yamuna do merge but the Sarasvatī is missing. The *Vāmana Purāṇa* lists the Ganga in Kurukshetra, *Vāmana Purāṇa* 13.6-7; 15.62.

Bharata caravan, praying to the river to lie low and let them pass,[28] in what is a commemoration of the Viśvāmitras' association with Bharata migration. Book VII has more material on Bharata migration across Punjab, and also mentions the BOTK.

Curiously, Book VII calls the Sarasvatī as *Vināśanā*, i.e. *that which disappears*, in contrast to the epithet *Nadītamā—Best amongst Rivers*, used for the *Sarasvatī* in older books and passages. Evidently, the Ghaggar–Hakra channel (considered the *Sarasvatī* in historical times, one of whose tributaries is the modern Sarsuti) is meant. In what was an immensely old hydrological event, rising of the intervening terrain, i.e. the Indo-Gangetic Divide, had caused the Yamuna and Satluj to slide away to either side, denying the later Sarasvatī their mass of meltwater and leaving a set of faltering, rain-fed relic channels known as the Ghaggar–Hakra. Although the event was pre-human, appearance of IVC sites along the watercourse, reference to the rivers in an agrarian context, subsequent conversion of the sites into ruins, and the *Mahabharata* story of Vaśiṣṭha throwing himself into the Satluj which would not let him pass, but which then prevented his getting hurt or drowned by dividing itself into a *hundred channels*,[29] suggest that the system of rivers had not stabilised till well after these regions had been populated.

Significantly, the Sarasvatī is singled out as *the* place to find potsherds for ritual purposes, which indicates that the IVC settlements on its banks, like Pīlibangan, had been abandoned. These ruins—*armaḥ/ka*s and (*mahā*) *vailasthāna*s—are mentioned in Vedic literature as navigation aids. Book VIII is also from this period, but concentrates on the west, referring to camels, *mathra* horses, wool, sheep, the Sindhu, its seven sister–streams (the *sapta–śvasā*), mountains and snow.

To the *Late Ṛgvedic stage*, 1350–1200 B.C., belong Books I (1–50), hymns 67–103 of VIII (Aṅgirā), and Book X. These hymns deal with descendants of the Pūru chief Trasadasyu (like Kuruśravaṇa) and emergence of the Kuru super-tribe (under the post-*ṚV* Pārikṣita). They also display assimilative features common to later Indian religion and society. It is difficult to discern any stratification beyond this; also, Books

28 *ṚV*, III: 33.

29 *Mbh*, I: 167.8

I and IX, being assorted collections, and Book X, being a late addition, carry scattered references and cannot be mapped easily. [30]

The above mapping indicates a familiarity with a wide swathe of terrain from Herat and the sand seas of Hamun in the west to the plains of the Yamuna and Ganga, with later generations of chiefs and priests being more familiar with the eastern parts. Also, *Nadītamā Sarasvatī* of the early Vedic hymns, which refer to the Helmand (and also the Arghandab, in a curious convention in which river names could fluctuate), appears earlier than the Indus hymns, which in turn appear before references to the *Vināśanā Sarasvatī.* Though the situation is somewhat complicated by Witzel's suggestion that the Vedic Sarasvatī was not a river at all but the *Milky Way*, crucial to the celestial religion of the Aryans,[31] there is an overall feel of eastward shift.[32] Book II makes the statement '*for the Ārya you opened the light; the Dasyu was left behind, on the left*',[33] suggesting increasing familiarity from west to east.

Such indication of any eastward shift is absent from later texts because their composers had already migrated to the plains by then, and in an un-self-conscious manner. There nevertheless exist two crucial concepts which indicate not only memory of migration but also its continuance, namely, the Āyu–Amāvasu duality first pointed out by Witzel several years ago, and the idea of *vrātya*, which has not been subjected to thorough academic analysis, respectively. These will be inspected in the next two subsections.

The Āyu–Amāvasu duality—Late References to Relocation

Witzel pointed out a till-then-unnoticed passage in the *Baudhayana Śrautasūtra* (*BŚS*) which says:

---

30 The stratification provided in Parpola's 'The Face Urns of Gandhara and the Nasatya Cult' is different, but it too points to a west to east movement. See Asko Parpola, 'The Face Urns of Gandhara and Nasatya Cult', in Michael Willis (ed.), *Migration, Trade and Peoples*, Proceedings of the Eighteenth Congress of the European Association of South Asian Archaeologists, London, 2005, the British Association for South Asian Studies, British Academy, London, 2009, pp. 149–162.

31 M. Witzel, 'Sur le Chemin du Ciel', *BEI*, 2, Leiden, Institut Kern, 1984, pp. 213–279. Also avalable at www.people.fas.harvard.edu/~witzel/CheminDuCiel.pdf (last seen 07 April 15).

32 *ṚV*, I: 130.7–8; 131.4–5; III: 31; VII: 100.4.

33 *ṚV*, II: 11.18.

> *'Ayu went east. His (people) are the Kuru–Pañcāla and the Kāśī–Videha. This is the Āyava. The Amāvasu stayed at home in the West. His* [people] *are the Gāndhārī, Parśu and Āraṭṭa. This is the Amāvasava.'*[34]

Here, Āyu and Amāvasu are sons of Purūravas from Urvaśi, and Kuru–Pañcāla and Kāśi–Videha (later Kosala–Videha) the two socio–political moieties on the Indo–Gangetic plains among whom the *Mahabharata* and *Ramayana* are set respectively. The Gāndhāra, Parśu, and Āraṭṭa are mountain peoples west of the Indus, and *Amāvasu* in Vedic grammar is '*stayed at home*'. The obvious interpretation of the passage—that peoples of the plains had migrated thither from a western homeland where their brethren still remained—has stirred up the hornets of controversy. Agarwal has cited the very next stanza of the *Baudhayana Śrautasūtra* which already places Purūravas, Urvaśi, and their sons at Kurukṣetra,[35] arguing that far from the Āyu *migrating to* Kurukṣetra, it was the Amāvasu who *migrated from* Kurukṣetra to the west.[36]

While Witzel has himself defended his arguments sufficiently,[37] Agarwal's objection can be countered even otherwise. The *Baudhāyana Śrautasūtra* is a late work, its lateness evident in its anachronistic use of the terms Kuru–Pañcāla for folk for whom Pūru, Bharata, or Sṛñjaya would have been more appropriate, and was written when the folk were *already* at Kurukṣetra. Its purpose was not to document migration—in the stanza quoted by Agarwal, Purūravas' semen and the earthen pitcher that held it, when placed next to the lake Bisvaṭi in Kurukṣetra, turn into the *aśvattha* tree surrounded by śami tree. A variant of this legend appears in the *Śatapatha Brāhmaṇa*[38] where the fire and sacrificial pan, given to

34 *prāṅ Ayuḥ pravavrāja. Tasyaite Kuru-Pañcālāḥ Kāśi-Videhāity. Etad Āyavam. Pratyanamāvasustasyaite Gāndhārayas Parśavo 'raṭṭāity. Etad Āmāvasyam*, see *BŚS*, 18, 44: 397.9 sqq.

35 *BŚS*, 18, 45.

36 Vishal Agarwal, 'On Perceiving Aryan Migrations in Vedic Ritual Texts', *Puratattva* (Bulletin of the Indian Archaeological Society), New Delhi, no. 36, 2005–06, pp. 155–165. As per translations of Willem Calland and C. G. Kashikar, while the Āyu went east, the Amāvasu (far from staying at home), *went west*.

37 For Witzel's defence and justification, see Witzel, 'Autochthonous Aryans?', n. 45 and 46.

38 ŚB, xi.5.1.

Purūravas by the Gandharvas (Urvaśi's people), on being placed near the lake Anyataplakṣaḥ in Kurukṣetra, turn into the *aśvattha* and śami. The story, whose purpose was to ascribe divinity to the two trees—the *aśvattha* (*Ficus Religiosa* or *peepul*) was the source of the fire drill to kindle the sacrificial fire, while the *śamī* was the base of the drill and also important in funerary rites—and underline the holiness of Kurukṣetra, only incidentally testifies to an *awareness* that Kuru, Pañcāla, Kosala, and Kāśi (all late names) had come from the western mountains where their *brethren remained.* An incidental contradiction is evident here—the Gandharvas, who are one of the Amāvasu, are already Urvaśi's people in the *Baudhāyana Śrautasūtra*! The situation will appear clearer if we recall that origin myths were created generations after the 'origin', i.e. when the tribe or family in question had become, or perceived itself to have become, important enough to require an origin myth (!), and were built around eponymous ancestors.

The *Vrātya*—Wolf of the Twilight

Migrations are no earth-shaking truth in themselves. Afghans have forever moved to the plains till the days of the Rohilla colonists, and continue to do so now. What is important is that Aryan immigration was not one exclusive wave but an endless trickle which continued even after the bulk of the IA had relocated to the plains and had lost recollection of any immigration. This trickle, very similar to the Rohilla migration, is poignantly represented in the ambiguous concept of the *vrātya.*

It is commonly held that *vrātya* stood for non-Aryan 'outcasts' from Brahmanic–Aryan society, but it has been shown that they really were IA groups who enjoyed high position in archaic levels of IA tradition, becoming renegades only from mid-1st millennium B.C. agrarian society. In archaic references, the *vrātya* is revered, mentioned respectfully eight times in the *Ṛgveda*, and has a dedicated section of the *Atharvaveda* (Book XV) where the king is called upon to honour a visiting *vrātya*. The *vrātya* is also crazed warrior, known for extreme, mystical practices represented by the *pañca–vrata* or five vows (thus the name), and forms of austerity like self-mortifying *askesis* of the Greeks which later developed into the systems of the *sāṅkyha*, *yoga*, and *tantra*.[39]

39 Mircea Eliade, trans. W.R. Trask, *Yoga: Immortality and Freedom*, New Jersey, Princeton University Press, 1990, pp. 103f, 256f.

Now, Wikander had postulated that the PIIr term **marya*, root of Old Avestan and Vedic terms *mairya*/ *márya*, denoted a *männerbund*,[40] i.e. an age-set undergoing rites of passage into adulthood, at the end of which its members would be initiated. This was vehemently, and derisively, opposed by Mary Boyce,[41] who denied evidence for any form of initiatory periods among PIIr youngsters, arguing that they were expected to act as householders immediately after initiation. She further argued that the term *mairya/ márya* indicated a generic fighting tribesman and had nothing to do with a *männerbund*. Both Wikander and Boyce would have had to considerably modify their views had they noted the IA institution of *vrātya*, which had overwhelming associations with initiatory practices. The *vrātya* is associated with the *sattra*, the original form of the Vedic *yajña* before it was taken over by the *soma* cult, and which survives only in some ceremonies like that of initiation. Other initiatory rites, including ritual intercourse with ceremonial 'harlot' *puṅścalī*, are associated with them. In later material, *vrātya* is labelled as disruptive to society,[42] called *uninitiated*, and are required to undergo the cleansing rite of *vrātyaṣṭoma* before admittance to Vedic society. It is in these 'initiatory' reference that lies the gap in understanding.

Very significantly, *vrātya*s are associated with the hounds of Rudra,[43] which at once places them in the liminal world of shape–shifters and shamans[44] alongside the *berserkr* and *werewolf* which are associated with the bears and wolves of Odin, Rudra's Teutonic counterpart. Now, the *berserkr* and *werewolf* were really Teutonic *männerbund*s which functioned under similar harsh vows, living and hunting in bear and wolf skins (thus their names), till they completed their period of initiation. Such *männerbund*s featured in many early societies, in which initiates lived

40 Stig Wikander, *Der arische Männerbund*, Lund, 1938, pp. 22ff.

41 M. Boyce, 'Priests, Cattle and Men', *Bulletin of the School of Oriental and African Studies*, University of London, vol. 50, no. 3, 1987, pp. 508–526, especially pp. 514–16.

42 D.G. White, *Myths of the Dog-Man*, University of Chicago Press, Chicago, 1991,p. 96.

43 White, *Myths of the Dog-Man*, p. 61. They were associated with liminal groups of Teutonic mythology, like *ulfhednar* and *halfhundingas*, i.e. wolf headed men and half hounds.

44 Mircea Eliade, *Essential Sacred Writings From Around the World*, New York, Harper San Francisco, 1992, p. 294.

under extreme, self-mortifying, and mystical vows, which included sexual promiscuity, genital mutilation, and even homosexuality. In Vedic society, we see youngsters undergoing rites of passage in *āśrama*s, spending part of the year roaming under harsh vows, indulging in cattle-lifting from rival tribes in order to establish their military prowess, enhance the stock of ones' tribe, use as seed capital to start new ventures, or even use as bride-price (quite like the Masai *morani* and the Turkana *ngingoroko*, discussed later). At the end of the initiatory periods, youngsters went through specific rituals after which they were acknowledged as adults. In Vedic practice, there were the *vrātyaṣṭoma* and *dīkṣā*, after which initiates were born again, i.e. *dvi-ja*.

Also, the *vrātya* were highly reputed as crazed warriors and associated with the colour black, using black cloaks and metal rings,[45] just as the *berserkr* '... *black their shields and dye their bodies black, and choose pitch nights for their battles. The terrifying shadow of such a fiendish army inspires a mortal panic, for no enemy can stand so strange and devilish sight*'.[46] In fact, these military fraternities everywhere served their societies as pools of manpower at the top in protocol of mobilization to deal with emergencies. They were also always young, being age-sets turned over frequently, often every year. In battle, they often acted as shock troops, able to inspire terror in enemies by their furious looks and antics—Mircea Eliade has called them the advance guard of Aryan invaders.[47] Comparing this institution with the medieval South Asian practice of using *sanyasi–faqir* irregulars will be an interesting exercise. The only theoretical difference between the *vrātya* and the Teutonic *männerbund* is that the *vrātya* stage passed with the *vrātyaṣṭoma* but the *berserkr* could never be 'cured' of his unpredictable, ungovernable nature which could relapse at any time.[48]

---

45 *Lāṭyāyana Śrautasūtra* (*LŚS*), 8: 6–7, *PB*, 17, 1.9–15.

46 H.R. Ellis Davidson, *Gods and Myths of Northern Europe*, Penguin Books, Middlesex, 1964, p. 67

47 Eliade, *Yoga*, p. 105.

48 G. Dumézil, *The Destiny of the Warrior*, University of Chicago Press, Chicago, 1970, p. 142, has the story of how a retired *berserkr*, though venerated for his wisdom, tended to relapse to his animal nature in the evenings, thereby getting the epithet *kveldúlfr* or *wolf of the twilight*.

With the above in mind, we can thus say that Boyce was only partially correct in disagreeing with Wikander's interpretation of the IIr term *marya*as *männerbund*, and *haumavarka* as *soma–wolf* (*vṛka* being wolf), and his equating the idea of the two and four-legged wolf with the shape-shifting *werewolf*, were overambitious.[49] In fact, she is not correct in saying that there was no institution resembling the *männerbund* among the IIr peoples. *Merak*, the Pehlavian cognate of *mairya*, also mean 'husband/ lover', which associates the idea of *mairyā* women in the *Avesta*in the sexual content with the *puṅścalī* ritual harlot.[50] Further, an intoxicating drink used in many early rituals is the *maireya*(*ka*), while the godhead *Aēšma*, the personified spirit of the *mairya/ márya* in Iranian lore, is armed with a knobkerrie-like wooden club which is a typical Stone Age weapon.[51]

Taken together, the above suggests that the term *mairya/ márya was indeed a sort of initiatory age-set, but from an even more archaic, near-*Stone Age period, when its members were armed with clubs, maces, and knobkerries. Logically, such age-sets would have been rendered *irrelevant later with the appearance of more effective* bronze weapons and better organization. The term *vrata* or vow, which was behind the term *vrātya*, is also one of the un-comprehended organizational terms associated with the Vedic militia, the others being *sardha* or *gaṇa*. The Vedic militia itself appears to have had a triangular–cum–hexadecimal organization, the *Marut*s, followers of the idiosyncratic Rudra who is intimately associated with the *vrātya* motif, being thrice six, and thrice sixty.[52] After the older institution *was superseded by the vrātya, mairya/ márya came to mean* generic herdsman–warrior.

Later, even the institution of *vrātya*, whose raison d'être was cattle rustling, faded out as cattle rustling grew unsustainable under the new conditions of South Asia. Even initiatory associations were lost, when *dīkṣā*, the ancient rite of passage, was replaced by the simpler rite of sacred–cord (*yajñopavīta*) and *upanayana* (second-eye, like the Iranian *naojot* or new-light), after which the youngster *directly* becomes householder. It was then that the term was re-appropriated to denote western mountain

49 Boyce, 'Priests', p. 515.

50 The *vrātya*s spent part of their year in the āśramas, where they often made advances towards the Guru's wife—*gurutalpagāmī.*

51 Boyce, 'Priests', p. 524.

52 *ṚV*, VII: 56.3; V: 59.6, 60.5.

folks, like the Malla, Madra, Aśvaka, Kekaya, Śākya, or Licchavi, inspired by their unkempt appearance, disrespectful egalitarianism, dangerous unpredictability, penchant for aggression, and fondness for raiding and cattle-lifting. In fact, the term came to mean something like *noble savage*, as these same tribes, though feared, were also venerated for handsome looks, purity of blood, preservation of original features of religion and language, and sublimity, uprightness, and courage—they were called *bhraṣṭa* (degraded) *Kṣatriya*, wooed for a range of socio–political reasons, and eagerly inducted into the regimented society of the plains *via* the old *vrātyaṣṭoma* rite of passage.

On their part, these '*vrātya*' tribes displayed migratory propensities, being always on the move. The Malla can be traced from the Indus, through Punjab, Rajasthan, Central India, the Nepal Terai, to Bengal, while the Aśvaka on the Swat can be traced to the Assaka on the Godavari.

The detour into these archaic concepts gives an insight into early PIIr military institutions and religious practices. In the epics, princes are recruited out of *āśrama*s to fight—in the *Ramayana*, they are taken, quite anachronistically by Vaśiṣṭha, to fight the 'ogress' Tāṭakā, while in the *Mahabharata*, they are taken by their preceptor Droṇa to fight the Pañcālas on behalf of the Kuru. We will later inspect in detail the mechanics of evolution of these terms and the forms of warfare associated with them. Their cult practices also provide insight into the origin of several South Asian religious themes, like mystical, extra–, even anti–sacrificial, religion that evolved into the *sāṅkhya* philosophy of the *Gīta*, or *yoga*, *tantra*, Buddhism, and Jainism (whose founder, the first *tīrthāṅkara* Ṛṣabhadeva, is hailed as *Mahā-Vrātya*). Most importantly, it underlines that naming of so many western tribes after a most archaic IA institution indicates an awareness of community of settled plainsmen with them, a tacit acknowledgement that the former were, at one time, just like the latter. We will see later that most participants of the *Mahabharata* war were such *vrātya* groups.

Genealogies and Migrating Groups

The Literary Picture

Having established the backdrop of immigration into South Asia of a host of nations, this section will try and see if mythical groups that populate South Asian lore, which can be divided into several classes, correspond to real and archaeological ones. One class, comprising the *Rakṣa* and *Asura* (and their affiliates) and perceived of as beyond the IA groups, will be discussed later. Another are the semi-mythical, -magical, -divine Gandharva, Kinnara, and Yakṣa, beings of the mountains, expert musicians, but allegedly with loose morals. Then there are the Amāvasu—Gāndhāra, Paraśu, or Āraṭṭa (king-less) tribes, kin of the a-cephalous peoples inhabiting these lands even today. And finally, there the Āyu, 'mainstream' IA on the plains represented by peoples who would in time bear the nomenclatures of Kuru–Pañcāla or Kosala–Videha. Before we progress, it is reiterated that no one-on-one identification is either being attempted or proposed, and nor is such a thing possible.

The plasticity of the genealogies and patterns is evident. As per the *Baudhāyana Śrautasūtra*, both Kuru–Pañcāla and Kosala–Videha were descended from Āyu (son of Purūravas, himself son of Iḷa/Iḷā, the hermaphrodite offspring of the Moon). The Kuru–Pañcāla can be traced to the *Pañcajana* or *Pañca-kṛṣṭi*, i.e. the five 'nations' or five 'furrows' that included the tribes of the Yadu, Turvaśa, Anu, Druhyu, and Pūru,[53] 'descended' from Yayāti, a descendant of Āyu and thus of the Lunar race. At the same time, as descended from Ikṣvāku, son of Pūru's descendant Tridhatu (at places son of Pūru himself), the Kosala–Videha are also Lunar. Elsewhere however, Ikṣvāku is descended from Manu *Vaivasvata*, i.e. *son of Vivasvat* the Sun, making the Kosala–Videha *Sūryavaṅśa* or Solar–clan.

Now, the Kosala–Videha may well have been a Pūru branch that had dispersed to the east, but it must be remembered that the Ikṣvāku always refer to themselves as *mānava* or *mānuṣa*, cognate with Germanic *Mannus*, and regard all but themselves as non-human, *a-mānuṣa*. Even the Lunar *Pañcajana* seems to have been a newly formed or imposed identity, as seen in its constituents forever deriding and denouncing one another as foreigners and barbarians. The Pūru, for instance, are derided as *mṛdhravācaḥ*, i.e. 'barbarous in speech', in the *Ṛgveda*, and as foreigners in the *Vāyupurāṇa*. To take this a step further, as sons of Yayāti from Devayānī and Sarmiṣṭhā, daughters of the *Asura* king Vṛṣaparvan and his high priest Śukra respectively, the five eponymous ancestors of the

53 Distinct from the *Pañca-Gaṇa* or Five Hordes, who are associated with later cavalry tribes like the Śaka, Cina, Hūṇa, etc. Also called *Pañcakṣiti*, *Pañcacarṣaṇi*, and *Pañcamānuṣa*. See Witzel, 'Ṛgvedic History', p. 202.

Pañcajana are also *Asura*. The affiliations of the Turvaśa are most suspect. The army of their chief Kāla–Yavana comprises Śaka, Tuṣāra, Darada, Tangana, Pārada, Khasa, and interestingly, Pāṇḍava, all Central Asian tribes, while the 'Yavana' part of his name suggests Ionic or Hellenic association.

In the Solar lore, Manu's son Ikṣvāku occupied the east and *became Kośala and Videha*, while Saryāti, another of his sons, *remained* on Anarta or lower Indus in the west, this theme of 'brethren' left behind in the west paralleling that of the Ayu–Amāvasu. Possibly, the Solar groups represent a more southerly route of immigration into South Asia. Pargiter thought that the *Mānava* were distinct from the *Aiḷa* or Lunar line, and were a westerly people who engaged with the Central Asian Haihaya and Śaka, classed as descended from Nariṣyanta, another son of Manu. Thus, it can be seen that applying any strict tree–branch model to formation of identities is fallacious, which is substantiated with the help of an example from Gothic genealogy. Jordannes, a Goth based at Constantinople, wrote that the Ostrogoth and Visigoth nations emerged abruptly when the bridge on the Dnepr which the Goths were crossing was washed away, stranding them on either side.[54] In reality, a long and complex stream of migration from the Wielbark culture in the Black Forests to the Chernyakhiv culture in the North Pontic steppes explains the origin of the Ostrogoths.[55] Similarly, of the five Mongol septs descended from their eponymous ancestors, two were strongly Turkic, while Subedei the general who defeated the Russian–Kipchak alliance on the River Khalka was himself Kipchak.[56]

However, convolutions in origin myths and genealogies, important to understanding the *Mahabharata*, can be best comprehended if seen not as genetically accurate genealogy but as conscious, politically motivated interpolations based on perceived affiliations and using eponymous characters. In addition to serving a political or social motive, they also deliberately or unconsciously conceal various types of succession—father-in-law to son-in-law (actually, mother–daughter), succession by sister's son, by brothers and adopted sons, and violent or non-violent political succession by outsiders—which coexisted with the usually presumed

54 Jordannes, *Gothic History*, 57–8 and Heather, *The Goths*, 21–49.

55 Christian, *Inner Eurasia*, pp. 221–222.

56 See Christian, *Inner Eurasia*, p. 404, on an analysis of Mongol alliance patterns.

patrilineal succession. In other words, genealogies and origin myths seek to propagate, reinforce, justify, ignore, or simply wish away events and associations. Another contributor to the convolution is the fact that often contemporaries were placed in succession, an ancient practice in the absence of common chronometry.

All that can be made out from the above is that Vedic, pre-Vedic, and extra-Vedic tribes, jostling along the migration routes over pastures that were increasingly at a premium, underwent endless realignments and developed varied identities, which they used selectively. Another aspect of the political structure of these tribes is that they often appear in pairs—not only the Kuru–Pañcāla and Kosala–Videha, or the latter's forerunner the Kāśī–Videha, but also Yadu–Turvaśu, Anu–Druhyu, or Pūru–Bharata. Such pairing is observed in the *Mahabharata* and later: Sindhu–Sauvīra, Andhaka–Vṛṣṇi, or Kṣudraka–Mālava. Now, while Anu–Druhyu and Yadu–Turvaśa appear in the earliest Vedic stage, only the latter is consistent through the early books which retain recollection of their migration. The Yadu–Turvaśa are '*brought from afar*',[57] and were helped by Indra to '*cross many waters*'[58] and '*narrow passages*'[59]; in Book IV and V, they are saved from drowning by Indra[60]; they feature in the slaying of *Dasyu*s like Cumuri or Dhuni. In the pro-Yadu–Turvaśa Book VI, they are glorified, and appear in association with Pūru–Bharata and Anu–Druhyu; they are not explicitly mentioned in Book VII but were presumably identical with the Yakṣu who are.[61] The Turvīti and Vayya, who crossed the Sindhu and defeat Āyu, Kutsa, and Atithīgva[62] with Indra's help,[63] are probably identical with the Yadu–Turvaśu, who are praised in the older portion of Book VIII (Kaṇva)[64] as giver of gifts.[65]

57 *ṚV*, VI: 45.1.

58 *ṚV*, I: 174.9; VI: 20.12.

59 *ṚV*, II: 11.18.

60 *ṚV*, IV: 30.17.

61 *ṚV*, VII: 18.14; also see H–P. Schimdt, 'Notes on the Rigveda, 7.18.5–10', *Indica*, Organ of the Heras Institute of History and Culture, Bombay, 1980, pp. 17, 41–47.

62 *ṚV*, II: 13.12.

63 *ṚV*, I: 54.6.

64 *ṚV*, VIII: 1-67.

65 *ṚV*, VIII: 45.27.

In contrast to the Yadu–Turvaśa, Anu–Druhyu appear only intermittently in early material, though they grow important in later works. Taken together, it appears that the Yadu–Turvaśu were an independent, politically influential people since the early Vedic times, while the Anu–Druhyu had a more chequered and unstable political career. The Pūru–Bharata appear on the scene later but steadily grow in power and influence. Their oldest discernible chiefs are Durga and his son Girikṣit, whose descendent Purukutsa was related to both Pūru and Bharata in Book I. They seem to have had an old rivalry with the Yadu–Turvaśa whom they often fight; they are defeated by Vayya and Turvīti, while one Kutsa, probably Purukutsa, and his Bharata ally Atithīgva, are defeated by Turvayāśa.[66]

The Pūru chief Trasadasyu (also called Paurukutsya, i.e. son of Purukutsa), is celebrated in Book VI as breaker of autumnal forts (*śāradi*) and conductor of an *aśvamedha* wherein his horse, the famed Dadhikravān or Dadhikra,[67] *spread his wings over the Pañcajana.*[68] This probably indicates the welding of a *Pañcajana* identity among the competing tribes under Pūru initiative. The Pūru are now said to be at the centre, with the Yadu–Turvaśu to their northwest and Anu–Druhyu the southeast; elsewhere, the Pūru are on the Irāvati or Rāvi, which suggests that the *Pañcajana* assimilation encompassed the northern plains of the Indus and extended across the Punjab towards the Divide. It was in this milieu that the rift between the Pūru and their Bharata partners appeared, precipitating the *Daśarājña* or BOTK. Some other Pūru names come across are Tryarjuna, Trivṛṣam, and Tridhātu.

Constructing history out of such liturgical material is at best tentative—for instance, the geographical directions of the various tribes *vis-à-vis* one another indicated above may be of ritual significance only and not represent reality. However, the directions *somewhat* correspond to the archaeological picture which we shall inspect, before trying to situate the *Daśarājña* and determine its relation with the *Mahabharata*.

---

66 *ṚV*, VI: 18.13.

67 This reflected the nomad practice of singing of famed horses. See James Hutton, *Central Asia: From the Aryan to the Cossack*, New Delhi, Manas, 2005, first published, 1871, p. 249.

68 *ṚV*, IV: 42.

The Archaeological Picture

The Indo–Gangetic plains and upper Deccan had been under dispersed occupation since the Palaeolithic times. Through the Neolithic, the region witnessed an increase in occupation, with settlements spreading across Mehrgarh near the Bolan, Galighai in the northern Indus plains, Burzahom and Gufkral in Kashmir, Mahagara and Chirand on the Gangetic plains, and Pandu-Rajar-Dhibi in deltaic Bengal. In time, many of these sites were supplanted by metal using cultures, mostly concentrated in or around the Indus though some sites extended as far east as the Belan Valley near Allahabad.[69] These diverse cultures, with a thriving copper industry (but with low bronze component), either arsenic or tin, formed the *regionalization era* of the IVC, and were later assimilated into the remarkably homogenous Mature Harappan civilization.

The Mature Harappan phase of the IVC, concentrated along the Indus and Hakra–Ghaggar valleys, was able to establish distant colonies and trading locations. These colonies extended not only to the Divide, but also to the Makran and Gujarat coasts (Prabhas), Central India (Rangpur, over the Malwa culture sites marked by Lustrous Red Ware), Northern Deccan (Daiamabad on the Pravara, a northern tributary of the Godavari, though Ratnagar doubts if it was Harappan), and as far north as Shortughai in Balkh. The impetus that created this remarkably homogenous, almost monotonous culture, or caused it to disperse or fall apart later, does not seem to have been military, nor does the homogeneity appear to have been enforced by one consistent physical type. Harappan prosperity, probably created by the *cotton rush* postulated by Shaikh and Ashfaque,[70] led to the ethnically striated[71] but predominantly mercantile people creating a functioning, homogenous culture, whose rules were enforced by socio–political means more than the military. Also, though Harappa had trade contacts with Mesopotamia as supplier of copper, which also gave it its

69 Two intriguing finds at Belan are rice in burnt clay pot, dated C_{14} at 5500 B.C., though many scholars do not agree, and a bone figurine from the late Paleolithic which represents a (hunter) mother goddess.

70 Khurshid Hasan Shaikh and Syed M. Ashfaque, *Mohenjodaro—a 5000 Years Old Legacy*, Geneva, UNESCO, 1981.

71 Shireen Ratnagar, *The End of the Great Harappan Tradition*, New Delhi, Manohar, 2002, p. 25.

Mesopotamian appellation of *Meluhha*,[72] cognate of Dravidian *milakkhu* and Sanskrit *mleccha* and *mlecchamukha* for copper, the Mesopotamian pattern of endless city warfare does not seem to have affected the IVC.[73]

The 'Decadent' Post-Harappan Phase

The Mature Harappa phase passed in the early 2nd millennium, but references to *Meluhha* in Mesopotamian records continued till mid-2nd millennium B.C., i.e. till the Hittite sack and Kassite takeover of Babylon. This indicates that trade contact had survived the passage of Mature Harappa. The question that automatically arises is, what exactly was implied by the passage of Mature Harappa. There is no evidence of any cataclysmic *collapse*, and few indicators of military catastrophe, unlike in Babylon. A few hastily secreted caches or hesitant signs of burnt walls apart, there are no signs of sack or pillage, and the much touted 'skeletal evidence' based on which Mortimer–Wheeler, T. Burrow, or Vere Gordon Childe had arraigned Indra[74] have been refuted as anachronistic.[75]

Largely, the passage meant *declining* civic standards, and gradual abandonment of the sites. Houses of recycled material, weakening drainage systems, squatter tenements, or kilns *within* municipality limits, all begin appearing in post-mature layers of Harappan towns, like in the Jhukar Phase in and around Mohenjo-Daro, Chanhu-Daro, or Amri on the lower Indus. Enumerating the indicators from Harappa,[76] Mukhtar Ahmed concluded that the dissolution had come about due to failure of one or more of the influences whose fortuitous conjunction had created the civilization in the first place.[77] It is also unlikely that the countryside was depopulated by the collapse of the cities—Possehl sees, in the continuance of Harappan motifs like the bullock cart, mathematics, or *kullaḍh* clay cups, evidence

72 As per Mukhtar Ahmed, the local word for sailor, *mallah*, comes from *Meluhha*. Mukhtar Ahmed, *Ancient Pakistan: An Archaeological History*, vol. 3: Harappan Civilization—the Material Culture, Foursome Group, Reidsville, 2014, p.8.

73 Doyne Dawson, *The First Armies*, London, Cassel, 2001, p. 105.

74 T. Burrows, 'The Early Āryans', in A.L. Basham (ed.), *A Cultural History of India*, pp. 20–29.

75 J.M. Kenoyer, 'Cultures and Societies of the Indus Tradition', in R. Thapar (ed.), *India: Historical Beginnings and the Concept of the Aryan*, Delhi, NBT, 2006, pp. 41–97.

76 Ahmed, *Ancient Pakistan*, pp. 449–450.

77 Ahmed, *Ancient Pakistan*, pp. 443–44.

against any civilizational collapse.[78] It was only much later that sites were abandoned; they are found under thick layers of earth, showing that they were not reoccupied for a long time. There was also a corresponding movement of population eastwards.

To Ratnagar, the collapse was violent, and far more thorough.[79] Pointing out that while desiccation may have triggered emigration from the Ghaggar–Hakra valley, it does not explain concurrent abandonment of sites in Makran, Baluchistan and Sindh, she denies that ecological reasons were the only ones behind the collapse.[80] Rather, though she does not spell it out, her constant comparison of the Aryans with the so-called 'Sea Peoples' who raided West Asia suggests that she had them in mind as behind the collapse of the civilization.

Signs of military emergencies do indeed appear in the later stages of the Mature period, including improved military architecture. Walls were raised, given packings of brick, and pierced with gates secured with towers and salient. At Harappa, a citadel-like structure was added near its northern gate. Taken together, there appear a sense of insecurity, which perhaps had caused movement of refugees who beleaguered the cities, as indicated by falling civic culture. The cities themselves seem to have been girding up against the force which the refugees were fleeing. In fact, Chanhu-Daro does seem to have been destroyed militarily, refugees from this place creating the Jhukar phase at Amri (though Mukhtar Ahmed points out that Amri, *west* of Chanhu-Daro, was likely to have been attacked before the latter by a western raider).

The destruction of Chanhu-Daro is contemporaneous with *military* conquests then going on in what are now modern Baluchistan and Southern Afghanistan. Contemporaneous signs of destruction have been obtained at Shahi Tump, Dabarkot, Rana Ghundai, Mundigak, and Nausharo and other sites, alongside evidence of new cultures with North Afghanistan affinity.[81] To the east of these sites, there is no compelling sign of sack but only of abandonment, though it must be realised that absence of signs

78 G.L. Possehl, 'The End of a State and the Continuity of a Tradition', in R. Fox (ed.), *Realm and Region in Traditional India*, Delhi, Vikas, 1979, pp. 234–54.

79 Ratnagar, *End of Harappa*, p. 28.

80 Ratnagar, *End of Harappa*, p. 60.

81 Ahmed, *Ancient Pakistan*, p. 450.

of sack does not rule out military defeat of a city's forces in open battle and its subsequent occupation by the victors. Also contemporaneous is evidence of population displacement towards the Divide and south, probably corresponding with Harappan settlements like Daiamabad. More importantly, the homogenising influence disappears, leading to pre-assimilation or unassimilated cultures, like Mithathal IIIB, Siswal C,[82] Bara (near Ludhiana), Sanghol, Kotla Nihang Khan, or the Banas, Kayatha, and Malwa cultures in the Aravalli, reasserting themselves in what is the *localization era* of the IVC.

This is also the time when several *new* cultures appear west of the Indus, like at Pirak, Nausharo, Sibri, Mundigak, or Mehrgarh South Cemetery. These sites, which remained under occupation up to 700 B.C., have yielded regular, multi-chambered houses on square plans that are significantly different from Harappan plans, pottery, evidence of domesticated animals including horse and camel, and other artefacts. These features display affiliations with Iranic cultures along the Balkh and Murghab rivers, i.e. the Bactria–Margiana Archaeological Complex (BMAC).[83] Furthermore, Pirak has yielded terracotta figurines of mounted horsemen, the oldest equestrian indication in South Asia,[84] and Mundigak and Shahi-Tump bronze straight-swords, exquisite bronze axes with well casted shaft-holes,[85] and spiral-headed copper pins,[86] all similar in design to those found at Luristan in Iran.[87] Such affinities are also noted in the uppermost layers of several post-Mature Harappan sites, and of the Jhukar and later layers.

Taken together, it is evident that affluent, warlike peoples possessing the horse were on the move from Central Asia, possibly across the Gurgan

82 Ratnagar, *End of Harappa*, p. 138.

83 F.T. Hiebert and C.C. Lamberg–Karlovsky, 'Central Asia and the Indo-Iranian Borderlands', *Iran*, vol. 30, 1992, pp. 1–15. Also see Ratnagar, *End of Harappa*, pp. 113–117.

84 Parpola, 'The Coming of the Aryans to Iran and India and the Cultural and Ethnic Identity of the Dasas', *International Journal of Dravidian Linguistics*, vol. 17, no. 2, June 1988, pp. 85–229; see especially pp. 150–151.

85 S. Piggott, *Prehistoric India*, pp. 220.

86 Ratnagar, *End of Harappa*, p. 136.

87 These copper pins are remarkably similar to the pins of the headless Śākambhṛ, and the Yellama–Maryamma pins from Southern Deccan.

plains, to South Afghanistan, and thence to Bolan and the Kachchi plains. These movements triggered the rash of refugees that mark Harappan townships, and led to subsequent abandonment of many sites. However, though the four ash layers between Harappan and post-Harappan layers at Rana Ghundai[88] suggest that these groups were not non-violent, largely the IVC was spared the devastation that was visited on contemporaneous cultures in Mesopotamia and Asia Minor.

Now, atop Harappan and Kot Dijian layers at Gumla, other spots along the Gomal River, on the Pothwar plateau, and at Sarai Khola near Taxila, there have been found graves in the form of circular pits layered with wood, containing clay figurines of women, bulls and horses, and personal effects of the deceased, all sealed with a layer of clay and burnt.[89] Closely associated with this culture, called the *Gomal Grave culture*, are graves in the Taxila–Peshawar region where the pits have greater number of sacrificed animals and large clay urns in the shape of stylised human faces.[90] The Swat valley to the north of Taxila is dotted with hill-slope or hilltop habitations that reveal at least two, if not more distinct peoples. These sites, like Ghalighai, Loebanhr, Timurgarha, Kalakoderay, Katelai, and Aligrama in Swat, and also Hathial in Taxila, grouped as the *Gandhara Grave culture*, were equated with the *Assekenoi* enemies of Alexander by the Italian archaeologists who discovered them,[91] but have since been shown by Dani to be far older and from the period of transition from bronze to iron.[92]

The Gandhara Grave culture has also yielded pottery which is reminiscent of the Dzharkutan Phase (2034–1684 B.C.) of the BMAC, which is in turn similar to ceramic yielded by a disturbed aristocratic grave in Tajikistan. This grave has also yielded two horse-bits and two

88 Ratnagar, *End of Harappa*, p. 125.

89 A.H. Dani, 'Pastoral–Agricultural Tribes of Pakistan in the Post-Indus Period', in A.H. Dani and V.M. Masson (eds.) *History of Civilizations of Central Asia*, vol. 1, Paris, UNESCO, 1992, pp. 395–420.

90 Dani, 'Pastoral–Agricultural', p. 404.

91 GuiseppeTucci, 'The Tombs of the Asvakayana–Assakenoi', *East and West*, nos. 14, 1963, p. 27.

92 Dani, 'Pastoral–Agricultural', pp. 417–18 and A.H. Dani, 'Gandhara Grave Complex in West Pakistan', *Asian Perspective*, vol. 9, 1968, pp. 99–110. These sites have yielded jade artefacts showing Chinese influence; see Ratnagar, *End of Harappa*, p. 143. Also see Mukhtar Ahmed, *Ancient Pakistan*, pp. 459–60.

pairs of cheek-pieces of the Sintashta–Arkhaim type (where Kelekna has shown several styles of cheek-pieces were being experimented with[93]), along with a bronze rod or sceptre with a horse-capital. Evidently, these post-IVC sites were associated with the pastoral and equestrian world of the steppes. Interestingly, some sites near Pirak, which as mentioned above yielded the earliest horse figurine from anywhere in South Asia, have yielded material evidence to suggest that trade through the Bolan had ceased prior to establishment of Pirak, and resumed thereafter. The old trade must have been disrupted by the unsettled conditions, and renewed when the Pirak people arrived through the Bolan in the post-IVC period.

Though some scholars insist upon the local evolution of the Gandhara and Gomal Grave cultures,[94] Dani has associated these with the IA, tracing their funerary practices as a continuum through BMAC to the steppes. Elaborate, multi-decked tumuli graves of the steppes, some so large that they require pillars for support, are indeed reminiscent of the Vedic wooden sarcophagi, *House of Yama*, a concept common to all IE world like *House of Hades* or *Hall of Heljarann*.[95] Also, two burials at Katelai in Swat have horses buried with their masters, Timurgarha

93 Pita Kelekna, 'The Politico–Economic Impact of the Horse on Old World Cultures: An Overview', *Sino–Platonic Papers*, no. 190, June 2009, p. 11.

94 Kuzmina does so, but this is opposed by Stacul. Even Parpola is against any one–on–one identification. To Tusa also the cultures had developed out of regional cultures. Sebastiano Tusa, 'The Swat Valley in the 2nd and 1st Millennia B.C.: A Question of Marginality', *South Asian Archaeology*, vol. 6, 1977, pp. 675–695 (especially pp. 690–92). Important survey of the discussions is available in Edwin Bryant, *The Quest for the Origins of Vedic Culture: The Indo-Aryan Migration Debate*, Oxford University Press, 2001.

95 The house is often associated with mortuary rites. In Greece and Rome, the deceased were represented as though in houses, and Mycenaean chamber tombs were often painted to resemble houses. Benedicte Gilman (ed.), *Masterpieces of the J. Paul Getty Museum: Antiquities*, The J. Paul Getty Museum, Los Angeles, 1997, p. 93. Even Late Bronze and Classical period coffins imitated houses, while actual house structures have been found at the Únetice burials at Leubingen in Saxony and elsewhere; see Marija Gimbutas, *Bronze Age cultures in Central and Eastern Europe*, The Hague/London, Mouton,1965, pp. 260–265, fig. 172 and 173. The link between funerary *house* and *vessel* is observed in the Villanovans culture, which decorated funerary houses with *swastikas*, just as clay vessels in Sintashta graves were decorated, as shown by Geninget *al* (eds.), *Sintashta: archaeological sites of the Aryan tribes of the Ural-Kazakhstan Steppe*, (trans. from the Russian), vol. 1, Chelyabinsk, 1992, fig: 47. In the *ṚV*, the '*house of clay*' is metaphor for grave (*ṚV*, VII: 89.1) but could also refer to urns containing cremated bones like the *face-urn* in the *gharmya* ritual of the Aśvins, evidence of which have been unearthed from the Swat Culture.

has yielded an iron cheek-piece from a bridle which can be traced to similar designs in the Ukrainian and Romanian steppes, and the horse is represented in artefacts like pins, brooches, or on handles of concave lids of the face–urns at a grave in Loebanhr in Swat.[96]

At the same time, these sites are highly striated.[97] They have yielded dwellings ranging from pits to rubble masonry, widely varying pottery styles (though the most frequently encountered is a coarse grey–black ware reminiscent of Iran and Gurgan), and diverse methods of disposal of the dead. And yet, their uppermost layers are marked by assimilative trends characterised by a fine red pottery patterned in black, more restrictive types of disposal of the dead, and so on. These assimilative evidences have been grouped as the *Cemetery H culture* centred on Harappa, and Bahawalpur from where alone 72 sites were discovered.[98] As per Meadows and Kenoyer, Period 4 on Mounds E and AB at Harappa marks the transition from Harappan to Cemetery H, after which Harappa is marked by a decadence in civic practices[99] till it is finally abandoned.

Features of steppe affiliations found covered in Gandhara and Gomal sites by Cemetery H layers are found preserved in *new* sites in Swat, Chitral, and the upper Indus. For instance, the Koshtaki valley in Nuristan has yielded *sarcophagi* or boxes of neatly arranged (not joined) stone slabs with gargoyle-like ends. Apparently, elements had 'escaped' the assimilative influence then underway on the plains, perhaps violently imposed, by withdrawing into the mountains. The warlikeness of these cultures brings back the question of collapse of the Mature Harappan phase, which requires us to survey the literary evidence of violence among migrating Vedic tribes.

96 Asko Parpola, 'Face Urns', Figure 1.

97 Kochhar, *Vedic People*, pp.181–83.

98 M. R. Mughal, 'New archaeological evidence from Bahawalpur', in A. H. Dani (ed.), *Indus Civilization: New Perspective*, Islamabad, Centre for the Study of the Civilizations of Central Asia, Quaid-e Azam University, 1981, pp. 33–41 (especially p. 37).

99 Ahmed, *Ancient Pakistan*, p. 452.

The Migration

Violence Implicit in the Migration

A reading of Vedic textual material shows that the tribes were a violent lot, constantly fighting with 'despicable others' whom they call *Dāsa, Dasyu, Dānava, Paṇi,* and so on, one of their chiefs even taking the epithet *Dāsyave Vṛka*, 'wolf for the *Dasyu'*.[100] They also fought among themselves. The endless references to violent interactions amongst gods, demons, and humans in Vedic literature can be grouped into two classes, one associated with the dread war-god Indra, and the other with identifiable human chiefs. Indra '*destroyed ... Dāsic forts which had Blacks in their laps;* [and],[101] '*dispersed the 100,000 men of Varcin*',[102] '*overcame for Jiśvan, the son of Vidathin, the mighty Pipru Mṛgaya* [,] ... *put down the 50,000 Blacks...* [and] ... *wore thin the forts like a garment*',[103] '*at once destroyed the 99 forts of Śambara ... when ...* [he]... *helped Divodāsa Atithīgva*',[104] '*destroyed 100 stone forts for the offering Divodāsa*',[105] and '*put to sleep with his sorcery 30,000 Dāsa for Dabhīti*'.[106]

In the other class, Indra *assists* humans like Namī Sāpya kill the *Dāsa* Namuci,[107] Purukutsa destroy the *Dāsa*s' '*autumnal forts*',[108] Divodāsa destroy forts of Śambara,[109]Abhyāvartin Cāyamāna defeat the Vārāśikha,[110] and Daivavāta kill '*130 Vṛcīvats...on the Yavyāvatī.*'[111] Indra is also associated with fighting Aryan lords—he '*killed the two Āryas, Arṇa and Citraratha, on the other side of the Sarayu*'[112] and helped Daivavāta

100 *ṚV*, VIII: 49.9; 55.1; 56.1-2.

101 *ṚV*, II: 20.7.

102 *ṚV*, II: 14.6.

103 *ṚV*, IV: 16.13.

104 *ṚV*, IV: 26.3.

105 *ṚV*, IV: 30.20.

106 *ṚV*, IV: 30.31.

107 *ṚV*, VI: 20.6.

108 *ṚV*, VI: 20.10.

109 *ṚV*, VI: 31.4.

110 *ṚV*, VI: 26.5.

111 *ṚV*, VI: 27.6.

112 *ṚV*, IV: 30.18.

'*beat down Dāsa and Ārya enemies*'.[113] One explanation of the two lists is that while the first referred to remote battles whose human heroes had been forgotten, the second featured more recent battles whose human heroes were in human memory. Also, is it significant that Agni was also the champion in many such contests.[114]

Several of the above contests were targeted at forts, resulting in the identification of these forts with the IVC citadels as soon as the latter were discovered. Even Dani endorsed the view that the Hariyūpiyā of Varcin the Dāsa and his Vṛchivant associates, destroyed by an Aryan chief with the help of Indra, was none other than Harappa.[115] Reaction to such identifications has varied, ranging from complete rejection of the idea of 'invasion' to a willingness to be more circumspect about Aryan role in the IVC collapse. For instance, Basham concedes that the Aryans could not have sacked Mohenjo-Daro because it lay *not on the direct line* of ingress.[116] Basham's view is however based on the assumption that the Aryans were using the Khyber—actually they were using the Gomal, Kurram, or Bolan, which would have brought them close enough to Mohenjo-Daro.

Significantly, IA ingress into South Asia, contemporaneous with IIr activity in the West, would have occurred not long before the 16th century, and thus *centuries after* the Mature Harappan phase had passed. Thus, the IA would have encountered only the successor cultures of the localization era of the IVC. Even the destruction of these is not supported by archaeology—four of the largest sites, Mohenjo-Daro, Ganeriwala, Rakhigarhi, Dholavira, and Harappa, and 101 of the 132 smaller sites, were not *sacked* but *deserted*, probably due to the shifting rivers. Also is it not easy to equate the 'adversaries' of the IA with the IVC folk, as they were complex identities defying equation with humans. For instance, *Cumuri*,

113 *ṚV*, VI: 31.3.

114 *ṚV*, VII: 5.3: *Out of fear of you, the black tribes moved away, leaving their possessions behind, without a fight, when you Agni Vaiśvānara, shone, flaming for Pūru and breaking their forts*'; *ṚV*, VII: 5.6, '*You, Agni, drove out the Dasyu from their home; creating wide light for the Āryas*'.

115 Dani, 'Pastoral–Agricultural', p. 396; It is *generally accepted* today that the Hariyupiya was the Haliab River, and not the city of Harappa, just as the Yavyavatī associated with the first river was the Zhob.

116 T. Burrow, 'Early Āryans', p. 25, n. 3.

Dhuni, *Pipru*, Śambara, *Balbūtha Taruka*,[117] or *Bṛṣaya*[118] are demoniac-cum-mortal, and in a few cases only are human foes discernible.[119] Many of these names are complex—*Anarśani* or *Arbuda*[120] are Iranian, while *DāsaAhīśu*[121] (*Dāsa* as quick as the dragon) and *Varo Suṣāman*,[122] are IA–Ir composites.

The problem identification led to elevation of the Vedic encounters above the human plane, adding spiritual overtones—*winning of light from darkness*, or *extraction of restrained water*, prizes of victory being *seed, water, and bodily progeny, the sun*,[123] or just *light*.[124] And yet, against a wider backdrop of migration, archaeological data matches the literarily created picture in many ways as long as we do not attempt one-on-one identification. The Elamites of Susa in Iran, after bringing Mesopotamia under their control *c.* 2200 B.C., looked east in search of sources of copper and tin. If the Dravidian *Eelam* is associated with them, we may surmise that they made their way across the lower Indus to the Deccan, and were responsible for the unsettled conditions discernible in the IVC, at least in its southern parts. As per Fairservis, they were also responsible for introducing the several pastoral features discernible in the IVC. The oldest layers at Pirak are associated with Proto-Dravidian speakers; it is possible that they first brought the horse to the Indus.[125]

The Migrations in a Wider Context

The above model of IA and IIr migrations into SouthAsia meshes with the overall pattern of migration of horse-using pastoralists across Eurasia. Development of captive wheel technology, and secondary products revolution in felt, milk products, wool, and carpentry enabled horse-domesticating Neolithic culture on the Danube and Dnepr to adapt to

117 *ṚV*, VIII: 46.32.

118 *ṚV*, VI: 61.3.

119 *ṚV*, VI: 20.7.

120 *ṚV*, VIII: 32.3.

121 *ṚV*, VIII: 32.2.

122 *ṚV*, VIII: 23.28, 24.28 - cf. VIII: 60.18.

123 *ṚV*, VI: 31.1; *ṚV*, VI: 46.4.

124 *ṚV*, II: 11.8; VII: 5.6.

125 Witzel, 'Substrate Languages', pp. 33–34.

pasturage and colonise the steppes. By the 4th millennium B.C., Yamnaya (Pit Grave) people were using ox-drawn carriages to migrate east,[126] and by the end of the 3rd millennium, the Sintashta–Arkhaim–Petrovka culture astride the Urals, discovered by the Russian archaeologist Gening and his team in the 1970s,[127] had been formed. Locations of these semi-urban sites suggest that they were agrarian settlements at the hub of pastoral economies, probably serving also as ore collecting and forwarding centres.[128] Rau has shown that these ovals or radial–annular sites, with semi-permanent defences comprising perimeters of clay blocks and palisades of logs, matched descriptions of the Vedic *pura*.[129]

In the first half of the 2nd millennium, by when carts and wagons were in use from the Rhine to the Indus, the Sintashta–Arkhaim cultures started expanding southwards, creating the agro–pastoralist *Andronovo Cultural Horizon* which would have been PIIr. The Urals themselves were concurrently taken over by the Okunosevo and Karasuk cultures from the Mongolia–China borderlands. The southern frontiers of the Andronovo culture marched with urban cultures on the Murghab and Amu rivers, initially founded by Mesopotamian settlers, the BMAC.[130] Urban centres

126 For a good discussion on Indo–European migrations, see J.P. Mallory, *In Search of the Indo–European: Language, Archaeology, and Myth*, Thames and Hudson, 1989, J.P. Mallory and D.Q. Adams, *Encyclopaedia of Indo–European Culture*, London, Fitzroy Dearborn, 1997; J.P. Mallory and Victor H. Mair, *The Tarim Mummies*, Thames and Hudson, 2008; D.W. Anthony, *The Horse, the Wheel, and Language—How Bronze-Age Riders from the Eurasian Steppes Shaped the Modern World*, Princeton University Press, Princeton, New Jersey, 2007.

127 V.F. Gening, 'The Cemetery at Sintashta and Early Indo–Iranian Peoples', *JIES*, vol. 7, 1979, pp. 1–30, trans. of the earlier Russian article of 1977.

128 Kelekna, 'Impact of the Horse', p. 10. Also see Kuzmina, *The Origins of the Indo-Europeans*, pp. 32–33.

129 Wilhelm Rau, *The Meaning of Pur in Vedic Literature*, Abhandlungen der Marburger Gelehrten Gesellschaft, Munich, Munich Willhelm Fink Veerlag, 1976.

130 This region, i.e. the plains of the Murghab and Amu Rivers, was first settled by Mesopotamian colonists, its oldest layers, *c.* 7000 B.C. being contemporaneous with early Mehrgarh. Later, the BMAC culture expanded into Zerafshan, probably attracted by tin deposits of Ferghana and the Amu–Balkh Rivers. The Jeitun sites in the Kopet Dag foothills were probably the *Harali* of Mesopotamian records which as per Harmatta was a Dravidian term; see J. Harmatta, 'The Emergence of the Indo–Iranians: the Indo–Iranian Languages', in A.H. Dani and V.M. Masson (eds.), *History of Civilization of Central Asia*, vol 1, pp. 357–78. Mature layers of these cultures are similar to the IVC and Mesopotamia in being urban, with seal–controlled trade; there are many similarities in iconography as well. See H–P. Francfort, 'La Civilisation

of the BMAC, like Dashli, Togolok, Gonur, or Namazga, are laid out as citadels with square plans and perambulatory passages along insides of their walls, motifs which reappear in the square temple complexes inside them with whitewashed walls, perambulatory passages, sacerdotal chambers, and fire altars.[131] The temples also contain curious large baths with channels, suggestive of ritual preparation of some fluid substances. While B.B. Lal observed the resemblance of these plans with the complex, post–Vedic sacrificial hearths, and with fire altars used in *tantra* goddess worship, these structures also match the accounts of the *vara*, citadel of Yima the Iranic culture god, and those of the *Paṇi*, a Vedic adversary.[132]

Surrounding these citadels are hundreds of campsites of Andronovo affiliation,[133] which have yielded superior weapons like battle-axes with cross-guards and tanged spearheads.[134] Apparently, the prosperous urban culture coexisted with northern nomads, with an ambivalent relation between the two. Though in possession of the countryside and able to dominate trade and transit, the nomads looked upon the cities with awe and dread. However, as they became confident, the dread wore off and they grew aggressive, at times taking over the cities. This endless cycle—nomads taking over cities and more nomads taking over the countryside—marks the history of Transoxiana, where Samarqand, Balkh, or Merv were forever contested by nomads.

---

de l'Oxus et les Indo–Iraniens et Indo–Aryens en Asie Centrale', in G. Fussman, J. Kellens, H–P. Francfort, and X Temblay (ed.), *Âryas, Aryens et Iraniens en Asie Centrale*, Paris, 2005, pp. 253–328, especially pp. 258–61.

131 V. Sarianidi, 'Temples of Bronze Age Margiana', *Antiquity*, vol. 68, 1994, pp. 388–97.

132 Names of peoples, especially as expressed by other peoples, should not be taken at face value and too much read into them. While foreigners do not coin names indiscriminately but use the *heard* pronunciation, these pronunciations are only as close to the original as the phonemes of their native language will permit. People also name other peoples after some of the latter's characteristics, or also as slang. Further, meanings and implications of names can change, as we have seen in the case of the Naga or Yavana, or Slav which later came to mean *slave*. This is true for *Paṇi* and *Dāsa*, kin to the North Iranic **Parna* and the equestrian *Parnae* and *Dahae*. Now, *Dāsa* too would in time mean *slave*, like the Iranian *dāha*(*ka*), Mycenaean *doero*, or Greek *doulos*.

133 A. Gubaev, G. Koshelenko, and M. Tosi, 'The Archaeological Map of the Murghab Delta: Preliminary Reports 1990–95', *IsIAO*, and also Francfort 2005, pp. 295–304.

134 V.M. Masson, 'The Decline of the Bronze Age Civilization and Movements of the Tribes', in Dani and Masson, *History of Civilization*, vol. 1, pp. 337–356 (especially p. 343).

The endless pressure also set up a southward migration from the BMAC, bringing sections of these folk into Iran and South Asia. Ch Ehret has used the model of a billiard ball hitting others to set them off, while stopping itself, to explain movements and migrations that occurred in BMAC. Parpola has gone further, suggesting that no real steppe physical type entered South Asia or Iran but only 'Aryanised' BMAC folks. This theory assumes that 'Aryanization' of the BMAC was so thorough that it came to resemble the IIr in all literary records,[135] and is not accurate as it is often the incoming group, even if victorious, that adopts the language of the conquered and 'submerges' in them, as was to happen with the Mitanni or Normans, as long as they were not in overwhelming numbers. It was only if ingress was massive and 'national' that subjugated peoples adopted the language of the victors in order to 'rise in life'. Parpola himself acknowledges that IA speakers in the BMAC were continually replenished, which was why the BMAC retained its Aryan speech.[136] Thus, part of the Andronovo ethnic component could not but have moved into South Asia and Iran.

The difficulty that arises here is that not a single evidence of steppe *material culture*, or a single sherd of Andronovo pottery, has been found in South Asia. Parpola, in support of his theory of only acculturated BMAC folk entering South Asia, says that the few examples of steppe decorative styles found in South Asia were results of commercial exchange. This at once draws our attention to the theory that IIr folk typified in South Asia and moved to Iran and Eurasia, in other words the *out of India* theory, but it has already been rejected on grounds of implausibility. Another explanation of the absence of steppe culture in South Asia that has been forwarded

135 The entire constellation of these cultures was remarkably aware of the ethnic continuum, which had been made possible by long distance migration, trade, warfare, and control over transport technology. The situation was similar to that of the Scythians, who at Balkh reminded the Greeks that they were neighbours across the Thracian frontier even at 'home'. See Quintus Curtius, VII.8.30. It has been shown that the horse was domesticated by early manifestations of these cultures on the Dnepr, i.e. at Derievka and Srednij Stog. The Andronovo culture, even the Sintashta–Petrovka culture, was PIIr at least as a *lingua franca*. M. Witzel, 'Linguistic Evidence of Cultural Exchange in Prehistoric Western Central Asia', *Sino–Platonic Papers*, no. 129, Philadelphia, December 2003.

136 See Parpola, 'Face Urn', in Michael Willis (ed.), *Migration, Trade and Peoples, Proceedings of the Eighteenth Congress of the European Association of South Asian Archaeologists*, London, 2005, the British Association for South Asian Studies, British Academy, London, 2009.

is that the zone of IIr typification was Anatolia and the Caucasus, where sites like Demirchiuyuk, Pulur, and Mercin (Anatolia), Rogem Hiri (Syro–Palestine), or Uzerlic-Tepe (Trans-Caucasus) display archaic features of Sintashta–Arkhaim.[137] This theory argues that the IIr emigrated eastward from this region, traversing Mesopotamia and Iran to Dasht-e-Margow, from where some went to the steppes and others descended to the Indus; Drews goes a step further and suggests that the IA reached South Asia by boat.[138]

This hypothesis has difficulties, not the least of which is that boats appear nowhere in the context of Vedic migration. Further, Iranians have always placed their *urheimat* of *Aïriiyanam Vaejo* to the northeast of each preceding generation, which means that they *came from the northeast* and not *went there*. Rather, it is the BMAC and the mountains of the Tajikistan where many archaic features of Zoroastrianism still survive. This theory also cannot explain the strong pre-IIr, IE presence in the steppes, like that of the Tocharians. These difficulties, and the overwhelming commonality of *moral culture* between the peoples who have left their records in steppe archaeology and the IIr of South Asia, render theories of movement *to* the steppes untenable. Instead, we will see that Parpola's model[139] is workable with some adjustments.

As per Parpola, early PIIr immigrants from *Andronovo* took over the BMAC cities, becoming their elite and adopting their religion centred on the veneration of *Asura* and the promiscuous siblings Yama–Yami.[140] This led to the acculturation and elevation of the *Asura* to *Deva* status, and its identification with Varuṇa, i.e. *night light* or darkness, alongside Mitra the *day light*, in the duality of *Mitra–Varuṇau* as part of the cosmic law-

137 S.A. Grigoriev has drawn our attention to these similarities, also citing the reports on the archaeological investigations in some of these places. See S.A. Grigoriev, 'The Sintashta Culture and Some Questions of Indo-Europeans Origins', *Institute of History and Archaeology*, Ural Branch of Russian Academy of Sciences, Chelyabinsk.

138 Robert Drews, *The Coming of the Greeks: Indo–European Conquests in the Aegean and the Near East*, New Jersey, Princeton University Press, 1998, pp. 183.

139 Discussed above, and best given out in Asko Parpola, 'The Formation of the Aryan Branch of the Indo–Europeans', in Roger Blench and Matthew Spriggs (eds.), *One World Archaeology and Languages*, London, Routledge, 1999, pp. 188–207 (especially p. 200).

140 The *Dāsa*s did not possess the chariot, as per Parpola. Asko Parpola, 'The Coming of the Aryans', pp. 85–229.

and-order mythology. These abstract deities were the result of Assyrian influence *c.* 1900 B.C.,[141] *via* the tin trade of Central Asia with Syria and Cappadocia, which co-opted on the early *Aśvin* system of the Aryans.[142]

As early nomads took over as the city elite, they gradually softened and lost touch with their nomad brethren, who were constantly refreshed with more immigrants. Thus, the rivalry between the city-elite, largely of nomad origin, and the nomads continued in the cycles mentioned above, which is reflected in the ambivalent relation between the *Deva* and *Asura*. In fact, the relation at times worsened, and violence, religious persecution, and forced conversion are part of *Asura* lore. As the split widened, worshippers of *Ahura Mazda*, *Saurva*, *Miθra,* and *Nāŋhaiθya*, more attuned to the Varuṇa of the Mitrā–Varuṇau duality, broke away from the worshippers of the *daeva*, underminers and upsetters of *Ahura Mazda*'s order, causing the *Asura* to fade out of Vedic mythology.

The above is not to say that the split occurred specifically in the BMAC, and in a later chapter we will inspect the nature of the split as it has major military implications on steppe warfare. It is only suggested here that the BMAC was significantly affected by this rivalry, and that substantial segments of its acculturated, *Asura/Ahura* worshipping populations moved to Iran or the Indus, as much responsible for leaving unsettled conditions in their wake as the Elamites before them. Thus, while the *Ahura* theme survives in Iran, in later times IA migrants into South Asia would encounter *Asura* adherents in South Asia, who would reappear in *Puraṇic* lore, both as benevolent (Bāṇa, Bali, or Prahlāda) and malevolent (Hiraṇyākṣa, Hiraṇyakaśipu, or Mahīṣa).

The above is not to say that the *Deva–Asura* rivalry was in the human–historical realm alone, as is supposed by Elst who, eager to support his *in-from-Tibet–out-of-India* hypothesis takes it as the fight between the Kashmir-based Anu and Indus-based Pūru.[143] In reality the *Asura* theme is far older than any Anu–Pūru rivalry (and the Anu were not based in Kashmir), and it also appears in the *Aesir* and *Vaenir* theme in Teutonic

141 AskoParpola, 'The Nāsatyas, the Chariot and Proto–Aryan Religion', *Journal of Indological Studies*, nos. 16 & 17, 2004–2005, pp. 1–63.

142 Parpola, 'Nāsatya', p. 19. The ideological influence is evidenced by Syrian and Egyptian motifs in BMAC seals.

143 KoenradElst, *Update on the Aryan Invasion Debate*, p. 207.

mythology. Also, there are crucial pointers to a western origin of the Vedic lore—the river *Danu* whose plains were in thrall by Vṛttra, the dragon killed by Indra, seems part of the set of river–names which includes the Don, Danube, Dnepr, Dnestr, or Donetz, while the *Rasā* or *Raŋha* river, on whose bank was the *vala* or *vara* of the Paṇi where the 'primordial cows' were concealed, is cognate with the Greek *Rhā* or Volga. Indeed, the fluid ambiguity of these themes takes the conflicts out of human–geographical realms; Witzel is reasonable to say that they represent annual nature conflicts to uphold *ṛta* or order. It however is suggested here that these were *also* used as models to portray or explain ideological, social, or military rivalries, and that the celestial 'wars' of IA lore, often erroneously associated with Indra's destruction of the IVC, really took place in the BMAC and along the mountain paths of Afghanistan, up to the foothills of the Bolan and the Kachchhi plains.

Migrations south of the BMAC are unlikely to have been a whirlwind phenomenon but a gradual process during which many phyla of ethnic *Andronovo* folk passed through the BMAC, discarding those features of steppe *material culture* that were no more *needed* or *affordable*—like replacing real horses in burials with models, or sealing graves in different manners. This makes detection of steppe material culture difficult; Huns left little archaeological record of material culture in Europe, as did Turkmans in South Asia, but this does not render Attila or the slave sultans fictional. Also, as mentioned above, there is an overwhelming Steppe moral impact on South Asia—several steppe motifs like the camp–capital, veneration for horse, predilection for cattle-raid, or *kurgan* burials,[144] survived among the IA, as did aspects of moral culture like family organization, religious lore, shamanism, and trance worship.

Reconciliation of the Archaeological and Genealogical Picture

Steppe folks making their way across the BMAC and jostling among themselves or with relic populations of older cultures on the plains were by no means of homogenous physical or cultural type. This, and wide ecological variations, forced them to adopt diverse survival strategies which resulted in divergences not only between sites, but also between

144 Burials is a regular motif in the *Ṛgveda*—*open up, Earth, do not crush him* (*ṚV*,X: 18.1), or *Let him live a hundred full autumns and bury death in this hill* (*ṚV*,X: 18.4) which probably indicated a Kurgan.

layers at the same site, most markedly evident in variations in funerary practices.[145] Now, while no one–on–one identification is possible between the archaeologically discerned cultures with literarily learnt ones, some trends can be detected. For instance, the assimilative Cemetery H or Painted Grey Ware (PGW) cultures may or may not find reflection in literarily defined assimilative phases like the *Pañcajana*, the Bharata conquest (the eponymous Bharata is considered the *first* emperor of India), or the Kuru–Pañcāla. Also, archaic cultures found beyond the fringes of the Indus cultures may or may not find reflections in literarily defined 'fringe' groups like Amāvasu, Gandharva, or Āraṭṭa.

A literally concrete association has been suggested by Parpola, who draws our attention to the more-than-meter thick walls of iron-hard mixture of gravel and clay surrounding the *q'ala* or fortress–manors of eastern Afghanistan, like the Afridi villages below the Khyber. These walls, locally called *pakhsa* and first recorded by Whitehouse,[146] have been found in the oldest Qandahar layers (c. 1000–600 B.C.), and have been equated by Parpola with the 99 *āyasī pura*s or iron forts of the *Dasyu*s that were destroyed by Indra's protégé, the Bharata Divodāsa. [147]

145 Xinru Liu, 'Introduction', in Xinru Liu (ed.), *India and Central Asia; A Reader*, New Delhi, Permanent Black, 2012, p. 13.

146 D. Whitehouse, 'Excavations at Kandahar, 1974: First Interim Report', *Afghan Studies*, 1, pp. 9–39.

147 Asko Parpola, 'Pre-Proto–Iranians of Afghanistan as initiators of Śâkta Tantrism: On the Scythian/Saka affiliations of the Dâsas, Nuristanis and Magadhans', *Iranica Antiqua*, vol. 37, pp. 233–324, especially pp. 260–273.

CHAPTER 3

Imperial Assimilation by the Bharata

Locating the Assimilation

Despite the caution required in equating archaeological cultures with literarily defined groups, Parpola boldly associated the destruction of the *pakhsa* walls of Qandahar with the Bharata chief Divodāsa. He also associated the Yadu–Turvaśa specifically with the Gandhara Grave culture.[1] We are therefore tempted to go a step further and situate the Pañcajana, and their assimilation in Trasadasyu's *aśvamedha*, across the swathe of territory from the Sarasvatī–Dṛṣadvatī–Āpayā valleys, i.e. the *Horax$_v$aiti* or Helmand and its tributaries, through the Peshawar region where the Yadu–Turvaśa lived, to regions to upper Punjab river valleys occupied by the Pūru, and terrain to their east occupied by the Anu–Druhyu. The independent identifiability of the Yadu–Turvaśa despite the assimilation suggests that the assimilation was no more than a temporary realignment, as *aśvamedha*s always were.

The Bharata seem to have begun as a component or ally of the Pūru[2] in their contest against the Yadu–Turvaśa. They fight the latter on the Sarayu, i.e. *Horayu*, *Hari-rud*, or Herat,[3] in the reign of Arṇa and Citraratha they are raided by the Yadu–Turvaśa, their chiefs Sṛñjaya Daivavāta, Sahadeva, and Somaka defeat an unidentified Turvaśa chief, and the Yadu chiefs

1 Asko Parpola, 'The Face Urns of Gandhara and the Nasatya Cult', in Michael Willis (ed.), *Migration, Trade and Peoples, Proceedings of the Eighteenth Congress of the European Association of South Asian Archaeologists, London, 2005*, the British Association for South Asian Studies, London, British Academy, 2009, pp. 149–162.

2 *ṚV*, V: 17.1. For another possible synchronism see I: 63.7; also, *ṚV*, VII: 19.3.

3 Kocchar, *Vedic People*, pp. 12, 120, where the Herat is the Tedzhen.

Prastoka and Vītihavya respectively.[4] However, under Atithīgva, they do not fare well against the Turvayaśa (Turvaśa in a different dialect) to whom Indra *hands* ... [him] ... *over along with* ... [his] ... *allies Kutsa the Pūru, and Āyu.*[5] Perhaps this battle is also referred to in the defeat of the Pūru–Bharata at the hands of the Vayya and Turvīti,[6] Yadu and Turvaśa in yet another dialect. Through these battles, the Bharata are observed growing increasingly independent and assertive. Cayamāna, son of Abhyāvartin, defeats the Varaśikha on the Hariyūpīyā[7] and '*130 armed Vṛcīvats*' on the Yavyāvatī,[8] while an alliance of their chiefs Sṛñjaya, Prastoka, and Aśvattha defeats the *Dāsa* Varcin at Udavraja.[9] Atithīgva defeats Arśasāna, an Iranic name, Satrājita Satānīka defeats Dhṛtaraṣṭra Vaicitravīrya, identified with the chief of Kāśi,[10] and the Bharata are associated with an obscure battle with twenty Aryan chiefs.[11]

It is Divodāsa Ātithīgva (son of Atithīgva) who seems to have brought the Bharata over the passes, capturing the 99 *iron* hill-forts of Kulitara's son Śambara.[12] Book II of the *ṚV* barely mentions the Yadu–Turvaśa or Pūru but is full of Bharata references in the context of tribes moving eastwards.[13] It can only be guessed if the Bharata were allies or subordinates of the Pūru, but the association seems to have lasted till the time of not only Divodāsa, who has even been called 'Pūru Divodāsa'[14] and whose son Parucchepa Daivodāsa, a *rājarṣi* like Devavāta/ Devaśravas, has been called Pūru at one place, but also that of Sudās Paijavana, probably a grandson of

4 *ṚV*, VI: 27.7.

5 *ṚV*, II: 14.7.

6 *ṚV*, I: 53.9–10

7 *ṚV*, VI: 27.5–8.

8 The *Hariyūpiyā* and *Yavyavatī*, through perceived phonetic similarities, have been equated with the Harappa of the granaries—*Yavyavatī* is 'she who is full of grain'. However, a closer etymological fit are *Haliab* and *Zhob* Rivers of the Bolan.

9 *ṚV*, VI: 47.

10 A. Berriedale Keith, 'Age of the Rigveda', in E.J. Rapson (ed.), *The Cambridge History of India*, vol. 1: Ancient India, pp. 105–6.

11 *ṚV*, I: 53.

12 *ṚV*, VI: 43.1; 47.2 and 61.1; Divodāsa had also engaged with the Paṇi, Pārāvata and the Bṛṣaya. See Uma Prasad Thapliyal, *Warfare in Ancient India: Organizational and Operational Dimensions*, Manohar, Delhi, 2010, p. 27.

13 *ṚV*, II: 13.8; 14.6.

14 *ṚV*, I: 130.7.

Divodāsa. One *ṛk* praises Indra for helping both Sudās and Trasadasyu in battle, and in another, Sudās's priest Vaśiṣṭha praises Agni for having vanquished the 'black' enemies of the Pūru.[15] It is shortly after this that the Bharata are seen striking off on their own under Sudās; Trasadasyu being a near contemporary of Divodāsa,[16] this event would not have been too long after the Pañcajana 'unification' under the Pūru.

The *Dāśarājña* or *Battle of the Ten Kings*

In their battle against Sudās, the Pūru lead the Pañcajana, of whom the Anu–Druhyu supposedly had '*600609 men*', and who are allied with the Paktha, Alīna, Bhalāna, Śiva, Viśānin, Pṛṣṇigu, and Vaikarṇa. Though these latter tribes have often been considered non-IA, their Amāvasu affiliations are evident, and they may be represented by the Pakhtun, Bolan (a name surviving in the Bolan Pass), Alan,[17] and the Sibioi of the Greeks.[18] The identity of the Vaikarṇa, Viśānīn, and Pṛṣṇigu are not conclusive. The florid description of battle suggests that Sudās, with the aid of Indra, broke '*a dyke and made the opponents flotsam on the Ravi, one following the other*'.[19] The victory seems to have been an upset, as it has been likened to victory of lamb over lion and paring of column with needle.[20] Also, Sudās apparently attacked westwards, scattering the *ten tribes* to the west, an idea that has been seized by the *Out-of-India* proponents as conclusive proof of a *westward migration* from India.

15 *ṚV*, VII: 5.3.

16 Witzel, 'Ṛgvedic History', p. 239.

17 See Witzel, 'Substrate Languages', *passim*. Witzel argues that the Dravidian were a pastoral people in the Ir highlands who migrated into the IV later, when the earliest Aryans were already there. This argument he bases on his contention that whereas 300 Munda words have been identified in the early *ṚV* I layer, there are no Dravidian words which start appearing only in *ṚV* layers II onwards.

18 The Sibis, mentioned in the *ṚV*, II: 192; III: 39; IV: 50, 103, 142, are the Sibioi of the Greek whose capital was at Aristapura or Sibipura. They are mentioned as clad in skins and armed with clubs by Alexander's chroniclers. In the *Mahabharata*, they appear as mountain people, *Mbh,* VIII: 45.

19 *ṚV*, VII: 33.3; VII: 16.

20 R.C. Majumdar, H.C. Raychaudhuri, and Kalikinkar Dutta, *An Advanced History of India*, MacMillan, London, 1963, pp. 26, very reminiscent of Guru Govind Singh's statement '*chiriya de naal baaz larāwān ... I shall fight the falcon with the sparrow*'.

However, a closer inspection of the hymns reveals that Sudās was only counterattacking, after an attack on them *from the west* across a water-obstacle faltered. In any case, in pre-modern battle, location of armies on a battlefield and actual direction of attack had little to do with relative directions of their homes, especially if there has been marching and countermarching. At Panipat the Afghans were *south* of the Marathas. The role of Indra in releasing the waters, which may or may not have had led to the faltering of the crossing, requires more study.

After the battle, Sudās is seen defeating the Yakṣu chief Bheda, and his two allies Aja and Śigru,[21] on the Yamuna. He then performs an *aśvamedha*, overcoming the north, east, and the west, but not the south where the Kīkata under Pramaganda and Naicaśākha resisted him.[22] The picture that emerges is that the Bharata, situated in the Pañcajana heartland with their Pūru allies, were attacked by the others from across a river obstacle, but they successfully counterattacked and scattered them, emerging unopposed in the Punjab and also quite able to extend their influence to the Divide. The rivalry with the Pūru persisted—the *Jaiminīya Brāhmaṇa*,[23] written long after the BOTK and by a descendent of Vaśiṣṭha, says that the Bharata were hard pressed by the Ikṣvāku, probably a Pūru sub-tribe.[24] However, this is clearly anachronistic as it places the Bharata *west of the Sindhu*, whereas they were already on the Ravi at the time of the BOTK.

This war and the continuance of rivalry indicate that the Pañcajana combine was more significant than a mere short-lived assimilation by the Pūru and involved more lasting interests. Also, though *Aja* (goat) and *Śigru* (horse-radish) have been taken as totemic names of non-Aryan autochthones,[25] *aja* is cognate of Circassian *ača* and Kabardian *aza*, where too it means goat.[26] Probably these groups were part of the many nations

21 *ṚV*, VII: 18.19 and VII: 33.3. This battle appears before the BOTK in the *ṚV* because the hymns are not chronologically ordered.

22 *ṚV*, III: 53.14.

23 *Jaiminīya Brāhmaṇa of the Sāma Veda*, (*JB*), ed. Raghu Vira, Lahore, International Academy of Indian Culture, 1937, 3.238.

24 Witzel, 'Rgvedic History', p. 264.

25 *ṚV*, III: 33, 53.9–12; VII.18. Aja and Śigru are taken as totemic names, which has prompted some to call them autochthonous. See Keith, 'Age of the Rigveda', p. 74.

26 Harmatta, 'Emergence of the Indo–Iranians', p. 360.

that then were on the move across South Asia. Unfortunately, literary evidence is too flimsy to permit a reconstruction of the battle, one of the difficulties arising in the name of the Pūru chief in the battle himself—to Keith, it was Purukutsa who was killed in battle,[27] whereas elsewhere it is Saṁvaraṇa. It is also difficult to determine the nature of the war, but its association with river-crossing and 'releasing of waters' suggests infantry-predominant action with some sort of combat engineering operation. This sets the BOTK apart from the *Mahabharata*, which is described as an open battle with a lot of chariotry action.

The Bharata; Constructing a Model of Migration

It is wrong to take the Bharata as a homogenous entity. There are two traditions about them, one the Vedic, which is not historically oriented, and the other that of the *Mahabharata*, which is 'historical' in so far as it meant to eulogise the Bharata. In the former, Sudās Paijavana is *allied* with other Bharata chiefs like Devaśravas, Devavāta, and Sṛñjaya Daivavāta, i.e. son of Devavāta,[28] which names probably represented clans and septs. The relation of the Bharata elements Tṛtsu and Kṛvi with the rest is unclear. The older view, that the Tṛtsu were Bharata enemies,[29] has been discarded—Ludwig equated the two,[30] while Hopkins, Majumdar, and others, based on the statement that after the war '*the people of the Tṛtsu prospered*', take the Tṛtsu as the Bharata ruling clan. Yet others have taken them to be their priests; to Oldenberg, Vaśiṣṭha was Tṛtsu[31] while Sṛñjaya was the ruling house.

The Bharata reappear in the *Mahabharata*, where Bharata Dauhśanti, son of the Pūru king Duḥṣanta/ Duṣyanta/ Duṣmanta, defeated the Sātvata (Yadu) on the Yamuna and Ganga. Kochhar takes these rivers as tributaries

27 Keith, 'Age of Rigveda', p. 74.

28 *ṚV*, IV: 15.4; VI: 27.7.

29 John Muir, *Original Sanskrit Text on the origin and history of the people of India, their religion and institutions*, 2 vols., Trübner, London, 1868, vol. 1, p. 354.

30 Alfred Ludwig, *Der Rigveda oder die Heiligen Hymnen der Brâhmana*, verlag von F. Tempsky, Prag, 1881, vol. 3, p. 172.

31 Oldenberg, 'Uber die Liedverfasser des Rigveda', in *ZDMG*, vol 42, p. 207. Also, '... *You Indra and Varuṇa sought to help Sudās ... while the Tṛtsu, walking about in white, composing poems, performed the sacrifice*', *ṚV*, VII: 83.8; also, '*the ones walking about in white, with the braid on the right side ... I cannot assist my Vāsiṣṭhas from far away*', *ṚV*, VII: 33.1.

of the Helmand, but as the Bharata victory over the Yadu (Yakṣu) was *after* the BOTK, and thus probably *after* Bharata Dauḥṣanti, undoubtedly an eponym representing the Bharata on the Divide, these were probably the rivers that answer to these names at present. Significantly, as per the *Mahabharata* Bharata's father Duḥṣanta was son of Rathāntara, the *Pūru* ruler of Gandhāra, while Bharata was brought up at the hermitage of the *ṛṣi* Kaṇva, the Kāṇva being associated with the Yadu–Turvaśa of the Gandhara grave culture.[32] Bharata, in the *Mahabharata*, is thus a forefather of the Kuru house which is lauded as Bhārata, though it uses the term more for the Pandu branch than for the Kuru themselves. We will return to the question of the Bharata affiliation of the Kuru.

No discussion of the Bharata can be complete without a look at their curious Iranic affiliations. The Bharata are associated with the *Uśij*[33] who are none other than the *Usig* of the Old Avestan *Gāthās*. The regnal titles of several Bharata chiefs, like Cayamāna or Kavaśa, was *kavi*, which resembled the Persian regnal title of *kavi* or *kai*, as in *Kavi Vištaspa*, *Kai–Kobad*, or *Kai-Khosru*. Cayamāna, son Abhyāvartin, is called Pārthava, i.e. Parthian, while their 'priest' Vaśiṣṭha compares favourably with the Avestan clan name *Vehišt*, calls himself Aṅgirā,[34] claims descent from Mitra–Varuṇau and Urvaśī,[35] and comes from eastern Iran.[36] In Book VII of Vaśiṣṭha, neither Iḷa/ Iḷā nor Manu is the primordial man, but Yama, which agrees with the position of Yima in Iranic lore.[37]

Having seen the advent of the Bharata, who have defined the cultural identity of a large part of South Asia (as the modern Bharat, i.e. *Bhārata* or *of the Bharata*), and where the eponymous Bharata is considered the first emperor of the Indians, we will now construct a model of the migration and distribution of the early IIr and IA ethnicities. C.N. Hoernle, among others, forwarded a model of the Aryan advent in South Asia occurring in two waves. There is indeed a curious correlation of this model with

32 Parpola, 'Face Urns', p. 153.

33 *ṚV*, I: 131.5.

34 *ṚV*, VII: 42.1; VII: 52.3.

35 *ṚV*, VII: 33.1.

36 *ṚV*, VII: 33, 3.

37 *ṚV*, VII: 33.9; compare with *ṚV*, X: 13.4 and see also I: 83.5 (composed by Gotama Rāhugaṇa/ Uśanas Kāvya).

the modern linguistic groupings in India—Nepalese, Assamese, Bengali, Oriya, Marathi, Gujarati, and Sindhi, spoken *around the Gangetic heartland*, preserve more archaic features of the Aryan tongue than the variants of Hindi spoken in the core regions, which indicates apparently that the first wave had been pushed out to the fringes by a second wave which occupied the core. This simplistic model has been challenged by Witzel, to whom the dichotomy arose due to a homogenising influence in the 'core' failing to reach the edges.

Kochhar has advanced a more flexible construct of the waves which considers migration routes. To him, one 'wave' descended the Bolan to create the Pirak culture and spread to Rangpur in Kutch and Ahar in Rajasthan, while another descended the Gomal and Khyber, creating the Swat IV culture and the assimilative Cemetery H, which to Kochhar was similar to but not identical with the Ṛgvedic people. An even later wave along the latter passes, as per him, created Swat V, which pushed the Swat IV people into the hills and absorbed the Cemetery H to form the Painted Grey Ware (PGW) culture. Kocchar goes so far as to equate the Swat V people with the Bharata, who created the assimilative Book X of the *ṚV*.[38]

Kochhar's model is more realistic in that it acknowledges *several* waves and not just two, and different 'streams' of migration. However, it still imagines migrations in terms of *waves* whereas in reality there was an endless trickle punctuated by occasional flushes, along several streams that changed course, split, merged, and divided, in response to a variety of stimuli. Migrations were seldom unidirectional and sequential, as seen in the highly convoluted tracks of the Uzbeks, Kazakhs, and Kirghiz.[39] Also, Kochhar's identifying literarily discerned folks with archaeological cultures, and periodizing such early events given the indifferent technology of chronometry, is extremely risky.

38 Kochhar, *Vedic People*, pp. 185–97.

39 The Kalmyk had followed Genghis and later the Golden Horde to the Volga, from where some of them returned to Kashgarh. Hutton, *Central Asia*, p. 316. The Kirghiz moved from Tuva in Russia to Central Asia during Mongol rule. When in 1930s they were forcibly settled in modern Kirghizstan, one group moved away and established a migration circuit between upper Afghanistan, Wakhan, and Xinjiang. From here a part of the group moved to Pakistan, which they found oppressive due to the heat and the *purdah* and tried to migrate to Alaska but failed. A large group managed to move to Turkey where they were welcomed by the Turcomans but faced the hostility of the Kurds. Some others returned to Wakhan.

The model proposed here, which owes much to the independent structures of Kochhar and Witzel,[40] may help better understand formation of early South Asian groupings and events leading to the *Mahabharata*. There was an endless trickle of migrant groups along the many routes through the passes, historically demonstrated to support human movement. The earliest groups, who we have met in the last chapter, were known to later peoples as the mysterious, semi-mythical Gandharva–Kinnara, marked by association with mountains, sheep, and music, and notorious for promiscuity, and the Yakṣa. These were followed by early IIr groups like the Anu–Druhyu who pass in and out of Vedic and post-Vedic material. The mainstream groups followed them in several waves, each comprising several tribes. The Yadu–Turvaśa, really a blanket term, migrated along the *Herat* (Hari-rud, Sarayu) to the Hamun region, and encountered the Pūru–Bharata, who had possibly migrated across northeast Iran, on the *Horax*$_{v}$*aiti* or Helmand. This was also the region where other tribes, like the Ikṣvāku, appeared, possibly along a more westerly route across Iran.

It was thus that the Hamun, i.e. the Dasht-e-Margow plains, and the neighbouring valleys of the Helmand and its *Sapta–Śvasā* (Seven Sisters) tributaries, became the jostling ground for endless branches and tribes, all gravitating towards what was to later become the Afghan 'promised land' of the Indo–Gangetic plains and the Ganga–Yamuna *doābā*. Endless plastic identities formed as a result of the jostling, one of which was the *Pañcajana* which the Pūru seem to have obliged the others to *also* use. As the mass of these tribes gravitated eastwards, there was an awareness of branches and septs 'left behind', reminiscent of the Rohillas each of whose tribes had a 'colony' on the plains and a homeland in the mountains, which is acknowledged in the Urvaśī story.

While the Anu–Druhyu barely managed to maintain their independent identity in this mass of movement, many older groups withdrew into the mountain fastness north of the Khyber–Peshawar–Punjab axis, climbing along the Kunar, Panjshir, Panjkora, Swat, Gauri, and Chitral valleys. It is they that have left archaeological evidence in these valleys, which display the archaic features found in the lower layers of the Gandhara Grave and other cultures on the Indus. In a wide arc along the remotest Himalayan valleys are found a remarkable host of nations—the Nuristani Kafirs of Hindukush, Kalasha–Chitrali–Hunza of Karakoram, Darada of

40 Witzel, 'Linguistic Evidence', *passim*.

Gurais and Kargil, Brog-pa of Ladakh and Zanskar, Kinnaura of Himachal Pradesh, and Jaunsari, Khasia, and Raji of Garhwal and Kumaon—that display various levels of archaic Proto-Indo–European (PIE) features in physique, physiognomy, and material culture, and lexical features older than Vedic and Avestan.[41] They are also marked by other peculiarities, like the use of chairs and shirts with pockets, and possess relic languages like *Buruδaski*.[42]

Popular identification of these nations with the soldiers of Alexander is incorrect. As Greek soldier–settlers did not travel with women but married local girls, their descendants gravitated towards the local language, culture, and physical type. Thus, although influence of Greek colonists like *Iavones* or *Yavana*, Tibetan or *Böd* peoples from across the mountains, or PIE elements from as far as Yarkand, cannot be ruled out, these nations are more likely the descendants of the architects of the earliest IE layers at Gomal or Swat who had *escaped* assimilation by moving up the rivers, and thereafter traversing the lofty Razdhanangan, Karakoram, Kunjom, Rohtang, and Shipki passes.[43] It being unlikely that they had *chosen* to live in such harsh locations, it is reasonable to suppose that they had been obliged to go there, perhaps as a result of military defeat. The isolation made their archaic customs and cultures grow more distinctive. The Kaffir godhead Imra is none other than Indra, but worshipped as an an-iconic stone with flour, blood and milk.[44] The cult-god *Jamlu* in the Beas valley near Manali has a violent and unpredictable reputation, Kinnauras make blood libations to Vishnu, whose worship is bloodless elsewhere,

41 *ṚV*, X: 18. Significantly, it is the Tenth Book.

42 G. Morgenstierne, 'Orthography and Sound System of the Avesta', in G. Morgenstierne (ed.), *Irano–Dardica*, Wiesbaden, 1975, pp. 31–83, has shown that the Kafirs or Nūristānīs constitute a third branch of the Indo–Iranians which had been isolated in the impenetrable valleys of the Kunar and its tributaries quite early, and then migrated along the height. It must not however be supposed that these groups were descended from *one* mother group, for there would have been late arrivals joining their ranks, some from the Tibetan Plateau. It is also possible that these groups dwelt along the Himalayan foothills and were pushed up to their current location independently along the rivers like the Satluj or Tons, and that they had not migrated along the heights.

43 Also, not all elements of pre-Vedic cultures were pushed northwards, as seen in the existence of relic languages like Nahali and Kusunda on the Narmada–Tapti plains and in Nepal respectively.

44 Hutton, *Central Asia*, pp. 420–2. Most of them who had accepted Islam had only nominally done so—the *Maula'is* of Agha Khan actually *rejected* the Koran, and preserved traces of animism. The Kaffirs have since become staunchly Islamic.

and Jaunsari enjoy a reputation for sorcery and witchcraft among their Garhwali brethren. The epithet Āraṭṭa suits them eminently, as they live under a-cephalous political conditions like in Hunza–Nagar, each of whose villages is an independent republic despite there being an overall *Thum*. It was thus that mysterious groups like the Gandharva, Kinnara, or Yakṣa, were modelled on them.

On the plains, the Āyu moved east leaving the Amāvasu *at home* in the west, moving not in two waves but in endless streams along the many routes which interacted and intermeshed with one another, which has confused not only the genealogies, but also the identities of their two overarching identities, the Lunar and the Solar lines. They also underwent several cycles of assimilation, some superficial but others fundamental. Overall, it appears that while the Lunar groups concentrated in the north and west, i.e. along the *Uttarāpatha*, the Divide, and the *Aparānta*, as the Kuru–Pāñcāla and Yadu, the Solar groups took a more southerly route, leaving behind *brethren* in the Ānarta or lower Indus, and gravitating further east as the Kāśi–Kosala–Videha on the Gangetic plains. The above shows the better efficacy of using the delta model of endlessly meandering, flooding and drying streams, rather than a neat tree–branch model with one or two waves, better represent the migrations. It also shows why the diverse groups inter-digitating on the plains always denounced one another as demonic, barbarous, and *mṛdhhravāc*, i.e. *of unintelligible speech*, and also using the overarching identity of Ārya for themselves, an ambivalent term derived from *ari* which meant *stranger* more than its modern meaning of *enemy*.[45] In addition, the numerous *vrātya* nations leavened the milieu.

The conflict of the *Dāśarājña* seems to be one such assimilative phase, which resulted in the spread of Bharata hegemony over the Pañcajana. What the appeal that brought so many nations to mobilise against the Bharata was can be guessed from the result of the Bharata victory, which logically must have been what the others had wanted to prevent, and which shall be inspected in the following sections.

45 Romila Thapar, *From Lineage to State: Social Formations in the Mid-First Millennium B.C. in the Ganga Valley*, Oxford University Press, 1984, p. 27.

Socio–Cultural and Religious Developments

Animism and Shamanism

The earliest religious consciousness of the Vedic people was an intense animism, expressed best in the *Atharvaveda*'s *Pṛthvi–sūkta*,[46] and centred on venerating the elements, and sacrificing to celestial gods like Indra, Sūrya, Rudra, Agni, Vāyu, or the Aśvins, who were invited to the hearth, praised with hymns (*śaṅsa*), and offered food and drinks (*purodaśa* and *soma*). Offerings were poured into the hearth and transported to the gods in the form of smoke, rendering Agni, the conduit in this homoeopathic rite, the 'priest' of gods. In return, the gods were expected to bestow benevolence.[47] The hearth was a temporary fire-pit erected at any spot meeting defined requirements of auspiciousness, and oblations were offered not by any special class of priests but by the *gṛhapati* or patriarch himself, with the other members of the family, including women, touching elbows in series. The concept of morality, which marked the mass religions of the Axial Age, had not yet developed.

In addition to this form of domestic worship, people also offered worship through *shamans* who interceded with gods and spirits. The *shamans* could foretell and influence the future, work up great magic, and invoke the gods in their own selves during which they were in trance or had fits. Ratnagar has contested the common assertion that *shamanism* was not prevalent in early South Asian religions, indicating that the seated figure of the ithyphallic horned man bearing a drum and surrounded by animals, found on a Harappan seal and generally called the *Paśupati* or lord of the animals, was really a *shaman*.[48] Now, while it is natural for Neolithic agrarian religions like that of Harappa to contain an element of *shamanism*, a closer look at Vedic material will also reveal strong indications of *shamanism*, though it has only been reluctantly acknowledged by Vedic scholars. One of the names of the Vedic poet–seer is *vipra*, the 'quivering one', like the later Kashmiri school of *shamans* called *spanda*, i.e. to shake, palpitate or quiver. The Vedic corpus has a large class of hymns called *ātmastuti* or self-praise; distinct from the main

46 *AV*, XII: 1.12.

47 Renou, *Religions of Ancient India*, p. 10.

48 Ratnagar, *End of Harappa*, p. 71 *et passim*.

genre of śaṅsa or praise, these were used in *Theyyam*-like impersonation of gods by the *shaman*.

In fact, Indra the Vedic god *par excellence* himself displays *shaman*ic traits. Though taken only as a war-god by Bergaigne,[49] Indra is not a belligerent *deva* in the earliest layers of the Vedas. Even his identification as primarily Thunder–God by Perry[50] requires a relook as the Vedic thunder god was the little-known deity Parjanya (Lithuanian Perkunos). Perry also denies his association with Aśvin–Uṣā, who have been called *indratamā*, on grounds that the word here meant *most impetuous* and not *better than Indra*.[51] Several aspects of Indra point in a different direction. He is praised in several ātmastutis,[52] which obviously were used by *shamans* to impersonate him. He assists his protégés by using sorcery[53] and is associated with shape-shifting—'*they ... made Indra into a cudgel for battle*'.[54] All these point to his being a *shaman* himself; after a later-to-come phase of primacy and belligerence, Indra reverts to sky/ air/ rain god, his cult fading away quickly in the ordered religion that emerged.

Even the trance, always an important ingredient in *shaman* cults, has a major presence in the Vedas wherein two methods of inducing it are discernible. One of these is the use of *soma*, a hallucinogen or stimulant derived from the *ephedra* weed (though imperfect substitutes were used later), and the other is the *Oṅkāra*, most misunderstood, and misused (even commercially) aspect of modern Hinduism, which is the *drone* audible across nomad Eurasia from Kamcatzka to Lapland, which marks the service in *Vajrayāna* monasteries, and which has evolved into several genres of throat singing like the Mongol *Khoomei*. Also important here are the class of *munis* or seers who are associated with retirement, solitude, fasting, silence, and self-mortification, all *shaman* motifs (see later).

49 Abel Bergaigne, *La Religion Védique'après les hymnes du Rig-veda*, 3 vols, Paris, 1878–83, p. xvi.

50 Edward Delavan Perry, 'Indra in the Rig-Veda', *JOAS* vol. 11, 1881, 1885, pp. 117–208. (120–121).

51 Perry, 'Indra', p. 124; also see *ṚV*, VII: 99.3.

52 *ṚV*, IV: 26–27; IV: 42.3; X: 48.

53 *ṚV*, IV.30.31, Indra *put to sleep with his sorcery* 30,000 Dāsa for Dabhīti.

54 *ṚV*, X: 48.6: *indraṅ ye vajraṅ yudhāye kṛṇvatā.*

Shamans were also important in politics, especially nomad politics, as they could intercede with the gods and *help* win battles. For instance, Mongol *shamans*, both male *böge* and female *idughan*, were venerated for their power and played kingmakers, but were liable to pay dearly, even with their lives, in case of failure. So strong was the hold of *shamans* that great kings and chiefs, like Genghis Khan, claimed to be and were recognised as *shamans*.[55] It is in this light that the role of the *ṛṣis* in the BOTK, Viśvāmitra and Vaśiṣṭha, must be inspected.

Evolution of the Vedic Religion

A study of Vedic stratigraphy reveals how the elementary religion outlined above evolved over the next centuries, one of the earliest steps in the process being the rise of the *Soma Pavamāna* cult when all *soma*-pressing hymns were compiled into the Book IX, and that of the cult of Indra the *soma*-drinking war-maker. Also is revealed the growing complexity of the sacrifice—from a domestic ceremony with offerings made by laymen led by the *gṛhapati*, it became a complex procedure where multiple hearths were used instead of one, and offerings were made by a class of specialist, regimented priests on behalf of the sponsors. Also, whereas at one time the sacrificial spot was selected based on only a few requirements of auspiciousness like slope and direction of winds,[56] fastidiousness in selecting the spot increased, and hearths and the sacrificial ground acquired an elaborate sacred geometry given out in the measuring instructions of the *Śulbasūtras*. In fact, while the Vedas barely mention fixed places of worship (only three late mentions of *devāyatana*, i.e. house

55 Christian, *Inner Eurasia*, p. 424. Also see J.A. Boyle, *The Mongol World Empire, 1206-1370*, London, Variorum Revised Editions, 1977, p. 181. Lattimore has shown how Genghis Khan has entered regional mythology, replacing the river god as the hero in old rites involving the sacrifice of pre-pubescent girls and 'marrying them off to the river', for instance; see Lattimore, *Mongol Journeys*, pp. 36–38. As late as the middle of the last century, in the festival of Genghis Khan an altar and casket containing his relics, including bow and arrow (some of the relics are replicas) was carried in procession, begging and robbing at will, and set up shows in tents where the relics were adored (compare adoration of Humayun's bow); Lattimore, *Mongol Journeys*, pp. 46–59. The Genghis festival marks the vernal equinox and has imported aspects of agrarian cults through the influence of the Buddhist lamas from the south, like the mass–like procedure or the *obo* or cairn which is treated like the Maypole; Lattimore, *Mongol Journeys*, p. 243.

56 Like slope and direction, like Mongol practice of locating family altars which later evolved into Chinese *Feng Shui*.

of god or temple),[57] references to fixed places of worship increase in later times, all indicative of increasing sedentization.

The Vedic corpus is also found reorganised, and now appended by a series of new manuals, of which the *Gṛhyasūtra*s and *Dharmasūtra*s describe comparatively less complex sacrificial rites for householders but the Śrautasūtras and *Brāhmaṇa*s detail extremely complex national and imperial sacrifices like the *rājasūya*. These sacrifices, especially of the latter class, were performed by specialist *priests* led by a *hotṛ* who made the offerings on behalf of the *yajamāna* or sponsor of the sacrifice. The *hotṛ* was assisted by the *adhvaryu* who was responsible for selecting plot, erecting altar, and lighting and nursing the fire in accordance to their manual the *Yajurveda*, the *udgatṛ* who sang the *ṛk*s set to music in the *Sāmaveda*, and the *Brāhmaṇa* who performed generic sacrificial tasks. The *adhvaryu*, once the independent priest of the *Aśvin*s, was now merely *suhastya* or skilled of hand, just as the *udgātṛ* was *suvāc* or auspicious of voice.

In fact, the sacrifice, which was now known as the *yajña* rather than by the archaic term *sattra*, was increasingly looked upon as an end in itself rather than a means to an end, and treated like a god. Concomitant with the above was the exalted status of the officiant–priests due to their expertise, and the appearance of numerous analyses and exegeses of the *ṛk*s, often based on speculative application of philology bordering on sophistry. The latter indicates that the meanings of the *ṛk*s had been lost and they were now used as magical formulae or *mantra* that must be pronounced perfectly, which reinforced the monopoly of the priest–experts. Correct performance of the *yajña* was essential in keeping the world going, and in many tales the *yajña* runs away, often in the shape of a deer, if there were errors in its performance.

At the same time, in many early popular stories, *muni*s or anchorites, through powers obtained by penance, fasting, silence, and self-mortification, come to the verge of upsetting the order of the gods and have to be coaxed or tricked out of their intention. In other words, these are nothing but the story of the suppression and supersession of the unpredictable, individualistic *shaman*s by regimented priesthood, which is the original plot of the story of Prajāpati Dakṣa, organiser of the *world–*

57 Irawati Karve, *Yugānta: The end of an Epoch*, Disha Books, 2007, p. 194, n. 1.

sacrifice; in popular mythology this story appears as the quarrel of Dakṣa with his *shaman–yogi* son-in-law, Śiva.[58] The Book X of the *ṚV* refers to these and more complex rites, while the *Atharvaveda*, supposedly the newest Veda but in reality the relics of the oldest, IIr *shaman* lore, is looked at disapprovingly.

That Book X was composed, or compiled, shortly after the BOTK, possibly under Bharata patronage, and that 'priests' like Viśvāmitra and Vaśiṣṭha played major roles in the war, calls for a closer inspection of these themes *vis-à-vis* the war. The popularity of the 'warrior sages' of the *Mahabharata* often forces us to take these men as priest–generals, but we see that in the BOTK, the contribution of these 'priests' was in the form of invoking Indra's help. The Bharata are associated with the Viśvāmitras in Book III,[59] but are lauded in Book VII as victors of the BOTK (the *people of the Tṛtsus prospered*) by the Vaśiṣṭha, who are rivals of the Viśvamitra.[60] Apparently at some point of time after the migrations and before the BOTK, the Viśvamitra had been replaced by the Vaśiṣṭha. However, neither can the circumstances of the changeover be discerned, nor did the Viśvamitra lose interest in the Bharata—Book III lauds Bharata dominance in Kurukṣetra,[61] mentions Sudās's *aśvamedha*, and notes the

58 Many early societies went through the process of the suppression of the *shaman* and his replacement by the priest. See Joseph Campbell, *The Masks of God*, vol.1: Primitive Mythology, London, Condor, 2000 (first published 1959), pp. 235–239 for the discrediting and regimentation of the *shamans* among the Jicarilla Apache by the group-oriented god Hactcin of the complex, agrarian society, and his priests. We see *Mi-chos* (*religion of man*), the earliest *shaman*istic religion of Tibet, superseded and suppressed by the Lamaism of first the Bon-pos and then the *Vajrayāna*. Nevertheless, *shamans* persist—most Himalayan deities, like Hiḍimbā of Manali or Narasiṅha of Joshimath, has, alongside its establishment of temple and hierarchical priests, the *guḍa* or *guṇa*, from the archaic *guṇin*, a revered figure who is maintained by a stipend throughout the year and who appears once or twice a year only when they perform special rites, impersonate the deity, and act as oracles. The last *guṇin* of the Sikkimese mountain god *Kāṅ–chenjaṅg-ha* passed away a few years ago, taking the lore of the mountain worship with him.

59 *ṚV*, III: 33.

60 *ṚV*, VII: 21.4; VII: 34.8; VII: 61.5; VII: 81.1; VII: 104, and X: 66.14. Also see *ṚV*, VII: 83.4, the late *ṚV*, X: 150.5 and also the *Śāṅkhāyana Śrautasūtra* 16.11.14. Book III of the *ṚV* refers to the BOTK but only as a past event, which suggests that this verse was probably a later interpolation.

61 *ṚV*, III: 23.2 and 3.

death of Sudās's son and the survival of his grandson,[62] all of which were events *later* than the BOTK.

The above can be reinterpreted as follows. The Bharata dismissed Viśvāmitra, an idiosyncratic, unpredictable, and ambitious character, with the placid and grave Vaśiṣṭha who was successful in invoking Indra's help for them in the battle that they won. In other words, Viśvāmitra and Vaśiṣṭha represented two forms of religion, the former that of the individualistic *shaman*, and the latter of the more organised religion of the Book X and after. The Iranic affiliations of the Bharata and Vaśiṣṭha require us now to look at corresponding developments in Iranian lore in which one can discern a similar reorganization despite only a quarter of the verbal material surviving Islamic conquest.

Thanks to a *padapāṭha*–like transmission system,[63] the five Old Avestan Gāthās (with 17 individual *Gāthās* = *Yasna* 28–53) of Zarathustra, which are like the Vedic family books and match the *Ṛgvedic* language very closely (they can be understood by one who speaks the other language), survive nearly unchanged. These early works are supported by ritual texts like the *Yasna Haptahaiti* which contain *Yajurveda*–like *mantras* for fire worship. The post-Zarathustran *Yasht*, which praises the gods *Miθra, Vaiiu*, or *Yima* in the *śaṅsa* style of the *ṚV*, and the *Yasna* 19.9–14 and 20–21 which are more *Brāhmaṇa*-like in content, are in Young Avestan which is quite divergent from the Indian *mantra* texts. Similarity in genre and purpose continues in the *Nirangistan* and *Videvdad*, which are similar in purpose to the *sūtras*, or the *Farhang-i-oim* which echoes the *Nighaṇṭu* of the *Nirukta*. At the same time, the now discredited *Atharvaveda* is seen to preserve ancient mythic elements like the Mesopotamian story of the archer god who killed the sacred boar *Emuṣa* with his bow *drumbhūlī*,[64] highly reminiscent of the Iranian *Verethragna* who runs before the Sun in the form of a boar.

62 *ṚV*, III:53

63 S.W. Jamison and M. Witzel, *Vedic Hinduism*, 1992, p. 30, www.people.fas.harvard.edu/~witzel/vedica.pdf, seen 17 April, 15. It is easy to agree with Witzel that the similarity is little observed.

64 F.B.J. Kuiper, 'An Austro-Asiatic Myth in the Rigveda', *Medeleengen der Koninklijke Nederlandse Akademie van Wetenschappen, Afd. Letterkunde*, Niewe Reeks, Deel 13, no. 7, Noord-Hollandsche Uitg. Maatschappij, Amsterdam, 1950.

The similarity of the Bharata- and Vaśiṣṭha- sponsored reorganization of religion, replacing the *shamanic* Viśvāmitra now despised as an overambitious *Kṣatriya* aspiring to become a *Brāhmaṇa*, with changes elsewhere in the IIr world forces us to look across a wider panorama of Eurasia, especially because the post-BOTK Book X is also reminiscent of elaborate burial practices of Sintashta–Arkhaim. At the same time, we must remind ourselves that we are treading dangerous waters, and selective reading of the scanty, ambiguous evidence can lead to whatever conclusion a reader desires.

Customs and Conflicts

This section casts across the Avestan world of the Eurasian steppes to understand evolution of early IIr and IA societies and evolution of warfare among these societies, the primary concern of this book. Geiger had equated Sintashta–Arkhaim with the world of the Old Avestan *Gāthās*, divided between into 'priests' (*aθravans*) and farmers (*vāstrya/ vaster/ vāstrya fšuyant*),[65] but had to be corrected by Boyce who showed that rather than farmers, the latter were really *herders who also fought when necessary.*[66] Boyce also insisted that, though graves and formalised burial rites show that priests existed in this world, there was little status differential in it except that some people were richer and thus more elaborately buried. This world of cattle and men—*paśu vīra* in *Old Avestan* (*Y.* 31.15, 45.9)—also parallels the early Vedic world of the herdsmen–householders, both with their *shaman* and *aθravan* priests and the common theme of **márya/ mairya/ vrātya*. The earliest lore of this world is preserved in the *Atharvaveda*.

This PIIr world was a patchwork of pastures of varying capacities linked by corridors that could support migration, though not prolonged occupation. Each group, composed of varying numbers of clans/ tents (*kulānām samūhastu gaṇah samparikīrtitaḥ*),[67] identified and maintained the optimal combination of animals (sheep, goat, cattle, camel, and horse)

65 W. Geiger, *Civilization of the Eastern Iranians in Ancient Times*, trans. D. P. Sanjana, London, 1886, vol. 2, p. 64. However, Geiger had translated the men not as herders but as farmers.

66 Mary Boyce, 'Priests', pp. 510–11.

67 Sharad Patil, 'Myth and Reality of Ramayana and Mahabharata', *Social Scientist*, vol. 4, no. 8, 1976, pp. 68–72.

best suited for its environs, and established an annual circuit with suitable staging areas.[68] Political authority took the form of regulating protocols of using and traversing pastures and corridors, and was highly diffused. Trek leaders or *grāmiṇis* (*grāma* being trek), assisted by *shaman* diviners, set dates and led migrations; those who could influence movements, and grant or deny permission to traverse pastures or camp on these, were *vrajapati*s or lords of the pastures (*vraja*) who in return for their 'service' obtained the use of the best pastures. Above them were a loose structure of power and authority holders like *viś-pati*s, *jas-pati*s, and *rājan*s who held authority more by custom and usage. Such a loosely diffused political authority can still be observed among the nomads of Rupshu and Kharnak in Eastern Ladakh, who elect a *goba* or headman from among themselves for a brief period, who then allots pastures for use by the different families and different animals and also arranges revenue collection for the Korzok and Thukje monasteries; the *goba* is seen to have hardly any coercive influence.[69]

The nomad's wealth was marked by two features—mobility and perishability. As it was pointless to fight over land—a piece of land could be all-important one season and mean nothing the next—territory was reckoned not in terms of square miles *occupied* but linear miles a tribe was *free to traverse*.[70] Rivers were obstructions and fords and bridges paramount, their importance seen in naming religious guides *tīrthāṅkara*, i.e. keeper of fords, like *pontiff* or bridge–keeper in Europe.[71] Secondly, perishability of wealth made it impossible to hedge against the future; unlike farming societies where the poor became poorer and the rich the richer in times of adversity, an *equality of uncertainty* permeated the nomad world, making it egalitarian with easy vertical and horizontal mobility.

68 Earlier pastoralists were noted to move up to 180 kilometers a year, but pastoralists of the early twentieth century, their terrain cut by political frontiers, barely moved 30 kilometers. Lattimore, *Mongol Journeys*, p. 188.

69 Wenche Hagalia, 'Changing Rangeland Use by the Nomads of Samad in the Highlands of Eastern Ladakh, India', M.Sc. Thesis, Noragric, Agricultural University of Norway, 2004, pp. 12–13.

70 Lattimore, O., *Mongol Journeys*, Varanasi, Pilgrim, 2006, first published 1941, pp. 186–88.

71 In the mountain world of Vajrayana Buddhism, the guide is *La-ma*, i.e. he who guides across the passes; the crossing, yet again, is important. Association of the BOTK with rivers, floods, and crossings suggest that its *casus belli* was control of fords on the Punjab rivers, a theme that will resurface in the context of the *Mahabharata*.

Men could rise and fall easily, making lineage–hierarchies extremely volatile, while men could transfer from one tribe to another just as tribes could merge and separate, making 'tribes' open status, heterogeneous, and cosmopolitan groups with multiple identities.[72] Conflicts in this world arose more on questions of the right to traverse, rather than possess, land, as also over other tangible and intangible goals like livestock, wives, sacrificial victims, revenge, and honour; while for the most these could be resolved by custom and powwows, at times they precipitated forms of ritual combat, one of the most dramatic of which was the cattle-raid, an endemic combat from which we shall commence our enquiry into the warfare of the IIr peoples.

Gaviṣṭi and Aśvamedha

In a little noticed statement, the Vedas justify '*since God gave the cattle to us, what use are cows to the Kīkaṭa*?'[73] This mirrors the Masai claim-statement—*since god had given cattle to our ancestor, we may take cattle away from our Kikuyu neighbours at will.* Such statements have been the justification of cattle raiders across the world, like the Mongol or Sakha, or the Nilotic Nuer, Isiolo, Murle, or Tutsi. Such desire for cattle—*gaviṣṭi*—was a prime IA predilection and the Vedas celebrate its champions as *gojit* or winner of kine.[74]

The horse is often supposed essential to the cattle-raid, as raiders required means of swift locomotion and controlling stampeding cattle. The idea is however not supported by East African evidence of the Masai, Kuria, Turkana, Samburu, or Isiolo, who were never associated with the horse, and whose pre-assault–rifle infantry tactics can be reconstructed from accounts of African travellers. Turkana raids, for instance, started with ceremonial exhortation by the *Dream Prophet* or *emuron* who gave out direction, routes, obstacles, and even type of cattle to be lifted. This was followed by an approach march on foot with scouts tracing 'enemy' cattle by dung, chewed grass and so on; raiders killed anyone they

72 Lattimore, *Mongol Journeys*, p. 149.

73 *ṚV*, III: 53.14, an attitude that is replicated in that of Visigoth Spain which enacted laws dealing with the cattle of the Goths but neglected to do so with regard to the land and property of the Celto–Iberic farmers, even though Spain was then one of the 'breadbaskets' of the Roman Empire.

74 The *govid* or *knower of kine* was also venerated; he was perhaps the scouts in cattle-raiding operations.

encountered during the march, leaving their path strewn with corpses as a warning against resistance and pursuit. Night raids were slightly different, involving cultivation of agents to gather intelligence of corrals, gates, and sentry routines, followed by night marches when navigation was difficult but concealment easy, infiltration of stockade and opening the gate (the bravest act), and abortion of raid if surprise was lost.[75] Night raids were less destructive and more ceremonial.

Drews postulated, in the context of stealing horses, that it was possible to lead an entire herd away by simply roping its leader.[76] As free-ranging herds of the early pastoral world operated in the follow-my-leader style, such tactics could have been used by pedestrian cattle-raiders as well, rendering the horse not a pre-requisite. However, absence of horse from East African raids was due to the fact that East Africa did not have horses (which could not counter the *tse-tse* flies of the grasslands); steppemen had them in copious numbers and could well have used them, especially as Littauer and Crouwel argued that acceptable riding existed in the steppes since late 4th millennium B.C.[77] Anthony suggests that raiders did use horses, at least to approach and escape in the case of horse-stealing raid, though they may have conducted the raid on foot.[78] Thus, the involvement of proto–cavalries, for approach, scouting, and rear-guard, cannot be ruled out in the case of the *gaviṣṭi.*

Denying the anti-essentialist idea that poverty and proliferation of firearms alone were behind cattle raiding in Africa, Kelvin Lines has shown that raiding was part of pastoralist culture and psyche,[79]

75 Michael L. Fleisher, *Kuria Cattle Raiders: Violence and Vigilantism on the Tanzania/ Kenya Frontier*, Michigan, University of Michigan, 2000, pp. 43–47.

76 Robert Drews, *Early Riders: The Beginnings of Mounted Warfare in Asia and Europe*, New York, Routledge, 2004, p. 23.

77 M.A. Littauer and J. Crouwel, 'The Origin of the True Chariot', in M.A. Littauer and J. Crouwel, *Selected Writings on Chariots, Other Early Vehicles, Riding and Harness*, ed. Peter Raulwig, Leiden, Brill, 2002, pp. 45–53, (especially p. 48 and 51) originally published in *Antiquity*, no. 70, 1996, pp. 934–939.

78 D.W. Anthony, *The Horse, the Wheel, and Language: How Bronze-Age Riders from the Eurasian Steppes Shaped the Modern World,* Princeton, Princeton University Press, 2007, pp. 222–24.

79 Kevin P. Lines, 'Is Turkana Cattle Raiding a part of Turkana Ethnicity? An Anti Anti-Essentialist View of both Internal and External Factors for Ngingoroko', *Intercultural Studies*, Asbury Theological Seminary, Wilmore, KY, December 2009, pp. 1–14.

and practiced by *männerbunds* like the Masai *morani* or the Turkana *ngingoroko* as proof of virility and bravery of the age-set as much as to gain glamour or reputation.[80] Youngsters launched raids to obtain bride-price which in some societies like that of the Turkana could be very high, or to take human captives who could be ransomed later for cattle. This is seen in the feting of the successful raiders after their return by sprinkling of milk and with ululation; the *emuron* divided the catch, giving the fattest head to the one who had shown the most bravery. Raids were considered beneficial as they rotated ownership of cattle, and in fact, except times of economic emergency (like the depopulation of the savannahs after the 1890s rinderpest outbreaks) when raids became economic necessities, it was usually a sport.[81] Rather than the popularly believed lion–hunt, the cattle-raid was main ingredient of Masai rite of passage.

At the same time, raids were also closely monitored and coordinated by elders, and had in-built measures like prohibition of killing women and children, abortion of night raids the moment surprise was lost, or assurance of sanctity of brideswealth cattle being transmitted through the land of other tribes. The attitude was similar to Afghans convening *jirgah*s before combats to determine acceptable number of casualties on reaching which battle would cease, and arrangements for upkeep of families of the killed, and so on, and also is reflected the controlled insertion of *vrātya*s into one another's territories by the Kuru and their neighbours. It was thus that, in line with Turney–High's postulation that wars of pre–literate communities could not rise above the military horizon despite the violence, butchery, and face painting, the cattle raid or IIr *gaviṣṭi* of the Eurasian steppes would have remained endemic. This is borne out by the experience of Shaka Zulu, the perfect Clausewitzian to Keegan, who could build no more than a one generation military success as his soldiers' style of warfare was traditionally endemic.

One early military endeavour of the steppes which definitely involved the horse was the *aśvamedha*. Known better as a spectacular imperial sacrifice–campaign in later times, in its original form the *aśvamedha* was in violence just a notch higher than the cattle raid, entailing little more

Also see Ian Skoggard and Teferi Abate Adem, 'From Raiders to Rustlers: The Filial Disaffection of a Turkana Age-Set', *Ethnology*, vol. 49, no. 4, Fall 2010, pp. 249–62.

80 Fleisher, *Kuria Cattle Raiders*, pp. 41–42.

81 Fleisher, *Kuria Cattle Raiders*, pp. 6–8.

than letting loose a special horse (or perhaps an entire herd) to sniff out the best grass it wanted, daring anyone to obstruct its progress.[82] In other words, it was a means to challenge and rearrange existing protocols of pasture usage.

Both *gaviṣṭi* and *aśvamedha* could be conducted without military riding, though involvement of some forms of proto-cavalries may not entirely be ruled out. However, it is extremely unlikely that chariots were used in these procedures. While Anthony and Vinogradov see the 'birth of chariotry' at Sintashta,[83] and Nicolo di Cosma sees the Sintashta chariots as fully formed,[84] Littauer and Crouwel have convincingly shown that the narrow dimensions and short naves (20 cm) of these chariots, discernible from impressions left in grave floors, rendered them unstable and wobbly.[85] Anthony and Vinogradov themselves concede that the Sintashta chariot was a little top-heavy.[86] In fact, military chariots convincingly appear only half a millennium after Sintashta, violently shaking the Eurasian world, raising cattle raid above the military horizon (much to the chagrin of Zarathustra), introducing massive tribal conflicts known as *saṅgrāma* (coming together of the treks) wherein treks laagered their wagons into strong points and fought around them with chariot and horse. These upheavals also brought about enormous socio–religious changes, all of which we shall see through the evolution in the ceremonial status of the horse.

The Horse and Chariot

The Horse in Eurasian Religions

The earliest horse was only used for food, and probably almost eaten out of existence once before its numbers were restored and the animal saved. Since then, it had grown to be part of religious and funerary rites from the Danube to the Yenisei, sacrificed, ritually eaten, and even interred

82 Anne Hyland, *The Horse in the Ancient World*, Sutton, Gloucestershire, 2003, p. 23.

83 D.W. Anthony and N.B. Vinogradov, 'Birth of the Chariot', *Archaeology*, no. 48, 1995, pp. 36–41, especially p. 40f.

84 Nicolo Di Cosma, 'Northern Frontiers of Imperial China', in Michael Loewe and Edward Shaughnessy (eds.), *The Cambridge History of Ancient China from the Origins of Civilization to 221 BC* (*CHAC*), Cambridge, Cambridge University Press, 1999, pp. 885–966, esp. p. 904.

85 Littauer and Crouwel, 'Origin of the True Chariot', p. 47.

86 Anthony and Vinogradov, 'Birth of the Chariot', p. 38.

in graves. Neolithic layers at Cucuteni and Tripolye have yielded horse–head sceptres indicating veneration of horses if not their use in war, old graves on the Volga, like at Khvalynsk, Syezzhe, or Varfolomievka, have yielded horse figurines and icons carved into bone, while one grave in Botai, Kazakhstan, yielded human skeletons encircled by the skulls, vertebrae, and pelvises of 14 horses.[87] The horse represented many things in the religions of early steppe peoples, like the sun, life, or spirit; in one rite, the skin of a horse, with skull, hoofs, and tail in place, was suspended so that it retained shape and swayed in the air, giving the impression of flight.[88]

Horse products were also ritually used. The Vedic *surā*, a word which in later times came to mean rice or barley beer, was cognate with the Iranian or Khotanese *hura* or mare's milk, presumably fermented like the *kumiss* or *ayräg*.[89] Honey mixed with *dadhī*, i.e. curd of mare's milk, was *madhuparka*, a ceremonial welcoming drink with the magical property of making people speak sweetly; mixed with *surā*, it became the *madhumantha*, funerary drink in the *pravargya* rite associated with the Aśvin cult. The seer Dadhyāñc, named after *dadhi*, is temporarily decapitated and revived with a *horse's* head by the Aśvins so that he could teach them the secret of horse–lore and *madhu-vidyā*, i.e. honey-knowledge; significantly, *madhu* here is not honey, but the fermented drink *mead*, one component of which is honey. Very curiously, a grave in Potopovka has yielded a decapitated human skeleton with a horse's head placed on its knees, reminiscent of this story.

Closely associated with the horse in religious practices are chariots. Many graves, like those at Sintashta–Arkhaim, have yielded chariots, largely as impressions on the floors alone, with sacrificed horses laid out symmetrically in galloping position along with retainers, wives,

87 Sandra L. Olsen, 'The Exploitation of Horses at Botai, Kazakhstan', in Marsha Levine, Colin Renfrew, and Katie Boyle (eds.), *Prehistoric Steppe Adaptation and the Horse*, Cambridge, Macdonald Institute for Archaeological Research, University of Cambridge, 2003, pp. 83-103, esp. pp. 94, 98–99.

88 David W. Anthony and Dorcas R. Brown, 'Eneolithic Horse Exploitation in the Eurasian Steppes: Diet, Ritual, and Riding', *Antiquity*, vol. 74, 2000, pp. 75–86 (especially pp. 80–81).

89 *BŚS*, 11, 11: 79.8–9, p. 1. *Hura* is mare's milk or a drink made from it both in ancient Iranian and Khotanese. Also, Parpola, 'The Nāsatyas, the Chariot and Proto–Aryan Religion', *Journal of Indological Studies*, nos. 16 & 17, 2004–2005, pp. 1–63, n. 251.

concubines, or slaves of buried chiefs. These graves, some of them so large that they required pillars to support the roofs in a manner reminiscent of *ṚV*, X: 18, have been (erroneously) associated by Anthony and Vinogradov with Vedic practices like the *vājapeya* 'funerary race', or the *aśvamedha* (see later). Further, there exist countless petroglyphs of chariots across the steppes, especially across the Mongolian Altai and the Chinese frontiers. The petroglyphs, which depict chariots in plan but in a squashed manner—with the horses 'split' like kippers on both sides of the pole[90] and the wheels 'laid out' on either side of the bucket—indicate an advanced pastoral technology, depicting several types of animals, including stallions and camels, accurately drawn halters, yoking arrangements, and outriders. It is difficult to discern the stratigraphy of the drawings, which may have been made over a long period, as they are etched one over the other.

Novgorodova argued that these petroglyph chariots were combat vehicles and indicate a warrior-elite—one such chariot with a large, snaky animal advancing towards it she associated with the myth of Indra, and *Vṛttra* the dragon.[91] Her theories were seconded by Novozhenov,[92] and reinforce the argument in favour of a steppe origin of the chariot advanced by Anthony and Vinogradov, and Piggott to a guarded extent.[93] However, Littauer and Crouwel, who have shown that the Ural vehicles were fragile and wobbly, with poor fore–aft stability, argued that the steppes did not *need a vehicle* because the horse was tolerably ridden there since the 4th

90 Karl Jettmar, 'The Origin of Chinese Civilization: Soviet Views', in David Kingsley (ed.), *The Origins of Chinese Civilization*, Berkeley, Univ. of Calif. Press, 1983, pp. 206–07.

91 Eleanora A. Novgorodova, *Drvniaia Mongolia[Ancient Mongolia]*, Moscow, Nauka, 1989, p. 153–4.

92 Victor Novozhenov, *Chudo Kommunikatsii I drevneishii Kolesnyi Transport Evrazii* [The Miracle of Communcation and the Earliest Wheeled Transport in Eurasia], Moscow, Taus, 2012.

93 Anthony and Vinogradov, 'Birth of the Chariot', pp. 36–41; Stuart Piggott, 'Chariot Burials in the Urals', Antiquity, vol. 49, 1975, pp. 189–90, Stuart Piggott, 'Chinese Chariotry: An Outsider's View', in P. Denwood (ed.), *The Arts of the Steppelands*, Colloquies on the Art and Archaeology of Asia, no. 7, London, 1978, pp. 32–51, and Stuart Piggott, *The Earliest Wheeled Transport: From the Atlantic Coast to the Caspian Sea*, Cornell, Ithaca, 1983, pp. 103–04.

millennium, and suggested that these *proto*–chariots was imitations of West Asian and Egyptian chariots as status–conferring vehicles.[94]

Association of chariots with the otherworld in *ṚV*[95] leads one to agree with Littauer and Crouwel, and Jones–Bley[96], that Sintashta chariots were funerary and not combat vehicles. Even the petroglyphs were not combat vehicles—there are no combat scenes and few of hunting if any, and they are always found in high, remote, and rocky places where chariots could not have possibly operated. Kenneth Lymner has shown such high and remote places in the steppes as associated with *shamanic* practices;[97] to Esther Jacobsen–Tepfer, chariot petroglyphs are indicative of *sky burials*.[98]

Chariot races were also part of funerary rites, begun perhaps with the practice of warriors racing one another for possession of armour, equipment, and chariot of the deceased which were considered charmed. In the *Iliad*, Nestor relates how he was defeated in a funerary chariot race by the *twin sons* of Aktor, one holding the rein and the other the whip. These were none other than the *Celestial Twins* of P-IE mythology: the *Aśvin*s, *Kastor* and *Peleudykos*, *Castor* and *Pollux*, *Hengist* and *Horsa*, or the Latvian *Dieva Deli* and Lithuanian *Dievo Suneliai*, which mean *Sons of God* just as the *Aśvin* are also *Divo Napāta*, *(Grand-)Sons of Heaven*. These twins, a detailed survey of whose association with the horse has been presented by O'Brien,[99] were part funerary cults everywhere, as all early

94 Littauer and Crouwel, 'The Origin of the True Chariot', p. 50. Indeed, not all graves in Sintashta–Arkhaim contain chariots, which somewhat challenges Boyce's assertion that there was no social ranking. Also, existence of defences suggests that some form of social ranking was involved.

95 *ṚV*, X: 135; see also *ṚV*, VI: 28, 'O Divine chariot etc …' which also appears in *AV*, VI: 125.1–3.

96 Karlene Jones-Bley, 'The Sintashta "Chariots"', in Jeannine Davis–Kimball, Eileen M. Murphy, Ludmila Koryakova, and Leonid T. Yablonsky (eds.), *Kurgans, Ritual Sites and Settlements: Eurasian Bronze and Iron Age,* BAR International Series, 890, Oxford, Archeopress, 2000, pp. 135–140.

97 Kenneth Lymner, 'Petroglyphs and Sacred Spaces at Terektye Aulie, Central Kazakhstan', in Jeannine Davis–Kimball et al ed., *Kurgans, Ritual Sites, and Settlements: Eurasian Bronze and Iron Age*, BAR International Series, 890, Oxford, Archaeopress, 2000, pp. 311–321.

98 Esther Jacobsen–Tepfer, 'The Image of Wheeled Vehicle in the Mongolian Altai: Instability and Ambiguity', *The Silk Road,* vol. 10, 2012, pp. 1–28.

99 S. O'Brien, 'Dioscuric Elements in Celtic and Germanic Mythology', *Journal of Indo–European Studies*, vol. 10, 1982, pp. 117–36.

religions, before the advent of the concept of morality, were preoccupied with making arrangements for the soul in the next world.

In Transport and Military

Littauer and Crouwel's idea that the horse was being tolerably ridden in the steppes since the 4th millennium B.C. has several difficulties. Firstly, the donkey or ass, domesticated in Nubia *c.* 4000 B.C., remained in use in West Asia despite its several problems. These animals had a gentle walking gait, but its forward sloping back and low neck gave a feeling of sliding forward, requiring the rider to perch on the croupé.[100] Its other gait was a break-neck, bone-dislocating trot which was difficult to control from the donkey-perch and was uncomfortable for rider and mount, damaging the kidneys of both. If the horse was indeed being ridden in the steppes already, there would have been no way its knowledge and technology would not have percolated to West Asia and enthusiastically adopted.

Unsuitability for riding led the donkey, and the more spirited ass and onager hybrids, to be used for traction, using the bovid yoke, developed in the agrarian context, modified to suit their slender spines and yoke them to four-wheeled wagons. However, though such wagons appear in the military context on the *Standard of Ur* and some pictograph from Uruk IVa, 3200–3100 B.C.,[101] they were slow and cumbrous, and to Littauer and Crouwel, suited only for civil transport.[102] Now, the development of even this contraption would have been stymied if the horse was being already ridden in the steppes, as the knowledge would have percolated to West Asia quickly enough. Therefore, though some rudimentary and experimental riding in Eurasia cannot be ruled out, most indicators of domestication from the wide zone of the ancestral horse, the earliest from Derievka and Srednij Stog on the Don to Botai in Kazakhstan, are in the form of equine bones in kitchen middens, mare's milk residues in potsherds, or dung deposits.

100 Littauer and Crouwel, 'The Origin of the True Chariot', p. 48. Ordinary travelling donkeys were ridden crosswise, which also suited the robes and gowns of the riders.

101 Littauer and Crouwel, *Wheeled vehicles and Ridden Animals in the Ancient Near East*, Leiden, Brill, 1979, pp. 13–14.

102 Littauer and Crouwel, *Wheeled Vehicles and Ridden Animals*, p. 45.

The horse does not seem to have been used for much more than as food in this early period.[103] It is true that some hesitant signs of bit-wear on equine teeth and articles like reindeer horn 'cheek-pieces' do appear in East European sites, but these are no conclusive proof of riding. Reindeer horn was used for several purposes and the articles may not have been cheek-pieces at all.[104] In fact, the barrel girth, hollow spine, uncomplimentary gait, and weak back all together rendered early horses unsuited for riding, which was consequently discouraged as inelegant. King Zimri–Lim of Mari was admonished by his priest for riding,[105] and one Vedic priest compared riding to a woman spreading her thighs at childbirth.[106] Only in late 2nd millennium is riding noted for the first time[107]—the Mesopotamian king Shulgi boasted of a long hike with a horse between two cities, though even here it is not clear if he rode or drove.[108] All that can be said yet is that the animal was *probably* used for traction, and there is no sign of tactical cavalry before the 1st millennium B.C., more correctly before 800–600 B.C.

103 D.W. Anthony, *The Horse, the Wheel, and Language*, pp. 206–13. Also, D.W. Anthony, 'The Domestication of the Horse', in R. Meadow and H.P. Uerpmann (eds.), *Equids in the Ancient World*, vol. 2, Weisbaden, Dr. Ludwig Reichart Verlag, 1991, pp. 256–57; Dmitriy Y. Telegin and J.P. Mallory (eds), *Derievka: a Settlement and Cemetery of Copper Age Horse Keepers in the Middle Dniepr*, (trans.) V.K. Pyatkovskiy, BAR International Series 287, 1986; Brown and D. Anthony, 'Bitwear, Horseback Riding and the Botai Sites of Kazakhstan', *Journal of Archaeological Sciences*, vol. 25, 1998, pp. 331–347. (especially p. 331). Parallel domestication of horses around the steppe fringes happened when the animals became habituated to farming settlements which they visited for food, just like reindeer got used to Esquimaux settlements which they visited to lick urine patches for salt. Horse bones have also been discovered at BMAC sites like Gonur in Turkestan, and Godin III and Malyan in Eastern Iran.

104 Marsha Levine, 'The Origin of Horse Husbandry on the Eurasian Steppes', in Marsha Levine, Yuri Rassamakov, Y. Y. Rassamakin, A. M. Kislenko, and N. S. Tatarintseva (eds.) *Late Prehistoric Exploitation of the Eurasian Steppe*, Cambridge, McDonald Institute, 1999, pp. 5–58, especially 11–12, and Drews, *Early Riders*, pp. 11–12, 16–18.

105 See also Hartmut Scharfe, *The state in Indian tradition*, Handbuch der Orientalistik. Zweite Abt, Indien, Dritter Band, Geschichte. Zweiter Abschn, Leiden, Brill, 1989, p. 193.

106 *ṚV*, V: 61.3.

107 For a summary of the evidence against riding before 2000 B.C., see Drews, *Early Riders*, pp. 31–34.

108 Drews, *Coming of the Greeks*, p. 83–84.

Also, Littauer and Crouwel's assertion that the steppes had no *history of wheeled conveyance*[109] requires inspection. It has been convincingly shown that East European Neolithic cultures advancing on to the steppes since the 4th millennium used ox-drawn carriages and other wheeled transport, and that by 3400–3000 B.C. wheeled transport was known across a wide swathe of territory from the Rhine to the Indus. Pastoral colonization of the steppes was made possible only by wheeled transport, which gave agro–pastoralists access to more land, ability to transport manure, and venture with herding camps to greater distances from mother sites. Massive plank-wheeled carts, often made of 400–500-year-old oak, have been found on the Rhine, some in preserved states, from 3000–2500 B.C., while a complete wagon fitted as a house has been found in a Pit Grave.[110] In fact, Littauer and Crouwel contradict themselves somewhat by acknowledging elsewhere a tradition of wheeled vehicles in the steppes since the time the horse was good only for eating.[111]

Adams and Mallory postulated that as the horse grew stronger, the steppe cartwright used them to replace bovids,[112] creating lighter, two–wheeled vehicles like the Sintashta proto-chariots. This proto-chariot *c.* 2000 B.C.,[113] though structurally weak, had two spoked wheels and thus was superior in design to the West Asian battle wagon which had four plank-wheels. The oldest two-wheeled design found in West Asia is from Anatolian cylinder seals *c.* 1900–1800 B.C.,[114] which suggests that the two-wheeled design was probably taken to West Asia from the steppes, making it difficult to agree with Littauer and Crouwel that the steppes had *imitated* the West Asian chariot, that too only for decorative purposes.

109 Littauer and Crouwel, 'The Origin of the True Chariot', pp. 50–51.

110 V.P. Shilov, 'The Origin of Migration and Animal Husbandry in the Steppe of Eastern Europe', in Juliet Clutton–Brock (ed.), *The Walking Larder: Patterns of Domestication, Pastoralism, and Predation*, London, Unwyn Hyman, 1989, pp. 119–126 (especially p. 123).

111 Littauer and Crouwel, *Wheeled vehicles and Ridden Animals*, pp. 28–29.

112 Mallory and Adams, *Encyclopaedia*, 1997, p. 627.

113 See Piggott, *Earliest Wheeled Transport*, pp. 1–63.

114 Littauer and Crouwel, *Wheeled Vehicles and Ridden Animals*, pp. 50–72.

Emergence of the Steppe Warrior

Hindus cremate their dead in rickety litters, but no anthropologist will conclude that it is beds of this type that they use in life! Chariots in Sintashta graves may have been just that, imperfect replicas of vehicles functional enough for travel if not racing or warring, and too expensive to be wasted in graves. Painstakingly drawn harnesses in Altai petroglyphs show that steppe chariots were functional, as no real care would have been taken to develop harnesses had the vehicles themselves been used only for symbolic transportation of the dead. It may thus be surmised that practical chariotry did exist in the steppes *c.* 2000 B.C. and was used for review, travel, and supervision of infantry, though their numbers remained small due to heavy resource requirements,

The first indication of military use of chariot in the PIIr world comes from *c.* 1500 B.C. when Zarathustra is seen castigating the warriors Fraŋrasyan and Arəjaṱ.aspa, enemies of his patron *Kavi* Vištāspa and his forebears, as '*slayers of men, harmers of men*' who assail law-abiding herdsmen, killing, robbing and stealing cattle. Boyce has shown that the title of both men, *mairya*, from the old *márya*, is hereafter used in the negative, pejorative sense of 'scoundrel', and that it soon falls out of use in Young Avestan which is marked by a rash of cattle-raiders. Significantly, Avestan texts call the raiders *a-vāstrya* or *a-fšuyant*, i.e. negative constructs that shows that they were *not herders* and *not pastors*. This has been rightly interpreted by Boyce as indicating a *recent* phenomenon—some men *gave up* being herders and pastors and *took to* raiding.

Also, a third class crystallised between *āθravan* priests and *vāstryō.fšuyant*—the *raθaēštar* (*standing in a chariots*) or *raiθi*, making steppe society tripartite, as against the older bipartite society.[115] While rivalries would have marked the early, bipartite society (it was only after Genghis Khan outlawed the cattle raid that Mongol society stabilised and flourished), violence was technologically limited and also regulated by custom and convention. The established order of unranked descent groups was not upset beyond rearranging protocols and recycling wealth. However, the appearance of the *raθaēštar* or *raiθī* upset this ordered world, introducing

115 M. Boyce, 'The Bipartite Society of the Ancient Iranians', in M. A. Dandamayev *et al* (eds.), *Societies and Languages of the Ancient Near East: Studies in Honour of I. M. Diakonoff*, Warminster, 1982, pp. 33–34.

nobles and chiefs (the *dušəxšaθra*, *Y.* 48.10), and warrior-dom, which triggered folk movements and raised steppe warfare above the military horizon. Concurrently, there emerged a series of chariot based empires in West Asia; in the 'state' of Naharin or Mitanni, the IIr (correctly IA) aristocracy over the Hurrian substrate called itself *Maryannu*, which to Winckler was derived from **marya*[116] though it has been also argued that it was a chance coincidence with a similar sounding Hurrian word.[117]

The question why all this took more than half a millennium after Sintashta can be answered through a re-inspection of the concepts of *márya/ mairya* and *vrātya*, which have been discussed in the previous chapter.

Horse and Chariot in West Asia; and the Chariot Empires

Horse bones were less than 1% of equine bones in 8th–5th millennium Anatolia. Horses appeared at Maikop north of the Caucasus at the end of the 4th millennium, and in Syria in 24th–22nd centuries B.C. Thus, there was limited import of horses into West Asia from across the mountains, either for food or traction, before the 2nd millennium. Contact with the steppes increased in early 2nd millennium,[118] when the horse at last became usable as transport, and West Asian words for the ass were adapted to the horse—ANŠE.KUR, i.e. *ass of the mountains*, and ANŠE.ZIZI, *ass that goes rapidly*. West Asian cartwrights began experimentation with the horse, one of their first products being the curious, scooter-like straddle car drawn by four horses, with seats lavishly folded in leopard skin, a copper model of which has been found at Tell Agrab in addition to sculptures elsewhere.[119]

The light, two-wheeled vehicle is noted for the first time in West Asia some two hundred years after Sintashta, implying that the vehicle was a steppe import. Through the next few hundred years, it grew militarily and politically, with powerful states of the Hyksos, Mitanni, Hittite, and Kassite appearing across Egypt, the Levant, Syria, Anatolia, or Mesopotamia. The

116 H. Winckler, *Orientalistische Literaturzeitung*, vol. 13, 1910, pp. 291–300, especially 291, n. 1. The word first appears in Assyrian inscriptions of Boghaz Koi, and is a composite of the words *Marya* (*RV*., young warrior), and the Semitic appellate *Nnu*

117 Littauer and Crouwel, *Wheeled Vehicles and Ridden Animals*, pp. 68–71 with n. 93 for the literature.

118 Anthony, *The Horse, the Wheel, and Language*, pp. 421–35.

119 Littauer and Crouwel, 'The Origin of the True Chariot', pp, 48–9 and Fig. 2.

Hyksos occupied Egypt in the 1750s. Moorey thought that the war-chariot was well-established in West Asia by 1650 B.C., which was soon after the Hittite Mursilis sacked Babylonia, a city soon occupied by the Kassites. The Mitannians established an elite state at Wassukhani, *c.* 1500 B.C.

These changes have often been seen as created by chariot-borne warrior elites who had *burst* out of the steppes, sweeping away 'civilized' communities of West Asia whose four-wheeled battle-wagons could not withstand them. Though perfectly effective among themselves, these wagons could have stood no chance against fleet and agile horse-drawn chariots, primarily because they were slow and cumbrous. It is unlikely that they had freely swivelling front axles, and with the equids guided by nose-rings, they would have been extremely difficult to turn. One experiment with a reconstructed battle-wagon achieved a turning radius of no less than 33 meters, undoubtedly because of the asses' thick, inflexible neck and high pain threshold;[120] the figure could have been better for practice, or worse under battle conditions. In reality, these vehicles were used to transport rulers, as static anvils for infantry to quash the enemy against, to reposition archers and reserves, and pursue fleeing foot.[121]

However, rather than 'bursting out', chariots seem to have grown in strength and dominance only gradually. Drews posits a much later date for Hyksos domination, saying that chariots were still a novelty in the 1650s. Deconstructing the idea of chariot-borne invasion, he suggests that these groups were not self-conscious nationalities from Central Asia but regional communities of Eastern Anatolia which developed the chariot, and then imposed their manners and social mores across West Asia, and even Mycenaean Greece, after peacefully *taking them over.*[122] He is prepared to take only the Aryan conquest of North India as a violent one.

The idea of the gradual emergence of chariot based powers is supported by the evidence regarding the chariot as such. A seal impression from Kultepe (Karum Kanesh II), 1950–1850 B.C., shows a vehicle with *two* wheels with four spokes each, with its two horses controlled by nose

120 Experiment by Duncan Noble cited in Gail Brownrigg, 'Horse Control and the Bit', in Sandra L. Olsen, Susan Grant, Alice M. Choyke, and László Bartosiwicz (eds.), *Horse and Humans: The Evolution of Human–Equine Relationships*, BAR International Series 1560, 2006, pp. 165–171.

121 Doyne Dawson, *The First Armies*, London, Cassell, 2001, pp. 84–85.

122 Drews, *Coming of the Greeks*, pp. 48–69.

rings. Though this model was a development from the Sintashta model in that it had spoked wheels, use of the painful and suboptimal nose-ring at a time when the bit was already in use in the steppes indicates that Anatolian chariotry was not yet battle–ready.[123] The oldest evidence of more agile chariots in West Asia comes from the 18th–17th century Syrian seal where a *single* crew drives a light chariot, the reins wrapped around his waist.[124] It was also from around this time that chariots started appearing in moderate to large numbers—Hittite texts from *c*. 1700 B.C. mention 30, 40, and even 80 chariots in battle.[125]

After 1550 B.C., chariots appear in larger numbers with the Egyptians who had thrown off the Hyksos by then. Thutmose III *captured* 894 chariots from the Mitanni at Megiddo, while the Egyptians captured 730 and 1092 chariots from their enemies in two other battles around this time.[126] If so many were *captured*, one may surmise that *many more may have been in use*; indeed, a total of 7000 chariots seem to have fought at Kadesh in the early 13th century, and 3943 chariots were arrayed against the Assyrians at Qarqar in 853 B.C. Obviously, whereas the sparse steppes, which had engendered the idea of the war–chariot, could barely sustain large parks of war-chariots, resource-rich West Asian states could. Naturally, groups that could control expertise in chariotry and dominate supplies of horses developed chariot based armies which ousted the battle-wagons easily.

Militarization of the Steppes

Though every trace of ritual or otherwise use of horse and chariot should not be taken as IE or Ir footprint—rituals such as ceremonial suspension of horse-skin was and is prevalent among Turkic tribes like the Altay or Sakha—there is a strong correlation between the early spread of the horse and chariot, and the PIE. One indicator of this is the commonality of terms: *mā* in Chinese is the English *mare*, Irish *mark* (horseman), or Persian *māl*, and while cartwright's and wainwright's terms are common in all PIE languages, indicating a self-sufficiency in the technology, Bauer

123 Drews, *Coming of the Greeks*, pp. 93–5.

124 Littauer and Crouwel, *Wheeled Vehicles and Ridden Animals*, p. 63, fig 36.

125 Edward L. Shaughnessy, 'Historical Perspectives on the Introduction of the Chariot into China', *Harvard Journal of Asiatic Studies*, vol. 48, no. 1, June 1988, pp. 189–237, especially p. 211.

126 Shaughnessy, 'Historical Perspectives', p. 212.

has also shown that even Chinese words of chariot technology, primarily the wheel, are of IE origin.[127]

Ghirshman connected a cylinder seal depicting a chariot at Tepe Hissar IIIB, *c.* 2000 B.C., a trumpet discovered at Tepe Hissar IIIC, *c.* 1900–1750 B.C. and others found in Syria,[128] and references to horses being trained to obey sound signals, to trace a Mitannian migration from Central Asia to Syria *via* the BMAC.[129] The Mitannians spoke IA[130] and called upon IA gods like Indra, Mitra–Varuṇau, or Nāsatya, as they did in a treaty with Egypt in 1380 B.C. The Hittites seem to have been another IIr (more correctly an IE) people, though Drews has argued that this was an artificial construct based on the *Old Testament* term *Khittim*, while the Mitannians were a branch before the IA–Ir split on its way east.[131] Now, the Hittites learnt chariotry from the manual of Kikkuli the Mitannian, several baked clay copies of which, giving a day-by-day, seven-month regimen for training of the chariot horse, have been found in their Hittite capital of Hattushas. The texts are in Hurrian or Anatolian but all its technical terms are in IA.[132]

Littauer and Crouwel deny any association of these texts with the IA based on their language, and the fact that other copies of the texts, and other manuals, have no Aryan terms.[133] However, there being no reason why a manual should be written in a native tongue but use foreign words

127 Robert S. Bauer, 'Sino–Tibetan *Kolo "Wheel"', *Sino–Platonic Papers*, no. 47, August, 1994. Bauer has shown the transformation of the PIE word k^wék^w*los* into all IE words like *wheel, cakra, circle, gola, ball*, and so on.

128 Bo Lawergren, "Oxus Trumpets, CA, 2200–1800 BCE: Material, Overview, Usage, Societal Role, and Catalog", *Iranica Antiqua*, vol. 38, 2003, pp. 41–118.

129 R. Ghirshman, *Iran: From the Earliest Times to the Islamic Conquests*, London, Penguin, 1954, pp. 10–19 and 30–31. That the Mitanni were not an isolated offshoot is seen in other evidence of Deva worship on the Caspian Sea and the Elburz. See Asko Parpola, 'Problem of the Aryan and Soma: Textual–Linguistic and Archaeological Evidence', in George Erdosy (ed.), *The Indo–Aryans*, pp. 353–381, especially p. 359.

130 O.R. Gurney, *The Hittites*, Penguin, 1952, p. 105.

131 Drews, *Coming of the Greeks*, p. 61.

132 Dawson, *The First Armies*, p. 121. For instance, *ashshushshani* was horse trainer. All equestrian and technical terms in Kikkuli's manual, whose language otherwise is Hattic, are Mitannian or Indic—for instance the words for colours, *babru, pinkara,* and *palita* correspond to *babhru* or brown, *piṅgala* or golden, and *palita* which is green.

133 Littauer and Crouwel, *Wheeled Vehicles and Ridden Animals*, pp. 83–84.

for technical terms unless those terms alone were understood, one must conclude that IA was the international language of chariotry just as Italian was to be that of music after the Renaissance; translators of Kikkuli's texts left foreign words un-translated initially, and translated them later. We cannot deny an association between the chariot, the IIr, and the steppes. However, though steppe communities had an advantage in control over the most exclusive element of the chariot system, the horse, they had to pay a premium on its other elements, viz. wood and metal, and perhaps to some extent technologically skilled manpower. Thus, the idea of the chariot had been stymied by lack of resources in the steppes, till it was brought to the edges of the steppes where resource availability and access to technological innovations was greater.

Another reason restricting the chariot to subsidiary and supervisory roles in battle was absence of a suitable weapon. Consequently, warrior nobles, who alone could afford chariots, dismounted to fight when necessary, a theme that is common to the *Iliad* or the *Li* oriented fighting of the *Spring and Autumn period.* Early steppe chariots must have used variations of clubs, hammers, or hammer–axes. The stone mace–club is associated with Aēšma, while Indra's *vajra,* from PIIr *vazrah* and cognate with the Lithuanian *vaecera/ uzere* and Finno–Ugric *waśarah,* was probably the perforated hammer–axe.[134] The *paraśu* associated with the early IA Bhārgava *Rāma,* cognate with the Greek *pelekuσ,* both from the PIE root **peleku,*[135] was a battle–axe. The Chinese used variations of the *ge* halberd. None of these weapons, as Shaughnessy[136] and Barbieri–Low[137] have shown in the specific case of the *ge,* were suitable for use from chariots, just as wasn't the spear, either thrown or thrust, as shown by Littauer and Crouwel (the mechanics of these weapons will be discussed later). In fact, there is a large component of ceremony associated with these weapons—the hammer–axe *labras* was ceremonially significant in Minoan mythology, Miθra wields the *vazra* as he runs after the boar-shaped Vereθraghna, god of victory, the Zhou king addressed his troops leaning on a *great yellow battle-axe*, and decapitated the corpses of the

134 J. Harmatta, 'The Emergence of the Indo-Iranians', pp. 346–370.

135 Piggott, *Prehistoric India*, p. 249.

136 Shaughnessy, 'Historical Perspectives', pp. 194–98.

137 Anthony J. Barbieri–Low, 'Wheeled Vehicles in the Chinese Bronze Age (c. 2000–741 B.C.), *Sino–Platonic Papers*, no. 99, Feb 2000, pp. 1–98, especially p. 37.

Shang king and his concubines with the *great yellow battle-axe* and the *black battle-axe* respectively, both of which were ceremonially paraded later.

A very crucial indicator appears in the account of the Battle of Kadesh on the walls of the Karnak temple in Egypt, which suggests that the Egyptians used bows which the Hittites did not possess, and thereby won. While this idea was result of Egyptian iconographic convention, it being unlikely that the Hittites still did not use archery,[138] it does indicate a recollection that chariots were at one time used without bows, and also represents a claim that chariot–archery was an Egyptian innovation. Obviously, a bow had to be small if it were to be used from a chariot, and thus composite unless it were to lose power drastically.

Composite bows are difficult to discern from sculptures and stylised illustrations, but Littauer and Crouwel's assertion that they were extant in the steppes since long[139] is unlikely to be correct, especially due to absence of metal tools essential in constructing them. The early 2nd millennium seal of Karum Kanesh II depicts a single charioteer with a battle–axe; composite bows possibly started appearing shortly after this, an early prototype being the ∑ bow on the *stele of Naram–sin*. Moorey attests that pharaohs were using composite bows since this time.[140] Stable and penetrative bronze arrowheads also become available *c*. 1650 B.C.,[141] from which time numbers of chariot archers in illustration increase, like in Syrian seals associated with the Kassites.

This brings us to Drews's succinctly stated need to differentiate between *where chariots developed* and *where chariot warfare developed*.[142] Evidently chariots originated in the steppes which developed the easily

138 Gurney, *Hittites*, p. 106.

139 Littauer and Crouwel, *Wheeled Vehicles and Ridden Animals*, pp. 36, 56–58, Figs. 76 & 78.

140 P.R.S. Moorey, 'The Emergence of the Light, Horse-Drawn Chariot in the Near East c. 2000-1500 B.C.', *World Archaeology*, vol. 18, no. 2, 1986, pp. 196–215, especially pp. 208–10.

141 Hermann Genz, 'Chariot and the Role of Archery in the Near East at the Transition from the Middle to the Late Bronze Ages: is there a Connection?', in André J. Veldmeijer & Salima Ikram (eds.), *Chasing Chariots, Proceedings of the First International Chariot Conference (Cairo 2012)*, Leiden, Sidestone, 2013, pp. 95–106.

142 Drews, *Coming of the Greeks*, p. 109.

accessible horse for traction, but their subsequent development was stymied by lack of resources and weaponry. This drawback was overcome in the steppe fringes, where chariots evolved in the hands of resources-rich ruling houses which could tap the resources required including bronze technology, gradually increasing in military effectiveness though it is doubtful if the appearance of chariot-using elite was all that dramatic. Though there was a tradition of fighting vehicles (albeit far less efficient), development was initially associated with IIr groups which infused the bloodlines of West Asian ruling houses (Mitannian girls were married by Egyptian and Assyrian royal families in large numbers, and Nefertiti was probably a Mitannian princess), thus bridging the two worlds.

The IIr groups could maintain their dominance through monopoly over horse-supplies. The Kassites were looked to for horses by all, and even the Hittites, whose own land was called *Cappadocia* or land of fine horses, said that in Babylon they were 'more plentiful than straw'.[143] Pharaohs obliged chariot–warriors to *buy* chariots from the state at great expense (ensuring that they had invested in the state) but then *provided* horses *free of charge*, indicating their monopoly over the horse which was maintained by matrimonial relations with the Mitanni, who gave Nefertiti her famous black horse. The *pharaoh*'s monopoly prevented the emergence of rivals, and the Berbers to their west could acquire the horse only after their defeat by the Egyptians under Seti I.

It was probably under Egyptian pioneer-ship that chariot designs evolved, acquiring among other things bronze fitments as also the more effective composite bow and bronze arrowheads. The idea of the greatly improved chariot now percolated *back* to the steppes where tribes along the frontier adopted it eagerly, mounting their nobles and young men, the mobilised *mairya/ márya* bands, on chariots to trounce the *mairya*s of other tribes still fighting on foot, dispersing or absorbing them. It was thus that the term *mairya/ márya* changed from *männerbund* to *generic warrior*.

The dangerous mobility and lethality of their new toy enabled these groups to run riot across the steppes, disrupting the orderly world of Zarathustra preoccupied with code of laws, dualism between good and

143 J. Oates, 'A Note on the Early Evidence of Riding of Equids in Western Asia', in M. Levine, C. Renfrew, and K. Boyles, (eds.), *Prehistoric Steppe Adaptation and the Horse*, Cambridge, 2003, pp. 115–25, (especially p. 122).

evil, sin, judgment, punishment, and ordeal. The word thus obtained its negative sense in New Avestan, becoming not only *raθaēštar* and *raiθī*, '*harnessed to horses racing ahead*', but also brigand. The predatory nature of the *Maryanni*, the Mitannian warrior elite named after *mairya/ márya*, is evident in the names of their kings: *Tusratta* = *Tveṣaratha* or 'Reckless Chariot', *Sattiwaza* = *Sativāja* or 'Booty Acquirer', *Saustatar* = *Savyaṣṭhār*, 'he who sits (in the car)', that is, 'Chariot Archer'. Even Vedic and Avestan gods acquire chariots.

Diffusion of the Chariot

One set of evidences for the steppe origin of the chariot is the similarity of cheek-pieces for chariot-horses from Mycenae, Rumania, southern Ukraine, the upper Don, and mid-Volga, all of which can be traced back to the southern Urals.[144] Apparently, chariots arrived in East Europe around the Black Sea and across the Aegean. Large parks of chariots and stores of arrowheads are reported in Mycenae by the *Linear B* tablets.[145] However, while charioteering developed in Mycenae and evolved into formalised fighting by the late 2nd millennium,[146] it appeared west of the Rhine and Marne only in the 5th century, and remained operational there till the 1st century.

Even in China their dispersal appears a little late. Some scholars, like Bagley, denied use of wheeled transport with animal traction in China before Anyang,[147] but Barbieri–Low has presented reasonable evidence to counter this.[148] But what are specifically chariots appear abruptly in Shang

144 Sylvia Penner, *Schliemanns Schachtgräberrund und der europäische Nordosten: Studien zur Herkunft der frühmykenischen Streitwagenausstattung*, Saarbrücker Beiträge zur Altertumskunde, v. 60, Bonn: Rudolf Habelt Verlag GMBH, 2004.

145 Drews, *Coming of the Greeks*, p. 167, where up to 10,000 arrowheads are mentioned.

146 Stuart Piggott, *Wagon, Chariot and Carriage: Symbol and Status in the History of Transport*, London, Thames and Hudson, 1992, pp. 58–63.

147 Robert Bagley, 'Shang Archaeology', in *CHAC*, pp. 124–231, especially p. 207. Also, Piggott, *Wagon, Chariot and Carriage*, p. 63, and Shaughnessy, 'Historical Perspectives', pp. 192 and 208. This is not altogether improbable for any society—the Tibetans did not have wheeled transport till the nineteenth century, and made do with yaks and horses.

148 Barbieri–Low, 'Wheeled Vehicles', pp. 11–13 (agricultural cart at Qinghai) *et passim*; also see Victor H. Mair, 'Mummies of the Tarim Basin', *Archaeology*, March/April 1995, pp. 28–35. Wheel ruts with hoof prints have been observed in several heartland cities.

graves at Anyang *c.* 1200.[149] Shaughnessy has rightly shown that stories of invention of the chariot by Xia and ancient Shang kings were nothing but Zhou plants,[150] and insists that the Shang grave chariots, closer in design to the Lchaschen chariot in Anatolia[151] than that of Sintashta, were not military vehicles. He discounts the reading of the set of five chariots in one grave complex as representing a military array as fanciful.[152]

However, his statement that '*no society could accept and adapt to such a sophisticated package of machinery as a horse-drawn chariot so smoothly without extensive previous experience with wheeled vehicles*',[153] has to be taken carefully, because the acceptance of the chariot in China was not at all smooth. In fact, it was rather jerky and painful—one prince called Yang is recorded to have been thrown from a chariot and suffered severe injuries in a rhinoceros hunt. While a single accident does not imply poor skills (rally drivers meet with them all the time), to Shaughnessy the only inscription from the period being that of a hunting accident is indicative.[154] Further, mere awareness of the wheel does not essentially mean that the wheel was being used in transport, as Barbieri–Low has himself pointed out in the case of Mesoamerica where wheeled toys existed but not carts.[155]

Some late Shang chariots in graves appear in more military contexts. They have *ges* and what look like fragments of compound bows arranged around them, while Chariot 175 at Dasikomgcun is buried with a human skeleton with 22 bronze and 10 bone arrows, stone halberd, bronze knife, knot detangler, adze, and axe (for maintenance), along with other scattered

---

149 William Watson, *Cultural Frontiers in Ancient East Asia*, Edinburgh, Edinburgh University Press, 1971, p. 65, and Stuart Piggott, 'Chariots in the Caucasus and China', *Antiquity*, vol. 49, 1975, pp. 289–90.

150 Shaughnessy, 'Historical Perspectives', p. 208, n. 29.

151 Shaughnessy, 'Historical Perspectives', pp. 200–201; Stuart Piggott, *The Earliest Wheeled Transport: from the Atlantic Coast to the Caspian Sea*, Ithaca, Cornell University Press, 1983, pp. 95–7; and Piggott, *Wagon, Chariot and Carriage*, pp. 63–6.

152 Shaughnessy, 'Historical Perspectives', pp. 194–98.

153 Barbieri–Low, 'Wheeled Vehicles', p.9.

154 Shaughnessy, 'Historical Perspectives', p. 217.

155 Anthony J. Barbieri–Low, 'Wheeled Vehicles', pp. 1–XX.

weapons and whetstones.[156] The shallow-curved bronze knife in the above list is of northern frontier origin,[157] and has been also found in the grave of Fu Hao, the northern consort of the Shang king.[158] Combined with textual evidence that mentions chariots with *frontier enemies*,[159] we may conclude that it was frontier peoples that possessed the war-chariot, and it was from them that the Shang obtained chariots by way of trade, gift, or dowry.[160] They also engaged northerners as drivers. Also, the oracle-bone pictograph for the chariot resembles the chariot petroglyphs of the Altai and Mongol plains.[161] Nevertheless, even for the later Shang, the primary roles of the chariot centred on burial, royal hunts (to show the prince as provider of food or display athletic prowess), and reviews.

The Western Zhou, Sinicized frontiersmen or nomadized Chinamen, and kin to the *Rong* and *Di* 'barbarians' whom Nicola di Cosma calls nomadic, had perhaps begun their career as Shang lords–marchers.[162] To Shaughnessy, Zhou expertise in chariots armed with the compound bow and improved *ge*s was responsible for their victory over the Shang at the ford of Muye,[163] though the exact role of the 300 chariots in this battle is difficult to discern. These chariots, though of the same overall pattern as the Shang chariots, were sturdier and appear in more military contexts, and were used against the Guifuang, Xianyuan, and Huai Yi foreigners. Western Zhou graves of not only kings but also ministers and nobles contained large numbers of dismantled chariots of varying designs, showing greater proliferation, wider research and development, and diffused ownership; the chariot regiment which *counterattacked* the Huai Yi was owned by a

156 Barbieri–Low, 'Wheeled Vehicles', pp. 60–64.

157 The knives had integrated hilts unlike the separate and stuck on hilts of the Shang, and were shaped into animals and griffins like the Scythian and Xioung Nu *animal art*. See di Cosma, 'Northern Frontiers', pp. 894–95, 902–903. This is the Ordos style.

158 Di Cosma, 'Northern Frontiers', pp. 902.

159 Barbieri–Low, 'Wheeled Vehicles', p. 36.

160 Barbieri–Low, 'Wheeled Vehicles', p. 47.

161 Shaughnessy, 'Historical Perspectives', p. 215, fig 4; also, Barbieri–Low, 'Wheeled Vehicles', p. 39, figs. 13 and 14.

162 Di Cosma, 'Northern Frontiers', p. 887. The Zhou intermarried with the Jiang, one of these associated tribes; see *ibid.* p. 890.

163 Shaughnessy, 'Historical Perspectives', p. 229.

duke and not the king.[164] In other words, while the Shang had only used chariots as an elitist veneer, war chariots were more integral to Western Zhou society.

IA Chariots, and Chariots in South Asia

Pointers to chariot proliferation are discernible among IIr migrants from Sintashta–Arkhaim towards the BMAC,[165] but there is little physical evidence of chariot or sacrificed horse from South Asia where there already existed a tradition of wheeled transport. Models of bullock-drawn carts with yokes and disc wheels have been found at Harappa, Mohenjo-Daro, Chanhu Daro, and Alamgirpur,[166] followed by representation of horse and rider at Pirak *c.* 1700 B.C.,[167] but none of chariots. However, some Italian archaeologists working in the heights above Swat, regions where the archaic PIE–PIIr cultural elements survived, have drawn our attention to some petroglyphs which seem to represent the chariot. Olivieri has pointed out one at Gogdara I which shows a topside view, with flattened wheel, in the manner drawn across Mongolia and Siberia.[168] At Thor, near Chilas in Gilgit, a wheeled vehicle, with horses in elevation one above the other and not split like kippers on either side of the yoke, has been compared by Jettmar with similar figures at Saimaly-tash in Ferghana, Kyrghistan.[169] At Kakai–Kandao appears a group of figures in which one, with a crossed

164 Shaughnessy, 'Historical Perspectives', pp. 224–26. The Marxist interpretation of the Western Zhou victory over the Shang is the replacement of slavery by feudalism!

165 Asko Parpola, 'Formation of the Aryan Branch', p. 200.

166 C. Margabandhu, 'Technology of Transport Vehicles in Early India', in D.P. Agarwal and A. Ghosh (eds.), *Radiocarbon and Archaeology*, Bombay, Tata Institute of Fundamental research, 1973, pp. 182–88. Also S.D. Singh, *Ancient Indian Warfare*, p. 24.

167 Asko Parpola, 'The Coming of the Aryans', pp. 85–229.

168 Luca M. Olivieri, 'The Rock-Carvings of Gogdara I (Swat) Documentation and Preliminary Analysis', *East and West*, vol. nos. 1–2, Rome, 1998, pp. 57–91, figs 4 and 15.

169 K. Jettmar, 'Non-Buddhist Traditions in the Petroglyphs of the Indus Valley', in J. Schottsman–Wolfers and M. Taddei (eds.), *Asian Archaeology 1985: Proceedings of the Seventh International Conference of the Association of South Asian Archaeologists in Western Europe (Bruxelles)*, Naples, Instituto Universitario Orientale, pp. 751–77; especially 755–57.

wheel on a trapeze apparently pulled by a running animal,[170] seems to represent a chariot, while another figure at Dandi-Sar I has been read as a chariot by Olivieri.[171]

These petroglyphs in lofty, un-chariotable places indicate adoration of the sun or the stars, but more importantly, are reminiscent of funerary connotations of the chariot, including *sky burials*, associated with the Aśvins, quiet, celestial, charioteering twins who had replaced the promiscuous Iranic twins Yama–Yamī in the religious lore of the earliest Vedic peoples like the Yadu–Turvaśa.

In seeking to differentiate *soma* offerings to Indra from older practice, Lincoln had suggested in his paper '*Priests, Warriors and Cattle*' that for the celestial sovereign, '*libations of milk or butter* ... [were] ... *appropriate* ...',[172] but, having provided no evidence in support of this, had ended up drawing caustic comments from Boyce.[173] Both esteemed scholars evidently overlooked the *gharmya* offerings to the Aśvins in which a mix of cold cow and goat milk was poured suddenly into a red-hot clay urn full of boiling butter (*ghṛta* or *ghee*), causing a pillar of smoke and fire to issue out of it. Parpola has shown how this rite had been assimilated into the *soma* cult of Indra, where in the *pravargya* rite performed by the *pratiprasthātṛ* priests and with the full complement of multiple fires including the *gārhapatya* and *āhavanīya*, the *adhvaryu*, once specialist priests of the Aśvins, pour the libations of milk on a boiling pan or pot placed on the *gārhapatya* alter. Interestingly, some of the anthropomorphic face urns used in these milk offerings have been found at the Gandhara grave sites at the foothills of the Swat which have been specifically associated with the Aśvin worshipping Yadu–Turvaśa.[174]

170 Massimo Vidale and Luca M. Olivieri, 'Painted Rock Shelters of the Swat Valley Further Discoveries and New Hypotheses', *East and West*, vol 52, nos. 1–4, December, 2002, pp. 173–224.

171 Luca Maria Olivieri, 'Painted Rock Shelters of the Swat-Malakand Area From Bronze Age to Buddhism—Materials for a Tentative Reconstruction of the Religious and Cultural Stratigraphy of Ancient Swat', *Zur Erlangung des Doktorgrades eingereicht am Fachbereich Geschichts- und Kulturwissenschaften der Freien Universität Berlin*, Rome, November 2010.

172 Bruce Lincoln, *Priests, Warriors and Cattle*, University of California Press, 1981, pp. 63–69, cited in Mary Boyce, 'Priests', p. 523,

173 Boyce, 'Priests', p. 523, fn. 119.

174 Parpola, 'Face urns', p. 157.

This brings us to the new religion of **saoma/ soma/ haoma* now elevated to into the full-fledged cult of *Soma Pavamāna*, ingredients of which were elevation and glorification of joyous war-gods like Indra, Agni, and Maruts. Indra, not too violent a god in older strata of Vedic mythology,[175] now appears as a charioteering warlord *par excellence*, quite different from the quiet Aśvins.[176] This was accompanied by a militarization of the chariot, which was now given superlative, warlike metaphors[177] like *bolt of Indra, vanguard of the Maruts, close knit to Varuṇa*, or *child of Mitra*',[178] and associated with the bow which was evidently composite as it is said to be drawn *to the ear* (and not the breast), and have tips of metal or dear horn.[179]

These changes are mirrored in Iranic lore. *Haoma* increases in prominence and there appear priests like the *zaotar* who offer oblations, *mąθran* who chant the formulae, *usig* who aid the *raθaēštar*, and the general duty *karapan*. These terms and offices were obviously counterparts of the *hotār* or *hotṛ*, the chant(er) of *mantra*, the *uśij* who aided the chariot–warrior, and the *Brāhmaṇa* who was generic officiant at the *yajña*. Also, *marya* is replaced by *raθaēštar/ arθaēštar* in Iranic lore and *kṣatra* in the Vedic (Boyce calls it *Kṣatriya*, but that term appeared later[180]), both of which groups represent newer styles of fighting.

The Zarathustrans (*Mazdayasnas*), fed up with the depredations of these *haoma* drinking *Daevayasnas* who had lately taken to a life of predatory warfare, dispersed, demonising the *daevas* and Indra. Probably under Assyrian influence, they developed the cult of the celestial twins into the more sombre and grave religion of *Mitra–Varuṇa*, *Amәša Spәntas*, and

175 Parpola, 'Face Urns', p. 158.

176 See Edward Delavan Perry, 'Indra', 117–208 for Indra's origin as a peaceable nature god. The relation with the Aśvins appears when the twins, and even Uṣas, are called *indratamā*, which as per Perry means 'most impetuous', and not the *best among the Indras*. In contrast, Bergaigne has looked at Indra only as a war-god, in Bergaigne, *La Religion Védique d'après les hymnes du Rig-Veda*, Paris, 1878, p. xvi.

177 *ṚV*, I: 20.3; III: 15.5; IV: 4.10; 16.20; X: 103.10.

178 *AV*, VI: 125.

179 *ṚV*, I: 282and VI: 75.

180 Boyce, 'Priests', pp. 512–13.

Ahura Mazda.[181] At the same time, while they retained the *aθravan* as the so-called fire–priest, the *atharvan* disappeared from Vedic lore except the archaic, offbeat *Atharvaveda.* Vedic groups instead celebrated the *marya* and Indra, developing a loud, warlike religion based on sacrificing to the *deva*s, demonising the *Asura* for hanging about ready to 'gobble up' the sacrifice if the *hotṛ* did not perform it properly, and castigating the *dasyu*, i.e. *daiŋhyu* of the *Gāthās*, which simply meant the '*the land over which the Iranic tribes wandered*'.

The Bharata, an amorphous conglomerate as seen earlier, the Iranic affiliations of whom and their Uśij and Vaśiṣṭha associates have already been noted, seem to have been associated with these changes. The new, sacrificial religion is especially associated with them. Book X was compiled shortly after their victory in the BOTK over the Pūru, whom they castigate as *enemy of the sacrifice*, who *speak ... ill of the sacrifice*,[182] and some of whose allies were the Aśvin-worshipping Yadu–Turvaśa. Their *priest* Vaśiṣṭha, who replaced the *shaman* Viśvāmitra, belonged to the Bhṛgu clan intimately associated with the sacrifice, the regimented compilation of Vedic material, collection of all *soma* hymns into Book IX, sanitization of the *Atharvaveda* (the Śaunaka recension), and development of the epics. As we shall see later, the Bhṛgu, were also associated with charioteering and fire. In other words, the Bharata were intimately associated with the chariot-based '*revolution in military affairs*' that had transformed IIr Eurasia and brought about warlords and chieftains.

Perhaps engaged as mercenaries by the Pūru due to their expertise in chariotry, they had grown ambitious and, aided by their warlike Vaśiṣṭha priests, upset the world of the Pañcajana. Their success brought about new religious and political formats—a new sacrificial cult which assimilated the Aśvins in the cults of *soma* and Indra, and formats like feudalism and chiefship. It must be remembered that the eponymous Bharata was considered the first emperor of the IA. It may be safe to conclude that it was to resist these fundamental changes that the Pañcajana and their allies had got together to resist the Bharata, precipitating the *Dāśarājña.*

---

181 Georges Dumézil, *Naissance d'archanges (Jupiter, Mars, Quirinus III): Essai sur la formation de la théologie zoroastrienne*, Paris, 1945, p. 56.

182 *ṚV*, VII: 18.13.

However, despite the primal position of chariots, not only ritually but also militarily, accounts of the BOTK do not talk of it much. Also, while some clay models of chariots from the Śuṅga period have been found, the earliest chariot illustrations to appear in a military context are petroglyphs at Morhana Pahar in western Uttar Pradesh which Bridgit and Raymond Allchin believe are no older than the 1st century B.C., though others place these at 8th century.[183] In the next few chapters, chariot warfare in South Asia will be reconstructed from literary and oral references, but it would do well to remind ourselves here that as chariots were to remain operational for more than a millennium in different geostrategic spheres, there naturally developed diverse traditions of chariotry, and diverse social systems to support them.

183 D.D. Kosambi, *The Culture and Civilization of Ancient India in Historical Outline*, London, Routledge and K. Paul, 1964, Fig 8.c, says that the rider represents Krishna with the wheel, while Bridgit and Raymond Allchin maintain that these are from no earlier than the 1st century B.C. See Bridgit Allchin and Raymond Allchin, *The Birth of Indian Civilization: India and Pakistan before 500 B.C.*, Baltimore, Penguin Books, 1968, p.154.

CHAPTER 4

Formation of the Kuru–Pañcāla Moiety

Occupation of the Divide

Victory in the BOTK had made the Bharata tribe dominant over the Punjab plains and the Divide, the world of the post *Ṛgvedic* texts, the *Brāhmaṇa*s and *Āraṇyaka*s. This was also pastoral country inter-digitated with streams and rivers like the Sarasvatī, i.e. the Ghaggar, and its tributaries. In the *Mahabharata*, the neck between the Punjab and the Divide, through which the Sarasvatī flowed, has been called Kurukṣetra—land of the Kuru. We will consider the relation between the Pūru–Bharata and the Kuru, among whom the epic is set, in a later section. In this, we will have a look at the geomorphology and hydrology of the region, to understand their impact upon the peoples passing over it.

It is known that the Divide and the Indus plains used to receive substantial rainfall in B.C. 3000–1800.[1] As per experts, the quantum of precipitation reduced over the ages, and by historical times, the Ghaggar was left carrying much less water, finding it hard to reach the Indus and unable to sustain habitation below its upper courses. Even the Indus, heavy with sediments, habitually veered to and fro across a wide floodplain, creating braided channels, as much due to the effect of Coriolis' force as due to heavy alluvial deposits that caused the watercourse to 'slip' from the 'top edge' of the alluvium. Habib has shown that as late as the Mughal times, the Jhelum, Chenab, and Ravi joined the Indus at Ujh, while Beas

1 J–F. Jarrige, 'Excavation at Nausharo,' *Pakistan Archaeology*, vol. 23, 1987–8, pp. 149–213. Also, Gurdip Singh, 'The Indus Valley Culture,' in G.L. Possehl (ed.), *Ancient Cities of the Indus*, Vikas, Delhi, 1979 (first published 1971), pp. 234–42. Also see Ratnagar, *The End of Harappa*, pp. 15–16.

and Satluj joined the Indus further downstream, at spots far from where they do so today.[2]

At some point in time in the past, the Indus slipped away towards the west, stranding the Ghaggar–Hakra in the sand seas of *Vināśanā*. The Satluj too veered away to the west, while its palaeo-channel, the Hakra, dried, leaving the howling Cholistan desert. All this caused the Ghaggar to falter beyond Anupgarh–Lunkaransar.[3] Later IVC and Painted Grey Ware (PGW) sites on the Sarasvatī/ Ghaggar are *not on top of old Harappan layers* but on to the erstwhile bed of the river,[4] showing further desiccation of the river.

Mughal has argued that the river was not as desiccated as is supposed, and the Hakra still carried some water from the Satluj into the Ghaggar, and thence the Indus.[5] The region is even today marked by numerous 'Ghaggarettes' and Yamuna proto-channels, and that the system of rivers has not yet stabilised is seen in the existence of many *būḍhi* (old) Yamunas marking its shifting course, still collecting and carrying water, and often disgorging into marshes.

It is an entirely different matter that the Ghaggar and Hakra are traced through the Nara, the *easternmost* alignment of the shifting Indus, into a *political* Sarasvatī, which is distinct from both *Naditamā* and *Vināśanā*! Also, to complete the impression, one of the Ghaggarettes east of the Ghaggar, the Chautang, has been called the Dṛṣadvatī.[6] The Kurukṣetra at the time of the epic was thus marked by pastoral wedges between shifting and braiding river channels which could support varying levels of cultivation. Beyond these rivers, and the Indo–Gangetic Divide, lay uncharted territory, occupied by the Kīkaṭa to the south, and under dense

2 Irfan Habib, *Atlas of the Mughal Empire*, OUP, Delhi, 1982, pp. 11.

3 The Ghaggar–Hakra channel, extended up to the sea along the easternmost of the many alignment of the Indus, is neither the *Naditamā* nor the *Vināśanā*, but the *Political* Sarasvati. One look at the map will demonstrate the impossibility for two rivers—the Sarasvatī and the Indus—to flow parallel to one another up to the, as alleged.

4 See V.N. Misra, 'Climate, a Factor in the Rise and Fall of the Indus Civilization', in B. B. Lal and Gupta, *Frontiers*, pp. 461–89 for a reasonable reconstruction.

5 M.R. Mughal, 'The Post-Harappan Phase in Bahawalpur District', in B.B. Lal and S.P. Gupta (eds.), *Frontiers of Indus Civilization*, Books and Books, Delhi, 1984, p. 501.

6 M.L. Bhargava, *The Geography of Ṛgvedic India,* Upper India Publishing House, Lucknow, 1964, p.71.

mahāvanas of the Gangetic plains, infested by forest tribes, to the east. The Divide was held by pastoralists, their pride in cattle evident in their Masai-like remark '*since God gave the cattle to us, what use of cows to the Kīkaṭa*?', but alongside them there also survived an agrarian tradition, which supplied the agrarian terms to the Vedic language[7] just as unknown, Neolithic substrate supplied the agrarian and domestic vocabulary to English, like *farm*, *home*, or *wife*.

Identifying some 300 Muṇḍāri words in the earliest strata of *Ṛgveda* itself, Witzel suggested that the IVC, at least its northern cluster, was ethnically Munda. Rather than the IVC being Munda, it is more reasonable to conclude that the Munda formed a considerable part of the agrarian substrate population of the IVC and later, across the upper Indus and the Punjab.

Kurukṣetra was also important because it formed the confluence of the migratory–trade corridors from Multan along the Ghaggar and the *Uttarāpatha* from Peshawar across the fords of the Punjab rivers. Vedic seers found the region so dear, strewn as it was with all the potsherds they needed for their rituals, that they hailed it as *varāpṛthivyā* or centre of the world,[8] and also *Uttara-vedi* or *Northern Altar*, *Madhyadeśa* or *Centre of the World*, and *Brahmarṣideśa, Land of the Venerable Sages*. Puranic literature also celebrates Kurukṣetra for prosperity, moral conduct, and a culture of being sagely without being unworldly and material without being avaricious, like its idol king Kuru. Tributes to Kuru humanity, material spirit, and sound economy were paid by Paṇini and Kauṭilya.

Curiously however, though the battle of the epic is situated at Kurkṣetra, its Kuru protagonists are not based here at all but on the Yamuna–Ganga interfluve, the ruins of their city of Hastināpura being identified near the modern town of Meerut at the edge of the rich *bangar* terrace overlooking the wide expanse of *khadar* along the Ganga to the east, covered in high grass and rich in game. So definitive, renowned, and evolving a people as the Kuru deserve to be independently inspected and

---

7 The Vedas are aware of wheat (*godhūma*, i.e. kine-dust, cognate of Iranic *gantüm*), and barley (*yava*), but not rice, till the time of the *Atharvaveda*, whereas rice was known in Mehrgarh since the 7th millennium B.C. and implicitly, in the IVC. Also, in early Vedic literature agrarian terms are few and far between, like *sītā* (furrow), *kṛ* (to plough), *kṛṣi* (agriculture), or *bhāṅga* (hemp).

8 *ṚV*, III: 53.11.

not lumped together with Pūru–Bharata, and so fleshed-out characters as the Kuru deserve to be considered by themselves and not written off as eponyms.

The Kuru

The Kuru origin is unclear. In the *ṚV*, the oldest *Kuru* name encountered is that of Kuruśravaṇa, descended from Trasadasyu,[9] whose death is deplored in Book X.[10] The epic and Puranic literature trace their descent along the Pūru line through Ajamīḍha, Saudyumni, Pūru, Yayati, Nahuṣ, and Āyu, ultimately to Aiḷa Purūravas.[11] The Bharata[12] are also found grafted into them, as Bharata Dauḥśanti, son of Duḥśyanta between Saudyumni and Ajamīḍha, as we have seen earlier.

In the *Mahabharata*, a king named Kuru appears several generations after Ajamīḍha, his four sons supposedly ruling Hastināpura, North Pañcāla, South Pañcāla, and Kānyakubja, an obvious attempt to associate these places with the Kuru. This Kuru is followed sixteen generations later by Dhṛtarāṣtra, the king or chief during the war, some discernable names between the two being Ṛkṣa, Uccaiśravas, Upaśramaṇa, Pratisūtana, Pratīpa *Prātisūtana* or *Prātisatvana*, and Śāntanu. Curiously, there appear two father–son pairs—one Parīkṣit and his son Janamejaya before Pratisūtana, and another pair, two generations after the Dhṛtarāṣtra. Such a pair also appears in the *Atharvaveda*, while in the *Śatapatha Brāhmaṇa*, a Kuru Janamejaya performs *aśvamedha*s with which the priests Indrota; Daivāpi Śaunaka and Tura Kāvaṣeya, the son of Kavaṣa Aiḷūṣa, are associated.

It must be remembered that king-lists, especially those of the *Purāṇa*s, are extremely unreliable, peppered with eponyms, glossing over several types of succession, and mentioning contemporaries in sequence. For instance, Bahīka Prātipeya and his brother Śāntanu, sons of Pratīpa, ruled *different* realms at the same time but appear sequentially in several king-lists. Even the name Kuru seems eponymous.

9 *ṚV*, IV: 38.1; VII: 19.3; through Mitrātithi and Tṛkṣi.

10 *ṚV*, X: 33.

11 Migrated from Bāhli or Bactra in Central Asia.*Rmn,* VII: 103.21–22.

12 H.C. Raychaudhuri, *Political History*, pp. 21–22.

While internal evidence of the *Mahabharata* suggests that the Kuru had supplanted the Pūru as the nation drifted towards the Divide, we cannot conclude that the Pūru had disappeared entirely, as seen in the existence of two Porus's in the 4th century B.C. on the Jhelum and the Indus. The Kuru are associated with the Kṛvi and Vaikarṇa,[13] Pañcajana allies which had got badly mauled at the BOTK; possibly the Kṛvi supplanted the Pūru house during or after Kuruśravaṇa, grafting themselves into the Aiḷa line with the eponymous Kuru, who is *not the first* ruler of Hastināpura.

Now, the Kṛvi also are part of the Pañcāla combine, which includes several Bharata affiliates like the Sṛñjaya, suggesting that not the entire Kṛvi tribe had converted to Kuru. Apparently, in the turmoil at the wake of the BOTK, tribes and clans underwent endless realignments and redefinition of identities, creating a situation where everyone was anxious to gain the legacy of the Pūru or the Bharata. Thus, while the Kuru call themselves *Dakṣiṇa-Kuru* or Southern Kuru, and associate themselves with the *Uttara Kuru*[14] or Northern Kuru, indicating awareness of a Trans–Himalayan mother-race, the Pandu also play up their Bharata affiliations, using Bharata Dauḥśanti to graft themselves into the Kuru line with which they are kindred through the Uttara–Kuru. This reinforces the suggestion that one must not equate the Kuru and the Pandu with the Pūru and Bharata, and write the *Mahabharata* off.

The Kuru Country

In the *Taittiriya Āraṇyaka,*[15] Kurukṣetra or the Kuru country extended from *Turghna* (Srughna or Yamunanagar, or the modern village of Sugh in Punjab) in the north, to *Khāṇḍava* in the south (of Delhi), and *Maru* in the west to *Pariṇah*, i.e. the Divide, in the east. A strong Neolithic agrarian tradition is found to have existed here, including human sacrifice, which seems to have been encountered and partly assimilated by the IA groups. Pehoa or Pṛthodaka (*Pṛthu's Pool*), a town on the Ghaggar, is revered as the spot where the *Brāhmaṇa*s killed the wicked king Veṇa (Pṛthu's father) and churned his body to create the world. In the original form of this story,

13 *ṚV*, VI: 51.128.

14 *Mbh*, VII: 109.10.

15 A.A. Macdonell and A.B. Keith, *Vedic Index*, 2 vols, Delhi, 1958, vol. 1, pp. 169–70; *Taittirīya Āraṇyaka* 5.1.1.

Veṇa was loving son, sole witness to the act of creation,[16] generous patron,[17] and '*the original seer*',[18] and it was only in Purāṇic times that he was recast as demoniac king *killed* by the *Brāhmaṇa*s, whose churned corpse gave rise to Niṣāda who became ancestor of foresters and barbarians, and whose son Pṛthu (Pṛthīn Vaiṇya), consecrated *by the Brāhmaṇa*s, ruled as a righteous king.[19] Several mythic themes are seen at work here. Creation of the world from the pulverised corpse of the primeval man is the origin-myth of many ethnicities. Given a Brahminic veneer in the *puruṣamedha*, or the *puruṣasūkta* of the *Manusmṛtiḥ*, it joins the theme of ritual regicide, where the king's body is mashed and is reborn as his son. *Veṇa the noble* becomes *Veṇa the wicked*, and his son, *consecrated by the Brāhmaṇa*s, rules as a just king, underlining that kingship is subservient to the priesthood, another Neolithic theme.

Pehoa is also associated with the sage–king Kuru who in the *Mahabharata* is seen cultivating here with passionate devotion. Using a golden ploughshare yoked to a golden chariot drawn by Śiva's bull and Yama's buffalo, he sows the seeds of goodness and virtue, making the land prosperous. The *Vāmana-Purāṇa* extols his courage, devotion and asceticism, and his insistence on the eight-fold path of ethical conduct (*aṣṭāṅga-mahādharma*), which included austerity (*tapas*), truth (*satya*), forgiveness (*kṣamā*), kindness (*dayā*), purity (*śauca*), charity (*dāna*), yoga and continence (*brahmacarya*). Significantly, in the *Vishnu Purāṇa* his arms were cut off by Vishnu with his discus (quoit) named *Sudarśana* and planted in the earth, another hint at royal sacrifice.[20] It was also at Pehoa that, in some versions of the *Ramayana*, Sītā appeared at the tip of the plough (variously of Janaka Sīradhvaja, Daśaratha, and even Rāvaṇa in the renegade versions).

In fact, the whole of Kurukṣetra is associated with the Neolithic human sacrifice. Its curious name of *Sāmanta-pañcaka* (lit. five barons) is explained with the story of *five pools of Kṣatriya blood* created by the

16 *ṚV*, X: 123.1–5.

17 *ṚV*, X: 93.14.

18 *AV*, II: 1; IV: 1. Some Rajput clans, like the Bachhal, claim descent from Veṇa, as also from Kīcaka.

19 Vijay Nath, 'King Vena, Niṣāda and Pṛthu', *Indian Historical Review*, vol. 29, nos. 1 and 2, January–July 2002, p. 52.

20 *Viṣṇu Purāṇa*, IV.19.

Bhṛgu hero Paraśurāma after avenging his father's murder, which were later turned into holy pools by the manes (*pitṛ*s), obviously to accommodate the Bhṛgu with Neolithic cults of sacrificing to water bodies. Other associations of Kurukṣetra with the Neolithic blood sacrifices are its name of *Nardak*, supposedly from *nirdayaka* or pitiless from the story of a child sacrifice at the tank of Ratauli near Kaithal by his father, and existence of the spot called *Nara-Kaṭāri*, or *cutting of humans*.

Such cults, which had taken roots in the patches and pockets along rivers and lakes of the Divide that could support agriculture, were adapted into the Aryan mythic system when they took to agriculture because in that age, knowing the exact mythology of sowing, harvesting, or winnowing was just as important as knowing the technology of sowing, harvesting, or winnowing. However, the mark of wealth and supremacy remained cattle, resulting in a strong agro–pastoral economy in the region, which also remained the happy homing ground for pastoral tribes till the late nineteenth century; Hsuen Tsang (visited 629 to 645 A.D.) called it a settled country with joyous peoples but also mentioned herders with no government or social distinctions.[21] In fact, an attitude of pastoralism and loose brigandage, permeated the region till the time the country was settled by the English, and is summed up succinctly in '*ék din mār liya, pandrah din khāliyā ... nā kare khet, nā bhare dhānd.*'[22]

Kurukṣetra gradually acquired the reputation for being the ideal spot for Vedic sacrifices and the home of several schools of philosophy, so much so that the legends of Indra, Dadhīci, Āśvin, and Vṛttra were recast around the lakes, primarily Saraṇyavat or Brahmasara. Later however, the honour of being the first choice for sacrifices was increasingly shared with the country east of the Divide, i.e. the Ganga–Yamuna *Doābā* and Pañcāla. This region, especially the latter, had a strong throwback to Neolithic agrarian cult of the serpent or Nāga. Its cities have Nāga association. Hastināpura, originally *Nāgasyahva*, was founded by a Nāga king, its name derived not from elephant or *hasti*, but snake or *hastin*.[23] The capital of North Pañcāla was *Ahicchatra, Umbrella of the Snake Ahi*, while Indraprastha is built by the *demon* Maya who is of Takṣaka affiliation and thus kindred

21 T. Watters, *On Yuan Chwang's Travels in India*, London, 1905, p. 252.

22 Trans.—*Robbing one day and surviving for the next fifteen, neither do they cultivate nor pay taxes*, see *Karnal District Gazetteer*, 1892, p. 57.

23 Note the *Hastin* association.

of the Nāga. A Nāga and agrarian tradition existed on the Yamuna south of Indraprastha with ambivalent relation with the pastoral Yadu—Krishna was helped by a Nāga during his birth, the Nāga Kāliya turned worshipful after being subdued by him, and his brother the Bacchic Baladeva had curious affiliations with the Neolithic culture god.

Nāga cults prevailed into historical times when many venerated clans derived Nāga lineages—the Bhāraśiva-Nāga king would carry a śiva-liṅga or phallic icon of Shiva on his shoulders at all times. Yet, it is impossible to attach an ethnic tag to the name; like the word *Yavana*, it implied different groups at different times.

At the time of the *Mahabharata*, building activity at Kurukṣetra centred on excavating 'tanks' and settling tribesmen on the mounds thus created—the lake of Brahmasara is said to have been excavated by Kuru himself. The building tradition took a firmer hold in the Gangetic plains, where a prosperous agrarian–urban civilization, based on the Neolithic fertility cults, would eventually appear.

Against this backdrop of agrarian settlement, prosperity, and taxability, the Aryan sacrificial religion grew complex. Their procedures were given out in the *Śrautasūtra* manuals, which the priests muttered under their breath as they performed, like the mutterings of a helicopter pilot in pre-flight check routine. The logic and procedures of the sacrifices were 'explained' and elaborated in the exegetical *Brāhmaṇa*s. There also appeared speculative *Āraṇyaka*s, some of which evolved into *Upaniṣad*s. The language of these texts was more modern than the Old Avestan-like *Ṛgvedic*. Further, there appeared no canonical corpus, and the different *śākhā*s or schools, marked by dialect differences, indicate development under different tribes in different regions. However, that it was the Kuru–Pañcāla country that had a lead role in formalization of sacrificial rituals and compilation and standardization of the manuals is seen in the manuals requiring the performers to address the sponsor, of whichever tribe, as '*O Kuru*' or '*O Pāñcāla*'. It was at Naimiṣāraṇya in the Pañcāla country that the Vedic and post-Vedic corpus and the *Mahabharata* were rearranged in their current form.

The relation between the Kuru and Pañcāla seems ambivalent. The early *Yajurveda saṁhitās*[24] state that the Kuru move eastwards and southwards victoriously, while the *Taittirīya Brāhmaṇa* suggests that the Kuru–Pañcāla raided the east in the season when the dew falls, i.e. the autumn.[25] There are indications of a Kuru defeat at the hands of the Śālva, and the raids were no longer practiced by the time of *Śatapatha Brāhmaṇa*.[26] In later times, the Pañcāla are seen more dominant. As many of the passages refer to iron, it is presumable that these events occurred after 1000 B.C,[27] Somewhere between these affiliations must have occurred the *Mahabharata* war.

An Archaeological Correlation

A correlation is faintly discerned between the literary picture outlined above and the archaeological evidence of occupation of the Divide and the lands to its east. Eastward emigration after the 'collapse' of Harappa brought agrarian cultures from Baluchistan and the Indus to Haryana and modern Uttar Pradesh (UP) along the Sarasvatī floodplains, as per Possehl, and Shaffer and Lichtenstein.[28] Thakran has reconstructed a reasonable picture of this movement.[29] Showing that while sites contemporaneous with mature Harappa lay on the *bangar*, i.e. low-productivity terraces of conglomerate, wind–blown sand and globular *kankar west* of the Yamuna proto-channels, later sites lay on the *khadar* or alluvial loam along the river, more productive but difficult to occupy, Thakran suggests the import of better civic technology from the IVC, presumably by Harappan immigrants. He goes on to compare this west–east movement with the north–south movement of *Painted Grey Ware* (PGW) sites along the Punjab fords and the Yamuna, which appear along the *eastern edge* of the *bangar* and even on the *khadar*, which he sees as people skirting the older sites around the east.

24 *YV: Kāṭhaka Saṁhitā*, 26.2; *YV: Maitrāyani Saṁhita*,4.7.9.

25 *Taittirīya Brāhmaṇa*, (*TB*), I.8.4.1

26 ŚB, v.5.2.3–5.

27 M. Witzel, 'Autochthonous Aryans?', p. 19.

28 G.L. Possehl, 'The Transformation of the Indus Civilization', *Journal of World Prehistory*, vol. 11, 1997, pp. 425–72. Also see J.G. Shaffer and Diane A. Lichtenstein, 'The concepts of "cultural tradition" and "paleoethnicity" in South Asian archaeology,' in G. Erdosy (ed.), *The Indo-Aryans*, p. 126–154, especially p. 138.

29 R.C. Thakran, *Dynamics of Settlement Archaeology*, Delhi, Gyan Publication, 2000.

More than 1000 PGW sites have been discovered over a 1400 by 700 km quadrilateral from Lakhiyo Pir on the Indus and Harappa on the Ravi to as far east and south as Tehri, Sravasti, and Ujjain. Of these, the early sites, which evolved out of *Plain Grey Ware c.* 1300 B.C., are centred on the upper Ghaggar and the Divide, over Late Harappan, Siswal or Bara layers—in other words, in and around Kurukṣetra. These sites display an evolution of material culture—Bhagwanpura on the Ghaggar evolved from non-urban, wattle, daub, and thatch constructions, through large, mud-walled buildings, to elaborate, many-roomed houses of baked brick. In contrast, eastern sites on the Gangetic plains display only the developed and finished features.

Another feature of PGW sites is that western sites, like at Noh in Rajasthan, Atranjikhera in Pañcāla, Jodhpura, Jogna Khera (part of the Bara culture on the Ghaggar), Kohand, Mirzapur near Raja Karan Ka Tila, or Daulatpur near the Chautang, succeeded the *Black and red Ware* (BRW), a sturdy pottery with a red slip decorated with linear designs in black on vegetal and animal motifs, which lies above the *Ochre Coloured Pottery* (OCP). This is in contrast to PGW sites on the Gangetic plains which seem to directly succeed OCP.

Contemporaneous with the above are numerous 'hoards' of copper weapons and implements—hatchets, barbed harpoons sometimes with tangs and mid-ribs, celts, adzes, axes, curious 'antenna–swords'—, and religious items like rings, anthropomorphic figures of cut sheet, and painted figurines of humped bulls and snakes, found on the Divide and its south and east. Predictably called Copper Hoards (hoards found west of the Indus should not be included in this group as the latter's contents are fundamentally different),[30] their bulls and snakes at once remind of Neolithic agrarian cults. Also, the anthropomorphic figure, which some notables insist is nothing other than Indra's *Vajra* because if thrown in a certain way they could bring birds down, overlooking the fact that even brickbats thrown in a certain way can bring birds down, are reminiscent of the cult of Śaṇi in which the god is worshipped in the form of a similar icon immersed in a pot of oil.

30 V.K. Jain, *Prehistory and Protohistory of India: An Appraisal*, Perspective in Indian Art and Archaeology, No 7, D.K. Printworld, New Delhi, 2006, p. 113. At Gungeria in Balaghat, 424 copper objects and 102 sheets of silver have been discovered.

Consistency in designs across the hoards shows that they were created by a single people, which has variously been identified with Neolithic hunter–gatherers, Pre-Aryan Munda, Harappans, Aryans,[31] and even specifically the *Mahabharata* people by Waradpande. Association of the Copper Hoards with OCP, which have at places been found together, links them with the IVC though the identification must be taken with a *caveat*—B.B. Lal says that the *Ochre Coloured Pottery* (OCP) is not a distinctive type of pottery at all but BRW spoilt from lying in waterlogged areas, and also doubts that an advanced culture like the IVC, which possessed technology like closed mould casting, would also have used poor quality pottery like OCP. At the same time, BRW has been associated with the Cemetery H culture, as it corresponds to its two foci, Punjab and Bahawalpur at the 'confluence' of the Ghaggar and Indus.

PGW culture, associated with the initial spread of iron,[32] appears to have succeeded older cultures on the Divide, evolving materially there, and then expanded eastwards in a more advanced form. Dating the PGW has been difficult. Though Jain sees it as fully established in the Gangetic plains by 700 B.C.,[33] Lal warned that when PGW sites were first excavated in 1951–52, technology of C_{14} was not available in India and the specimens had become contaminated by the time they were put to the test. However, discovery at Taxila of mint condition Greek coins above the *Northern Black Polished Ware* (NBPW), an elite pottery that succeeded PGW on the Gangetic valley in the 7th century B.C., helps establish a convincing relative stratigraphy, placing PGW at the turn of the millennium.

Can we now attempt a reconstruction of distribution of peoples and ethnicities indicated by distribution of pottery types and other archaeological data?

31 Jain, *Prehistory*, pp. 113–8.

32 B.B. Lal, 'This is How an Archaeologist looks at the Historicity of the *Mahābharata*', in Shastri (ed.), *Mahābhārata*, pp.1–25, especially p. 10, fig. 3. Also see B.B. Lal, 'Archaeology and the Two Indian Epics', *Annals of the BORI*, vol. 54, no. 1/4, 1973, pp. 1–8.

33 Jain, *Prehistory*, p. 104. Neolithic, rice growing cultures along the river valleys of Eastern U.P., Bihar, Bengal, and Orissa, which depended more on bone than stone (stone being rare on the alluvial plains, whereas animals were available in the dense forests), had evolved into Chalcolithic cultures that used copper from Singhbhum.

BRW-using Cemetery H culture represents a phase of assimilation and acculturation in the Copper–Bronze Age, possibly like the one represented literarily by the Pañcajana–Bharata conquest. Such a phase covered the upper plains of the Indus and the Punjab, one of its results being the emigration of the post-Harappans towards the Divide. On the Divide, socioeconomic form of these groups merged with those of the pastoral migrants following them, creating inter-digitating economies that were agrarian along rivers, and pastoral away from them, with an agro–pastoralism bridging the two.

There is no evidence of a military conquest of the Divide by distinct, iron using tribes. Also, it is unsafe to equate pottery styles with specific peoples.Thus, discovery of PGW over BRW in the sites on the Divide suggest evolution of technology among the Cemetery H people themselves who had succeeded the OCP using 'peoples'. Iron must have evolved in this milieu itself, as seen in the evolving PGW culture at Bhagwanpura.

This PGW culture matches the turn-of-the-millennium Late Vedic or *Mantra* period, based on the agro-pastoral opportunities of the Divide, conforming to Lal's associating them with the *Mahabharata*—the oldest layers of *Mahabharata* sites, except Hastināpura, being PGW.[34] Subsequent appearance of PGW sites with sufficiently developed civic technology directly above the OCP, without any intervening BRW, suggests 'colonization' of the plains by culturally advanced, iron-using cultures, which also carried its pottery technology. Appearance of NBPW, an expensive, elite pottery made by adding a slip of alkaline substances to get a glossier finish, in these PGW sites shows emerging social stratification.[35] This phase seems to correspond to the period of the *janapada*s that followed the epic. It was during such tumultuous movements that communities migrating east, adapting to iron, may have ceremonially cached obsolescent copper–bronze tools and weapons, creating the Hoards. Such ceremonial deposits are known in Europe.

The above discussion questions Kochhar's theory that the epic was pre-PGW,[36] because he himself placed it in the early 1st millennium. Also, it shows how incorrect it is to equate pottery styles or material hoards

34 B.B. Lal, 'Historicity of the *Mahābhārata*', p. 18.

35 Thus, it was at best a technological change. See Erdosy, 'Origin of Cities', p. 86.

36 Kochhar, *Vedic People*, p. 84.

with specific peoples, and how much more reasonable it is to see them as a continuum of technological change among relocating peoples of various ethnicities.

Evolution of Society and Polity

As mentioned earlier, pottery styles, and changes in them, do not necessarily indicate changes in ethnicities. Pottery styles or techniques can be long-lasting, often due to conservatism. Older conventions might be adopted by newcomers and conquerors, who would thus not show up in archaeological records. Or styles or conventions could be changed by the same people, if better technology were available, which would suggest new groups. Nevertheless, comparing associated material technology and literary indications in the previous section suggest, first an enhancement of the importance of the Kurukṣetra region which became a cradle for a new material culture, and then a reduction in its primacy as the material culture gravitated towards the more fertile (including literarily) ground of the east, which became the new cultural hub. Corresponding with the reduced importance of Kurukṣetra was a reduction in its geographical extent—from the vast area in the *Taittiriya Āraṇyaka*, it came to be reckoned as a restrictive quadrilateral between the Ghaggar and the Chautang in the *Mahabharata* and later texts.

The *Mahabharata* actually divides Kurukṣetra into three provinces—*Kurukṣetra* proper, the *Kurujaṅgala* wilderness along the Sarasvatī, and *Kuru* in the upper Yamuna–Ganga *doābā*.[37] This diffusion of territorial identity and application of tribal name to fixed territory, the upper Yamuna–Ganga *doābā*, anticipated the *territorial janapada* colonization of the plains. An early step in these change, which would culminate in the urban civilization of mid-1st millennium B.C. Gangetic India, was the *increasing sedentization* reflected in changing import of the term *grāma*. At one time, the term *grāma* had denoted a nomad *trek*, in which sense the word was remembered by Patañjali till as late as c. 150 B.C. In the *Brāhmaṇa*s and later texts, the term *grāma* is used in the sense of *settled village*. Obviously, reducing pastoral opportunities led to treks settled in fixed homesteads with ranches and stockades, with more permanent constructions like bamboo sheds or *śālā*. They also took to farming, sending out herders to satellite ranches or *ghoṣa*, which themselves might also turn sedentary. The exact

37 *Mbh*, I: 49.17–26; also see Raychaudhuri, *Political History*, p. 19.

form of land tenure in this early agro–pastoral economy is unknown, but may have resembled the Afghan system where agrarian land was parcelled out as *daftar* while commons were parcelled out as *inām*, all of which were periodically recycled in the procedure known as *wesh*.[38]

These changes, accompanied by the sharing of ritual primacy with Pañcāla and an eastward migration of the Kuru, were also complemented by encouragement of agriculture, glorification of Pṛthīn Vaiṇya, and transformation of tribal chiefship to feudal kingship. They also led to the deracination of the tribal folk, the *viś*, as underlings of the *Brahma–Kṣatra* combine. Thapar has outlined these changes, but her insistence upon the *lineage society*, which she describes as '*corporate group of unilineal kin with a formalised system of authority*',[39] as the representative Vedic political format, is questionable.[40] The *Mahabharata* war was a crucial staging point in these changes.

In fact, there was no single 'Vedic political system' or society, but shades of primarily patriarchal formats marked with matrilineal features of varying strengths. Political authority lay with the *rājan*s, a term which meant *chief* or *noble* and not *king*, who were for the most *elected head of oligarchies*. The *rājan* was associated with the folk or *viś* through the open assembly or *sabhā* resembling the Germanic *sippe*, and his *rāṣṭra* not as much territory as *sphere of influence*. Its synonyms—*gopa*, *gopati*, or *janasya gopati* and *nṛpa*, *nṛpati*, or *nareśa*—implied lordship over cattle and men, and not terrain. In fact, the *āraṭṭa* or kingless political format of later tribes represents an archaic form where the *rājan* is temporarily war-leader, selected by *rota* or acclaim, which is commemorated in the gods *choosing a leader* to deal with emergencies, like rise of a particularly pugnacious titan.[41]

The *rājan* led the *viś* militia in war and cattle-raid, afterwards distributing the proceeds among them, i.e. among the *sva* (own, followers)

38 James W. Spain, *The Way of the Pathans*, Karachi, OUP, repr. 1972 (1st 1962), pp. 74

39 Thapar, *From Lineage to State*, pp. 1–4.

40 J. Middleton and D. Tait, *Tribes Without Rulers*, London, 1964, cited in Thapar, *From Lineage to State*, p. 10.

41 The gods make a *raja* to fight the *Asura—rājānāmkaravāmahe*, *Aitareya Brāhmaṇa*, (*Ait.Br.*), i.3.3; also, Agni, Indra and Varuṇa agree to become *rājan* to fight Vṛttra, ŚB, ii.6.4.2–3.

standing poignantly *on his chariot* in what is called the *vidatha* ceremony.[42] In return, the *sva* offered the *rājan* the voluntary *bali*, and hosted him on his visits, i.e. *ātithya* (a form of tax consumed *in situ*). As resource-sharing procedures grew formalised, gains were distributed by officials called the *bhāgadugha*, i.e. distributor of milk, and *akṣavāpa* or 'keeper of the dice', two of the *ratnīns* or 'gems' of the chief's council.[43] The *rājan*'s title of *ṣaḍbhāgin* shows that he kept a *sixth* of the gains and distributed the rest, like the Islamic *khums* or *peñcik* where the chief was to keep a fifth.

The term *rājan* gravitated towards the modern sense of king in later times, in a process similar to the career of the term *basileus* between the Mycenaean and Macedonian periods.[44] The *rājan* gathered more authority, acquiring closed *pariṣad*s or councils from which the *viś* was excluded. Even distributive practices were subverted and the *rājan* took more than he gave. That kingship grew out of the household of the successful *rājan* is seen in the use of household terms for administrative officials—*govyaccha*, *akṣavāpa*, *takṣaṇa*, *saṅgrihatṛ*, or *rathakāra*, just like that of the *lord chamberlain* or *chancellor*. Such evolution of rulership and distributive practices between chiefship and kingship, brilliantly traced by Kumkum Roy,[45] was completed well after the Ganges valley was covered by *janapada* proto-states with complex, stratified societies.

The evolution affected the state sacrifices. The *rājasūya*, which in its original form required a chief to launch raids and bring back spoils, which he would then distribute, now only retained a stylized cattle raid wherein the *rājan* had to merely *touch* a herd with the tip of his arrow, and shoot an arrow lightly at a man on a chariot,[46] nominally signifying victory over cattle and men. The gifts were no more required to be violently captured and then distributed, but in a reverse process, peaceably deposited, by those sufficiently impressed or intimidated, or wishing to impress, i.e.

42 *ṚV*, III: 3.3, and *ṚV*, III: 26.6

43 Other officiants possibly complemented the process. The *govikartṛ*, whom Hiltebeitel sees as the official slaughterer, was possibly responsible for the distribution of captured cattle.

44 W.G. Runciman, 'Origins of States: The Case of Archaic Greece', *Comparative Studies in Society and History*, vol. 24, no. 3, 1982, pp. 351–77.

45 Kumkum Roy, *The Emergence of Monarchy in North India: Eighth to Fourth Centuries B.C.*, Delhi, Oxford, 1994, p. 124*et passim*.

46 *ŚB*, v.4.3.1.

allies, tributaries, and feudatories, and even the *viś* or *sva*, which were *re*-distributed. In other words, instead of distributing captured booty to the *sva*, the *rājan* now took from the *sva* and distributes it among his interest group, the *kṣatra* and *Brāhmaṇa*. The meaning of *ṣaḍbhāgin* changes—from one who *retained* a sixth and *distributed* the rest to the *viś*, it became one who *took* a sixth of the *produce* of the *viś* as *tax*.

Also, increasing proportions of gifts changing hands at the *rājasūya* were non-livestock items of conspicuous consumption, and even land,[47] which indicates a change from pastoralism to agriculture. Roy points out that the *rājasūya* had become a means of controlling the *viś* or *sva*, not only indicating control over givers of gifts but also over receivers of gifts through obligation.

As the position of the *viś* decayed to that of the deracinated *Vaiśya*, its role as militia diluted. In contrast, the *kṣatra* rose in prominence due to its monopoly over the prohibitively expensive chariot. The *senānī*, commander of the royal host, was increasingly associated with the chariot—*rathagṛtsa*, *rathasvana*, *tārkṣya*, and so on—while *Brāhmaṇa*s extolled the chariot as gainer of wealth.[48] The decaying relation between the *kṣatra* and the *viś* is evident in the falling position of the *viśaḥ* gods—whereas in the *Śatapatha Brāhmaṇa*, *Sarvadevaḥ* or all-god, who is *viśaḥ*, shares in the conquests of Indra, who is *kṣatra*,[49] later works doubt if the same cup of oblation could be offered to Indra (*kṣatra*) and to the Maruts (*viś*).[50]

The agrarian sedentization led to a rise in aggressive masculinity at the expense of older matrilineal formats. Communities stopped holding land in the female line and transferring land with women; instead, women were transferred independently in a system, which resembled that among sedentising nomads in China when they took to agriculture.[51] This is seen

47 All the sacrifices, *aśvamedha*, *rājasūya*, and the *vājapeya*, increasingly include non-livestock gifts which include food, drinks, gemstones, servants, effulgence, though *paśu* or animals is also included. See *PB*, 18, 7.3–4, ŚB, xiii.1.2.3, *Āpastambha-Śrautasūtra* (Āp.ŚS), 18.10.6.

48 ŚB, v.1.4.3

49 ŚB, ii.4.3.6.

50 Roy, *Monarchy*, pp. 47–48.

51 See Owen Lattimore, *Inner Asian Frontiers of China*, Oxford University Press, 1940, pp. 294–96.

in the conflict with *sapatna* or *bhrātṛvya*, i.e. co-husband, and the appeal to Agni to destroy them. There was also a growth in the institutions of *jyeṣṭha* and *śreṣṭha*, elder and best among equals respectively, which are indicative of male dominance. In fact, polity was marked by ambitiousness and adventurism, the term *śreṣṭha* being used like the moniker *malik*, which was adopted by any and every Afghan who could gather a dozen followers. All śreṣṭhas wanted to be *śreṣṭha svanām*, i.e. first amongst śreṣṭhas, first among the *sva*, and so on.

Above these minor lords appeared grades and types of 'gift devouring kings'—*samrājya* of the east, *bhaujya* of the south, *svarājya* of the west, or *vairājya* of the north. To Raychaudhuri, these were different styles of authority, *samrājya* being diarchy, *svarājya* chief-ship, *vairājya* kingless-ness, and so on. On the other hand, gradations like *rāṭ*, *samrāṭ*, *ekarāṭ*, *virāṭ*, and *cakravarti* indicate progression, but even here the lexicography is ambiguous—*samrāṭ* could well denote equal-chief or dual-chief rather than be a grade above the *rāṭ*.

It may be surmised that current political thought attempted to co-opt diverse sovereignty styles extant across South Asia into a single system, and offered the means of progress through them by manipulating the prestation-oriented, sacrificial religion. Sovereigns could promote themselves in grade and ritual protocol through the great sacrifices. However, the gradation is unclear. To Roy, the *rājasūya* elevated one to *rājā* (here meaning king) and *vājapeya* to *sāmrājya*, which could be followed by *aśvamedha* and *aindra-mahābhiṣeka*. In the *Mahabharata*, the *rājasūya* elevated one to *samrāṭ* through a *digvijaya* (victory over the quarters) in which another *samrāṭ* had to be defeated.

In addition to the stylised cattle-raid mentioned above, the *rājasūya* included a mock game of dice at which the king was made to win,[52] symbolising distribution of spoils after victory over cattle and men. This does not essentially mean that the performer was a parvenu—he would in reality have actually gone through these stages, i.e. victory over his neighbours, which was then formalised through the *yajña* to promote him formally to *samrāṭ*. However, successful completion of the *yajña* could require more diplomacy than battle, like a *potlatch* among the Indian tribes of North America, and in its fully mature form, in which the battle-content

52 Raychaudhuri, *Political History*, p. 141.

was formalised, it could take over two years.[53] In other words, position of sovereigns depended not as much on success in battle as on performance of great *yajña*s aimed at not only promoting spiritual and material prosperity of their people but also at tapping out and recycling wealth, creating a pecking-order of social privileges.

The *rājasūya* was just one of the immensely complex *yajña*s. It was accompanied by great slaughter of victims, including humans (*puruṣamedha*), and the sovereign retained large shares of the gifts that were recycled, while the *Brāhmaṇa*s clamoured for more, encouraging the formers' generosity by the *dānastuti*, i.e. extolling of benevolence.[54] Another sacrifice, the *vājapeya*, was designed to elevate one above *sāmrājya*. It included a *simulated* race of 17 chariots in which the performer was made to win, and had probably originated from the archaic procedure of a chief being required to periodically prove his fitness to rule in a test of physical prowess, in this case a chariot race.[55] The *yajña* gathered a concoction of other rites, like the funerary chariot race wherein warriors contested for the armour and weapons of the deceased, supposedly endowed with magical powers,[56] or the sympathetic magic of compelling the earth to turn on its axis, or, like the *gavāmayana*, the sun to turn at the solstice from *dakṣiṇāyana* to *uttarāyana*. The royal couple mounted a chariot wheel stuck on the ground to make obeisance to the earth.[57]

The *aśvamedha*, originally an endemic operation to rearrange protocols and precedence of pasture usage, gathered aspects that compared well to sacrifices to the sun like the Roman *October Equus* and certain

53 ŚB, v.2.3.

54 Kochhar, *Vedic People*, p. 17–19. This distribution may be contrasted with those of Hopkins and Witzel referred to elsewhere.

55 Defeat in a physical contest, like in a chariot race, was an old format of transfer of mandate or legitimacy to rule. We see this in the old tale of Pelops, who defeated and killed Oenemaus of Olympia in a chariot race and won the hand of his daughter Hippodamia along with his kingdom. As per the tale, Oenemaus had earlier defeated and killed eighteen suitors for the hand of his daughter, whose heads he displayed. This tale, which is associated with the foundation legend of the Olympic Games, is essentially one of the transfer of matrilineal legacy through contest—interestingly, Pelops is associated with royal sacrifice and cannibalism.

56 At the funeral of Atilla, his body was placed in a silken tent and horsemen raced around it.

57 J. Eggeling, 'Introduction', in Eggeling (trans.) *ŚB*, xxiv.

Irish rituals.[58] It too grew immensely in complexity, acquiring practices akin to the Neolithic fertility cult of the Apis Bull which included mock necrophilia and bestiality by the chief queen. It ultimately became an imperial sacrifice the most elaborate form of which, the *govitāta*, only a few dared to perform because it could easily ruin the performer.

As kings made their way through these sacrifices, they were consecrated to greater degrees of kingship, i.e. *abhiṣeka*, with increasingly complex procedures and anointing substances. If a king performed an *aśvamedha* after an initial *abhiṣeka*, he went through the *punar-abhiṣeka*, i.e. re-anointment. The *aindra-mahābhiṣeka*, or great consecration of Indra, was the most splendorous and elaborate, which made the king *cakravartin*. Interestingly, while these sacrifices were the means to realise imperial ambition, interrupting them or preventing their smooth completion was the means to challenge the ambition. The *aśvamedha* could be interrupted not only by arresting the horse but also by desecrating the sacrificial ground. In the *Śatapatha Brāhmaṇa*, Kākra Sthapati's efforts to restore Duṣṭaṛtu Pauṅsāyana to the Sṛñjaya *via* the *Sautrāmaṇi* sacrifice are interrupted by Bahīka Prātipeya who tries to vandalise the sacrificial ground.[59] It must not be concluded from the above that performers did not need to have real military prowess—they could ensure completion of the sacrifices only if few would dare to challenge them. This is seen from the negative evidence from later times when parvenus desirous of the reputation of having performed the *aśvamedha* performed quiet sacrifices, making sure that the horse did not stray too far!

The role of the new breed of sovereigns is ambiguous. They were enjoined to protect, but the 'seller of protection' motif does not easily apply to them because the task was often ritually waived.[60] They do not seem to have controlled labour like in the Cretan palace system, and labour was controlled more by custom in a command economy where each class had an allotted role. In effect, the role of the sovereign was largely limited to preserve the established system, i.e. the *ṛta*, a term originally with

58 Giraldus Cambrensis, 'Topographic Hybernia', in J. Puhvel, *Comparative Mythology*, London, John Hopkins University Press, 1987, pp. 269–276.

59 ŚB, xii.9.3.3

60 A king was supposed to make good the lost property of his subject; in practice, he seldom did any such thing, but merely *took over a part of a robbed subject's load of sin* (!)

close resemblance to the Greek *Moira*, but not interfere in its functioning beyond some public works like dams, irrigation tanks, or cities. In theory, the countryside was covered with self-sufficient villages which did not specialise in any commodity and traded little, conducting their internal function through barter of goods and services governed by custom and protocol, handing over part of their produce to the king, i.e. his residential garrison or his liege–lords who represented his authority, and who in turn deposited them in the giant sacrifices. In other words, commoners were left to their own devices, the 'state' being nothing more than a giant clearing house for conspicuous consumption, operated through the sacrifices. It was this tradition of absence of interference and *letting-be* that enabled English youngsters to function effectively as magistrates and collectors, as long as they warded off anarchy but left social procedures and protocols un-tampered.

This ritual-governed political economy, which perhaps had marked the IVC where there is little evidence of kingly interference or monumental work, became established in regions most advanced towards kingship. But the system was not as bleakly monotonous everywhere, as discussed admirably by Jayaswal.[61] All tribes were not equally deracinated, and vibrant *Vrātya*s created *gaṇarājya* oligarchies[62] whose political process were entirely different. *Vrātya* chiefs like Ajātaśatru[63] or Aśvapati Kekaya[64] opted out of the system, ready to beset the fragile *ṛta*. There was a rich tradition of trade operated by nomad *sārthavāha*s or caravan captains. It was among such groups that the vibrant religions of the Buddha or the Mahāvīra, which gave the individual man an identity, would in time thrive.

The above changes occurred over a thousand years, from the mid-2nd millennium Bharata ascendancy to the mid-1st millennium urbanization of the Gangetic plains. Midway was the establishment of the Kuru, who embodied many of the changes like assimilating old Neolithic customs to their pastoral culture. The Kuru and Pañcāla chiefs are called *rājan*, they do not have unbridled authority and have to constantly consult elders,

61 K.P. Jayaswal, *Hindu Polity: A Constitutional History of India in Hindu Times*, 2 vols, Butterworth, 1924, vol. 1, p. 5.

62 Terms which were interpreted as republic by Rhys Davis but which are better as tribal oligarchy.

63 *Bṛhadāraṇyaka Upaniṣad* (*Bṛ.U*), 2.1.15, distinct from the Ajātaśatru of Magadha.

64 *Ch.U*, 18.1–5.

priests, or councils (*kaṇika*) who even challenge them, and follow nomad procedures like cattle raids, *ghoṣayātrā*, or *vrātya* insertion.[65] In contrast,it was the The Kuru–Pañcāla political union, an outcome of the war, that spearheaded the changes represented in the sacrificial literature and manuals composed between 800 and 500 B.C.,[66] which have been rued as having brought about the *Kali-yuga*.

Situating the *Mahabharata*

That the terrain associated with the war is at quite a distance from Hastināpura and the Pañcāla country is not too disturbing in itself as in the pre-modern world, armies often met at designated places by appointment, or abruptly after marching and counter-marching. The situation is, however, confused by the mention of daily traffic between the battlefield and the court. Kochhar has sought to explain this by relocating the epic close to the Afghan foothills, a theory that not only contradicts all local traditions associating modern Kurukṣetra with the battle, but also places the battle *west* of the BOTK, which is anachronistic. It would be more reasonable to move the Kuru court closer to the battlefield instead. In the epic, the Kuru court is always referred to as āsandivat, i.e. the *throne–place* where the throne made of *uḍumbura* (fig) wood interwoven with straw was installed. This at once disassociates the court from a fixed spot and makes it a camp–capital, like that of the Mughals. Further, the region Hastināpura is said to lie in is called 'Kuru', one of the three provinces of the post-war Parīkṣit's realm. Such application of tribal name to fixed territory was a feature of the *janapada* period. This aspect shall be considered again in the last chapter.

All seems to have been going well with the illustrious line of the Kuru till their *rājan* Śāntanu lost his heart to Satyavatī, daughter of the chief of a fishing tribe though the convoluted story of her birth, which as per Yardi was part of the *Bharata*,[67] makes her an Aryan princess.[68] Satyavatī's father

65 Jamison and Witzel, 'Vedic Hinduism', p. 47. The Kuru and Pañcāla exchanged *vrātyas*, while the Jaiminīyas to their south sent *vrātyas* to them and not the Draviḍa.

66 See Kochhar, *Vedic People*, pp. 16–18 for an overview of organization of Vedic material.

67 See Yardi, *The Mahabharata*, pp. 1–2 for a précis of this story. The stories of the births of several of the other characters are equally convoluted, but they are not part of the Bharata, as per Yardi.

68 The family of Satyavatī is *Dāsa*, and may thus have been kin to the Iranic *Dahae*.

set the condition that Śāntanu must be succeeded by *her* children, and not by his son Devavrata, driving the *rājan* into depression. To help his father out of his predicament, Devavrata vows to neither accede to the throne nor marry and beget children who might contest it in future, this 'terrible' vow not only earning him the epithet of Bhīṣma *the Terrible*, but also sowing the seeds of trouble.

The impasse might have been avoided had Devavrata rescinded at the death of Satyavatī's childless sons Vicitravīrya and Citrasena and acceded to the throne, or married their wives in levirate. But he did not, and Satyavatī had to cause the widows to undergo the *niyoga* by her pre-nuptial son Kṛṣṇadvaipāyana Vyāsa. To this effort were born Dhṛtarāṣṭra and Pāṇḍu, while to a slave woman also offered to this sage was born the wise Vidura, who would play a pivotal role in the story. That these liaisons made the princes not biologically Kuru was not a difficulty, as *niyoga* was socially perfectly acceptable. What is significant here is that the generations hereafter are marked as Bhṛgu, being born of Vyāsa who was son of Satyavatī from the Bhṛgu sage Parāśara.

This was not the end. It turned out that both princes suffered physical defects, Dhṛtarāṣṭra being blind and Pandu having a skin condition. Physical perfection was an important requisite for kingship as rulers represented well-being of their people and physical blemishes were inauspicious—just two generations ago, Śāntanu's eldest brother Devāpi had been declared unfit to rule because of a skin affliction. In a later age, the Greeks noted that the Kathaioi and their neighbours selected their *handsomest* as king, and the *Dīgha Nikāya* says that the *Mahāsammata* or great–elect of the *gaṇarājya* must be the handsomest. The words used by the Greeks for handsome and handsomest are *kalos* and *kaliston* respectively,[69] which are better translated as auspicious, i.e. *kalyāṇa* or *lakṣaṇa*. The word *handsome* should rather be interpreted as he who bore the most auspicious marks.

His blindness rendering him inauspicious, Dhṛtarāṣṭra was denied the throne, but later when the probably leucoderma-afflicted Pandu was obliged to withdraw to the forests, the reason for which is nowhere specified, he was installed as the Kuru *rājan*. This rendered both *rājan*s, and their heirs, of questionable legitimacy. The above build-up is briefly

69 U.P. Arora, 'Fragments of Onesikritos on India—An Appraisal,' in *The Indian Historical Review,* vol. 32, no. 1, January 2005, pp, 35–102, especially pp. 81–2.

outlined in *Ādiparvan* 55–57 and about twenty scattered chapters of the *Udyogaparvan*, which Yardi says were in the original *Bharata*.[70] They were grossly exaggerated by later redactors, who added the entire second to fourth *parvan*s, i.e the *Sabhā-*, *Āraṇyaka-* and *Virāṭ*.

The name Dhṛtarāṣṭra appears in Vedic literature. In the *Pañcaviṅśati Brāhmaṇa* and *Baudhāyana Śrautasūtra*, one Dhṛtarāṣṭra Airāvata officiates as priest at the *sarpasattra* or snake–sacrifice of the *Nāga*s,[71] and while in the *Kāṭhaka Saṅhitā* of the *Yajurveda*, Dhṛtarāṣṭra Vaicitravīrya is a Kuru–Pañcāla king.[72] Elsewhere, this name appears in the context of Kāśī though Raychaudhuri disagrees with this interpretation.[73] Probably Dhṛtarāṣṭra was an important king who *may* have been of the Kuru line, but the *passivity* of the epic Dhṛtarāṣṭra—doing nothing while his son Duryodhana does everything, refusing to dissuade him from his nefarious schemes, helplessly getting upbraided for spoiling his sons with indulgence, a helplessness highlighted by blindness—has led to suggestions that he was a mere dummy interpolated to make Duryodhana's claim no stronger than that of Yudhiṣṭhira, the son of Pāṇḍu.

In this context, we must again look at the two father–son pairs, Parīkṣit and Janamejaya, which appear twice in the epic. To Hopkins, only the older pair was real, mighty Kuru chiefs who were reintroduced later by the past-their-prime Kuru at Hastināpura to obtain legitimacy. In contrast, Raychaudhuri takes both pairs as real, the older a pair of vague chiefs and the later ones the rulers of the powerful Kuru–Pañcāla combine. A closer inspection of the Kuru characters will reveal alliance and interest patterns that led to their line-up; this is a good time to remind us that tribes were amorphous groups with plastic, many-faceted identities that they could change and selectively use, and that there were many procedures of succession other than patrilineal.

---

70 Yardi, *The Mahabharata*, p. 156.

71 Janamejaya was one of the two *adhvaryu*s, the *Brāhmaṇa* priest being Dhṛtarāṣṭra Airāvata (*PB*, 25,15; *BŚS* 17,18).

72 *YV: Kāṭhaka Saṅhitā*, 10.6.

73 Raychaudhuri, *Political History*, p. 18, note 2.

Characters in the Kuru Constellation, including Kuru Allies

Duryodhana and Duḥśāsana

Duryodhana, though cast *yuvarāja* with his father Dhṛtarāṣṭra, had a prime position in the war, and had his own *yuvarāja* in his brother Duḥśāsana. The term *yuvarāja* is often understood as 'crown prince', but really meant junior–king in a diarchy, the common political format across the IE world as represented by the Aśvins or the Diouskouroi. There were two hereditary *dyarch*s of two houses in Sparta, in some kingdoms *dyarch*s succeeded through female lines so that males of different families became king, and diarchy made tracing descents of Scythian lines difficult as many of these kings had common names or titles. In the later days of Rome, which had legendarily originated from the rule of the brothers Romulus and Remus, two *imperators* returned by the army—the *Augustus* and the *Caesar*—governed in supposed deference to the senate with the younger, *Caesar*, leading the armies, a throwback to *dyarch*s ruling in concord with the *council of elders*. When the empire divided between the senior Rome and the junior Constantinople, the system snowballed and each of the emperors acquired his own junior emperors. Existence of dual kings, often with similar names or titles, makes tracing of descent amongst Śaka such a riddle, while from the early Turkic world appear several pairs of brothers–kings, El Terish and Qapaghan (which were titles), Istemi and Bumin, or Çagri and Tughrul.

Dvairājya or dual kingship is attested in the *Arthaśāstra*,[74] and was common in Aryan *janapada*s of north India as well as the Cola of the Tamil country.[75] Dhṛtarāṣṭra's ineffectuality, appearance of Duryodhana's brother (and not his son Lakṣmaṇa) as *yuvarāja* and heir apparent in what was a matrilineal custom, builds a strong case for rendering Dhṛtarāṣṭra a construct and taking Duryodhana and Duḥśāsana the real Kuru rulers. In this regard, it has been suggested that the other brothers of the duo were really Yakṣa *caecodemons*.

74 Kautilya, *Arthaśāstra*, http://www.sanskritdocuments.org/all_pdf/artha.pdf (accessed 10 May 2014), VIII: 2.5.7.

75 A.K. Majumdar, *Concise History of India*, vol. 2, New Delhi, 1980, p. 138.

The Gāndhāra

Duryodhana's prime counsel was his maternal uncle Śakuni, chief of the Gandhāra, a warlike *Vrātya* people from the foothills of Peshawar. Though despised and classed with the Mujavats,[76] the Gandhāra were respected as scholars, and as possessors of horses, chariots, and good wool. They are linked with the Druhyus in the *Mātsya-* and *Vāyu-Purāṇas*;[77] in Greek times they were ruled by a Porus, cousin or nephew of his more famous namesake on the Hydaspes or Jhelum.

In the epic, their ruler Śakuni seems to forever be at the Kuru court, which has at times been explained as the result of a Dhṛtarāṣtra being obliged to take on board all relations of his wife at the time of marriage. In the *Ramayana*, the prince Bharata is at the court of his maternal uncle the *Aśvapati Kekaya* (neighbours to the Gandhāra), whose sister tries to subvert the succession of Rama in favour of her son. This was nothing but a matrilineal procedure wherein a man attended to the affairs of his maternal uncle's household which he later inherited—Bah(l)īka Prātipeya, *son of the Kuru Pratīpa* and great-great-uncle of Duryodhana, had married the princess of Bahīka (Punjab) and inherited her realm. We see this motif repeatedly at play in the *Mahabharata*—the sons of the Pandu, like Abhimanyu, Ghaṭotkaca, Irāvan, or Babhruvāhana, were all brought up in their mothers' homes.

Returning to the *Mahabharata*, it may be concluded that Duryodhana, or his father who had married the Gandhāra princess (eponymously Gāndhārī who had also taken a vow of blindness and kept herself blindfolded), was heir to the Gandhāra realm, and Śakuni's closeness to the Kuru, especially to his sister's son, indicates that there had been some sort of an Anschluss between the Kuru and the Gandhāra, giving Duryodhana access to the latter's resources.

Karṇa

In the epic, Karṇa was the pre-nuptial, abandoned son of Kuntī, mother of the Pandu, brought up as a foundling by Rādhā, wife of the chariot-maker *Sūta*. When his being a *Sūta* disqualified him from duelling with Arjuna at a contest, he was ennobled as *Aṅga-rāja* by Duryodhana

76 *AV*, V: 22.14.

77 Raychaudhuri, *Political History*, p. 124.

who was eager to see Arjuna defeated. He became Duryodhana's friend and confidant thereafter.

The appointment as *Aṅga-rāja*, usually interpreted as king of the Aṅga country at the Rajmahal Gap, traditional eastern extremity of campaigning cavalry, is another example of Duryodhana's independent conduct. It also at once throws us into difficulties. At the time of the said contest, the princes are novitiates, making Duryodhana's authority to appoint vassals without reference to his father or the council questionable. It is also unlikely that chiefs of the Divide could appoint vassals as far east as Aṅga, especially as Magadha, acknowledged in the *Mahabharata*, lay between them. Nowhere in the subsequent narrative is Karṇa associated with *Aṅga*, though medieval legends associate some eastern places with him. Rather, he is associated with places on the Divide, like Karnal or *Raja-Karan-ka-Tila* (mound of King Karna) near Kurukṣetra.[78] His *digvijaya*, placed anachronistically in the *Karṇaparvan*, is around the fringes of Madhyadeśa and has nothing at all to do with the Aṇga we know.[79]

Of significance is that Karṇa is known not by his patronymic, but his matronymic Rādheya—the common appellation of *Sūtaputra*, i.e. son of the *Sūta*, does not qualify as *Sūta* is not a proper name. In the *Karṇaparvan*, the people of Karna's country are said to abandon the afflicted and sell their wives and children—*āturānaṃparityāgaḥsadāra-sūta-vikrayaḥ*[80]—which resembles the sale of daughters observed by the Greeks by certain tribes on the Indus.

Taken together, it appears that Karṇa was scion of a matrilineal, charioteering people on the *Uttarāpatha* which had been adopted by the Kuru as allies. His appellation of *Aṅgarāja* may have signified some sort of subordinate chief, as the word *aṅga* also means *part* or *section*. The

78 *Raja-Karan-ka-Tila*, a small mound about 3 miles W–SW of Thanesar, yielded PGW shards, flesh rubber, a terracotta reel, a mould for printing cloth, a human head, a double inkpot, a hollow terracotta rattle, a flattened bronze object appearing to be a late derivative of a celt with crescentic circle, an earthen *chati* (pot) having a line of *triśūla*and wheel carved on it, and an earthen pitcher ornamented round the shoulder, in addition to later potsherds and structures. That it was occupied from an early period is seen in the discovery of two ancient, wedge shaped bricks 2 or 3 feet above the virgin soil.

79 *Mbh*,VIII: 5.18.

80 Raychaudhuri, *Political History*, p. 119.

discomfort with his charioteering origin must have entered the epic in later stages of its development, by which time charioteering had come to be considered lowly. The curious story of his birth was probably fashioned to make grounds for the Pandu attempt to win him over, significantly as *Kuntī*'s son, a matrilineal motif—that he would also thus become Draupadī's senior husband, in other words the head of the Pandu, is the bait offered to him. That the 'secret' of his convoluted birth was an artificial construct is evident in it being *revealed* to him not once but twice, once by Krishna, and again by Kuntī herself. In all, it served to create the tragic–hero image for Karṇa, which was reinforced by his self-destructive generosity and the manner of his death.

Devavrata or Bhīṣma

Devavrata, whose vow it was that precipitated the issues, has an even more curious background. He was Śāntanu's son from the river goddess Gaṅgā who had agreed to marry him on condition that she must never be asked to explain any of her acts. When Śāntanu could not keep himself from demanding the reason for her drowning her seven babies just as she was about to do it the eighth time, she left him, taking the child with her, and only restoring him as a youth by when she had trained him into an accomplished archer.

The epic uses the story of the *Aṣṭa-Vasu*, a set of eight gods cursed to mortal birth from which they contrived to get themselves released by persuading Ganga to take mortal birth herself, give birth to them, and kill them immediately afterwards. In effect, this rather implausible story is reminiscent of the practice of trial by exposure common to IE peoples like Scythians, Celts, Spartans, and Persians,[81] and also observed among the Kathaians by Onesikritos,[82] in which children were killed unless they were strong and healthy or if they bore inauspicious marks. Further, the story is reminiscent of that of Purūravas, the first male of the Lunar race which before him was hermaphrodite (Purūravas was son of Iḷa/Iḷā, sex–changing

81 Diogene Laërtius, (trans. R. D. Hicks), *Lives of Eminent Philosophers*, 2 vols, Harvard University Press, Loeb Classical Library, 1925, VI, 59.

82 The Spartans inspected their children when they were two weeks old and put them to death if they were not found strong enough. See Matthew Dillon and Linda Garland, *Ancient Greece: Social and Historical Document from the Archaic Times till the Death of Alexander the Great*, Routledge Sourcebook for the Ancient World, 2000, 4:23, also Strabo, *Geography*, 3 vols, trans. H.C. Hamilton, ed. H.G. Bonn, 1854–1857: XV,1,30.

offspring of *Candra* the moon).[83] A foreigner, Purūravas was *permitted* by the Gandharvas to cohabit with Urvaśi for a short period on certain conditions, and was *sent away* when that condition was violated with *one* son, while the other was retained and brought up by the Gandharvas. This indicates that the Gandharvas were not only matrilineal but also matri–local, where the male joins the female's family where the child is brought up. Apparently, Devavrata was also offspring of a lady of one such tribe, and was brought up by them after surviving trial by exposure.

Irawati Karve has been a little too harsh on Bhīṣma, saying that his reputation as a great warrior was founded not on fact but only on convention, the only major action he had seen being a three-week long battle with Paraśurama, a sage who would in reality have existed generations before him. She also points out that he had *not joined* the campaign of Pāṇḍu, was routed by Arjuna in the cattle raid,[84] and stinted assistance to the Kuru. In fact, she insists that he was an extremely old man at the time of the battle, quite powerless to influence events but merely hanging on to power, perhaps spiteful that he was denied the succession.[85] It is difficult to confirm any of this—there are several instances of his heroic battles—but his special leaning towards the Pandu and hostility for Duryodhana must be noted. We will return to the theme of Bhīṣma.

Droṇa and Aśvatthāmā

Another set of important characters directly part of Kuru polity was Droṇa, the weapons master of the princes, and his son Aśvatthāman. Interestingly, Droṇa was the Kuru leader in their contest with the Pañcālas over North Pañcāla, i.e. modern Rohilkhand. As per the *Mahabharata*, Droṇa was a poor Brahman from the northwest who, when unable to provide a cup of milk to his child, approached his childhood friend Drupada who was now king of Pañcāla. But Drupada snubbed him on grounds of there being no possibility of friendship between the two as their circumstances were so dramatically different, at which Droṇa offered his services to the Kuru as weapons master to the princes. In what was now his personal vendetta against Drupada, he took the novices from his āśrama to attack Pañcāla, taking away substantial parts of it but restoring

83 The Kośala-Videha and other *Sūryavaṅśa* folk were also originally *Candravaṅśa.*

84 Karve, *Yugānta*, pp. 18–19.

85 Karve, *Yugānta*, pp. 19–20.

it later. 'Students', i.e. initiates, recruited out of *āśrama*s for warfare is reminiscent of the *vrātya* practice, which has been discussed earlier.

While the valley of Dehradun is associated with Droṇa (though the popular etymological derivation is improbable), many spots in Rohilkhand are strongly associated with Droṇa and his son. Further, the hoary fortress of Asirgarh rising above the Burhanpur Gap in the Satpura, called *Dakkhan-ki-kunji* or *key to the Deccan* by virtue of its strategic location, preserves ancient legends associated with Aśvatthāman. Asirgarh is associated with the Tak Rajputs, a branch of a once powerful Rajput group on the northern Indus plains (probably associated with the Takṣaka and encountered by the Greeks as *Paraitakai*), and also the Asa Ahir or Asa Jat of the NWFP, who were destroyed in the Ambela campaign 1863 at the Wahhabi stronghold of Mahaban. A little south of Asirgarh, in the valley of the Godavari, lay the Assaka *gaṇasaṅgha*, an Aśvaka/Aśvakāyana colony from Swat. These associations strongly place Droṇa and his son among the other people along the *Uttarāpatha*; even Aśvatthāmā's name associates him with the horse.

Other Allies

The other Kuru allies can be grouped into three—those from their north and west, those located close to the Divide, and those to their east. Though the use of eastern levies, allies, and mercenaries cannot be ruled out, we shall see that most of the eastern allies are not convincing, and their removal does not affect the storyline at all. They appear to have been included when geographical knowledge of the east increased, and eastern groups wanted the honour of being featured in the epic. An obvious pointer is that though Karṇa is Aṅga-rāja, the armies of Aṅga, by which is meant the Champaran region of Bihar, have nothing to do with him but are commanded by a different king. Also, it is extremely doubtful if the Prāgjyotiṣ of Bhagadatta really was Assam.

Of the peoples on or near the Divide, like the Videha, Vatsa, and the Yadu on the *Dakṣiṇāpatha*, some later moved east. The allies most convincingly present in the battle were from the north of the Divide, i.e. the *Uttarāpatha*. We have already noted the Gandhāra, and have seen that Karṇa, Bhīṣma, and Droṇa had north-western affiliations. Also on the Kuru side is their uncle Bhūriśravas, grandson of Bahīka Prātipeya; curiously, though Prātipeya is associated with Bahīka or Punjab, as a rival of the Iranic Kākra Sthapati, he must have been situated closer to Bahlīka or Balkh. Other important peoples in the Kuru camp are the Trigarta (today the Himachal foothills near Jalandhar), and the Sindhu–Sauvīra on the Indus, two tribes which executed a peculiar gambit in the battle that resembled the tactics of pastoral nomads.

The most curious of the northern allies are the Madra, whose chief Śalya was maternal uncle to two of the Pandu—Nakula and Sahadeva. As the *Mahabharata* is a family drama, compelling reasons were required to explain why such close family of the Pandu were on the side of the Kuru, and the explanation provided was that while passing through the Kuru country on his way south to join his nephews, Śalya was intercepted by Duryodhana and so regally feted that he decided to join him. However, when Śalya was confronted by Yudhiṣṭhira, he assured him that when Duryodhana would eventually ask him to drive Karṇa's chariot, he would nag him so badly that Karṇa would not be able to fight well.

As it is unlikely that Yudhiṣṭhira could encounter him (though sending missives cannot be ruled out), or that Śalya could have known then that he would be eventually asked to drive Karṇa's chariot, it is needless to say what is needless to say.

This is not to say that all other northern allies—the Tangana, Kulinda (Vaidya Kuninda), Ṛṣīka, Śaka, Hara-Hūṇa—were authentic entries just as it is not to say that all eastern ones were spurious. Vast numbers of migrants and mercenaries crisscrossed the area of our interest, many of whom may have been engaged or encountered. Also, it is often pointed out, as I too have done, that all mention of Śaka and Hūṇa were late entries as these peoples were operational in South Asia only from the late first millennium B.C. onwards. However, Śakas, and the associated Cimmerians and Medes, had been operating in Central and West Asia from early in the 1st millennium, and their use as mercenaries cannot be ruled out.

The Pañcāla

The name Pañcāla suggests a federation of five tribes,[86] which the *Mahabharata* lists as Kṛvi, Turvaśa, Keśin, Sṛñjaya, and Somaka and the *Brahma Purāṇa* as the Mudgala, Sṛñjaya, Bṛhadiṣu, Yavanāra, and

86 Romila Thapar goes with five tribes, *Panca–āla*, Thapar, *From Lineage to State*, pp. 23–24, note 8. See also ŚB, xiii.5.4.7. At the same time, some have compared āla in

Krimilāśva. Witzel has shown that there were really *six* and not five tribes in the federation, making the *pañca* part of the name irrelevant. The Turvaśa have often been associated with Yavana in early literature, and Turvaśa and Yavanāra of the two lists may be identical. The Kṛvi, which the *Śatapatha Brāhmaṇa* says was the old name of Pañcāla,[87] are related with the Vaikarṇa[88] and Kuru, and possibly identical with the Kṛmilāśva. Also, Sṛñjaya and Somaka of the first list are names of successful Bharata clans, which render the Pañcāla federation as composed of several groups, many of which were once antagonistic.[89]

In itself, this was not abnormal, as alliance patterns among early tribes, which were heterogeneous, open-status groups, could change kaleidoscopically, as they did in the case of the Mongols. In another example, the Yeuh Chi was not one tribe at all but a conglomerate of five autonomous *yabghus*, of which the Guishang/KiuShuang/Kushan obliged the others to *also* use the Kushan identity. Such arrangements were essentially fragile and could fall to pieces in defeat, defeat here meaning not annihilation or loss of independence, but simply dissolution and rearrangements of identities. In fact, such dissolution could occur immediately after the first flush of victory in war.

Each nomad tribe had several identities, reflected in contradictory origin legends, it being extremely difficult to unravel their metamorphosing threads from the conventional, heraldic, and eulogatory records whose intent was seldom historical. For instance, just as there is no conformity about the Pūru chief defeated at the BOTK, the *Jaminīya Brāhmaṇa*[90] mentions Pratṛd as the Bharata chief at the BOTK instead of his descendent Sudās.[91] Now, while references to the Bharata cease in Vedic literature

Pañcāla with the eel, and thus ultimately the snake. Also, in Dravidian, āḷ is *one who rules*; so ruler of the five tribes?

87 ŚB, xiii.5.4.7.

88 *Mbh,* VI: 51, 128.

89 A.D. Pusalkar, *Studies in Epics and Purāṇas*, Bharatiya Vidya Bhavan, Bombay, 1965, pp. 247. Pusalkar has shown how confused the Pañcāla identity was.

90 *JB*, 3.244.

91 Note the shifting of the tradition. *YV: Maitrāyani Saṅhitā* 3.40.6, *JB*, 3.244, and *PB* 15, 3.7 substitute other names for Sudās and Vaśiṣṭha. Such confusion is not uncommon in bardic tradition; parallels may be seen in the cases of Theodoric and Ermanric in Gothic history. The battle of twenty kings in *ṚV*, I: 53 may also point to such a shift in tradition.

with the defeat of Sudās's descendent Pratardana, they reappear in the *Mahabharata*.

The Pañcāla territory is divided into two spheres. The North or *Uttara–Pañcāla* capital of Ahicchatra, close to the later-day Rohilla capitals of Aonla or Bangarh, was associated with the Nāga, while the South or *Dakṣiṇa–Pañcāla*, whose capital was Kampilya has been identified with the mound abutting on the marshy channel of the *Buṛhi Ganga* in modern Kampila in Farrukhabad District. These sites have yielded PGW, dressed stone walls and defence against monsoonal floods in the form of mud embankment;[92] in other words, Pañcāla material culture was similar to that of the Kuru. North Pañcāla, across the Ganga east of Kuru, was wrested away by Droṇa and his students and retained by him as *gurudakṣiṇa*, opening a vendetta with the Pañcāla supremo Drupada, the Somaka *rājan* of South Pañcāla on the lower Yamuna–Ganga *doaba*, east of the Hindon and along the Chambal.

The Pañcāla region, where the Ganga disgorged on to the plains, had watered tracts, ample agrarian opportunities, and meadows of *dūb* grass which could support grazing. Just to its east were dense forests, hitherto occupied by pioneering *āśrama*s whose prime concern was to fight the foresters, which were being opened to agriculture by newly available iron technology. In other words, Pañcāla was astride the transition zone from the pastoral divide to the agrarian plains, and could exploit the opportunities of both; no wonder it was the happy homing ground for immigrants—Rohilla settlers came to these regions in droves till the Mughal times. Understandably, many tribes and clans which had fought the BOTK had gravitated towards this region, founding the Pañcāla identity under Sṛñjaya initiative.[93]

Their relative position makes intense rivalry with the Kuru only expected. The Kuru, who commanded the terminus of the *Uttarāpatha*, controlled migrations and trade on it. They also were advancing across the Yamuna, and eying *Uttarapañcāla* across the Ganga. This rivalry, anticipating the rivalry between Katehria Rajputs and Rohilla immigrants

92 K.M. Srivastava, 'Possible Location of Kāmpilya in the Mahābhārata,' in Ajay MitraShastri (ed.), *Mahabharata*, pp. 112–17. The mound of *Drupada Kila* in another part of the town, which enclosed only 50 hectares in a wall of brickbats, was a late construction when the original was evacuated.

93 Raychaudhuri, *Political History*, p. 60.

in the medieval period, was recast as personal vendetta between Droṇa and Drupada, the latter's son Dhṛṣṭadyumna said to be born for the express purpose of killing Droṇa. Probably this rivalry precipitated the war, which has been called a Kuru–Pañcāla or Kuru–Sṛñjaya war in several places.[94]

Unfriendly feelings between the Sṛñjaya and Kuru are averred to in the *Śatapatha Brāhmaṇa*[95] and the political union of the two, mentioned in later literature, was a result of the war. To Witzel, it was this new union, which he calls a 'state', that officially encouraged orthopraxy and societal changes. Naimiṣāraṇya, the hermitage where the Vedic and epic corpus were given their final shape, lay in Pāñcāla territory.

94 *Mbh*, VI: 45. 2; 60.29; 72.15; 73.41; VII: 20.41; 149.40; VIII: 47.23; 57.12; 59.1; 93.1.

95 *Mbh*, XII: 9.3.1ff.

CHAPTER 5

The Pāṇḍu and the Yadu

The Pandu

Hastināpura

The *Ādivaṅśāvatāraṇa* (*Ādiparvan*, 55–57)[1] outlines crisply the births and early careers of the protagonists, showing that the Kuru bloodline ended with Śantanu's sons Citrāṅgada and Vicitravīrya. It also shows that while the sons of Dhṛtarāṣṭra were at least biologically, though magically, his, those of his brother Pāṇḍu were really the sons of his wives Kuntī and Mādrī, princesses of Kunti–Bhoja and Madra, by a variety of gods. The convoluted mechanics of their births were developed in later redactions only. Now, merely being *not biological* sons was not a social disadvantage as long as the proper procedures of levirate or *niyoga* had been followed—what was of disadvantage was that both half-brothers Dhṛtarāṣṭra and Pāṇḍu suffered physical defects, the former being blind and the latter blemished in the skin, possibly leucoderma, making their fitness to rule questionable. Pāṇḍu was nevertheless elevated to the throne which was denied to his elder brother, but the trigger that led to his resigning it to Dhṛtarāṣṭra later and withdrawing to the forests is not clarified.

In the forests, Pāṇḍu suffered a fatal stroke while cohabiting with Mādrī, allegedly result of a curse incurred from a sage whom he had shot when the latter, in the shape of a deer, was cohabiting with a doe! Mādrī begged and obtained for herself the privilege of dying with him on the pyre, i.e. the *Satī*, while Kuntī returned to Hastināpura with the five princes. Here occurred a little noticed but highly interesting episode—after Kuntī

1 Yardi, *The Mahabharata*, p. 3.

reached Hastināpura, the remains of Pāṇḍu were interred. To Hopkins, Pāṇḍu had already been cremated in the forests and there would not have been much more of him left to inter at Hastināpura, and the episode was inauthentic. However, the case seems to have been one of *partial cremation* and *fractional burial*, a funerary format of several IIr groups wherein the body was not completely burnt but retrieved after charring, and then cut into pieces and buried.[2] Very curiously, a mound in Bengal, at the lowest level of which a fractional burial has been found, is called *Pandu-Rajar-Dhibi*, i.e. the *mound of king Pandu*. Does this suggest wider familiarity of fractional burial with the Pandu?

At Hastināpura, the princes were given an education alongside the Kuru prince Duryodhana and his 99 brothers, during the course of which their master Droṇa used them to attack the Pañcāla. As per Yardi, the *Bharata* redaction describes how Duryodhana, threatened by Pandu excellence in combat, perpetrated mischief on them like trying to poison or drown them (most efforts aimed at Bhīma), and how Vidura, half-brother of Dhṛtarāṣṭra and Pāṇḍu, stood by them through these vicissitudes. The persecution climaxed when Duryodhana prevailed upon his blindly doting father to send the Pandu and Kuntī to Vāraṇāvata, where he plotted to burn them down in the *lākṣāgṛha*, a residence made of lac. The Pandu were warned in time by Vidura, and after warding off Kuru agents for a year during which they dug an exit tunnel, escaped after themselves setting the house on fire.

Thereafter, the Pandu roamed as fugitives for an unspecified length of time, when Bhīma had adventures like killing the 'cannibals' Kirmira, Baka, and Hiḍimba, marrying the latter's sister Hiḍimbā and siring a child Ghaṭotkaca, and undergoing other trials like that of the *Yakṣa Praśna* episode, i.e. the *Quiz of the Gnome*. As per Yardi's estimates, these episodes, which appear in a concise form in *Adiparvan*, 55–57, are dramatized in *Adi-* 124–199 by Lomaharṣaṇa. In the end, they reach the town of Ekacakra in Pañcāla country where they remain *incognito* in the home of a pious Brahmin. Their identities are however revealed when they appear at the *svayaṁvara* of the Pañcāla princess Draupadī where Arjuna wins her hand in a spectacular feat of archery—they are feted by the

2 *ṚV*, X: 16.1—'*Do not burn entirely, Agni, or engulf him in your flames. Do not consume his skin, or his flesh*'. Also see W.D. O'Flaherty, *The Rig Veda: An Anthology 108 Hymns Translated from the Sanskrit*, Harmondsworth, Penguin Classics, 1981, p. 49.

Pañcāla, who are nonetheless scandalised by their polyandrous marriage with their princess. After the wedding, the Pandu return to Hastināpura where, thanks to their greatly enhanced circumstances, they are offered the tracts of Khāṇḍavaprastha south of Kurukṣetra.

Indraprastha

Significantly, in most episodes so far it is Bhīma who is the Pandu hero. He digs tunnels, leaps over the fire with the others on his shoulder, carries his brothers and mother when they are tired, and kills demons. It is only in the *Draupadī-svayaṁvara* and the *Caitraratha* episodes that Arjuna is hero. At this juncture, Arjuna is sent off by Yudhiṣṭhira, on a curious pretext, into exile on his own, wherein he has several independent adventures. Among other places, he visits Dvārakā at the terminus of the *Aparānta*, the base of the Vṛṣṇi Yadu, where he abducts Subhadrā, the Vṛṣni princess, with the complicity of her brother Krishna, though her other brother Baladeva (Rāma) is resentful. Arjuna returns to the Divide 'pursued' by Krishna where the wedding is solemnised. Later, Agni appears as an ascetic before Arjuna and Krishna and demands to be fed, and the duo burn the Khāṇḍava scrublands and establish the settlement of Indraprastha. The Pandu then launch expeditions in the *four directions* (Bhīma to the east, Arjuna the North, Nakula west, and Sahadeva south), collecting riches but also inciting the envy of the Kuru.

As per Yardi, this simple narrative was directly followed in the *Bharata* by the jealous Kuru challenging the Pandu at dice and cheating them with Śakuni's help, resulting in their being exiled for thirteen years with the proviso that the last year must be spent *incognito* failing which the term would have to be repeated. It was the later redactors who, according to Yardi, generously supplied the endless dramatic episodes. Sūta detailed how the duo drove around the fire at Khāṇḍavaprastha, slaughtering any and every animal that tried to escape, how Indra came to save his friend Takṣaka the Nāga who lived in that forest, retiring only when assured that he was safe, how a satiated Agni gave Arjuna many gifts, including a bow of knotted wood, the *gāṇḍīva*, an inexhaustible quiver, and a splendid chariot with the eagle standard, how the *Asura* Maya, flushed out of the forest, promised to build Indraprastha in return for his life, and how the Pandu, especially Draupadī, invite and then humiliate the Kuru princes when they visited their new city. Sautī expanded the Subhadrā episode, dramatizing

Krishna's complicity and Baladeva's indignation in the elopement, adding much humour to the plot. He also interpolated that Arjuna had been sent away in the first place under a vow of celibacy for having barged into Draupadī's chamber when she was with Yudhiṣṭhira, having failed to notice the pair of slippers left outside as a warning. Further, he rearranged the Pandu campaigns in *Sabhā*, 1–45, into the *digvijaya*, i.e. the conquest of the four quarters as part of the *rājasūya* sacrifice.

Hopkins has pointed out the inconsistencies in these stories. Arjuna's banishment is for thirteen years, which is the same as the time taken by Agni to burn the Khāṇḍava, and the duration of the brothers' joint exile. Also, though Arjuna goes off under an oath of celibacy, he immediately enters into liaisons with the Nāga princess Ulūpi and Citrāṅgadā the princess of Maṇipura, and puts up an elaborate pretence to elope with Subhadrā. Evidently the exile under vow of celibacy has the express purpose of accounting for Arjuna's solo adventures (of which there will be more in future), his personal matrimonial alliances, and his independent existence. The above, and the closer relation between the so called *rājasūya* and the dice game pointed out by J.A.B van Buitenen, will be inspected in a later section.

A Revaluation

Though the Pandu were tailed by Duryodhana's agents through their year at Vāraṇāvata, they are seen to have been quite free to move about, showing that they were not under any form of detention. Thus, the story of their 'escape' was really a dramatized one. Also, while in the older redaction, Bhīma *jumps across* the fire with the others on his shoulders and escapes, in later ones there appears the tunnel that the Pandu had spent a year digging out to the forest, and through which they escape one rainy night escape after setting the house alight, Bhīma taking everyone on his shoulder and *jumping across the fire into the tunnel*. While the element of fire was not discarded, the story of the tunnel, the term used for which is *suraṅga*, cognate with the Greek siege engineering term *syrinx*, was interpolated.[3] The story of the destitute woman who enters the *lākṣāgṛha* with her five children on the very night of the escape, and whose charred

3 The story of the house being burnt one rainy night when a few destitute people had taken shelter in it, their charred remains assuring the Kuru that the Pandu had really got burnt, are part of the later additions.

bones assure the Kuru that the Pandu had perished, was undoubtedly a late addition for didactic and tear–jerking purposes.

All that can be said of the plastic story so far is that the Pandu had become fugitives when they were attacked by arson, but later, when they had gained powerful matrimonial relations—Pañcāla, Naga, and Maṇipura, and probably Hiḍimbā's people—they were taken more seriously and offered territory to settle. It can be seen that they were offered land at the *edge of Kuru territory*, after which they stopped pressing their claim on Hastināpura, which is in line with the nomad practice of relocating to avoid conflict—the Śakas would avoid conflict with the Kushans by moving away from Mathura to Saurashtra.

From their new settlement at Indraprastha (identified with the mound under the Purana Quila or Old Fort of Delhi which appears to have started as a pre–Aryan settlement), the Pandu launch the operations which were later organised into the *digvijaya*. That the list of their conquests in the *digvijaya* is anachronistic is seen in its being more extensive than lists in later episodes like the *Dyūtaparvan* or the post-war *aśvamedha*, and showing wider familiarity with South Asia. Also, several entries are highly suspect. Bhagadatta of Prāgjyotiṣ, usually associated with the king of Pragjyotishpur in Assam, is attacked not in Bhīma's eastern campaign which went further east of Assam, but in Arjuna's *northern campaign*; Bhagadatta offers Arjuna fine horses, which is unlikely of an Assamese king. The list also reveals later attitudes—Bhīma avoids the malarial country of deltaic Bengal, which is derided as *Pāṇḍava-varjita* or *rejected by the Pandu*; it is unlikely a charioteering people on the Divide could have reached so far east yet.

In fact, the lists look like conventional enumerations. Sahadeva's 'conquest' reads like the itinerary of a traveller or pilgrim. Similar anachronistic organization of campaigns appears in the post-war *Aśvamedhika-parvan* which also includes new peoples like the Kṣudraka, Rajanya, or Kulūṭa, displaying geographical awareness of a later age. For instance, the Yaudheya, supposed descendants of Yudhiṣṭhira through a Śivi woman, are already defeated by Yudhiṣṭhira in this list, and forced to bring presents;[4] obviously, the redactor had forgotten himself. In effect,

4 *Mbh*, VII: 19.16; 161.5; 157.30. This is another case of blind redaction.

these lists were used to expand the epic's footprints, show geographical knowledge, and bring many diverse peoples within its folds.[5]

The expanded geographical awareness is most acutely demonstrated in the story of Jarāsandha, which as per Yardi appears not before the Sautī redaction. Krishna announced that no *rājasūya*, a sacrifice which promoted the performer to *samrāṭ*, could be consummated as long as a reigning *samrāṭ*, in this case Jarāsandha of Magadha, lived. At this, the Pandu decided to attack him, infiltrating into his palace at Girivraja and challenging him to a duel in which Bhīma tears him down the middle, the only way to kill him (the tale of *Jarā–sandha*, or *sutured down the middle*, is told here). Now, while it is unlikely that chiefs of the Divide could operate so far east, the timelines are also immediately confused when the epic says that after killing Jarāsandha, Kṛṣṇa, Arjuna, and Bhīma ride about in the dead king's chariot and celebrate by destroying a Caitya,[6] as such Buddhist monuments could not have appeared for another half a millennium at least.

The story is further confused by the existence of others Bhīmas, like the son of the Vedic Parīkṣit,[7] and sons of both *Mahabharata* Parīkṣitas,[8] each of whom is associated with the defeat of a Jarāsandha. It may be so that the later Bhīma defeated the eastern king of Rājagṛha, which exploit was attributed to his great-uncle the Bhīma of the *Mahabharata*. At the same time, Girivraja may have been identical with the town of Girjak near Murree, whose ruler must have been inimical to immigrants; in fact, as per Hemacandra's *Triṣaṣṭiśalākāpuruṣacarita*, Rājagṛha or Girivraja was established by Prasenajit, father of Śreṇika Bimbisāra, *after* the capital of Kuśāgrapura was destroyed by fire, an event which would have occurred centuries after the *Mahabharata*.

5 There are other issues with the lists. With the original meaning of *Tāmara* in the northern list lost, redactors substituted it with *Tomara*, a historical people from medieval times. A closer etymological fit would however have been *Ḍāmara*, the Kashmiri feudal elite. Similarly, in the Critical Edition, Professor Franklin Edgerton replaced *Aṭavī* with *Antakhi*, which to him implied *Antioch*, though he does acknowledge that it was no more than a personal speculation.

6 *Mbh*, II: 19.19.

7 Raychaudhuri, *Political History*, p, 13; also *Mbh*, Ādiparva, 95.42

8 Raychaudhuri, *Political History*, p. 13. *Mbh*, I: 94.54–55. Raychaudhuri points out that the name of four sons of the Vedic Parīkṣit, only three appear in this list, Śrutasena being absent; even Janamejaya is missed out in the *Java* text.

Overall, the Pandu campaigns out of Indraprastha had a northerly orientation; the Hātaka country (of the Guhyakas) conquered by Arjuna was probably Hotak in Aghanistan. Presumably, they were reorganised into the *digvijaya* in later times, which was when a northern Girivraja associated with a Pandu conquest, was re-associated with Jarāsandha's Magadha. This association is not merely an example of increasing familiarity with the east, or the commemoration of eastern kings vying with the Divide for primacy, a theme which appears in the Vṛṣṇi being ousted from Mathura (see later). The bulk of the *Mahabharata* was composed at a time when the imperial state of Magadha was supreme, and it was incomprehensible to the popular mind that a *rājasūya* could be completed without defeating this mighty state. The natural fallout was the recasting of a northern king as Jarāsandha, the pious and noble *samrāṭ* of Magadha, who had to be defeated. This association is also seen in the *sabhā* or hall at Indraprastha, which the *Asura* Maya constructs with stones saved from his construction of the hall of the *Asura* Vṛṣaparan which he travelled north to fetch; Persian style stone-masonry was the in-thing at the height of Magadhan city architecture.

After a short sojourn in Indraprastha, the Pandu once again are seen roaming as 'exiles' as a result of the dice game. Their vicissitudes of fortune, fugitive status, endless peregrinations, military campaigns, and tribute lists, when taken together, indicate that they were in the class of adventurers, semi-mercenaries, and nomads, their career resembling those of many nomad chiefs-turned-emperors. A dispossessed Tëmujin had roamed the steppes with his brothers and mother, Tëmur had roamed the Gurgan plains with 70 followers when his uncle Toghrul dispossessed him, in the company of one Amir Hussein who had likewise been exiled from his native Badakhshan, and Babur, dispossessed by his *Khungtaïji* uncles, had had to hang about for several years in the bleak mountains of Tajikistan with his immediate followers and several mothers. The fortunes of such chiefs varied—while the aptly named Humayun, whose fortune had reached an abyss by the time he reached Iran after being cast out of Delhi, could turn around with the help of his spiteful allies, Dārā Shukoh could never recover and was butchered by his brother.

Another common ground between the Pandu and such historical nomad chiefs was the role that women played in their polities, keeping them together and helping them turn around.

The Pandu Constellation

We shall inspect some components of the Pandu identity before we progress with the story and build-up of the war. To Parpola, the Pandu were a foreign tribe that had entered the Deccan across the lower Indus,[9] and then approached the Divide from the south. In this regard our attention is attracted to the 2000 or so sites in the Deccan which, along with similar sites from Baluchistan, Kashmir, Delhi, and Central India, the eastern Gangetic plains, and Manipur, have been called *megaliths*.[10] Indeed, though their oldest sites or lowest layers have yielded utilitarian results like homesteads, newer layers have yielded campsites, iron weapons, horse-harnesses and headgears, well-fired dual Black and Red pottery, and jewellery and other prestige goods; most importantly, they are associated with monumental graves of *massive stones* after which they have been named.

Location of these sites along trade routes, circular, temporary huts with fireplaces that resemble *yurts*,[11] association with weapons and high quality products including jewellery, and monumental architecture, suggest that these sites are the relics of a military people which controlled trade routes, dominated society as seen in their control over specialized skill groups like potters, blacksmiths, and goldsmiths, and venerated their dead. Associating these *megaliths* with Pandu legends of Madurai and Sri Lanka, and Sinhalese origin legend that places their homeland in Gujarat, Parpola traced a definite folk movement from lower Indus and Saurashtra to the Deccan, branches of which later moved north to occupy the Divide; to him, the etymological association of the name Pāṇḍu with the Dravidian term for *paleface* is significant.

Indeed, the Pandu are allies of the Vṛṣṇi of Saurāṣṭra, associated with several Deccan peoples and places like the Pāṇḍya and Nashik, and appear at Kurukṣetra from the south along the *Aparānta*, the obvious direction for any immigrant from Saurashtra. The difficulty with this theory is that all

9 Asko Parpola, 'Pandaiŋ and Sītā: On the Historical Background of the Sanskrit Epics', *Journal of the American Oriental Society*, vol. 122, no. 2, Indic and Iranian Studies in Honor of Stanley Insler on His Sixty-Fifth Birthday, April–June 2002, pp. 361–373.

10 U.S. Moorti, *The Megalithic Culture of South India: Socio-Economic Perspectives*, Varanasi, 1994, pp. 4–5. Moorti has identified more than 600 in Karnataka and Tamil Nadu alone.

11 Parpola, 'Pandaiŋ', p. 362.

South Asian peoples have always associated with the *Mahabharata* heroes, and the name Pāṇḍya of the Madurai ruling house does not automatically imply Pandu ethnicity. Further, it is reasonable to posit that not one but numerous immigrant groups had migrated to the Deccan, most of them fair-skinned pastoralists; the term Pāṇḍu, if it really meant *paleface*, would at best have been a generic label and not denoted a specific historical group. Further, the fact that the *megalith*s are associated with not one but many modes of disposal of the dead—urn burials, bodies inside double clay caskets inserted into cavities cut into the rock-face, various types of sarcophagi—indicates that a host of ethnicities were responsible for them; the Pandu themselves are associated at least with two funerary procedures, a partial cremation–fractional burial as seen above, and exposure on the Śamī tree.

What is more persuasive is that the Pandu are affinituous with the Bharata, Pūru, and Kuru, all of whom are northerners, their association with the Kuru–Bharata attested in them being addressed as *Bhārata* more than anyone else. It is doubtful if they peregrinated too far south—Ptolemy mentioned a tribe called *Pandooui* in the Punjab.[12] It is more reasonable to take the Pandu as a nomad warband closely related to the Kuru which at the same time displayed many distinctive traits: they are reasonably matrilineal, scandalise others by a polyandrous marriage, and are associated with fractional burials and Parthian-like exposure of the dead[13] unlike Vedic cremation or inhumation.[14] We shall later see that they fight far more violently than the Kuru, ignoring rules of warfare that the Kuru at least affect to follow, and also observe magical rituals. In fact,

12 IA, XIII, pp. 331, 349.

13 *Mbh*, IV: 5.27–29, and J.L. Brockington, *The Sanskrit Epics*, Brill, 1998, p. 227. Also see Karlene Jones–Bley, 'Sintashta Burials and their Western European Counterparts', in Davis–Kimball *et all* (eds.), *Kurgans, Ritual Sites and Settlements*, pp. 126–134. It must also be remembered that while exposure is the norm among Tibetans, under special circumstances other methods were adopted, like earth or water burial.

14 See *ṚV*, X: 16.1 for what appears to be partial cremation. Also, *ṚV*, X: 18.11. '*open up, earth; do not crush him. Be easy for him to enter and to burrow in. Earth, wrap him up as a mother wraps a son in the edge of her skirt*', see O'Flaherty, *The Rig Veda: An Anthology*, p. 53. Differences in funerary customs are noted elsewhere. In *ŚB*, xii.8.1.5, Kuru–Pañcāla built small square mounds about a yard high, with internal chambers, while 'easterners and others' made round graves called *Asurya* or daemonic. Such barrow graves, some of which have been found at places like Laurya on the Nepalese border, have a great affinity with the Buddhist *stūpa* and Kurgan grave mounds.

the *Mahabharata* itself, and some Buddhist texts, know the Pandu as marauders.[15]

To Hopkins, polyandry was not a Vedic custom and never practiced by the Aryans;[16] the existence of this practice among Tibetan, Kinnauri, Jaunsari, and Ladakhi peoples had at one time led to a theory that the Pandu were actually *pale-faced* Tibetans. However, notwithstanding quaint stories—Kuntī unknowingly making the brothers promise to share everything, or that of the old woman and the *five Indras*—to explain the polyandrous marriage, Kuntī is seen citing polyandrous marriage as the custom in the homeland of *Uttara-Kuru*.[17] In fact the Kuru themselves, and even Pañcāla, display several matrilineal traits—Kuru and Pāñcāla princes are related through their mothers, women like Satyavatī and Gāndhārī wield immense influence, Gāndhārī's *brother* Śakuni is always at the side of his nephews, Duryodhana's brother Duḥśāsana, and not his son Laksmaṇa, is *yuvarāja*, and the story of Śāntanu and Gaṅgā is as matrilineal and matri-local as that of the hoary Purūravas and Urvaśī. Tracing of descent from the wife's clan is seen in some Ahir and Banaphar Rajputs *gotra*s even today; Babur, a Turcoman, was known as a Mughal because he was descended from Grand Khan Yunus on his mother's side.

The fact is that IA tribes were at that time undergoing changes from matrilineal society, where the man joined the woman's breeding group, at least temporarily, his children being brought up there. We see many characters of the epic, like Devavrata, Irāvan, Babhruvāhana, Abhimanyu (the last three sons of Arjuna by Ulūpī, Citrāṅgadā, and Subhadrā respectively), Ghaṭotkaca, and also eponymous ones like Amāvasu,

15 *Mbh*, II: 23–29. and early northern Buddhist texts (cf. Weber 1853: 403).

16 Hopkins, 'Ruling Caste', p. 354.

17 Even Yudhiṣṭhira cites precedence to Drupada for the decision, *Mbh*, I: 195.29–31. Polyandry is in existence among several PIA groups like the Kinnaura, Jaunsari, or Khasiya in the Himalaya today. D.N. Majumdar notes that the Khasiya '... live in a joint family, the brothers sharing a wife or wives in common, ... [A]ll the husbands of the mother, who are brothers, are addressed as father. If there are four brothers, the eldest is addressed as "barā bābā" [*the big father*], the next as "choṭā bābā" [*the little father*], the third as "bheḍi bābā" [*father who tends sheep*], and the youngest as "gaiar bābā" [*father who tends cows*]. The family house belongs to the eldest brother, the garden, crops ... are owned by him and the wife and children, with the duty of maintenance and control, are his. He is the governor of the family and the brothers accept his rule and authority without grumbling." D.N. Majumdar, 'The Culture Patterns of Polyandrous Society', in *Proceedings of the Indian Science Congress*, Madras, 1940, p. 185.

were actually brought up by their mothers' peoples. However, patrilineal procedures were increasingly entering society, with many kings using patrilineal pedigrees and offspring of *niyoga* taking the father's, and not the mother's identity.[18] While as per original custom the groom selected through the *svayaṁvara* joined the woman's group, in the epic *svayaṁvara* the bride selects the groom *but joins* the latter's group, where she is required to marry all *brothers* (the eldest being the formal husband). That such a procedure was not fundamentally alien is seen in its being practiced in secret by some communities on the Divide even today. The changes are most poignantly represented in the story of the boy Jābāla Satyakāma, son of Jabāli, who could not provide his father's identity and thus was castigated.[19]

The above can be concluded as—it would be too generic to identify the Pandu with warrior–immigrants into the Deccan who created the megaliths, and that it would be too hasty to say, despite their 'unusual' practices, that they were foreigners with a distinct culture. As the Pandu enjoy great popularity and sympathy among the Kuru and are addressed as Bharata far oftener than them, it would not be erroneous to say that they were a branch of the Kuru mother–stock, also closely associated with the Bharata, which had newly arrived from the Kuru homeland—Kuntī calls *Uttara-Kuru* their homeland too. Having started in a subordinate position, probably as mercenaries as seen in them participating in Droṇa's assaults against the Pañcālas, and in the *rājasūya* episode as we shall see later, they go on to wax enough in power to challenge the Kuru. This is a recurrent theme wherein fresh nomad stock supplant their kindred predecessors who had sedentised into softer ruling classes which try to control their wilder brethren by recruiting or allying with them but in due course, invariably, lose their vigour and get ousted. The IIr went through several such cycles in the Balkh and Murghab valleys at one time.

What we may conclude is that the Pandu were not as 'foreign', and differed from the Kuru not in type but in degree. For instance, Bhīma's act of drinking Duḥśāsana's blood after felling him, taken as proof of his barbarous foreignness, was nothing but a magical rite practiced at one time

18 Procedures similar to the *niyoga* were practiced among the early colonists in America, where widows and women without sons from their husbands were expected to raise children through other men.

19 See the *Ch.U.* 4.4.

by the Danes as well.[20] Strabon has mentioned the head hunting habits of the Medes, among whom no man could marry till he had made a present of a slaughtered head to his king so that the king and his council could make a paste of the tongue and eat it; the king who was gifted the most heads was the most respected.[21] The *Mahabharata* was not a war between two cultures[22]—all that the Pandu required was legitimacy, to do which a little tweaking of the genealogies was required.

Yudhiṣṭhira

Yudiṣṭhira, the eldest of the Pandu brothers, is largely conceived of as a helpless dummy listening to advice from any and every person willing to give him some. A closer look at the epic, however, reveals that in reality he was a hot-headed leader of a clan with a predilection for gambling. His relation with *Dharma* or Righteousness, which is made much of, is curious and revealing. He is born of Kuntī from *Dharma*. Curiously, when towards the end of the epic Yudhiṣṭhira rushes to the forest to meet a dying Vidura, the latter embraces him and declares that he *transfers his organs and powers to him*, reminiscent of an Upaniṣadic context wherein the son of a dying man lies down atop his father who then says,'I give you my organs', to which the son replies, 'I accept'. At another place, Vyāsa says that Yudhiṣṭhira was born of the yogic powers of Vidura.

Vidura, brother of Pāṇḍu and Dhṛtarāṣṭra born of a *Dāsa* woman, is *Dharma* incarnate, said to have been born as a result of the curse of the sage Aṇimāṇḍavya.[23] Based on the above, Irawati Karve has suggested that Yudhiṣṭhira was really the son of Vidura by *niyoga*. Yudhiṣṭhira's paternity is very important to the Pandu claim to legitimacy; we will return to Yudhiṣṭhira's proclivity for dicing.

---

20 Drinking of blood and mutilating the body were ancient magical rites. Scalps were taken, skulls used as drinking cup (even by peaceable Tibetan monks), human skin were stretched to construct drums and other things, while quivers were made of arms. Christian, *Central Asia—Russia*, pp. 144–46. Herodotus has remarked upon blood–drinking by the Scythes. *Herodotus*, 4:64.

21 Strabo, 'Geography of Strabo', in R.C. Majumdar, *The Classical Accounts of India*, Calcutta, Firma K.L. Mukopadhyaya, 1960, pp. 101.

22 Yardi, *The Mahabharata*, pp. 69–71. Yardi also suggested that Kurus displayed several other 'tribal' characteristics like playing of dice to decide distribution.

23 Yardi, *The Mahabharata*, pp. 2–3. Now, Yudhiṣṭhira was also Dharma mortally born.

Bhīma

The general run of the story so far shows that while Arjuna is largely on his own, it is Bhīma who, thanks to his immense strength, bears most of the trials on behalf of the Pandu. He digs the tunnel, carries his tired brothers and mother on his shoulders, fights and kills cannibals like Kirmira, Baka, and Jaṭāsura, enters into a curious marriage with the 'demoness' Hiḍimbā, has his adventures while fetching the *saugandhika* flowers, and kills Jarāsandha. These legends, and the actual position of Bhīma, require closer inspection.

In the Himalayan town of Manali stands a temple to Hiḍimbā with an imposing cedar spire. If one looks closely at the sanctum under the spire, one sees a part–underground cave. Several other spots across South Asia are associated with the Hiḍimbā–Bhīma story, like Hiḍimbāḍāṅgā near Howrah in Bengal, Hiḍimbāvana near Patan, Hidimbāci Tekḍi near Nagpur, and Dimapur, a corruption of Hiḍimbāpura, in Kachhar whose kings trace descent from Bhīma and Hiḍimbā. The *Sindūra-giri Māhātmya* gives the procedure of Hiḍimbā worship, which includes a bath at the *Mansar* Lake, i.e. *Maṇikālasara* or *Lake of the Serpent's Jewel*, of which there are several associated with Hiḍimbā, one near Nagpur, and another near Samba in the Jammu foothills.

Association with the snake and cave motif at once associates Hiḍimbā with the Earth–Mother—the serpent has obvious symbolism, and the cave is part of many Earth–Mother cults like Vaiṣṇavīdevī (Vaishnodevi) in Jammu or Hiṅgulāja in Baluchistan. Curiously, the Bhīma associated with these Hiḍimbā cult sites is *son of Śiva*, thereby associating the Earth–Mother with the Father–Husband–Son. Evidently the agrarian, Nāga cult of Hiḍimbā and Bhīma was assimilated using the similarity of names with the Pandu Bhīma, through a part comic story reminiscent of that of the Cyclops in which Bhīma tricks and kills the demon Hiḍimba, Hiḍimbā's brother, who had impounded the Pandu in, significantly, a cave.

Returning to the Pandu Bhīma, we find that not only is he the only one who is caringly attached with Draupadī and the most understanding of her difficulties, he also is the commander of the only Pandu division in the battle, all others being, in actuality, supplied by allies. In the war, he kills all the Kuru brothers personally, which is significant. Taking the above together, one may make a bold surmise, that Yudhiṣṭhira and Bhīma formed a *diarchy*, with the former as the head of the clan, and Bhīma the junior and war–leader, mirroring closely the political situation in the Kuru where Duryodhana and Duḥśāsana appear to have a *diarchy*. The Pandu Bhīma probably felled the chief of Girjak, an exploit that later relocated at Girivraja.

Arjuna

In contrast to Bhīma, Arjuna is a free-ranger. Though it is he who wins the hand of Draupadī, the princess ends up marrying all the other brothers, of whom Yudhiṣṭhira is the senior husband. Also, he is away most of the time winning other powerful matrimonial relations. That the story of his twelve-years exile under a vow of celibacy was an interpolation is evident in his entering into at least three amorous alliances during its course—with Ulūpī the Nāga, Subhadrā the Vṛṣṇi, and Citrāṅgadā of Maṇipura, siring Irāvan, Abhimanyu, and Babhruvāhana respectively, all of whom would participate in the war. Curiously, the period of his exile is twelve years, the same as the period of the brothers' exile together. Also, while those of the other brothers appear formalised, only Arjuna's campaign alone in the *rājasūya* that appears authentic.

Even during the later exile, Arjuna would be away most of the time seeking specialist weapons from the gods. It will also be seen that in the war, his actions were highly independent of the others.

In all of Arjuna's later marriages, the brides marry a stranger (Arjuna), one even having to be kidnapped, and all offspring are brought up by their mother's peoples. This shows that Arjuna moved in a largely matrilineal context. Also, in one scene Arjuna is associated with exposure of the dead on a tree. Exposure or excarnation, prevalent among Iranians after Zarathustra condemned inhumation, burning, or burying, does not automatically imply Iranic or Parthian affiliations and must have existed as *one of the many* methods of disposal of the dead, as seen in the diverse funerary practices from Sintashta–Arkhaim or the Bactria–Margiana Archaeological Complex (BMAC). However, Arjuna alone among the brothers is called *Pārtha*, a name explained as *son of Pṛthā*, i.e. Kuntī, in what is a fallacious logic as that would mean that Yudhiṣṭhira, Bhīma, and even Karṇa should be called *Pārtha* which they hardly ever are.[24]

At the same time, mere association with the Parthians and tree *burials* does not automatically prove foreignness of Arjuna. While the tree burial was practiced by diverse peoples including Nande agriculturists of the Great Lakes region in Africa, we also know that the stretch from Eastern Iran, BMAC, the Indus, and Punjab plains was an immense transition zone where most groups belonged as much to the Iranian as the IA world. The Bharata Sṛñjaya, who were at one time led by a chief styled Pārthava, are a component of the Pañcāla, while the Pañcajana are descended from the daughters, Devayānī and Śarmiṣṭhā, of an *Asura* priest and an *Asura* king. Also, the *Asura* strategist, Śukra, like Bṛhaspati was of the *Deva*, was a Bhṛgu. The Kekaya, represented in later times by the Khakkaṭṭa, Khokhar, and Gakkhar, have strong Pārthava or Parthian affiliations, while Medes of western Iran are associated with the Madra of upper Indus, and the later Meḍs of Sindh. In fact, Manu classified Bactrian and 'Margian' peoples as Mārgava, son of *Niṣāda* father and *Ayogava* mother, *Ayogava* itself being cross (*sic*) between *Śūdra* and *Vaiśya*;[25] Mārgava, which appears in the *Bṛhatsaṅhitā* as *Mārgara*, is also *Dāsa*, which at once associates them with the Iranic **Maryu*, *Margava*, *Merv*, and *Dahae*. Significantly, one of the less used names of the Hamun plains in Afghanistan, in important staging area in the IIr migration, is *Dasht-ê-Margow*, or the Marg deserts.

In historical times, we find two *Vrātya gaṇarājya*s affiliated to Arjuna, the Arjunāyanas and Prārjunas, while the Yaudheya of Rohtaka are associated with Yudhiṣṭhira.[26] Though data from these historical periods is too scanty, and ruling houses may have simply traced origin fictitiously to these *Mahabharata* characters, taken with the other aspects it does seem that the Pandu were a composite identity of closely affiliated warbands

24 The others together are called *Pārtha*, as in *the Five Pārtha*s, but never individually.

25 *Mānava Dharmaśāstra* (hereafter *Manu*), x, 12, in Patrick Olivelle ed. and trans., *Manu's Code of Law*, Oxford, 2005, p.209.

26 Alexander Cunningham, *Archaeological Survey Report: Report of the Year 1878-79*, CASR, vol. 14, 1882, pp. 140. The *Yaudheya*s are said to be descended from Yudhiṣṭhira from the princess of the Śivis. At the sametime, they are *Mattamayuraka* or the *Charmed Peacocks*, while *Kārttikeya* appears in Yaudheya *gaṇasaṅgha* coins from the time when the peacock-riding war-god, *Kārttikeya* or *Skanda*, was extremely popular across Central and South Asia, and who grew popular in the Deccan as Murugan or Mañjunātha and in Central Asian Mahāyāna Buddhism as Mañjuśrī.

which often operated independently. The next section will inspect how and why this composite group required tweaking of the genealogies to obtain political legitimacy, in which context we shall discuss the other components of the Pandu alliance. But before that we shall have a look at the importance of Pandu women.

Pandu Women

While the mothers of Babur and Akbar had played strong roles at the time of their vicissitudes, three generations of women in the family of Genghis—his mother Hoelun, his wife Bortë, and his youngest son Tolui's wife Sorkhakhtani Beki—had kept the family together through thick and thin and made it prosper. We see two women playing similar roles in the case of the Pandu, their mother Kuntī, and their wife Draupadī. Far from being a helpless widow tagging along behind her sons, Kuntī guarded them against schemers in their boyhood, guided their fortunes in their youth, maintained good relations with the nobles at court during their exile, exhorted them to fight for their rights afterwards, even offering to stand them the money to raise an army. It was she who insisted upon the polyandrous marriage of Draupadī as a means of keeping the brothers united, and later, tried to win Karṇa over as *her* son. In fact, as adoptive daughter of the Kunti–Bhoja kings, she represented yet another of the powerful matrimonial relations of the Pandu.

During their exile, the Pandu were accompanied not by Kuntī but by Draupadī, who as their common wife was instrumental in keeping them together and exhorting them not to give up their cause. Significantly, the bait Karṇa would be offered when the Pandu tried to win him over was that as senior brother, he would replace Yudhiṣṭhira as *first husband* of Draupadī. Keeping the brothers united was perhaps more significant than is apparent, as we shall see later.

Successions, and Pandu Quest for Political Legitimacy

A democratic election, however spurious or laughable, is the most widely acknowledged source of political legitimacy in the modern world. Pre-modern societies too used several manners of discerning and establishing political legitimacy, one of which was descent from 'special' families which, in ancient times, claimed ancestors among gods, and in the medieval, among ancient kings descended from gods. Needless to say, all such claims were made only once these families felt sure that they required a genealogy to match their importance. Claimants from other families were considered pretenders unless they too could publicly establish a link with the first family, or a comparable pedigree from another. Holders of real power could thus find it difficult to assume sovereignty as long as members of the acknowledged families lived. Sher Shah could take over leadership of the Afghan *Risorgimento* only after the failed house of Lodi petered out, and the governors of the Mughals, vastly more powerful than the emperor, had to remain content with titles like *nawab* or *nizam*. Nadir Quli Khan or Ahmad Khan Abdali's assumption of the title of *Shah* was looked at askance, as the only three sources of legitimacy in the Islamic world then were the Caliph, the Shah of Persia, and the Grand Khan of the Mongols. Tipu's use of the regnal title of *sultan* showed that he sought legitimacy directly from the Caliph and not the Mughal.

Even in the case of special families, primogeniture was *one of the several* methods of succession. Junior rights, in which the youngest son inherited the home and hearth, was a Mongol practice and can be discerned from the myths of many early people. Among the Turco–Mongols, any member of the family of Tëmur or Babur was authorised to rule, a tanistry that led to bloody wars of accession on the demise of each emperor. In China, the *Heaven's Mandate*, discerned by painstaking inspection of omens, could devolve on anyone, including commoners, though all families that received it were quick to trace themselves from one or the other of the *Spring and Autumn* clans; even the Zhou, in underlining *their* mandate as distinct from their Shang predecessors, created the fictional line of the *Xia who had earlier lost the mandate to the Shang and which was now rightfully restored to the Zhou.*[27] The upstart but unusually able kings of meritocratic Magadha had to insist upon a *Kṣatriya* lineage.

27 As per Bagley, the universal position of the Shang monarchy at Anyang is not borne out by archaeological evidence, but was imputed by the Zhou in order to elevate their own primacy. Perhaps the Shang were only the most spectacular of several states that had existed then. The logic used by the Zhou was that, the Shang had been noble at one time, when they had received the mandate, but had later forfeited it by losing their nobility. See Bagley, 'Shang Archaeology', pp. 230–231. To underline their moral position, the Zhou king *hesitated thrice* before attacking the Shang, and also retained minor Shang princes as dukes. They also claim an agrarian descent to underline their Chinese–ness, so as to validate their legitimacy.

The overwhelming importance of genealogy is obvious from an inverse example. When Tëmur, chief of the relatively minor Barlas clan, felt he had become important enough to associate with Genghis, the only source of legitimacy in Central Asia then but too close to him in time, the latter's real descendants, the various Khanates of the Altyn Ordë (Golden Horde) and the Il, Yuan, and Chaghatay, and the diverse *Khungtaïji* princes, being extant, he designed a genealogy that traced him from the *brother of an ancestor of Genghis*. This put him on an equal footing with Genghis and his descendants as *equal bearer of the Mongol heritage*.[28] Thus we see the Mughal-sponsored fiction of Pakhtun descent from *Afghānān* through *Kaïs* being enthusiastically adopted by the Afghans, complementing hoary Pakhtun lore of having been settled from West Asia by the Assyrians or Persians.

A manner of regularising transfer of legitimacy was by *grafting* into the special families. Several manners were used to graft new families into established lines, depending upon the form of succession. This was easy in the case of matrilineal successions, wherein a conqueror could marry the daughter and heiress of a defeated king to authenticate the transfer. This is observed in the case of Achaean kings like Agamemnon and Menelaus, sons of Atreus, who inherited Athens and Sparta from their Mycenaean father-in-law by marrying his daughters Clytemnestra and Helen respectively (this can be made out through several contradictory tales all of which involve much violence, incest, and even cannibalism on the part of the Atridae). Indeed, it was this, and not that a powerful man like Menelaus had been cuckolded, that caused all hell to break loose when Paris took Helen away—as Helen's possessor, he could claim Sparta. When Paris and Menelaus decide to duel in *Iliad* 3:69–70, the condition was that the winner would 'take Helen *and all her possessions*'; there was no retribution against Helen after the war as she was Menelaus' ticket to fortune.[29] Such matrilineal succession was also why Penelope, wife of Odysseus who went missing in action, was wooed endlessly by suitors

28 See S.K. Bose, *Boots, Hooves, and Wheels: and the Social Dynamics Behind South Asian Warfare*, Delhi, Vij Books, 2015, p. 248 and n. 47.

29 There are other references to matrilineal succession in the *Iliad*. Odysseus turns down three such offers, from Circe, Nausicaa, and Calypso. After the war, Agamemnon is killed by Clytemnestra who then marries her lover Aygesthus who consequently becomes king. Servius Tullius, a commoner, had succeeded to the Roman king Ancus Marcius by marrying his daughter.

hoping to succeed to 'Odysseus's' fortune, and in many a fairy-tale the king gives away half his kingdom with the hand of his daughter, without his sons objecting.

Understandably, increasingly patriarchal societies could find such inheritance highly disruptive, and violently try to suppress them, as did Kaṅsa. Or they could try to explain them away, one clear case being the mixing of the story of the Mycenaean–Spartan Helen with that of the goddess Helen Tyrche—no brother of Helen inherited Sparta because they had *died and became the gods Kastor and Peleudykos*, the brothers of Helen Tyrche. Interestingly, some tribes like the Śākya and Licchavi trace their origin to a brother–sister marriage, while Arrian recorded a tradition of the Indian Heracles, which in this case could have been a southern king, *marrying his daughter* when he found no one suitable enough to succeed him. Diodorus Siculus recorded that this Heracles made his sole daughter queen while he made his various sons *kings in various parts of the country.*[30] Explaining the above as means to maintain racial purity does not stand to logic; the procedure was essentially a means of creating a precedence for retaining the legacy in the patrilineal line.

Another way of grafting into a family was the lost-and-found story. Paris of the *Iliad* is usually taken to be an effete prince who brought ruin upon his country by acting rashly and then chickening out of the fight, leaving Hector to bear its brunt. However, he *elsewhere* appears as an adoptive son of a mountain shepherd from Hittia who fights and defeats Hector in a contest over a prize bull (which in some versions belonged to Paris and had been impounded by Hector). At this contest, Hector's father Priam recognises Paris as the son he had abandoned as a child due to portents predicting him to be the cause of his ruin, and readmits him into the royal household, much to the chagrin of his wife and daughter who find the event foreboding. In addition to fighting Hector heroically, Paris, being a mountain shepherd, is seen fighting Scythian fashion with horses, chariots, bows, and arrows, which was the origin of his reputation for cowardice among the chivalric Greeks who at least pretended to detest such weapons. It is evident that Paris was a highly ambitious shepherd–prince, probably with Hittite, Parthian, or Scythian affiliation, who associated with the Trojan royal house as a long–lost son, and then tried to

30 Periplus, in Majumdar, *Classical Accounts*, p. 236.

gain Sparta by wooing the bearer of its legacy, Helen, bringing ruin upon his foster home.

Returning to the *Mahabharata*, we see that the lost–and–found theme was tried to co-opt Karṇa into the Pandu household.

Also, we see that the Pandu have *no direct bloodline with the Kuru house*. Pāṇḍu was born of *niyoga*, the *niyukta* being the Bhṛgu sage Kṛṣṇa Dvaipāyana Vyāsa, pre–nuptial offspring of his mother Satyavatī (thus half-brother to Bhīṣma and her other two sons), on one of the 'foreign' wives of the last 'ethnic' Kuru king. His sons were born of Yadu and Mādra princesses from 'gods'. Significantly, the Pandu were not born in the Kuru household but in the *wilderness*, arriving at Hastināpura as boys after Pāṇḍu died. Even though Dhṛtarāṣṭra was at least biologically (though miraculously) father of his sons, he too was born of the same *niyoga* as was Pāṇḍu.

The Pandu, so ambivalently related to the Kuru household, are hailed as bearers of the Bharata legacy, called *Bhāratārṣabha* (Bharata Bull), *Bhāratasattamas* (Mighty Bharata), or simply *Bhārata* all the time, and also said to come from the Kuru mother–stock of *Uttara-Kuru*. A hesitating conclusion that can be drawn here is that the Pāṇḍu and Dhṛtarāṣṭra never really existed, and were dummy constructs to graft the Pandu, a people kindred of the Kuru, into the Kuru genealogy. The helpless, ineffectual, and metaphorically blind Dhṛtarāṣṭra helped account for Kuru conduct, making their legitimacy appear at least as shaky as that of the Pandu. In this context, other Dhṛtarāṣṭras who appear as priest of snakes and king of Kāśī must be recollected.

Yet, both Pāṇḍu and Dhṛtarāṣṭra appear to have been real people who lived, as did their brother Vidura, born of a *Dāsa* woman in the same sequence of *niyoga*. Now, while Vidura's *Dāsa* mother is popularly considered Śūdra, she really might have been one of the many captured women who existed in royal households and need not have been Śūdra at all. In fact, Bhīṣma, having not learnt his lesson from the goof-up while capturing brides for his half-brothers, again captured three three brides for his nephews—a *Yādavīkanyā*, i.e. daughter of a Yadu, the daughter of Subala of Gandhāra, and the daughter of the Madra chief. These three are usually taken as Kuntī, daughter of the Yadu Śurasena and adoptive daughter of Yadu Kunti–Bhoja, and Gandhārī, and Mādrī. Now, there is no explanation as to why Bhīṣma should think of *two* brides for Pāṇḍu, i.e. Kuntī and Mādri, and only one for Dhṛtarāṣṭra. In fact, Pāṇḍu had independently married the Kunti–Bhoja princess in her *svayaṁvara*.

It is more probable that the *Yādavīkanyā* referred to here was Vidura's wife Sulabhā, daughter of a Yadu chief by a *Dāsa* woman who, not being a well-born princess, was treated less formally. In other words, Bhīṣma brought brides for Vidura, Dhṛtarāṣṭra, and Pāṇḍu, in that order. Now, the Madra were staunch Kuru allies who often give them brides—the Mādra king Śalya, despite being an uncle of the Pandu, fights on the Kuru side. In this light, it seems that Bhīṣma had arranged for a Madra bride for Pāṇḍu to strengthen the Kuru–Madra relation which had been somewhat compromised by Pāṇḍu's alliance with the less accommodative Kunti–Bhoja. The above suggests that Pāṇḍu was not fictional but of (the chief of) a branch of the original Kuru–Bharata stock, which had appeared on the scene at a time when the Kuru household was undergoing turmoil, and with which Bhīṣma was trying to establish relations.

It would also not do, despite his ineffectuality, to discard Dhṛtarāṣṭra—Duryodhana had to have a father. All that we can say at this remove in time is that the Kuru household had come to a juncture wherein neither prince, descended from or affiliated to the household by any one of several types of inheritances, could stake a strong claim to rule except the power of their matrimonial allies.[31]

The *Mahabharata* genealogies were subsequently tweaked by the victor Pandu who grafted the Bharata, their ancestors, as a *Kuru* king, as seen in the previous chapter, implying thereby that not only their own Uttara-Kuru but also their Bharata heritage were represented by the Kuru, whose legacy they had now succeeded to.

This is somewhat mirrored in the Western Zhou sequence of taking over legitimacy from the Shang. The Zhou start with affecting a reluctance to do anything violent, moralising on Shang misdeeds but feigning a

31 It is also important here to remind ourselves of the immense influence, and interference, that matrimonial alliances could perpetrate. Kings proudly retained their wives' native names or advertised the country of origin of their wives, as seen in the appellations of the wives of Daśaratha in the *Ramayana*, several women in the *Mahabharata*, and *Vaidehī* and *Pāñcālī* for Sītā and Draupadī respectively. Later Magadhan monarchs proudly proclaimed their Licchavi in-laws. This has been pointed out in the case of the Zhou also by Edwin Pulleybanks.

reluctance to topple them (making two abortive attempts), and then creating the fictional line of Xia whose mandate, lost to the Shang, they *rightfully* reclaim. They highlight that the last Shang committed suicide (in other words *they* did not kill him), that 800 Shang nobles *transferred* their allegiance to them, and that they also granted Shang descendants courtesy fiefs. The same the Pandu seem to be doing, grafting their Bharata heritage into the Kuru line first, and then reclaiming it, justifying the takeover with moralistic apologia and the 'wickedness' of the Kuru. Such archaic procedures are best understood only if the preconception that male primogeniture was the 'only' means of succession is discarded.

The Yadu Conglomeration

The appearance of Yadu on either side of the field at Kurukṣetra is explained by a quaint story in the epic. On reaching Dvārakā to seek Krishna's alliance, Duryodhana and Arjuna found him asleep. The former proudly sat himself at the head of the bed, but the latter stood humbly at its foot. On waking, Krishna's eyes first alighted on Arjuna, and pleased with his humility he decided to join him, though as a non-combatant, offering his huge army, the *Nārāyaṇīya*, to Duryodhana which the latter vainly accepted.

The story is however disturbed by the fact that not only Kṛṣṇa, but a substantial part of his Vṛṣṇyandhaka (Vṛṣṇi–Andhaka) tribe, including the warriors Sātyaki and Cekitāna, appear on the Pandu side despite his having given his army to the Kuru. On the side of the Kuru, not only *Krishna's army* but diverse other Yadu chiefs also appear. In another attempt to explain the confused participation of the Yadu, Baladeva, who had not received much attention in Vaiśampāyana's *Bharata*, is in Sūta's redaction (as per Yardi), approached by an embassy from Duryodhana which is turned away by him, as he says his brother had already joined the Pandu. Thus we see that this story is not a very convincing explanation of the Yadu choice of sides in the battle, and Ruben has drawn our attention to the Teutonic story of the waking god—both Langobards (Lombards) and Wandals (Vandals), when about to go to war, sue a sleeping Godan/Odinn for victory, and when the god wakes up, he chances to see the Langobards first and grants victory to them.[32] It would be more profitable

32 See Walter Ruben, *Krishna: Konkordanz und Kommentar der Motive Seines Heldenlebens*, Istanbul, Istanbul Yazilari, 1944, pp. 220–221; also see Alf Hiltebeitel,

to look closely at the composition of the Yadu in order to understand the confused participation.

The Yadu were really a large constellation of tribes, closely associated with the Turvaśa, and were divided into many septs and clans like the Bhaima, Kaukura, Sātvat, Bhoja, Andhaka, Vṛṣṇi, Yādava, and Dasārha, among others. Different lists of these tribes appear in various works, and there is little consistency among them. For example, the *Aitareya Brāhmaṇa* easily substitutes Sātvat for Yadu, at least for the Yadu who live south of the Satpuras,[33] but elsewhere the Vṛṣṇi, Dvaivavṛdha, and Mahabhoja have been called Sātvat. Manu calls the Sātvat and Śūrasena as *Vrātya Vaiśya*.[34] Also, while the Yadu are paired with the 'Scythic' Turvaśa, Yadu branches like the Haihaya have strong Scythic affiliations. The Haihaya, first seen fighting the Ikṣvāku in association with Śaka, Pahlava, and Kamboja, have branches called Vītihotra, Bhoja, Saryata, Avanti, Tuṇḍikera, and Tāḷajaṅgha, of which the Vītihotra have been called foreigners in the *Vāyupurāṇa*[35] and the Avanti, whose language was different from Sanskrit, have been called *Vrātya*.[36] In yet another twist, the *Harivaṅśa* calls the Bharata themselves as Tāḷajaṅgha, which is a branch of the Haihaya.

To Raychaudhuri, the Sātvat was the royal line of the Bhoja,[37] but it appears equally probable that the Kuntī and Kunti–Bhoja, associated with Avanti and Haihaya, was a Sātvat branch ruled by Bhoja kings.[38] In other words, the inverse of Raychaudhuri's position. At the same time, the Haihaya are seen in possession of Mahiṣmatī on the Narmada, i.e. the southern frontiers of Avanti along the *Dakṣiṇāpatha*, which had been conquered by their ruler Kārtavīrya Arjuna from the Karkoṭaka-Nāga whose troops were called *Nīlāyudha*, i.e. '*black warriors, unconquered*'.[39]

The Ritual of Battle: Krishna in the Mahabharata, Ithaca, Cornell University, 1976, pp. 107–109.

33 *Ait.Br.*, viii.14.

34 *Manu*, x, 23.

35 F.E. Pargiter, *The Purāṇa Text of the Dynasties of the Kali Age*, Motilal Banarasidass, Delhi, 1972 (First Published 1913), pp. 2–3.

36 Pargiter, *Kali Age*, pp. 54–55.

37 Raychaudhuri, *Political History*, p. 90.

38 Raychaudhuri, *Political History*, pp. 76–77.

39 *Mbh*, V: 18.

Probably the Haihaya were Yadu pioneers into the lands of the Nisadic Bhīla tribes who inhabit the area even today.

These convolutions are impossible to decipher against the background of lax records, but do indicate endless re-affiliations, and suggest that early Yadu groups—the Yakṣu, Sātvat, Avanti, Kunti, Bhoja, or Haihaya—once in possession of Mathura–Vṛndāvana, had been pushed out by the Śūrasena who were in possession of those regions at the time of the epic. The former group seem to have dispersed along the *Dakṣiṇāpatha* towards the Narmada, where Yadu presence is seen in the emperor of the south being called *Bhaujya* in the early texts. *Bhoja* was the regnal title of the king of Avanti till early 2nd millennium A.D.

Apparently, not all members of the Yadu conglomerate were at the same socioeconomic and political level. The Vṛṣṇi appear to have been far more nomadic and pastoral than the others, associating easily with the pastoral Ābhīra, or with the Haihaya Tālajaṅgha. They were branded *Vrātya* in the *Droṇaparvan*,[40] had an army entirely of cowherds,[41] and are located at the southern terminus of the *Aparānta*, one of the best places for breeding of animals in India. As per the *Baudhāyana Dharmaśāstra*, the people of this region were of mixed foreign origin,[42] and the *Purāṇas* call them *vrātya* and even Śūdra.[43] The violence inherent in them is seen in one episode from Krishna's youth, when he and Baladeva casually kill a reddleman, the incident extolled as one of his *līlā*s or *doings*.

The Yadu hero *Krishna of Dvārakā*, who has himself been called *Vrātya*,[44] is the effective Krishna in the *Mahabharata*.[45] In contrast, the lovable and pastoral Krishna of Hinduism is the *Krishna of Mathura*, who does not appear in the main body of the epic at all but only in its appendix called *Harivaṅśa-khila*, his story being developed in the *Purāṇa*s and popular literature thereafter. However, we can trace a strong link between the two.

40 *Mbh*, VII: 145.15; also 143.15.

41 *Mbh*, V: 7.17ff.

42 *BŚS*, 5, 1, 1.32–33.

43 Pargiter, *Kali Age*, pp. 54–55.

44 MRK, p. 95.

45 Yardi, *The Mahabharata*, pp. 98–99.

As per legend, *Krishna of Mathura* was born in a cell where his parents and maternal grandfather Ugrasena, chief of the Vṛṣṇyandhaka then located at Mathura, were held captive by his mother's brother, the tyrant Kaṅsa, who had been prophesied to be killed by his sister's eighth child. Kaṅsa had successfully killed the first six new-borns, the seventh was immaculately transferred from the womb, and the eighth, Krishna, survived by a series of miracles—his father's shackles fell, the guards slept, and a serpent helped his father cross a flooded Yamuna to the pastures of Vṛndāvana and deposit him with the Ābhīra chief Nanda and return with the latter's child, which was duly killed by Kaṅsa next morning. However, another prophecy was made damning Kaṅsa, which led to his letting loose on the new-borns reminiscent of the *massacre of the innocents*.

Many a tale and legend surround the upbringing of Krishna among Nanda's pastoral Ābhīra people, including tales of his amorous escapades with swooning cowgirls. Years later, Krishna kills Kaṅsa in a wrestling match, releases his parents, and restores Ugrasena to the chief-ship. This leads, as per the lore, to the Vṛṣṇyandhaka being attacked by Jarāsandha of Magadha, Kaṅsa's father-in-law, and forced to withdraw along the *Aparānta* to Dvārakā in Saurāṣṭra, thus joining the story of *Krishna of Mathura* with that of *Krishna of Dvārakā*. One of the many epithets of Krishna is *Raṇachoḍa-ji*, i.e. the *Lord, Quitter of Battle*, acquired due to his retreat several times in the face of Jarāsandha's onslaughts.

Some scholars, like Karve or Dandekar, have suggested that *Krishna of Mathura* was a fictional construct from an Ābhīra pastoral godhead whose tale was amalgamated with that of the historical Krishna.[46] There is however enough logical reason in favour of a real *Krishna of Mathura*. The political organization of the Vṛṣṇyandhaka, in the *Mahabharata* and *Arthaśāstra*, was the *saṅgha* or oligarchy, under the *saṅghamukhya*.[47] Kaṅsa's imprisoning his father Ugrasena, who was the *saṅghamukhya*, and his sister and her husband Vasudeva, an obvious attempt to subvert the matrilineal succession, proved by Ugrasena being actually succeeded by Vasudeva later.

46 Karve, *Yugānta*, pp. 179-80. Also, Dandekar, 'Vaiṣṇavism and Saivism', in R.N. Dandekar (ed.), *Ramkrishna Gopal Bhandarkar as an Indologist: a Symposium*, BORI, Poona, 1976, p. 73.

47 *Mbh*, XII. 81.25.

An ally of Jarāsandha was Bhīṣmaka of Vidarbha, who had a feud with Krishna because his daughter Rukmiṇi had eloped with him. In the *rājasūya*, the Pandu and Krishna kill Jarāsandha, and also deal severely with Bhīṣmaka who had tried to disrupt it. We have already seen that the Jarāsandha killed by the Pandu was probably not a Magadhan king but a northern chief. In the *Arghyābhiharaṇa* episode of the *rājasūya*, the Cedī chief Śiśupāla, who had rivalled Krishna over Rukmiṇi and was also a general in the slain Jarāsandha's army, denounces Krishna as an upstart and objects to his being given the seat, or gift, of honour (*arghya*) at the *rājasūya*. He demands that it be offered to Bhīṣma, if not to him, instead, and is beheaded by Krishna when he turns abusive and vituperative (the *Śiśupāla-vadha* episode).

Van Buitenen has shown that the recipient of the *arghya* was second only to the performer of the *rājasūya*;[48] possibly this close position of the Vṛṣṇi to the Pandu was resented by Śiśupāla, a Vṛṣṇi of a different faction. The episode shows that Krishna's position in the council or *saṅgha* was shaky and ill-defined, that Vṛṣṇi participation in the Pandu *rājasūya* had possibly resulted in a northern king ousted by them being 'confused' and equated with an eastern monarch who was enemy of the Vṛṣṇi, and that this could be the reason of Krishna's special hostility towards Bhīṣma evident later.

We can now draw the link between the Krishnas of Mathura and Dvārakā closer. We see that both are associated with pastoralism and the Ābhīras. The Ābhīra, who like the Yadu have been called *mleccha*[49] and *vrātya*,[50] and classed as sons of Brahman man and Ambaṣṭha woman,[51] had brought Krishna up as a fugitive at Vṛndāvana, were Vṛṣṇi neighbours at Saurashtra, and even *attacked* Vṛṣṇi caravan being led back to Indraprastha by Arjuna after the war. In other words, like the Vṛṣṇi, the Ābhīras, possibly the tall and swarthy *Abiria* encountered north of the Indus delta by the Greeks,[52] were associated with both termini of the *Aparānta*. They

48 J.A.B. van Buitenen, *Mahābhārata*, vol 2: Book 2: The Book of Assembly; Book 3: The Book of the Forest, Chicago, 1975, p. 23.

49 *Mbh*, XVI: 7.63.

50 Pargiter, *Kali Age*, pp. 54–55.

51 *Mbh*, X: 15.

52 R.C. Majumdar, *The Classical Accounts of India*, Firma KLM, Calcutta, 1981, VI. *Periplus Maris Erythraei*, p. 301. Also, *Periplus*, par. 41. Ptolemy calls Abiria inland

were possibly an associated group of the Vṛṣṇi that survived their demise, remaining powerful till the 9th century[53] when they dispersed to serve as mercenaries or establish principalities. Today, they are a prosperous community that bears the commemorative honorific of Yadav.[54]

Interestingly, both termini of the *Aparānta* are also associated with Madhu, the 'demon' of Naga affiliation. The Yadu 'capital' of Ānarta in Sindh, between Dvārakā and the Indus, was once part of the kingdom of Madhu, whose son Lavana was killed by Śatrughna, who also cut down his groves, the *Madhuvana*, and founded the settlement of *Madhula* or *Mathura*. Elsewhere, Krishna is *Madhusūdana*, i.e. slayer of Madhu, but also *Mādhava*, descended from Madhu on his mother's side. Now, while we have seen *madhu*, i.e. honey or mead, as an important accessory of the Aśvin cult (*madhumantha, madhuparka*) of the Yadu–Turvaśa of the Gandhara Grave culture, *madhu* was also an important ingredient of the Bacchic cult of Saṅkarṣaṇa, i.e. the plougher, popular around Mathura then and who later is associated with Baladeva (Rāma), always depicted with the plough. In other words, the Yadu were co-opting the agrarian substrate as much as they were retaining themes from their old Aśvin cult, as were the Kuru in the north.

The overall situation can be passably reconstructed. Yadu tribes, including 'have beens' like Bhoja and Haihaya (on the *Dakṣiṇāpatha*) and 'would be's' like Vṛṣṇyandhaka (on the *Aparānta*), aspired to Mathura–Vṛndāvana, then occupied by the Śūrasena. The Vṛṣṇyandhaka, who probably had a foothold there at one point of time, were themselves split, with Krishna, Sātyakī, and Cekitāna joining the Pandu, Baladeva holding out (though this aspect of holding out has more significant religious implications, as we shall see), and others being in rival factions. Closeness of the Vṛṣṇi to the Pandu, their matrimonial relation, their alliance in the *rājasūya*, all indicate that they too, like the Pandu, were a fresh branch of the 'mother' race, and aspired to a place on the Divide. One of the many possible reasons for the 'split' must have been the question of renewing attempts to restore themselves on the Divide. All this, however,

---

and north of Patalene, the delta, see Majumdar, *Classical Accounts*, Ptolemy, 372.

53 B.D. Chattopadhyaya, *Aspects of Rural Settlements and Rural Society in Early Medieval India*, Calcutta, 1990, pp. 3–4.

54 Shireen Ratnagar, *The Other Indians: Essays on Pastoralists and Prehistoric Tribal People*, Three Essays Collection, Gurgaon, 2004, p. 99.

was incomprehensible to later redactors who explained the split with the quaintly didactic story of Arjuna's humility, Baladeva's refusal to support to the Pandu, and the meaningless story of a Yadu free-for-all at the picnic in the *Mauṣalaparvan* (see later) that would eventually destroy their race.

The strong correlation between the stories of *Krishna of Mathura* and *Krishna of Dvārakā* suggests that there are enough reasons to take them as real and identical, demonstrating two phases in the career of one and the same person, whose tribe, nomadic as it was, was associated with the length of the pastoral corridor of *Aparānta*. In this regard, we remember the philosopher Krishna of *Chandogya Upaniṣad*, who is called Devakīputra or son of Devakī, mother of *Krishna of Mathura* though his foster mother was Yaśodā, wife of Nanda.

The Dice game

One of the most charged episodes of the epic is the dice game in which the Kuru challenge the Pandu and win everything away, forcing them into thirteen years of 'exile'. As per Yardi, only the above outline appeared in the *Ādiparvan* of the original *Bharata*, and it was Sūta who developed the lengthy episode of *Sabhāparvan* or *Dicing Hall*, *Sabha*-46–72, which dramatizes the game with the staking and losing of all by Yudhiṣṭhira, the lascivious humiliation of Draupadī by Duryodhana and his courtiers who drag her there in her *dishabille*, the inaction of the rest of the court, and her timely rescue by Krishna. The episode divides the dicing into two phases, the *Dyūta* and *Anudyūta*, of which the first contains the above orgy of victory and humiliation. Afterwards, the elders prevail upon Duryodhana to restore Yudhiṣṭhira and play another round, in which the Pandu are defeated again and exiled for twelve years followed by a year of living *incognito* on pain of repeating the first term.

The game itself is barely described in the epic. Rather, the sub-*parvan* concentrates on vassals bringing gifts, including gold dug up by ants, obviously, another attempt to exhibit new geographical awareness. However, the area these lists are familiar with is smaller than the *digvijaya* lists, i.e. the one that appeared with the Pandu *rājasūya*, showing that the earlier episode had been really added later.

Nature of the Game

Of the few works on the *Mahabharata* game, one considered the most reasonable is Heinrich Lüders's essay of 1906, no translation of which I have been able to get my hands on but which I have discussed with those who have read it in the original.[55] Lüders suggests that the game was indeed played in the manner as described in the epic—in each round of play a bet is placed, Śakuni, playing for the Kuru, calls a number, both he and Yudhiṣṭhira roll, and invariably Śakuni announces victory. Now, while Śakuni is seen naming the stakes and declaring victory in each of the 21 rounds, he is shown casting (or rolling) first only four times, and not in the other 17; Yudhiṣṭhira is *not even once* shown casting or rolling, but Śakuni is mentioned as throwing in return in a few of the remaining 17 rounds. Taken together, it probably means that Yudhiṣṭhira too did roll or cast first in a few of the 21 rounds at least.

Can we then surmise that they both named the stakes and rolled by turns, the thrower of the higher number winning the round? It has also been traditionally believed that Śakuni's dice were loaded, in some versions with lizards secreted within them who knew which way to turn and what scores to show! A survey of early Indian dice games shows several popular types, one of which was played with nuts of the *vibhītaka* (Hindi *baheḍā*) tree, so shaped that when thrown they fall on one of two distinguishable sides with equal probability. The *kapardaka* or cowrie shell also behaved similarly and became popular in later ages, but it is unlikely that the cowrie, a maritime product, was used by the *Mahabharata* people.[56] These games presumably involved more than tossing higher numbers, because tossing was a random event and needed no skill on the part of the players.

55 Heinrich Lüders, 'Das Würfelspiel im alten Indien', *Abhandlungen der königlich Gessellschaft der Wissenschaftlissen zu Göttingen,* Philologische–historischen Klasse, n.s. 9, no. 2, Berlin, 1907. Another paper on the dice game, a mimeograph by H.H. Ingalls for his class at Harvard, attempts to explain the dice game; this paper, mentioned in van Buitenen, *Mahābhārata* 2&3, n. 79, p. 29, is hard to come byand is also quite inaccurate. Also see M.A. Mehandale, 'Has the Vedic rājasūya any relevance for the epic game of dice?', in V. N. Jha (ed.), *Vidyā-vratin: Professor A. M. Ghatage Felicitation Volume*, Sri Garib Dass Oriental Series, No. 160, Delhi, Sri Satguru, 1992, pp. 61–67, and M.A. Mehendale, 'Is there only one version of the game of dice in the Mahābhārata?', in S.P. Narang (ed.), *Modern evaluation of the Mahābhārata, (Prof P. K. Sharma felicitation volume)*, Delhi, Nag Publishers, 1995, pp. 33–39.

56 In village and street corner games of modern India, played by children as well as by gamblers, tamarind seeds split into two are used. These too tend to behave in the same manner.

Another popular game was the *pāśaka*, known also as *pāśā*, which required some more skill and planning. This game was played with three cuboidal dice with figures from four to one (*kṛta*, *treta*, *dvāpara*, and *kali*) cut into its four long sides. Three distinct dice (different colours, material, or marks) were thrown, or the same one thrown thrice, giving a sequence of three digits; there could be 64 combinations, 324 being different from 234. B. B. Lal excavated some dice along with gamesmen from PGW sites, which may have been the type used.[57] Now, a number of different games from across the world use *pāśaka*-like or cubic dice, most of which are played on boards with movable coloured gamesmen like *tric-trac*, *ludo*, *pachisi*, and *chaupar*, the latter two in India.[58] Such games require planning, patience, and cunning in addition to throwing *good* numbers on the dice, which is not the same as throwing *high* numbers. These games also provide ample scope and opportunity of cheating. It is not clear at all as to what type of game was played in the *Mahabharata* and what the conditions of victory were.

In another episode of gaming in the epic, the *Nalopākhyāna*, a game is played between Nala, Ṛtuparṇa, and Puskara[59] in which skill seems to lie in quick estimation of number on the cast *vibhītaka* nuts, and determining quickly if the number thrown was a *kṛta* number, i.e. divisible by four. Lüders very hesitantly suggested that the Vedic game involved the casting of a certain number of dice on the board (*adhidevana*) by one gambler, which would be replied by the second gambler quickly estimating the throw and throwing another number which would add up to the first to a *kṛta* number. This explanation is not convincing. Quick estimation, an example of which is provided in Ṛtuparṇa's estimation of the number of nuts on a standing *vibhītaka* tree and then proving his accuracy to Nala, who was doubtful and wanted to cut down the tree to count them, by cutting down a sample branch and counting the nuts on it, is unlikely to work as the other gambler, especially when so much was at stake, would certainly insist on deliberate counting and verification. Also, throwing a second number that would add up with the first to create a *kṛta* number was an entirely random event, which could be modified by neither skill

57 B.B. Lal, 'Historicity of the *Mahābhārata*', p. 12, Plates III and IV.

58 There is the description in Amaracandra's *Bælabhærata* (II, 5, 10 sq) which shows the players playing a board game.

59 *Mbh*, III: 72.

nor trickery. Obviously, the *Mahabharata* game could not be as simplistic as this.

Now, the dice are called *akṣa,* i.e. an eye, in the epic, which suggests that they had spots or notches on them. This, alongside the fact that lizards could conceal themselves inside neither *vibhītaka* nor *cowrie*, but *could if they wanted to* inside longitudinal *pāśaka*s which have spots or eyes on them, suggests that the *pāśaka* game was the one being referred to. In a third gaming episode in the epic, the Mātsya chief Virāṭ angrily throws a die at Yudhiṣṭhira's (incognito as Kaṅka) face, drawing blood; as neither *cowrie* nor *vibhītaka* could draw blood, possibly metal or wooden *pāśaka* were meant. We may thus surmise that a form of game using *pāśaka* was used at court, but the exact nature of the game evades us. Some have even suggested that the rule was to catch the dice mid–air and toss them again (and again) till the desired number were thrown, but as this feat of arms is fantastic and quite improbable, we ought to look elsewhere. Just like it is impossible to decide which game—bridge, whist, or rummy—was being played from a statement that *players were slapping cards down on the table and declaring victory*, we cannot say any more than a board-game with dice was played whose rules are unknown to us. But we can certainly talk of the political significance of the game.

Political Significance of the Game

While it may not be too important to understand the exact nature of the game played except realise that it required skill in addition to chance, and also opportunity to cheat, it is important to understand why the Pandu, and other early rulers, would agree to stake so much and take such momentous political decisions on the outcome of a 'mere' game. It is known that early societies across the world used dicing to determine shares in spoils, allotment of pasturage, or distribution of conquered land;[60] dicing was a great leveller—everyone hoped to win but everyone faced equal probability of losing. No wonder an entire *ṛk* in the *Ṛgveda* condemns dicing.[61] That dicing was crucial to early IA political procedures is seen in the *akṣavāpa* or *akṣapāla*, or *keeper of the royal dice*, and the *bhāgadugha*

60 In Greek mythology, Zeus, Poseidon, and Hades play at dice to divide the universe among them. Among the Rupshu nomads, the chief or *goba* is selected among three candidates by the throw of dice. See Hagalia, 'Changing Rangeland Use', p. 31.

61 *ṚV*, X: 34.

or *distributor of milk*, being part of the nine *ratnīns* or important (gem-like) officials of the court.

Now, when after the first orgy of dicing in the *Sabhāparvan* the appalled elders at last decide to stop the game, it is *Yudhiṣṭhira* they *address their appeals to* and not the Kuru who had challenged him. In other words, it seems that it was the Pandu who were intent on the game. Van Buitenen has suggested a closer relation between the dicing episode and the Pandu *rājasūya*, suggesting that the dicing was part of the *rājasūya* which made it imperative for the Pandu to play.[62]

Dicing was indeed an integral part of several sacrificial rituals of the *Mantra* age. In the *agnyādheya*, 49 dice were divided between father and son, the former receiving 12, a *kṛta* amount. In the *rājasūya*, 400 dice were thrown in favour of the chief (a *kṛta* amount again), of which five were given to him though he did not play with them. Obviously, these formalised and ritualized procedures simulated victory of the performer in dice, just as his victories over cattle and men were simulated by touching cows with the tip of an arrow and shooting an arrow lightly at a man on a chariot.

The above rituals appear in the mature form of the sacrifice, as discussed by Heesterman, in which the *ratnin* officials like *akṣavāpa*, *bhāgadugha*, or *govikartṛ* appear to have lost their original importance and acted out.[63] In this sacrifice, the spot where the performer sat was the *nadir* of the universe (not used here in a negative sense), directly below its *zenith* where sat Brahmā. From here, he sent out armies in the four quarters, with the aim of ousting the reigning *samrāṭ*, securing the allegiance of the 'baronage', i.e. all *Kṣatriya* kings, and becoming *samrāṭ* himself.[64]

The Pandu *rājasūya* seems not to have been so ritualised or fossilised, primarily because the *digvijaya* episode seems to have been a later arrangement of their campaigns. Much of the expeditions come

62 J.A.B. van Buitenen, trans. and ed., *The Mahābhārata*, 2. The Book of the Assembly Hall, 3. The Book of the Forest, University of Chicago Press, 1975, pp. 16–21.

63 Heesterman mentions the possibility that these appointments were of Śūdra rank. Jan Heesterman, *The Ancient Indian Royal Consecration*, S'Gravenhage, Mouton and Co., 1957, pp. 49–57, especially n. 34 on p. 55.

64 Van Buitenen, *The Mahābhārata*, 2&3, p. 29. Killing Jarāsandha was supposed to at once win the allegiance of the 86 kings he had kept confined, and he himself.

across as spurious, as seen above, and only Arjuna's northern expedition appears authentic. Even Jarāsandha seems to have denoted a northern king. In other words, it appears that this *rājasūya* was from an older, less ritualised age, and it included a real military campaign astride the *Uttarāpatha*. Interestingly, we see that far from being targeted as their arch-rivals, Duryodhana (and significantly not Dhṛtarāṣṭra) receives the tributes brought by defeated vassals as *head of the clan*. This role of Duryodhana suggests that the *rājasūya* was probably a joint Kuru–Pandu venture, or probably a Kuru venture utilizing the Pandu as allies or agents, the primary military participant being the Pandu.

Now, if indeed such was the case, we are witnessing an extremely archaic episode here, from a time when the military element in the *rājasūya* had not yet fossilised and the performer not ritually *made to win* both war and dice games. Possibly, the gains, won largely by Pandu arms, were to be actually distributed by a real dice game, making it imperative for the Pandu to play. Apparently, the shrewd, sophisticated, and worldly-wise Kuru deputed Śakuni, a semi-nomadic Gāndhāra, ideally more adept at handling impetuous, rough-and-ready northerners like the Pandu, to play for them.[65] Whether they lost to trickery can no more be verified, but the defeat appears to have compelled the Pandu to revert to warband status, a reversal that they would have taken in their stride like any other nomad. Indeed, *jaṅgala* in the *Mahabharata* simply meant wilderness, and not dense, steamy forests as imagined. Even the wilderness need not be far from settlements, and the 'exile' was dramatically horrifying only for later, sedentary generations.

Further, the real political outcome of the game resulted from the *Anudyūta* section, while the *Dyūta* section, in which Yudhiṣṭhira staked and lost everything, including himself, his brothers, and their wife, only resulted in charged philosophical arguments. This makes it tempting to conclude that the former was an interpolation designed to cast the Pandu as wronged heroes, and bring to the front questions of logic and propriety. Further, the epic gives no answer to Draupadī's question, when dragged to the hall in her *dishabille*, if Yudhiṣṭhira's staking her *after he had himself lost his own independence*, was *legally* valid; it must be noticed that she,

65 There are other instances of dicing games being played by proxy. See Haricharan Bandyopadhyay, 'Akṣakrīḍā o Prāṇidyūta' (Bengali), in *Desh*, vol. 11, no. 1, Nov 1943, pp. 77–79.

or the epic, does not really ask whether it is valid at all to stake a woman. It is known that some Central Asian tribes, like the Hazlakh, were nations of gamblers who would stake wife, mother, and daughter when they got going. In fact, while the emotionally moving episode of Draupadī's humiliation may have been authentic, it was later dramatized in order to justify other events of the war, like Bhīma's drinking Duḥśāsana's blood, while her appeal to and rescue by Krishna was a step in the gradual deification of Krishna.

Interestingly, at the end of the battle when the Pandu catch up with the sole, surviving Duryodhana, Yudhiṣṭhira offers him a duel which would decide victory. This at once invites a reproach from Krishna who says that this would re-invoke the gamble—*dyūtārambham*.

The Exile and the Sojourn Incognito

The exile is discussed in the Āraṇyaka and *Virāṭ-parvan*s. Yardi suggests that in the *Bharata*, the exile had been treated briefly in the *Ādi* 55–57 itself, after which the narrative had moved to the preparations for the war in *Udyoga* 22, and that the exile was fleshed out by Sūta and Sauti who added the *Āraṇyaka* and *Virāṭ*. The *Āraṇyaka* is especially long, and it has been said that this is to simulate or replicate the duration of the exile by the bard or narrator.

Duration and Extent

The duration of exile, i.e. thirteen years, is close to the periods of exile in several other epics based on the theme of political exile and restoration that appeared in that period, viz. the IA *Ramayana*, the Kyrgyz *Manas*, or the Chinese *Zuozhuan*. In all of these, the protagonists—Rāma, Semetei, or Chönger, respectively—faced exile for between twelve and fourteen years, whereas in the fringe *Ramayana*s or the *Daśaratha Jātaka*, the exile was shorter or left vague. This suggests that the duration of exile was a formal one, and all that can be said is that the Pandu, after losing their position on the Divide and reverting to their peripatetic status, remained so for *several* years before managing to restore themselves.

What is more intriguing is that the Pandu seem to have covered a large part of the sub-continent, including the Deccan (*Araṇyaka* 99–140), in their peregrination. Almost all places and peoples of South Asia are mentioned, as are the many *tīrtha*s or shrines that they supposedly visited, their *māhātmya* or lore detailed in the *parvan*s. In other words, the Pandu peregrination shows greater familiarity with South Asia than was encountered in the *Dyūta* or *digvijaya* episodes described earlier. Is it possible that they had actually traversed such a large territory?

It is quite possible that the peregrination was limited to the area around the Divide. In the *Ghoṣayātrā* sub-*parvan* of the *Āraṇyaka-*, the Kuru visit their pastures to attend the annual branding of the royal herd, an ancient, worldwide custom marking the annual procession of herds to pastures.[66] While on this trip, they decide to mix business with pleasure and visit the Pandu encampment to taunt them on their fate, where they only end up shamefaced as they are attacked by the Gandharvas and have to be rescued by the Pandu. Though the second half of the story may have been added to glamorize the Pandu and provide comic relief, the episode, indicative of the pastoral nature of the *Mahabharata* people, also is geographically indicative. The Kuru herds would have been in pastures not far from their base, and if the Kuru could take a short detour and reach the Pandu encampment, the Pandu were not too far from the Kuru country either.

We know that in historical times, many of the tribes and peoples located earlier on the Divide moved away to the east and the south. Such people, who may indeed have had encounters with the Pandu, would have carried these recollections in their legends, as also their original place-names which they gave to their new places. Other peoples, who may have not encountered the Pandu at all, may have got themselves included to gain importance. These reasons were sufficient to give the peregrination a wide-ranging appearance. It can be seen that names are mixed up and associated with various places. Vāraṇāvata, near where the Pandu were attacked by arson, is identified with Barnawa in western U.P. This is a reasonable match as Barnawa lies close to the Pañcāla territory, where the Pandu repaired after the arson attempt. However, the curious little temple town of Lakhamandal at the confluence of the Yamuna and Tons in the lower Himalayas also claims the honour. Now, the Tons valley, i.e. Jaunsar, preserves archaic traditions like polyandry, shrines dedicated to Kuru heroes (though they have lately been converted to the Pandu and the

66 Like the annual transhumance practiced in the Pyrenees or the Cantabrian mountains, or the *kuch* migration of the Wakhi people of the Pamirs.

general pantheon under the influence of assimilation), and a reputation for sorcery in the rest of Garhwal. Possibly fugitive Kuru branches took shelter at Jaunsar after the war, also taking these traditions with them as also the recollection of the arson incident. Similarly, the story of Nala is associated with regions as far east as Nalhati and Dooars in Bengal.

And yet, the Pandu did have time on their hands and they may have easily hung about the *Aparānta* and the Deccan, and Deccan spots should not automatically be rejected as spurious. They could have indeed left at least some authentic legends in the Deccan. The pastoral Toda of Koṭagiri, an IA tribe, claim descent from Arjuna; the Pāṇḍya of Madurai may not have been as close to the Pandu as Parpola posits, however. The above makes it impossible to map the Pandu circuit.

Major Events

The Pandu camp was also within reached of Jayadratha, chief of Sindhu on the Indus and husband of Duryodhana's sister Duḥśalā. Jayadratha's attempt to abduct Draupadī starting a vendetta with the Pandu, and serves as a precursor to the major role that Jayadratha played in two episodes of the war. Episodes such as these are used to justify some or the other of the actions during the defining moments in the battle.

Two of the most significant episodes during the exile, or at least related in the Āraṇyaka, are, firstly, the independent adventures of Arjuna in search of weapons, and secondly, the miraculous birth of Karṇa.

Soon after the exile, Arjuna goes off on his own to seek divine weapons from his father Indra in what was another of his independent expeditions. Indra redirects him to Śiva, and when Arjuna approaches the mountains of Śiva he runs into a wizened hunter, the *Kirāta*, and fights with him over the boar they both shoot at the same moment. Arjuna is unable to beat the old hunter till he realises that he is none other than Śiva; the latter, pleased with Arjuna's prowess, presents him with the *Pāśupatāstra*. The story shows an increasing importance of the Śaiva religion—Indra redirects Arjuna to Śiva to get the *most potent* weapon, somewhat indicating the superiority of the *Pāśupata* or *Śaiva* religion over that of Indra. In fact, Yardi has detected a strong Śaiva influence in the early layers of the epic alongside the Bhāgavata religion, while Parpola sees the Pandu as Shiva worshippers from the presence of tridents or *triśūla*s in the megaliths. However, it must be noted that Śiva here is neither the *Neolithic culture god* associated with the Earth–Mother, agrarian rites, phallus, and the bull, nor the Aryan cult god, the idiosyncratic Rudra, but the Śiva of *the Kirāta* associated with *Bhūta*s or Bhoṭas, Mongoloid mountaineers of the Himalayas and *Cirrhidae* by the Greeks.[67] In other words, this was the cult of the Himalayan *shaman* associated with the hunt, snow, and eternal silence.

When Arjuna returns to thank Indra at his court, he has to resist the amorous advances of Urvaśī, arguing that she, in being a progenitor of his race (as wife of Purūravas), was a mother to him. He earns the curse of emasculation from a spurned Urvaśī, which however is ameliorated on Indra's intervention—he stood to variously lose his virility, become a woman, or a eunuch, for a period of one year which he could chose himself. This was the foundation of the Bṛhaṇṇaḍā/Bṛhaṇṇaḷā episode later.

The next important theme accounts for the 'virgin' birth of Karṇa. In return for having 'looked after' well the sage Durvāsā in her maidenhood during his visit to her father's court, Kuntī had been granted a boon which enabled her to call up any god she pleased. While it was this boon that had enabled her and her co–wife Mādrī to call up the gods and sire their five sons, it is 'revealed' now that she had called up Sūrya the Sun to test her new boon immediately after receiving it, and had ended up conceiving Karṇa. She had, as per the tale, abandoned the baby boy, floating it away in a casket on a river. The casket was retrieved by a 'poor' Sūta, not to be confused with the Sūta Lomaharṣaṇa but an unnamed chariot–maker, whose wife Rādhā brought him up.

This disadvantaged, pre-nuptial birth, and the fact that his natural armour given to him by his father was tricked away by Indra by exploiting his legendary generosity, cast Karṇa in the tragic hero mould. Even the miraculous spear he obtained in return for the armour, with which he meant to kill Arjuna, would be used up in the killing of another warrior later.

Though some role of Kuntī in his birth may not be denied, concluding that Karṇa was her maiden son by Durvāsā himself is a little too direct. Interestingly, while the 'secret' is revealed to him twice, once by Krishna and then again by Kuntī, even on the first instance he states that he is well

67 Periplus, in Majumadar, *Classical Accounts*, p. 307.

aware of the story of his birth. We have earlier seen Karṇa as leader of one of the many charioteering nations on the *Uttarāpatha*; it is probable that the redoubtable Kuntī, governess of her sons' fortunes, was trying a ruse to co-opt him into the Pandu lineage.

What is of significance is that Karṇa was known by the matronymic *Rādheya*, and it is along the mother's line, i.e. *not as son of Pāṇḍu but that of Kuntī*, that the Pandu attempt to assimilate him. Such grafting of princes as sons abandoned in their childhood is a common motif in early legends, like in the story of Paris of Ilium.

Other Episodes

In addition, later redactors provided much didactic padding that had little to do with the plot, like the encounter of Savitṛ–Satyavat with Yama, or the quizzing of Yudhiṣṭhira by the Yakṣa. The latter is a common mythological motif wherein the fate of a man's dependents hangs in balance as he enters in a contest of wits, like in the Sphinx–Oedipus riddles or the story of Ahikar, or even where Alexander quizzing the gymnosophists.[68] In this episode, Yudhiṣṭhira's wit rescues his dependants who had been poisoned as a result of drinking from the Yakṣa's pool. In another such episode, it rescues not only Bhīma from the coils of a python or *ajagara*, but also the python who was none other than Nahuṣa, an ancestor of the house, who was suffering from a curse.[69]

In many episodes, Yudhiṣṭhira serves as dummy to help brings out societal lessons like duties of the king, of the wife in a patriarchal household, or of the son. Episodes such as these recast him from the hot-headed leader of a warband into a pious, righteous, and composed man

68 Arora, 'Onesikritos', pp. 76–77. Alexander's interaction with and supposed admiration of Indian sophists was increasingly dramatized, from Plutarch's *Alexander* onwards, into direct confrontation with gymnosophists like Dandamis or Mandanis. What originally was philosophical query now becoming a witty quiz wherein Alexander asked each of the ten captured gymnosophists a query bordering on riddle, warning them that wrong or too clever answers could lead to execution; he was supposedly so impressed with their answers that he not only restored their liberty but also loaded them with presents.

69 Chandrashekhar Gupta, 'Yaksha Cult in the *Mahābhārata*,' in Ajay Mitra Sastri (ed.), *Mahābhārata: End of an Era*, pp. 243–53, shows the popularity of the Yakṣa cult during the period of composition of the epic. The Yakṣa cult may have arisen after Aryan and pre–Aryan deities like Kubera and Maṇibhadra, worshipped by traders, caravaneers and merchants were fused.

forced to listen to advice regarding kingship which he had little use of, often first made to ask inane questions to precipitate his predicaments. Yardi has shown that parts of the *Āraṇya(ka)* with little to do with the plot had been added by Harivaṃśakāra(s), like the Vaiṣṇava legends and tales—the deluge and the fish, the *Rāmopakhyāna*, or Bhima's encounter with Hanumat. These stories are all nested in the frame–in–tale style. Yudhiṣṭhira, ruing his misfortune in being exiled, is told the story of the misfortunes of Rāma who was similarly exiled.

The Sojourn Incognito

The *Ādiparvan*'s brief account of the Pandu sojourn at the Mātsya court is developed into an independent volume, the *Virāṭ-parvan*, later. The Mātsya, enemies of the Bharata in the BOTK[70] and called *Vrātya* elsewhere, resided in historical times in the Jaipur–Alwar region astride the *Aparānta*, where the town of Bairat is identified with Virāṭ–nagara. As per Sūta's matter-of-fact description, the Pandu took up *incognito* positions as household officials at the court of the *Virāṭ*, a regnal title and not a proper name.

Sūta also tells of Bhīma killing the Mātsya commander-in-chief Kīcaka when he tried to get fresh with Draupadī, and of the climax of the sojourn when the Kuru and their Trigarta allies raiding Mātsya cattle are trounced by Arjuna and Bhīma. As per Yardi, the dramatic episodes of Bhīma rescuing Virāṭ when captured by the Trigarta, and Arjuna driving the chariot of the panicking prince Uttara to the forest, retrieving their weapons cached in the shape of a *bundle containing a corpse* on the Śamī tree and then driving back to the battlefield, were added by Sautī. The Pandu disguise however was blown by the valiant acts, and *Virāṭ* offered Arjuna the hand of his daughter Uttarā. As he had been teaching the arts to the young lady in the guise of Bṛhaṇṇaḍā the eunuch, Arjuna accepted it as more befitting for Abhimanyu, his son by Subhadrā. We see here another matrimonial alliance being sealed with a strong people. The Pandu now camp at Upaplavya in Mātsya country and prepare for war.

It is known that most early polities grew out of households, and many early states were extensions of the royal household. The Mongol imperial government, for instance, grew out of the *keshiq*, i.e. the household, its

70 *ṚV*, VII: 18.6.

most intimate following being the *keshiqchiyān*. The same was the case in Europe, where political titles like chamberlain and chancellor grew out of household officials. Thus, use of appellations for household officials—Yudhiṣṭhira as dicing companion, Bhīma as cook, Arjuna as danseuse, Nakula and Sahadeva as keepers of the ranch and stables, and Draupadī as *Sairindhṛ* or lady-in-waiting—does not automatically imply menial positions.

Significantly, Kīcaka, whom Bhīma killed along with his 99 brothers for pawing Draupadī, was brother of Sudeṣṇā, the Mātsya queen, who was complicit in his lust. Both siblings have been called *sūta*. Kīcaka's adherents tried to burn Draupadī as *satī* at his funeral.[71] It is reasonable to presume that the Kīcaka were a mercenary people, like Karṇa, represented in historical times by the *Vrātya* Kīcaka mercenaries from whom medieval Bacchal Rajputs claimed descent in addition to claiming descent from Veṇa. In this light, it is reasonable to interpret the above as the Mātsya having replaced a troublesome mercenary, the Kīcaka, with the more reliable Pandu, who help them resist the Kuru and Trigarta. While Nakula and Sahadeva, of Mādra stock, were natural choices for being in charge of the stables, Yudhiṣṭhira's position as 'gaming partner', in which capacity he was once struck by *Virāṭ* with a pair of dice, may indicate that he held the appointment of keeper of the dice, i.e. *akṣapāla*.

Diplomacy, Negotiations, and the Battle-lines

The epic gives the subsequent diplomatic negotiations between the Pandu and the Kuru an intensely moralistic tone, casting the Kuru as obstinate and un-accommodative and thereby responsible for the war. To Yardi, these were later embellishments to the curt narrative that appear in a few chapters in the *Udyogaparvan* of the *Bharata*, which contained only the embassy of Sañjaya sent by Dhṛtarāṣṭra to cajole the Pandu with some sops, but which was informed that the Pandu are quite ready for battle.

As per Yardi, it was Sūta who dramatized the episode with details of the wedding of Abhimanyu and Uttarā, selection of an envoy at the wedding, the embassy to the Kuru court which is informed that the Kuru would themselves be sending Sañjaya shortly, and the anxious wait of Dhṛtarāṣṭra for the outcome of Sañjaya's mission when he is incited by

71 *Mbh,* IV: 23.8.

his council, the *kaṇika*. The *kaṇika* lecture Dhṛtarāṣṭra on the importance of expediency with the help of the embedded story of the jackal which tricked several animals to cooperate in hunting a deer but then made them fight among themselves and leave him in possession of the deer, the upshot of which is—when possible stick to the correct path, when not, innovate, when in a tight corner, use any means to get out. Such advice, portrayed as close to Dhṛtarāṣṭra's heart, is contrasted by the futile moralistic chastisement given to him by Vidura and others. The mention of a *Brāhmaṇa* envoy from the Pāñcāla court at this stage represents the memory that the Pāñcāla also entered the diplomatic fray.

The most spectacular episode of recasting of the 'peaceably inclined' Pandu in the 'wronged' mould was the embassy of Krishna, which, as per Yardi, was very briefly mentioned in the *Bharata* but which was greatly enlarged by Sūta and Sautī. Sūta introduced the rather curious justification of Krishna's choosing to join the Pandu (the waking god, discussed above). Sautī recast the embassy into a family drama, describing at length the sumptuous welcome given by Duryodhana, the intense, morally charged speeches at the Kuru court where even Gāndhāri tries to reason with her sons in addition to some long dead and gone sages, Krishna's refusal to accept Duryodhana's hospitality, his calling upon the Kuru to detain him and make peace, his escape after displaying his dazzling *Viśvarūpa* when Duryodhana's aides attempt to detain him, and the frugal meal he takes with Kuntī and Vidura afterwards. Sautī also includes Krishna's attempt to persuade Karṇa to join the Pandu, disclosing to him the 'secret' of his birth and enticing him with the position of the eldest brother and first of Draupadī's husbands. Karṇa would remain similarly unmoved to Kuntī's entreaties later, to whom he makes the concession that he would kill only Arjuna, who had always been rude and disrespectful towards him, and none of the other brothers.

As per tradition, the Pandu demand 'merely' five 'villages', even which the Kuru are disinclined to part with. From local legends, these villages are identified by B.B. Lal as Pāṇiprastha, Soṇiprastha, Vṛkaprastha, Indraprastha, and Tilaprastha, which are the modern Panipat, Sonepat, Bhagpat, Delhi, and Tilpat. These are all fords on the Yamuna, giving which away was akin to surrendering control of the river.[72]

72 B.B. Lal, 'Historicity of the *Mahābhārata*', pp. 3–4.

However, these names are as per local traditions only, Soṇiprastha being anachronistic as it is associated with king Soṇi who was 13th in descent from Arjuna. The names given in the *Mahabharata* are ambiguous, being Kuśasthala, Āsandi, Vṛkasthala, Vṛṇāvṛta, and 'one more place' which we may presume to be the original 'base' of Indraprastha.[73] Of these, Kuśasthala seems to be a place on the Ghaggar, Āsandi the camp–capital in Kurukṣetra, Vṛkasthala identical with Vṛkaprastha or Bhagpat, possibly Kakar in Bhagpat district which has yielded Hastinapura–style pottery, and Vṛṇāvṛta with Vāraṇāvata or Barnawa east of the Yamuna. Plotting both sets of names on the map shows that whereas Lal's five spots are *along* the Yamuna, giving control of the river, the other set forms a wide west–east traverse of fords from the Ghaggar–Sarasvatī route, more popular than the *Uttarāpatha* at the time of the *Mahabharata*,[74] along modern Hansi and Hissar, across Kurukṣetra, the Divide, and the *doābā*, up to the country of the Pañcāla. In other words, rather than seeking 'merely' five spots, the Pandu, who once held only one spot of Indraprastha, had now become emboldened enough to demand much more.

We have already seen that nomad sovereignty was reckoned not in terms of *square miles held* but *linear miles freely traversed*, making fords and crossings important. This is seen in the association of both Viśvāmitra and Vaśiṣṭha with them, as also the BOTK being set on river crossings. In such a scenario, the concern of anyone east of the Divide would be to keep open their access to the west, i.e. the Indus and the *Uttarāpatha*, if for nothing else then at least to get high quality horses which were not easily bred in the plains. This would have been reason enough for the Pañcāla, then being steadily hemmed in by the Kuru, to ally with the Pandu. The Pandu were also the ideal choice for Yadu branches on the *Aparānta* and *Dakṣiṇāpatha*, like the Vṛṣṇi or the Bhoja, who wanted to get at Mathura.

On the other hand, the Kuru, who held the Divide, were naturally averse to their heartland being split and separated from their Śūrasena

73 See V.B. Athavale, 'The Movements of the Pandavas', *Annals of the BORI*, vol. 29, 1948, pp. 85–95.

74 To Dani, the Bolan and Gomal passes brought the caravans to the lush green plains astride the Indus. From here, caravans passed along the valley of the Sarasvatī, which had sufficient water and grass for camping, to the Divide. This route, which was used by Baladeva to arrive from Saurāṣṭra on the penultimate day of the war, was also used by Razzia and Tĕmur in their operations. See A.H. Dani, 'Origins of Bronze Age Cultures in the Indus Basin: A Geographical Perspective', *Expedition*, Winter, 1975, pp. 12–18.

allies in Mathura. They were also the natural choice for tribes on the *Uttarāpatha* and Indus—Trigarta, Gāndhāra, Yaudheya, Ambaṣṭha, Mādra, Vṛṣadarbha, Bahlīka, Śibi, and Sindhu–Sauvīra, and even nomadic Yadu groups like the Śālva—all keen on gravitating to the Divide. At the same time, Kuru allies on their east, like the Aṅga or Kaliṅga, have been called Ānava,[75] while their Yavana[76] and *Mleccha* allies have been called Turvaśa, showing that Pañcajana elements were still on the Kuru side. On the other hand, the Pandu and the Pañcāla have strong Bharata affiliations, with only small Yadu and Anu components like the Vṛṣṇi, Kekaya, or Mātsya.

Taken together, the battle-lines start making sense now. Though the chivalric as also the endemic motif of vengeance may have been the motivation for some of its individual participants, the war was fought over reasons more significant than family vendetta alone. However, such macro reasons are however difficult to discern in epic poetry, which is more intent on glamorising chivalric elements of rivalry. This is the case in the *Iliad* as well. Menelaus's motivation was the title to Sparta, though the epic makes it appear more as the jealousy of a cuckolded husband. The motivation of the other contestants was the access to the Black Sea, which Troy was able to monopolise because it held the only harbour (on the Scamander) where ships had to wait out the gales in the torrential passage through the Dardanelles, but the epic portrays their motivation as the vow that all suitors for Helen's hand had taken, which was to help her winner recover her in case she was taken away. Obviously, this oath, such as which were not entirely abnormal in chivalric ages, was introduced later, by when the idea of matrilineal inheritance had become socially disturbing.

In the *Gītā*, Krishna states that Arjuna's wishes and concerns were insignificant compared to the reasons for which *he had arranged the battle*. This, and other reasons, have made many see Krishna's role as primal in bringing about the war. In fact, Patil sees Krishna, who went on to become the most popular god of India offering the philosophy of transcendental salvation (*Bhakti-yoga*), as the pioneer of the *gaṇasaṅgha* system which '*combined equality by birth and slavery by birth in its most developed form*'.[77]

75 This is intriguing, because the Ānava were mostly associated with the west.

76 *ṚV*, VI: 20.45.

77 Sharad Patil, 'Myth and Reality of Ramayana and Mahabharata', pp. 71–72.

It is easy to exaggerate Krishna's role, just as it is erroneous to call him *pioneer* of the *gaṇasaṅgha* system to which he was as much heir and inheritor as several other participants. Likewise, there is no way the monarchical opposite can be attributed to the Kuru—not only the Kuru but most of their allies were nearly *gaṇasaṅgha*, even *vrātya*, while it is only the post-war Kuru–Pandu, outcome of Krishna's efforts, that sponsored or patronised monarchical forms of government. Thus, though we can suppose that Krishna had had some role in bringing about the war, and that the war was fought for reasons greater than personal vendetta, it would not have been fought for more than immediate tribal goals; one should not fall into the socio-political trap of assigning long-term political agenda to the participants on either side.

Why Kurukṣetra

Kurukṣetra is the strategic junction of the *Uttarāpatha* and the Ghaggar corridor, south of which the passage towards the Divide is defiled between the Yamuna and the scrub deserts of Aravalli. Armies on their way to Delhi have always passed this corridor, which had led to it seeing many battles—Sirhind 40 kilometres northwest of Ambala, Ambala 40 kilometres north of Kurukṣetra, Taraori 20 kilometres south of Kurukṣetra, Karnal another 20, Panipat 15 kilometres south of Karnal, and Badli-ki-Sarai just north of Delhi. At several of these fields, like Taraori and Panipat, more than one battle has been fought. In the nineteenth century, the EIC used Karnal and Ambala as fulcrums for defence against the then current bogey, an Afghan–Russian advance, and also as bases for operations in Punjab and Afghanistan. That a battle among the immigrating Aryan tribes would have been fought at Kurukṣetra is therefore not at all out of the ordinary. What disturbs the above scheme however is that Kurukṣetra is at least 100 kilometres from Hastināpura, the capital of the Kuru in the epic.

Now, armies in chivalric ages often did meet by appointment as they lacked wherewithal to march and counter-march for too long. At the same time, most armies involved in the epic war seem to have been nomadic, who turned up at unexpected places to fight—the Egyptians complained that the Levantine nomads never disclosed when and where they would fight next. Either of these reasons may account for the engagement occurring so far from the 'capital'.

Now, the epic always refers to the Kuru court as (being at) *Āsaṅdivat* or *throne place*, which suggests a camp–capital and not a fixed city. Hastināpura, or the mound near Meerut identified by Lal as the Kuru capital, has yielded PGW but little evidence of civic constructions more than defensive walls, which is exactly how Erdosy posited cities of 1st millennium B.C. India to have commenced,[78] i.e. as earthen mounds (*vapra, caya*) surrounded by walls with a veneer of baked bricks. Such a walled enclosure would contain the fortified camp–capitals of sedenising nomad chiefs, made of tents and temporary clay–bamboo sheds or śālā, who dominated the surrounding country. When the fugitive Pandu at Ekacakra saw the Pañcāla capital of Kāmpilya for the first time, they had indeed called it *skandhāvara* or encampment.

This discussion at once removes the Kuru 'capital' from a fixed place. We may surmise that, at the time of the war, Hastināpura (the mound near Meerut) was a fortified outpost in the contested borderlands with the Pañcāla, while the Kuru 'camp–capital' or Āsaṅdivat, i.e. the base of their chiefs, was still in their heartland of Kurukṣetra. It was only after the war, during the *janapada* period, that Hastināpura emerged as a fixed capital of 'Kuru', one of the three provinces of the Kuru people. The pompously eulogising descriptions of Hastināpura are, like those of the cities of the *Ramayana*, from no earlier than post–Buddhist times, and have been shown by Hopkins to be not descriptions at all but phrases designed to aid narration from memory.[79]

78 George Erdosy, 'The Origin of Cities in the Ganges Valley', *Journal of the Economic and Social History of the Orient*, vol. 28, no. 1, 1985, pp. 81–109, especially pp. 95–96.

79 Hopkins, 'Ruling Caste', pp. 174–75; Hopkins points out a curious inversion—not only are descriptions based on variations of stock phrases (*saprākārāṭṭālikā*, i.e. *with walls and bastions*), while they generally are from a period *after* that of the epic events, but before that of the period of composition which was the late first millennium B.C., as though the poets '*even then did not describe what ... existed, but what had been set as a poetically correct method of description, and preserved as a model*'.

CHAPTER 6

The Armies, and Nature of Combat

Organization and Deployment, the *Vyūha*

The epic says that at Kurukṣetra, the Kuru had eleven *akṣauhini*s or divisions which were deployed on the west, under the overall command of Bhīṣma, and the Pandu had seven divisions that were deployed on the east. Of the seven Pandu divisions, three were commanded by Dhṛṣṭadyumna, Drupada, and Śikhaṇḍin, i.e. the Pañcāla, two by Sātyaki and Cekitāna, i.e. the Vṛṣṇi, one by Virāṭ the Mātsya, and one by Bhīma. This suggests that the Pandu were a small component of the alliance and the Pañcāla, who also held overall command—Drupada's son Dhṛṣṭadyumna being the overall commander—were the largest. This seems to bear out Lassen's position that the war was originally not as much Kuru–Pandu as it was Kuru–Pañcāla, though Hopkins disagreed with this.[1]

The war begins with a dramatic and poignant episode that has been crucial to the Hindu faith. On the morning of the first day's battle, reluctant to shed the blood of his kin and doubtful of the merits of a victory tainted with their deaths, Arjuna refuses to fight and has to be brought about by Krishna, his charioteer, the justifications and advice rendered by him being called the *Bhagavad–Gītā*, i.e. the *song of the god*. When the battle commences after this episode, there is little that sets apart one day from another through the first ten days. Each morning, the armies turn out[2] in elaborate arrays or *vyūha*s, clash through the day, and disengage at retreat. Through the day, hero–warriors and princes move about randomly, seeking

1 Hopkins, 'Ruling Caste', pp. 59.

2 Hopkins, 'Ruling Caste', start times of days' activities vary, sometimes the soldiers arising before sunrise, sometimes with it, and so on.

out and challenging one another. Combats between hero–warriors, largely in the form of archery duel from speeding chariots, are accompanied by much speechifying and posturing, and at least lip service to rules of chivalry and fair combat. It is only when chariots are immobilised or shattered do warriors dismount to fight with contact weapons, but are soon extricated by their companions or replacement chariots are driven up. These battles are thus different from those of the *Iliad*, where warriors are disdainful of archery and mostly fight dismounted, with heavy spears, swords, and even huge rocks, using chariots only to get about on the battlefield.

A Survey of the Vyūhas and a Run-through of the Battle

The *vyūha*s themselves are a spectacular aspect of these supposed battles. They are described with curious, often zoomorphic names, the simile carried to the locations of contingents and warriors forming necks, wings, beak, or eyes, or tails. Surveying these formations in the epic, we see that on the first day, the Kuru deploy an *unnamed* array which has only been called defensive, and which Hopkins thinks was a circle.[3] The Pandu respond by deploying the *vajra* or *thunderbolt*, which was probably a column modified into a needle. As per the descriptions, Bhīṣma buzzes Arjuna immediately after contact, though they were in distant part of their respective *vyūha*s, which must have thrown everything into confusion. At the same time, combat after initial contact is everywhere called *tumūla* or tumult, i.e. melee, which shows that formations disintegrated quickly. Several minor warriors were killed on the first day, including Virāṭ's sons Uttara and Śveta.

On the second day, the Pandu deploy the *krauñca* or *stork*, to which the Kuru respond with something called *mahāvyūha* or *great-array*,[4] but which the epic does not detail. Detailed descriptions are provided only for some arrays, like the *krauñca*, whose wings, neck, beak, and eyes are said to have been formed by various contingents and knights—it is such descriptions that have encouraged the schematic diagrams of Sensharma. The elephants, in the *krauñca* diagram by Sensharma, are deployed at tips of the wings. The highlight of the second day's fight is Arjuna's combat with Bhīṣma wherein the former is pinned, and extricated only when Sātyaki kills Bhīṣma's charioteer and makes his horses bolt.

3 Hopkins, 'Ruling Caste', p. 206.

4 *Mbh*, VI: 51.10–11.

On the third day, the Kuru deploy the *garuḍa* or *eagle*. In keeping with the metaphor, warriors are deployed at its beak, eyes, wings; many scholars, like Hopkins, suggest that this was a rhomboid with its points towards and away from the enemy. The Pandu respond with an *ardhacandra* or crescent, with Arjuna and Bhīma on the horns. Though Hopkins, in light of the fewer number of Pandu *akṣauhiṇi*s, has deemed the envelopment idea as ludicrous, smaller but better handled forces have been known to envelop larger ones successfully; enveloping the Kuru might indeed have been the aim of such a deployment. Of the major actions of this day was Sātyaki getting cast off his chariot by Śakuni, and his extrication by Abhimanyu. Also, on another part of the field, Krishna upbraids Arjuna for fighting Bhīṣma half-heartedly, in exasperation running to kill Bhīṣma himself with his discus till only just dissuaded by Arjuna.

On the fourth day, the opponents deploy *vyūha*s ambiguously described as *array like a cloud*, and *an array unseen before*.[5] Combat is monotonous and repetitive, one aspect of note being the ambush of Abhimanyu by several Kuru warriors from which he is extricated by the timely arrival of Arjuna. Also, Bhīma, when stunned by a blow, is extricated by his son Ghaṭotkac who fights with *Rākṣa* savagery; the Kuru fear that Ghaṭotkac will grow even more powerful with nightfall.

On the fifth day, the Kuru deploy the *makara* or mythical *crocodile* or *gargoyle*, its eyes, snout, head, trunk, legs, and tail staffed by various warriors. Hopkins has seen this array as two triangles joined at the apex, the broadside of the triangles towards the enemy. The Pandu attempt to pierce this array with the *śyena* or *hawk*, called '*king of all arrays*'. Bhīma appears to have been in the van because he plunges straight for Bhīṣma, from whose grip he has to be extricated by Arjuna. Later in the day, Sātyaki is attacked by Bhūriśravas and his chariot dashed to pieces, and is just extricated by Bhīma as Bhūriśravas attacks him with the sword. Bhīṣma, while wreaking havoc among Sātyaki's divisions, turns away when Śikhaṇḍin attacks him together with Bhīma; Droṇa manages to stop Śikhaṇḍin and make him withdraw.

The sixth day has repetitions of *vyūha*s, with the Pandu deploying the *makara* and the Kuru the *krauñca*. The major actions on this day are Bhima's two attacks on the Kuru line, once on a chariot, which falters and

5 *Mbh*, VI: 60.7,11.

he has to be extricated by the Kekaya (the only people of the *Uttarāpatha* on the Pandu side), and again on foot with mace, wreaking great havoc, till he becomes surrounded. He is reinforced by Dhṛṣṭadyumna and then extricated by twelve Pandu warriors led by Abhimanyu.

The *maṇḍala* or annular array of the Kuru of the seventh day, with the king in the centre and its borders 'packed with chariots, elephants and swordsmen', is pierced by the Pandu *thunder* or *vajra*, which, as no needle shaped modifications are mentioned, appears to have been a column. Important among the day's encounters are Śikhaṇḍin's defeat by Droṇa's son Aśvatthāmā, and Śalya's defeat at the hands of his nephews Nakula and Sahadeva. The Kuru array on the eighth day is un-described and only called *sāgaropama*, i.e. *like the sea*; the Pandu counter this with the *śṛṅgāṭaka* or 'horned', which Hopkins thinks as a triangle with the base as van. On this day, Irāvān, Arjuna's son by Ulūpī, is killed but only after severely mauling Duryodhana's cavalries under the demoniac Alambuṣa. Also, Ghaṭotkac attacks Duryodhana and the latter is just saved when the Vaṅga king interposes an elephant between the two.

The action seems to heat up hereafter, with the *vyūha*s on the ninth and tenth days being called nothing more than *devilish* or *infernal*.[6] On the ninth day, Arjuna half-heartedly resists Bhīṣma's onslaughts, exasperating Krishna into once again rushing at Bhīṣma, this time with his whip. Arjuna persuades him not to break his pledge of not wielding arms, promising to slay Bhīṣma the following day. On the tenth day Arjuna advances, supposedly 'protecting' Śikhaṇḍin in the van. Bhīṣma turns away on seeing Śikhaṇḍin and is peppered by the arrows of the two, of which he supposedly could identify which Arjuna's were because they bit his flesh sharper than those of the other. At last, porcupined with bolts, he falls headlong on the battlefield, where he remains immobilised till the end of battle. This is the first case of any major warrior being incapacitated or killed.

The course of combat changes hereafter, with the *vyūha*s become schematic variants of the *wedge and circle* motif and no more given fabulous, zoomorphic names. On the eleventh day, Droṇa who had assumed command of the Kuru, combines wedges into a rhomboid, calling it *suparṇa* which, like *garuḍa*, meant eagle. The Pandu counter

6 *Asurān akarod vyūhān paiśācān atha rākṣasān. Mbh,* VI: 16.

this with the *krauñca*. On the twelfth day, the Trigarta attack Arjuna in *crescent* formation,[7] while Droṇa advances in 'full array' (*vyūḍhānīka*) which the Pandu meet with the *maṇḍalārdha* or semi-circle. The Kuru array of the thirteenth day is the notorious *cakra-vyūha* or wheel, whose impregnability has been made much of and which shall be discussed later. On the fourteenth day they defend Jayadratha with a wedge with a circle at its end, within the latter there being another *concealed formation*. The Pandu *vyūha*s on these days, if any, are not named.

Combat of the fourteenth day rolls into the fifteenth; on the sixteenth day the Kuru deploy the *makara* and the Pandu reply with the *ardhacandra*. The seventeenth sees the Kuru deploying the *Bārhaspatya*, i.e. one of the arrays of Bṛhaspati, the Machiavellian counsel of the gods, which was countered by a '*suitable array*' (*nītir vidhīyatām*). The Kuru array of Śalya on the eighteenth day is not named, but has mouth, arms, flanks, and so on, to counter which the Pandu advance in *line*, i.e., *anīka*.

Organizations

The most obvious correlation between *vyūha*s and subsequent action is that there seldom is any. Combat is largely independent of *vyūha*s—warriors deployed at opposing ends fly at one another immediately after commencement of combat. Battles lose all semblance of order immediately after contact, turning into melees wherein heroes move independently. As Bhīma was in command of the Pandu *akṣauhiṇi*, it is presumable that Arjuna was part of it; yet on the day the crescent–array is deployed, they appear on opposite tips of the crescent. Also, while various levies—those of Bhagadatta or the king of Daśārṇa, Ghaṭotkac or Alambuṣa, or Hūṇa, Yavana, and Śaka—are seen forming the neck or head of such and such array (Śaka, Yavana, and Kamboja form the neck of *suparṇa*), in the battle narratives they drift in an out of action without order. And yet the appeal of the *vyūha* is so strong that even G.D. Bakshi, who started with distinguishing between those named after geometrical shapes and those after animal archetypes, and tried using a functional approach to understand them by a needlessly detailed description of the German *Laager*, then willingly suspends his disbelief and discusses the *makara* as designed by Sensharma, without pausing to think why the Aryans, a mountain and pastoral people, would design a *vyūha* that from the air

7 *vyūhyānīkaṅ candrākāraṅ*, *Mbh*, VII: 18. 1.

resembles a baleen whale on its side with mouth ajar and tail doubled back! He also overlooked the fact that the *makara* was not a whale but a mythical gargoyle that combined features of crocodile, eel, and fish.[8]

We must remember that semi–pastoral folk like the *Mahabharata* people would have possessed little organizational ability to deploy complex, zoomorphic *vyūha*s, in addition to having little use for them in battle. Yet, the concept must not be thrown out with the proverbial bathwater, as geometrically defined arrays, suited for defending, outflanking, marching obliquely, changing orientation, and so on, have always been used by armies and theorists to explain battle-formations and their purposes. As early as the Vedic times, tribal militia subunits like the *sardha* or *gaṇa* used elementary *vyūha*s; *vyūha*s are associated with the ancient Uśanas, Bṛhaspati, and the Ādityas.[9] While even no formation is also a formation, armies would definitely have deployed in block, like the mid-1st millennium *caturaṅga* which was a gigantic oblong of infantry fronted by elephants, or in oblongs and arrowheads like in the well-documented Chinese battle of Chengpu against the Chu in 634 B.C.[10] Philip of Macedon broke the monolithic oblong of the *phalanx* into the *quadruple phalanx*, which was more agile and manoeuvrable and could advance obliquely, while Jomini used geometrically shaped deployments to build his theories on warfare. Thus, despite their outlandish names and descriptions, one can still discern an underlying tactical scheme in the *vyūha*s.

At a few places, *vyūha*s do have relevance to ensuing battle—the Pandu launch the crescent to envelope the rhombus, and the needle to pierce the inverted triangle, while the Kuru deploy the wheel or circle to ambush Abhimanyu or defend Jayadratha. Also, at times a side detects the opponent's array and quickly redeploys to *counter* it, even while in contact. For example, on the sixth day the Pandu quickly reorganise themselves into a *needle-array* to extricate some warriors that had been surrounded by

8 Bakshi, *Mahabharata*, pp. 50–67.

9 P.C. Chakravarti, *The Art of War in Ancient India*, Low Priced Publications, 2010, First Published 1941, pp. 112–4. Of the poetic licence in naming *vyūha*s—demoniac, angelic, irresistible, and so on—Hopkins notes that on the Hindu battlefield, 'the irresistible force was always meeting the immovable body'. See Hopkins, 'Ruling Caste', p. 203.

10 Frank A, Kierman, 'Phases and Modes of Combat in Early China', in Frank A. Kierman and John K. Fairbank (eds.), *Chinese Ways in Warfare*, Harvard University Press, Cambridge, MA, 1974, pp. 52–53.

the enemy. Such detection and quick redeployment could not be possible if *vyūha*s were very large, and thus, rather than all *akṣauhiṇi*s on a side combining to form a *vyūha*, their units and subunits adopted different formations simultaneously. This is like a tank regiment advancing *one squadron up*, its squadrons moving *two* or *one tank platoon up* as fit, the platoons moving their tanks in *line ahead*, *file*, or *echeloned to a flank*, depending upon terrain and direction of threat.

Similarly, while the legion could deploy in the *quincunx* or checkerboard, individual maniples could adopt different formations like the *testudo*. Indeed, the epic at some places talks of *vyūha*s involving only selected bodies. We may thus conclude that, while military science contemporaneous with the epic war was aware of arrays or *vyūha*s, redactors who endlessly evolved and modified the epic, not being military men, were clueless about them and gave them zoomorphic names and forms, at times defining them only with adjectives—*sāgaropama* or vast like the sea, *paiśācān* or *rākṣasān*, i.e. devilish or associated with 'communities' considered devilish.

Also, while some passages describe *vyūha*s with the different arms—infantry (swordsmen and knifemen), elephants, horses, chariots, and auxiliaries—deployed in homogenous blocks within them, others describe *vyūha*s organised in pyramidal schema with all arms combined in the basic *paṭṭi*. This brings us to the organizational terms and schemes that appear in the epic and inspect their validity.

The size of the *paṭṭi*, the elementary unit of organization, varies widely in the epic. Some passages speak of it as comprising a single elephant accompanied by ten chariots, each chariot by ten horses, and each horse by ten footmen or archers, i.e. one elephant, ten chariots, hundred horses, and thousand footmen or archers, plus crews of chariot and elephant. Others are soberer, suggesting, for instance, one elephant, one chariot, three horses, and five swordsmen. Statements like hundred shield bearers to one archer (*dhanuṣke śataṅ carminaḥ*)[11] may of course be ignored as absurd. The *paṭṭi* was then aggregated in a triangular scheme through the *senāmukha*, *gulma*, *gaṇa*, *vāhini*, *pṛtana*, *camu*, and *anīkinī*, the last one being aggregated tenfold into the *akṣauhiṇi*.

11 *Mbh*, VI: 20.18; the full thing goes … *one hundred cars support each elephant, one hundred cavalry, each car, ten archers, each horse, and … dhanuṣke śataṅ carminaḥ*.

Such aggregation of *paṭṭi*, even for the more modest of the two *paṭṭi*s given above, would return the strength of the *akṣauhiṇi* as 21,870 chariots and elephants each, 65,610 cavalry, and 1,09,350 foot, figures that do not include crews of chariots and elephants and their logistics and ground staffs. Turn of the millennium Bronze Age societies, more so of the arid Divide, simply did not possess organizational ability to embody, mobilize, and maintain such massive organizations. Eighteen such gigantic bodies on one battlefield would simply eat and drink out the countryside in no time. Further, mixing of all arms in the elementary *paṭṭi* is against military logic, because it prevents exploitation of the inherent advantages of any of the component arm—the infantry would, for instance, only slow the chariot down. Historical observation indicates in an entirely different direction. Even if different arms were mixed in 'units', it would be for logistics and administrative purposes only, and in war they would deployed in separate wings—each Roman infantry battalion or *cohort* had a *turma* or squadron of cavalry, but in battle all *turmae* were 'brigaded' into the *ala* or wing. Groupings of different arms have usually been temporary.

The organizational hierarchy outlined above is one of the more popular ones and is not sacrosanct. Hopkins has shown that different sources give the levels differently, some suppressing one or more levels, others equating a few.[12] There is no reason to also believe that all armies used the same hierarchy; armies from different parts of the sub-continent would have varying proportions of the arms as per their resources. For instance, the organization of Alexander's Scythian mercenary cavalry was entirely different from his Thracian cavalry, with each Scythian squadron having far more number of horses than the Thracian ones. A different, logically more sustainable model is presented here, which is that different arms were organised in homogenous units which were integrated at a higher level of command. In other words, a *paṭṭi* was not a mix of all arms but a pure section of each arm, i.e. a chariot or elephant *paṭṭi* had one chariot or elephant and its crew, a cavalry *paṭṭi* three (or even ten, like the Turkic *khail*) horses, an infantry *paṭṭi* a squad of ten troops.

Such homogenous *paṭṭi*s would be aggregated upwards through a few levels to form battalions or regiments of each arm, the *gaṇa* or *vāhini*,

12 Hopkins, 'Ruling Caste', pp. 196–97.

which would yield entirely plausible figures of 81 chariots, 81 elephants, 243 horse, and 405 infantry, for homogenous *vāhini*s of each arm. At the same time, though 405 men is a good number for a commanding officer to control, it must not be believed that these were the figures everywhere, for they could certainly be greater or lesser depending upon native organization of any army or people.

Now, Yardi postulated that *pṛtana*, *camu*, and *anīkini* were synonymous with the *akṣauhiṇi*, a word that came from *akṣa* or four-sided die and denoted a combine of the four arms. This would at once remove three steps of aggregation, reducing the *akṣauhiṇi* to plausible figures; taken together, an *akṣauhiṇi* would comprise a battalion or *vāhini* each of the different arms. At the same time, just as we cannot say that an infantry *vāhini* always and everywhere comprise 405 men, so also we cannot say that the *akṣauhiṇi* everywhere had only one *vāhini* each of the different arms. Probably, the intervening organizational levels were used alternately and selectively, leading to the *akṣauhiṇi* having mixes of one or more battalions of the four arms as per human, animal, and material resources that it could draw upon.

In other words, in this model each major ally brought an *akṣauhiṇi*, i.e. a formation of varying proportions of the four major arms which were organised variously. Levies, allies, and feudatories were probably appended with one or the other of the *akṣauhiṇi*s for command and control purposes. Such a model supports the contention, often made in the battle-pieces in the epic, that infantry fought infantry, archers fought archers, cavalry, cavalry, and so on—though arms do not attack arms of their own type alone, such combat is more likely if there were homogenous wings than when all was mixed in a *paṭṭi*.

We thus have a plausible structure of the armies. What is left to be decided is whether such a schema was really operative at the time of the epic war, or did it belong to a later period when societies had developed better organizational ability. We will return to the issue after inspecting the nature of each component arm, starting with the horse, the animal with which most of the literature is obsessed.

The Hub of the *Akṣauhiṇi*—Horses and Chariots

Cavalry

The horse is associated with many of the epic peoples. The Kekaya and Madra rulers are called *aśvapati*, the root of the name Sātvat is *sāta* or horse, which also appears in Sātivāja, Sātavāhana and Sātakarṇi, while Śaka, Kamboja, or Yavana are called *aśvayuddhakuśala*, i.e. skilled cavalry. However, although riding and riders (*aśvasāda*) are mentioned in Vedic literature, like the *Vājasaneyi Saṅhitā* of the *Atharvaveda* or the *Taittiriya Brahmana*,[13] it is doubtful that true combat riding existed at the turn of the millennium when horse technology was still indifferent and mounted archery far from developed. As against common perception, bare-back riding is no indicator of great skill but of extreme discomfort—the constant banging is highly painful, can damage the kidneys of both riders and mount, and bring blood into the urine—and only indicates indifferent riding equipment and technology. True cavalry appeared south of the steppes only when Scythians, Cimmerians, and Medes took over West Asia in the seventh century B.C., and has not been convincingly detected in South Asia before the fourth century.

Yet the horse is of utmost importance in Vedic lore. Vedic groups like the Haihaya or Turvaśa, who have strong Turanic or Scythic affiliations (after their defeat by the Ikṣvāku, the Haihaya and their Śaka affiliates are forced to adopt outlandish hairstyles, which is reminiscent of the peculiar tonsure of steppe folk) are also strongly associated with the horse. The *Chāndogya Upaniṣad* says that the Kuru were once saved by the mare, perhaps a memory of the nomad horse which was oftener a mare or a gelding than a stallion. Greek accounts, like those of Pliny, mention a strong cavalry tradition in the western parts of South Asia[14] and attest that Gandhāra horse was surpassed only by the Nisaean horses of the Medes.[15]

It may be surmised from the above that while among the greatest part of the participants the horse, though ritually important, was limited to chariotry, there were some communities who were more adept at riding

13 *ṚV*, I: 162.17; 163.9; V: 61.1–3; also,*YV: VājasaneyiSaṅhitā:* XXX: 13, and *TB*, III.4.7.1.

14 Pliny, *Naturalia Historia*, VI, 22, 66 ff.

15 Herodotus, III. 106, in Majumdar, *Classical Accounts*, p. 4.

and which provided cavalries to act as auxiliaries and scouts. This makes it important to inspect whether or not the mythical and supernatural cavalry combat between Irāvān and Alambuṣa (sons of Arjuna and Duryodhana respectively), and the *aśvayuddhakuśala* Greeks and Scythians, were later interpolations.

Chariotry

Rather than cavalry, chariotry was the main arm of combat and strongly associated with the horse. That captive-wheel technology had proliferated sufficiently in the Vedic age is seen in mention of several types of animal-drawn vehicles (*yānāni vividhāni*, including *śakaṭa* and *ānas*, i.e. carts or wagons), as also different animals (*gokharoṣṭrayuktāi*, i.e. *harnessed to cattle, asses and camels*),[16] in addition to sedan chairs and litters (*śibikā*, *narayāna*). The war-chariot, called in the Vedas the *vipatha* or trackless,[17] was one of this wide variety of vehicles, but it is almost impossible to reconstruct it, there being no pictorial representation except highly stylised Swat petroglyphs and some etchings on early Scarlet Ware vessels.[18] The issue is further confused with fanciful descriptions of big, *golden* chariots, chariots covered by net or with elaborate standards and umbrellas, or even *flying* chariots. In the next few passages of this section we shall try to create a picture of how the *vipatha* looked and functioned, and consider if it was the same design that was used in the *Mahabharata* war.

Chassis and Body

As its name indicates, the *vipatha* would have been a light, two–wheeled chariot, and probably represented the model from across the high age of Bronze Age, with body open to the rear and drawn by two, though at times by four, horses. Piggott presented a diagrammatic reconstruction of the *vipatha* based on the many references in Vedic texts and other dimensions given in the Śulbasūtra manuals.[19] The *Āpastamba Śulbasūtra* gives the pole (*iśā*) as 188 *aṅgula*s or finger's width, a measure which usually is taken as ¾", i.e. 16 *aṅgula* to a foot. Arguing that the *aṅgula*

16 *Mbh*, XVI: 7.33.

17 *Ch.U*, 4.16.5; *Jaiminiya Upanisad Brāhmaṇa*, III: 16,7; *Kauśītaki Upaniṣad*, I: 4.

18 Piggott, *Prehistoric India*, p. 274.

19 Piggott, *Prehistoric India*, pp. 277–78.

should be taken as ½", instead of the usual measure as that exaggerates all dimensions, Piggott converted this figure to 7'10", which he said was reasonable after deducting the 1' or so of the *prauga*, i.e. part of the *iśā* ahead of the yoke, because it is comparable to the contemporary West Asian figures of 6'–7'6"[20] for the length of the pole *ahead* of the body.

Now, though some clay models of Śunga chariot, which I have seen at the Indian Museum Calcutta, but which I have not since been able to trace, have small holes at the front lower edge of the body for fixing the pole, it is doubtful if this would have been the case in real chariots. Attaching the pole in this way would transfer the draw to the wheels *via* the body, a suboptimal method as unless the body was extremely strong and heavy, and very securely lashed to the axle, it would simply get ripped off. In the *Veda*s, the *iśā* has been called *pṛṣṭha* (backbone) and *dhūri* (axis) of the chariot, in other words, the foundation on which the entire vehicle was built and not just a rod lashed to the front of the body. We can take this to mean that the pole extended under the body to its rear end, and that the axle was mortised and lashed directly to it, forming a chassis in which the draw of the horse was transferred directly to the wheels. The body or basket was built up on it. If the 188 *aṅgula*s is converted by the usual ¾", it would yield a figure of about 11'8", i.e. a pole long enough to act as the axis of the chariot from the tip, including the *prauga*, to the rear end of the bucket.[21] We need not thus reduce the size of the *aṅgula* to ½".

The problem of using the ¾" *aṅgula* is that it returns an immense 10' for the axle (*akṣa*), which is given at 164 *aṅgula*. The ½" *aṅgula*, on the other hand, returns a more reasonable 6'8". Now, the yoke or *yuga*, at 86 *aṇgula*s, is 5'4" with the ¾" *aṅgula* but only 3'6" with the ½" *aṅgula*, which would be too constricted for yoking two horses abreast. Though Piggott argues in favour of the shorter yoke in Egyptian and European vehicles,[22] most Mediterranean chariots had wide yokes, if only to accommodate the yoke saddle (to be discussed later). We can therefore conclude that the ¾" *aṅgula* is still the correct conversion, and that the length of the axle can be seen as a textual aberration. On the whole, Piggott's reconstruction of the

20 Piggott, *Prehistoric India*, pp. 280–81.

21 For other lists of chariot dimensions, see *Baudhāyana Śulbasūtra*, I.10–12, and *Kātyāyana Śulbasūtra*, II.1–4.

22 Though this is the figure that Piggott prefers, *Prehistoric India*, p. 280.

vipatha matches contemporaneous chariots in design, and the Śulbasūtra dimensions appear to be reliable and logical.

Notwithstanding the popularity of four–wheeled chariots in folklore, the Vedic and epic chariot were two–wheeled, like all war–chariots, though special purpose chariots with four–wheels may not be ruled out. Two–wheeled chariots appear in *Mahabharata* battle-pieces. Krishna's chariot, at one place, is said to have wheels like the Sun and Moon. Horses are said to be dragging chariots on one wheel when the other has been shot off, and so on. Piggott's reconstruction does not give details on wheel construction and hub arrangements except saying that wheels were about a meter in diameter. That wheels had spokes is evident from the Vedic word ārā, but number of spokes is difficult to discern from literary evidences; Piggott suggests eight to ten but without citing his source. Now, the Vedic poet's '*I bend with song, as bends a wright his felloe of solid wood*'[23] suggests that the felloe (*prādhi*) was made of a single piece wood[24] bent into shape, a technique which would require a large number of spokes to retain shape. Late 1st millennium stone sculptures, like the *Vessantara Jātaka* frieze on the Sanchi Stūpa, depict almost thirty spokes.

Outer ends of spokes would have been drilled into the felloe and secured by thongs through slots on the outside so as to prevent wear. Around the felloe was the tyre (*pāvi*), the two together forming the *nemī* or rim; the *Vedic Index* has *nemī* as tyre, but I would limit the tyre to the *pāvi*, which could have been made of a variety of material like leather and metal.[25] Iron was probably used in time, if the reputedly deafening rumble of the chariot is anything to go by.

As derived so far, the *vipatha* appears comparable to the Sintashta chariots in so far as the latter's wheels, all specimens of which have rotted away but which can be known from impressions in grave floor, were about a meter in diameter and had gauges of 1.3 or 1.4 meters. However, Piggott is silent on things like hub arrangement and width of nave, and neither does he provide the literary references his reconstruction is based upon. Now, while the short, 20 centimetre nave of the Sintashta chariot implied wobbly wheels, the smoothly spinning wheel of the Vedic chariot

23 *ṚV*, VII:32.20. Single piece rims require large number of spokes to retain shape.

24 *ṚV*, VII:32.

25 *Vedic Index*, vol 2, pp. 201–202.

is made much of and is the metaphor for stability in the Vedic language. This implied that the hub cylinder of the *vipatha* was wider than the less robust Sintashta proto-chariot. It is also mentioned that a bronze sleeve was inserted through the centre of the wooden hub, the nave or *nābhya.*

The *vipatha* was also different from Shang and Western Zhou chariots, which were typologically similar to one another. The oldest discovered Shang chariots from Anyang, ghost images of which were obtained by scraping away the earth packing to leave an image in mud (a technique first used while excavating ship remains in East Anglia), show large wheels of 137 centimetres, gauges of up to 227 centimetres, and wheels with 18–27 spokes.[26]

Western Zhou chariots have been found in more military contexts than Shang chariots. Some of them, found in grave relics, have been reconstructed with the help of dimensions given in 18th cent A.D. Qing philologies, and show more finished wheel constructions. For instance, the dismantled and jumbled chariots in pit M100 at Liulihe near Beijing, associated with the lord of grave M1046[27], show highly finished wheels of 135–140 centimetres diameter. These large wheels were attached to axles about three meters wide, which when lashed to a slotted pole, created sturdy chassis with floors far higher than either Sintashta chariots or the *vipatha*. Also, the wheels had wide naves of 40 centimetres, and 18–24 tapering spokes attached to two–piece felloes with an element of dishing, i.e. leaning outward so that the plane of the rim lay *outside* the plane of the hub.

The Chinese chariots also had tapering axles that ended in profusely decorated hub-caps, with elaborate bushings and lynch-pins to keep the wheels from sliding on the axle and grazing the body.[28] Some Western Zhou chariots, like those at Wei or at Shaanxi (Baoji, Rojiazhuang), have

26 See Shaughnessy, 'Historical Perspectives', p. 193 *et passim* for a survey of dimensions of the Anyang chariot. Barbieri–Low argues that planked wheels were never used in China because of the paucity of wood, which encouraged construction of spoked wheel. It is rather more likely that chariots introduced into China already had spoked wheels, and that they developed the mortising techniques to add as many as 30 spokes.

27 Barbieri–Low, 'Wheeled Vehicles', pp. 60–64.

28 Barbieri–Low, 'Wheeled Vehicles', p. 25, fn. 54. These were means to prevent the wheels from backing up towards the body, which could damage the vehicles badly, or away from it, which might call the wheels to shear at the hub.

metal reinforcements in the form of nave bands with raised edges or slots.[29] These techniques differed considerably from Egyptian and West Asian models. Egyptian chariot wheels, with gauges of 1.54 to 1.8 meters, had sectionized nave-hubs with half–spokes carved out of the same block of wood at 60 or 90 degrees. These were then put together to form the hub and the spokes, the longitudinal sections fused and lashed with wet rawhide and birch bark to make waterproof.[30] Sectionized hubs enabled axles to *bulge* on either side of the nave, obviating the necessity for bushings like in Western Zhou chariots. Such technique also warranted far fewer spokes—six and even four.[31] The segment of a 90 centimetre diameter bronze ring with six spokes, found at a grave at Shangxidui, China, had slots at the end of the spokes where they would join the rim. This has been taken as the metal cover of wheel and spokes of an Indian chariot by Barbieri–Low,[32] but it is more likely to have been the 'hub-cap' of a Mediterranean chariot that found its way there, possibly by trade.

The body of the Vedic and epic chariot has been called *koṣa*, *garta*, or *garbha*, all of which imply an enclosed space, a bucket open at the rear mounted on the chassis. Piggott's bucket is semi-circular in plan, with vertical rear edge, but the *Vessantara* and other illustrations, like the Morhana Pahar wall-painting, have rounded edges projecting rearwards, possibly for additional protection of the calves from low projectiles coming in at an angle. The material of the bucket, which reached the waist,[33] is difficult to discern as many fabulous substances, including gold, wood, tiger-skin, are variously mentioned. Possibly, wicker reinforced with planks

29 Barbieri–Low, 'Wheeled Vehicles', figures 23 and 24.

30 Littauer and Crouwel, *Wheeled Vehicles and Ridden Animals*, p. 79.

31 Littauer and Crouvel, *Wheeled vehicles*, p. 78; the chariots in the grave of Tutankhamun had wheels of 93 centimetres diameter with six spokes and gauge of 170 centimetres, but it has been considered a designer vehicle by Littauer and Crouwel. See also Littauer and Crouwel, *Chariots and Related Equipment from the Tomb of Tutankhamun*, Oxford, Griffith, London, 1985.

32 Barbieri–Low, 'Wheeled Vehicles', p. 58.

33 Upwards the crew was protected by the *varma* or armour:

Marmāṇī te varmāṇacchādayāmi sonastvān rajāmṛtetanu vastām |

urorvaśīyo varuṇaste kṛṇotu jayantan' tvānu devāmadantu|| 18,

yotasvī araṇe yaśca niṣṭayo jinghānsati |

dalastan' sarve dhurvantu bamha varma mamāntaram || *ṚV*, VI:75.19

or hide was used. Stitch marks along the edges on the *Vessantara* chariots suggest hide or leather, while the plaited material on a Gupta terracotta panel showing two combating chariots possibly represents leather strap.

Before we inspect one crucial indicator to the structure of the bucket, we will quickly survey the types of body constructions that have been in use. Shang and Western Zhou chariot bodies were rectangular plan with rounded corners (Anyang chariots were 134 by 85 centimetres, the M52 chariot as wide as 160 centimetres). These were surrounded by a wall with an opening at the back. The material of the wall is difficult to discern, and may have been nothing more than short bamboo stakes, of an average of 51 centimetres, grouted around the perimeter of the rectangular floors in the grave chariots. Possibly, wicker was woven between the stakes and reinforced with hide, lacquered wood, or bronze. However, such low height of the stakes means that a standing warrior had nothing to brace himself against and, given the high floor due to the large wheels, was very exposed and unsteady. Further, as Shaughnessy's illustrations[34] show, the upper edge of the wheels rose above the edge of the wall, making it extremely dangerous for robe-wearing Chinese men. The argument that warriors knelt on the floor is unreasonable as kneeling is not the optimal position to wield weapons in, and could be extremely uncomfortable after a short while. It is more reasonable to suppose that there was additional support, in the form of handrails, attached to the stakes but which have now rotted away completely.

In fact, some West Asian and most Egyptian chariots had little more than handrails or frames, like the light chariot of elm pole and ash felloes found at Thebes with wheels of four spokes.[35] In fact, even sparser chariots appear on Greek vases, though these can be dismissed as racing chariots as the broken terrain of Greece was not, *prima facie*, chariot country. There is no indication that leathern walls once stretched between the frame—Egyptian paintings and grave relics (Rameses and Tutankhamun respectively) or Greek vases, give little indication of any.

34 Shaughnessy, 'Historical Perspectives', p. 196, fig. 1.

35 For an illustration, see Y. Yadin, *The Art of Warfare in Biblical Lands in the Light of Archaeological Studies*, 2 vols., New York, McGraw–Hill, vol 1, pp. 89–90, 240–41. It has been represented in the plan presented with this book.

The handrail is indicated in the case of South Asian chariots. *Mahabharata* chariots have a fence–rim of leather called the *varūtha*,[36] while the *vipatha* is associated with a curious term, *kūbara*, which seems to have been a handrail.

Kūbara is a term significant in the context of chariotry. *Kubera*, lord of wealth in Indian mythology, was originally *Kubera Vaiśrāvaṇa*, chief chariot–raider, whose son is *Nala–Kūbara*, *nala* being reed or cane. *Naḍa Naiṣidha* or *Nala Naiṣadha*, who appears in the beauteous story of Nala–Damayantī, is a famed charioteer in the *Mahabharata* and the *Śatapatha* Brāhmaṇa. This chief is usually taken as an un-Aryan *Niṣāda*, i.e. forester, but chariotry being foreign to the Niṣāda, the name must have indicated something else. Use of the terms *kūbara* and *nala* in the charioteering context suggests that the cane frame was synonymous with the chariot, in turn suggesting that the *vipatha* as also the *Mahabharata* vehicle were lightly constructed, and closer to the West Asian in design.

The relation between *koṣa* and axle is important. Often statements like the *axle was attached below the koṣa with leather straps* are encountered, whereas in reality the *koṣa* could only be attached *above* the axle. A curious statement I have come across is that in Iron Age Celtic chariots, axles were *suspended* by ropes from the body thus making the ride less bumpy. Now, the axle could not be *suspended* from the body unless first the body was suspended from something higher. It just may be that two inverted 'U's were attached below the body, their ends joined by sturdy thongs on which the axle was placed and fixed. Needless to say, though such a device should act as a shock absorber in theory, its reliability is highly questionable. Rather, floors of supple material like leather or straw mats may have been used to make the ride smooth. Also, terms like *upastha* or lap, i.e. the place where the warrior stood, and *nīḍa* or nest which was the cockpit for the charioteer, are unlikely to have been applicable to the *vipatha*, and only to later, larger, or specialised chariots.

Thus far we see that the Vedic *vipatha* meets the definition of being a light, two spoke-wheeled vehicles drawn by horse,[37] and that the

36 *Mbh*, V: 155.8; '*vyāghra-carma-parīvārā dvīpi-carmāvṛtāśca te*'

37 The chariot has been defined as a '*light vehicle with two spoked wheels, pulled by horses and designed for speed*' in D.W. Anthony, 'The Opening of the Eurasian Steppe at 2000 BCE', in *The Bronze Age and Early Iron Age Peoples of Eastern Central Asia*, vol.1, 1998, pp. 94–113, esp. p. 105, fn. 10. This definition is inclusive, as against

Mahabharata chariot may have been similar to it. No contemporaneous illustrations of either the *vipatha* or the *Mahabharata* chariot are available, but we can say that the illustrations in Morhana Pahar caves or the *Vessantara* friezes at Sanchi, or the Śunga clay models, all of which are from later periods, do represent them somewhat. This is because tenacious forms have tended to be held on to tenaciously in South Asia, and the reliance on *Śulbasūtra* dimensions may have persisted.[38] Thus, we can say that while the epic chariot was more robust and advanced than the Sintashta proto–chariot, it was different from the elaborately finished Chinese chariots, which had higher elevations and design developments like felloes of trapezoidal sections held together by bronze clasps. Also, though the chariot found at Lchaschen in Anatolia curiously followed the Chinese design,[39] West Asian chariots more closely resembled the *vipatha* design, although their construction was far sparser. In other words, the *vipatha* and the *Mahabharata* chariotry belonged to the West Asian and Steppe tradition.

Pole and Yoke

Lightness of a chariot can be converted to effectiveness in battle only with efficient yoking arrangements. This arrangement, in the case of Sintashta or Lchaschen chariots, is difficult to discern because the poles have rotted away except for a stub closest to the axle. Some archaeologists have extended the stump in a straight line, concluding that the pole lay between the horses no higher than the axle.[40] This however would require the pole to be secured to the horses with thongs, making the vehicle unstable and causing it to lurch from side to side. It is more likely that poles were curved, and rose to the whither of the horse, as Piggott surmises in the case of the *vipatha* and Shaughnessy in that of the Lchaschen chariot.[41]

Piggott's earlier definition which had emphasised upon warfare. Piggott later relented in his definition, as it made the chariot too restrictive, leaving out hunting, travel, and ceremonial chariots, see Littauer and Crouwel define the charot as a '*light, fast, two-wheeled, usually horse-drawn vehicle with spoked wheels; used for warfare, hunting, racing and ceremonial purposes. Its crew usually stood.*' Littauer and Crouwel, *Wheeled Vehicles and Ridden Animals*, pp. 4–5.

38 S.D. Singh, *Ancient Indian Warfare*, p. 29.

39 Shaughnessy, 'Historical Perspectives', pp. 200–201.

40 Barbieri–Low, 'Wheeled vehicles', p. 28 fn. 65.

41 Shaughnessy, 'Historical Perspectives', p. 201.

The arrangement was different in Chinese chariots which had higher wheel diameters and thus higher axles, making the rise shallower. The Shang pole curved up gradually, while Western Zhou poles lay flat and then rose sharply. At the same time, chariot poles were not required to curve up too steeply, as horses were small—the one whose remains have been uncovered at the Gandhara Grave site of Dir was only 135 centimetres at the whither, while the Sintashta horse, as per Kuzmina, was only thirteen to fourteen hands,[42] requiring poles to rise less than a meter from the axle in its entire length.

The yoke was attached crosswise to the pole at a sufficient height, and to it the team was harnessed at the shoulders. The manner of attaching the yoke to the pole varied. To Chakravarty or Singh, the *vipatha*'s rising pole was tapering in section, and passed through a hole in the yoke, called the *kha* or *tardman* in the *Vedic Index*.[43] The arrangement is somewhat different as per Piggott, in whose model the yoke and pole had vertically aligned holes that were joined by a stout pin (*śamyā*) and lashed with thongs (*yoktra*). Though both arrangements gave flexibility in both planes, adjusting for uneven rise and fall of shoulders and variable speeds during turns, the latter was probably more efficient in terms of robustness; it is more reasonable to conclude that the *kha* was the slot in which the śamyā, and not the pole, was inserted.

More difficult than attaching yoke to pole was attaching horses to yoke. One device used in many places was the saddle yoke (or yoke saddle), an inverted wishbone shaped piece of wood that was lashed to the ends of the yoke and placed on the shoulders. It was secured to the horse with straps across the throat and through the mouth. While Kelekna sees it as an efficient arrangement[44] and even Littauer reluctantly agrees that it did take away some weight from the throat and transfer it to the bone of the horse,[45] to Barbieri–Low the yoke saddle was inefficient and an anachronistic holdover.[46] However, if axles were placed sufficiently

42 Elena Kuzmina, *The Prehistory of the Silk Road*, ed. Victor H. Mair, Philadelphia, University of Pennsylvania Press, 2008, p. 44.

43 *Vedic Index*, vol. 2, p. 202.

44 See Pita Kelekna, 'Impact of the Horse', p. 9.

45 See M.A. Littauer, 'The Function of the Yoke Saddle in Ancient Harnessing', *Antiquity*, vol. 42, 1968, pp. 27–31.

46 Barbieri-Low, 'Wheeled Vehicles', p. 29 note 68.

rearward under the body, the weight of the crew would cause the yoke to settle on the whither of the animals, taking away some weight of the chariot. Given its popularity in Egypt, Thebes, and China, the yoke saddle was not ineffective.

No indication of such an arrangement appears anywhere in Indian art or literature. Yokes in Sanchi or Bharhut chariots end at the whither in spherical hubs—the horses were presumably tied to the yoke with straps, though this is not clear from the illustrations. However, as straps around the neck were inefficient and choked the horses, the animals were probably tied *directly to the pole* around their girths (*kākṣya*), causing them to pull not with the throats against themselves, but with their bodies. We thus have a model in which two horses directly drag the chassis with its independently mounted, robust wheels, which do not impair turning. Built upon this was the body of the chariot.

The *vipatha*, which rose no more than 4½' above ground, would have been as light as the Egyptian chariot which to Piggott weighed as low as 34 kilos.[47] Such a light chariot could be easily carried by a man across difficult terrain. However, the effectiveness of a chariot depended upon distribution of this weight, and those of its crew and their equipment, on the chassis, the major determinant of which was the position of the body *vis-à-vis* the axle. In most illustrations, axles are directly below the centre of the floor if not placed forward, in which cases, especially in the latter, the crew's weight would tilt the chariot back around the axle, pulling the pole upwards and backwards against the animals. In contrast, axles placed at the rear edge of the body, as in West Asian chariots after 1500 B.C., made the crew's weight fall *ahead* of the axle, pressing the pole down, causing the yoke to settle upon the horses, and obviating the choking drag. The Sanchi chariot indeed has the wheels set quite forward below the body, which makes its distribution of weight somewhat questionable.

Horses

By definition the chariot is associated with the horse, though other animals, like asses (*gardhabha*) and mules (*aśvetara*), have also been associated with it. While ass-drawn vehicles appear in scenes of travel, in one curious reference to the chariot of the *Aśvin*s themselves is drawn

47 Piggott, *Earliest Wheeled Transport*, p. 89.

by *gardhabhas*, no doubt a pointer to a West Asian inspiration behind the steppe chariot. In the *Ramayana*, the chariot of Khara, a general of Rāvaṇa and whose name itself means ass, is drawn by 'speckled horses' which possibly were some sort of ass.

Also, the number of horses to each chariot has varied widely in records, and also includes odd numbers.[48] One-horsed chariots were known, but implied poverty. Four-horsed chariots are not only mentioned in literature but also their relics have been found in Chinese graves, like in Pit #2, also known as M168, at Fengxi in Shaanxi.[49] The *Mahabharata* calls some chariots *caturyuj*, i.e. quadruple-yoked, and mentions specialised charioteers, one driving the central horses (*dhuryayor hayayor ekaḥ ... rathī*) and two others, the *pārṣṇisārathi*, driving the outer horses (more on this later). However, before the advent of the whipple-tree, it was extremely difficult for the yoke to adjust to variations in rise and speed of four horses and keep them from dragging and choking one another constantly. It is quite likely that four-horsed chariots were ceremonial vehicles. The outer horses in grave M168 are found to have yoke-saddles but are not actually under the yoke bar. In other words, these were outriders, who added little to speed directly as their draw was not transferred to the wheels.

However, though the real purpose of outriders was to act as reserve horses, they did add to speed indirectly as, not encumbered by the pole, they set a higher pace for the pole horses. The trade-off here was the complication of harnessing arrangements, additional controlling problems to make sure outriders did not run in opposite directions, larger target presented to enemy archers, and greater vulnerability. The *Mahabharata* chariot appears to have been the two-horsed variety, though the four-horsed ones may not be ruled out. Even in the case of the latter, there appear to have been no *pārṣṇisārathi*; the knight and his charioteer, i.e. *rathī* and *sārathī*, are the quintessential duo, and though in a few places the *pārṣṇirathi* is said to be killed and the *sārathī* takes over the reins, the narrations are too formalised to be authentic accounts. Not in a single case where the *sārathī* is killed is a *pārṣṇirathi* seen taking over; it is the warrior himself who tries to control the chariot. Evidently, the *pārṣṇisārathi* was

48 Three horses in *ṚV*, X: 33,5; four in *ṚV*, II: 81,1, five in Kāṭhaka Saṅhitā, XV, 2—*rathapañcavāhi*.

49 Barbieri–Low, 'Wheeled vehicles', pp. 63–64. Their halters are in a good state of preservation and decorated with shells.

an interpolation from later days when larger chariots came in use, a survey of references to which is provided by Chakravarty.[50]

Also, while older chariots had only one seat, the *vandhura*, elaborate seats like *ati-vandhura* or *talpa* (cushioned) are mentioned in later references. At the same time, the *Atharvaveda* associates the *vipatha* with the *vrātya*.[51] Taken together, the above suggests that in later times the 'mainstream' IA peoples, among whom the epic and other sacred literature evolved, took to elaborate chariots with more than two horses, multiple charioteers, and many seats, relegating the sparse but fleet designs to the *vrātya*. It was at this time that the separate cockpit, *nīḍa*, for the charioteer appeared. In contrast, as most of the *Mahabharata* peoples were *vrātya*, it is unlikely that epic chariot-makers were really enthusiastic about four horses—despite popularity of the four-horsed chariot, all representations are from angles that obviate the necessity of depicting their yoking arrangements! References to horses attached directly to the wheels, which appear in some Indian tales, are absurd, while the whipple-tree was not known in India.[52]

The oldest known chariot illustrations show single charioteers using the nose-ring to guide horses, a suboptimal arrangement that could be extremely painful to the animals. Later, control techniques improved with the use of soft bits attached to reins, the reins themselves passing through loop-shaped metal guides on the backs of the horses[53] to keep them from flying about. Barbieri–Low has shown that the curious bow-shaped metal prongs, of northern frontier origin, found at Anyang and other graves, were really rein holders attached to the belt of the driver.[54] The bit (*śiprā*)

50 Chakravarty, 'The War Chariot', pp. 31–32.

51 S.D. Singh, *Ancient Indian Warfare*, p. 33.

52 Piggot, *Prehistoric India*, p. 279. Piggott finds indication of the trace and swingle tree in the words *raśmi* and *vāṇi* but efficient arrangements like the whipple-tree did not exist.

53 Position of the guide is ambiguous. If set too far back on the pole, it would be too low, causing the reins to touch the flanks of the horse and confusing it, but if placed on the yoke, in which case it would be high enough, it would cause the reins to be turned at right angles and interfere with the pull on the rein. It is more reasonable that rein-guides were placed on the backs of each horse.

54 Watson, *Cultural Frontiers*, pp. 61–66. Six pieces of such equipment, though no chariot, have been found in the grave of Fu Hao, the northern consort of the Shang king; Bagley, 'Shang Archaeology', p. 208, n. 143, which have been explained in many

and rein (*raśmī*) are mentioned in Vedic literature (Piggott takes *raśmī* as trace), but there is no mention of either rein-guide or holder. Probably Vedic charioteers wrapped reins around their waists, like the Pharaohs on Egyptian wall art which show them driving their own chariots, or attached them to projections on the front of the body of the chariot. Drivers used the whip or *kaśā* to control horses.

Now, though Littauer and Crouwel's view that riding was extant in the steppes since the 4th millennium may not be acceptable, horses had nevertheless been improving steadily in breed and strength. By the end of Thutmose III's reign, the Egyptians had developed specialised, Arab-like breeds that were resistant to heat.[55] However, it was the stocky Turki ponies, like the 135 centimetre specimen found at Dir in Swat, that were best suited for the chariot as they presented small targets to archers, did not obstruct forward visibility, and possessed stamina to draw weights close to 250 kilos (the chariot, two riders, their armour and equipment). *Dadhikra*, the epitome of Vedic chariot horse, was probably modelled on a real animal that had won fame and fortune in war or race.[56] However, though *Dadhikra* is referred to in the masculine, the king-making chariot horse of Eurasia was the mare, or the more tractable, patient, and abstemious gelding. In contrast, stallions could not be kept in free herds as they constantly quarrelled over mares and made herds restive, and were consequently

---

fanciful ways including as cover for composite bows, have been convincingly shown by reins.

55 C. Rommelaere, *Les chevaux du Nouvel Empire Ègyptian: Origines, races, harnechement*, Brusssels, 1991.

56 That *Dadhikra*, possibly modelled on a personal horse of the Vedic chieftain Trasadasyu, was a chariot horse can be made out from the description of his harness details. *ṚV*, IV: 40.4. Also, *ṚV*, IV:38.3–8. *Dadhikra* cascades down precipice, '*whirling the car and flying like the tempest*'; he gains precious booty in battle and moves among the cattle; he speeds away as a hungry falcon amongst enemy herds while the folk '*cry after him in battle, as 't'were 'a thief who steals away a garment*';

> *... this way and that with rows of cars he rushes, ... tossing the dust, champing the rein that holds him*'; '*at his thunder, like the roar of heaven, those who attack tremble and are affrighted; for when he fights against embattled thousands, dread is he in his striving; none may stay him.*

For other instances of probably real horses turned into celebrities, see H. Creel, 'The Role of the Horse in Chinese History', *American Historical Review*, 70, 1965, pp. 647–72.

culled or castrated.[57] Fascination with the stallion was a feature of later sedentary and masculine age of chivalry when horses could be kept in stalls.

Social and Strategic Relevance of Chariots

The above discussion shows that construction and maintenance of chariots was an immensely expensive procedure, calling for control over a vast range of knowledge, expertise, and skilled and unskilled labour like those of carpentry, metallurgy, horse-keeping, and so on. Chariots were not easy to replace—it reportedly took one group of 20th century German research scholars 600 man hours to construct one Egyptian chariot[58]—and armies could be put back by years in regional arms races if they lost their chariots. Naturally, all chariots captured as war booty went to the chief or king.[59] Great care was taken to preserve chariots—wheels were shod in metal tyres, spokes were tied through slots *on the sides* of the wheels so as to reduce wear, chariots were turned over to take the weight off their wheels during storage, wheels were removed completely when not in use and hung on walls. It appears from grave relics that chariots were parked on their chassis–frames, with their wheels suspended inside adjoining slots cut into the earth.

Being elitist instruments, chariots were richly done up, often in gold-trimmed trappings like the Vedic *hemabhaṇḍa*. One Western Zhou inscription says of a chariot bestowed as gift upon a nobleman that '*I confer on you ... a chariot with bronze fittings, with a decorated cover on the handrail; a front-rail and breast trappings of soft leather, painted scarlet, for the horses; a canopy of tiger skin, with a reddish brown lining; yoke-bar bindings and axle couplings of painted leather; bronze jingle bells for the yoke bar; a main shaft and rear-end fitting and brake*

57 The greatest number of bones found at Derievka was of young males, showing that stallions were culled from the herds.

58 Reported in *News, Décembre – December 2001, Part 1,* www.osirisnet.net/news/n12_01p1.htm, (accessed 24 April 2014). The "GEO Magazine" site with the paper 'Streitwagen: Die Superwaffe der Pharaonen', describing the construction, http://www.geo.de/themen/historie/streitwagen/index.html, has been discontinued.

59 *Gautama-Dharmasūtra*, 10.20–21, *jetā labhate sāṃgrāmikaṃ vittam/ vāhanaṃ tu rājñah.* See Harry Falk, 'Das Reitpferd im vedischen Indien', in B. Hänsel, Stefan Zimmer *et al* (eds.), *Die Indogermanen und das Pferd,* Akten des Internationalen interdisziplinaren Kolloquiums, Freie Universitat Berlin, 1992, Bernfried Schlerath zum, 70, Geburtstag gewidmet, Budapest 1995, pp. 91–101.

fittings, bound with leather and painted gilt; a gilt bow-press and a fish-skin quiver; a team of four horses, with bits and bridles, bronze frontlets, and gilt girthstraps; a scarlet banner with two bells'.[60] This suggests that Western Zhou chariot relics, found in more military contexts than the elaborate Anyang chariots, are pale reflections of real chariots, their accoutrements like leather bindings or tiger-skin canopies having decayed or been stripped.[61] It is however more likely that such lavishly decorated chariots were ceremonial gifts to demonstrate royal favour, like the coded jewelled daggers, *khillat* robes, or permission to build *kungurah* battlements awarded by the Mughals to their followers, and were used only with ceremonial vehicles.

Chariot Crew

It is natural that each chariot would require an establishment of combat crew and 'ground' staff to operate it. The combat crew itself came in several classes. The car warrior, the basic term for which in the *Mahabharata* is *rathī*, largely belonged to the *Kṣatriya* class though there were many accomplished *Brāhmaṇa* warriors too. Other terms associated with the chariot warrior are *marya*, encountered already as the member of a *männerbund*, and the *śūra* and *vīra*, which can be loosely interpreted as hero–'knight' without taking the word's feudal connotations literally. In all, the warriors—*rathī*, *śūra*, or *vīra*—belonged to a class of middling to exalted rank as everywhere else in the Bronze Age world, like the Mycenaean *hippeis*. They alone could afford the expensive chariot, command services of elaborate ground staffs comprising not only of unskilled members like servants, guards, grass-cutters, and foragers but also highly skilled ones like chariot-makers, grooms, arrow-makers, weapon-men, and scouts, afford expensive armours, composite bow, and endless supplies of arrows, and also the nutrition required for the stamina to wear and wield such equipment for long durations. Also, they alone had the leisure to practice aggressive driving, archery from spring-less chariots, and skills in close quarter weapons like swords and maces.

Ownership of chariots in most societies, except in Egypt where it was monopolised by the pharaoh, was diffused among the middling to exalted

60 Edward L. Shaughnessy, *Sources of Western Zhou History*, Berkeley, University of California Press, 1991, p. 81.

61 Barbieri–Low, 'Wheeled Vehicles', pp. 65–66.

elite which were not everywhere equally feudal. A chivalric attitude is observed among these classes, with injunctions to fight only men of equal status and that too honourably. In the *Mahabharata*, gradation of *rathī*s as *mahārathī*, *atirathī*, or *adhiratha* was based not on feudal rank but reputation and prowess, a chivalric attitude, though they are seen attacking their inferiors in droves and flouting other rules of chivalry easily.

In contrast to the elite *rathī*, position of the *sārathī* is ambivalent. He belongs to the *sūta* class whose ritual and social position is not very high, just like that of the act of driving chariots. *Sūta* is minstrel, is derided as illegitimate progeny of the *Kṣatriya*,[62] and is seen performing minor functions at court. Insult is heaped upon Karṇa on account of his being *sūta*, and he seems to face a glass ceiling;[63] he is derided by Bhīṣma as *ardharathī* or *half-a-charioteer*. Śalya is indignant at having to drive Karṇa's chariot, philosophical and pseudo–logical justifications, not always convincing, are advanced to explain Śalya, Krishna, and Arjuna driving Karṇa, Arjuna, and Uttara's chariots respectively. That the act of driving chariots had fallen out of fashion is seen in scions of Mycenaean nobility knowing how to drive but leaving it to lesser men; this is not a very difficult situation—rich men *can* drive cars, but usually leave the driving to chauffeurs!

Nevertheless, the fact is that Karṇa does attain great power and is taken very seriously, while great men like Arjuna, Krishna, and Śalya do drive chariots, that too of their peers. Elsewhere the *rathakāra* or wright is called *Brāhmaṇa*,[64] his importance is underlined,[65] and he is venerated

62 Karve, *Yugānta*, p. 2.

63 The modern–day community of carpenters in India are called the *Sutār*, a word that comes from *Sūtradhāra* or thread-bearer, i.e. the narrator of tales. He is none other than the *Sūta* who was charioteer and bard of Vedic India. The fall in position is illustrate by the unfortunate placement of the *Sūta* among less privileged communities, but the insistence of the *Sūta* that he is a Brahman.

64 S.D. Singh, *Ancient Indian Warfare*, p.30.

65 *AV*, III: 5.6; *YV: Kāṭhaka Saṅhitā*, XVII: 13; *YV: Maitrāyani Saṅhitā*, II: 9.5; *YV: Taittirīya Saṅhitā*, IV: 5.4.2; *YV: Vājasaneyi Saṅhitā*, XVI.17; *TB*, I.1.4.8; III.4.2.1; ŚB, xiii.4.2.17. For instance, *Taittirīya Saṅhitā* remembers to hail the carpenter, maker of chariots, alongside the warriors, charioteers, and hosts:

> ... *namo rathibhyau'rathebhyeśca vo namo namaḥ|*
>
> *namo rathaibhyo rathapatibhyaśca vo namo namaḥ||*

for his ability to handle and repair chariots.[66] Many *sūtas* are men and women of importance—Vidura (whose mother was a *sūta*) and Sañjaya are members of council, Vidura's wife Sulabhā is highly venerated, and Sudeṣṇā, daughter of a *sūta*, is queen of Mātsya. Charioteers are personal friends of warriors; in the hermitage, Dhṛtarāṣṭra and his charioteer–counsel Sañjaya live in the same cottage. In the *Śatapatha Brāhmaṇa*, the *sūta* is one of the *ratnins*, alongside *akṣavāpa* and *senāni*.[67] In one Vedic ceremony, all warriors, even chieftains, walked to the residence of their charioteers with milk products like the *apūpa* cake, which they had helped prepare, in their hands and fed them as brothers.[68] The *sārathī* was only functionally junior to the *rathī*; he was called *sthātṛ*, i.e. *he who stands*, against the warrior who was *savyaṣṭhār*, *he who sits*. He was also *saṅgrahyātṛ*, collector, perhaps it was his task to collect the booties of downed enemies.

It is evident that at one time, before egalitarian steppe society morphed into sedentary, feudal and agrarian ones, the charioteer had a socially exalted status. The strongest indication of equality was the joint deification of charioteer and warrior as the *Celestial Twins*. The *Aśvins* are of the same womb as the *rathī* and *sārathī* are of the same body, i.e. the *garta*.[69] Their alternate name of *Nāsatya* comes from **nasati*, i.e. *to bring back safely* ('safe return home'=**nas*); this is exactly what the two were to do with one another, one by driving well and giving counsel, which could be tactical advice like that of the spotter to the sniper, and the other by fighting well. The Greek Nestor, also from the same root, was a renowned charioteer or *hippóta*. This model of divinity, derived directly from the

---

senobhyaḥ senānibhyeśca vo namo namaḥ|

kṣatṛbhyeḥ saṅgrahītṛbhyeśca vo namo namastakṣebhyo rathakārebhyeśca vo namo namaḥ||

Or

Hail, that have chariots, and that are chariotless! Hail chariots, and you, lords of chariots!

Hail hosts, and you, lords of hosts! Hail, doorkeepers, and you, charioteers!

Hail carpenters, and you, makers of chariots! [translation mine]

66 Keith, 'The Age of the Rigveda', p.100.

67 *ŚB*, v.3.1.

68 *ŚB*, v.3.1.8.

69 *ŚB*, v.3.1.

charioteer–warrior pair, was also the model for diarchy—senior and junior chief, chief and *purohita*, chief and advisor–charioteer.[70] *Bṛhaspati* (or *Brahmaṇaspati*), *purohita* of the gods, is also *charioteer* of the gods—Zarathustra's condemnation of the priests who helped charioteers in the militarization of the steppes were perhaps directed at these *purohita* who helped the warrior with their armour, managed their weapons, and led them in saying the *apratirathaḥ* prayer before departure designed to make them invincible.[71] In this prayer it is none other than *Bṛhaspati*, chaplain–charioteer of the gods, who is addressed.

The exalted position of the charioteer, consequent of his technically complicated job which required skill in horse-lore as much as in aggressive and evasive driving, was common to many cultures. The Kassite king, in greeting the pharaoh, remembered to greet his charioteer and horses,[72] Bagley has shown that the Shang gave elite status to foreigners whom they employed as charioteers,[73] and at Kadesh, Rameses' charioteer Menna, who gives him tactical advice, is respectfully addressed by Rameses as '*shield-bearer*' and '*protector*'. We can surmise that the charioteer had a high social position in the *Mahabharata* period, but his position deteriorated in later centuries with obsolescence of the chariot; the discomfort and derision were interpolated now, as were the justifications for great men driving others' chariots.

The degeneration corresponded with changing role of chariotry. While the *vipatha* was retained by the *vrātya*, chariots became elaborate vehicles with 'mainstream' Aryans by mid-1st millennium who, obsessed with size, number of horses, and strength of crew, replaced *vipatha* manoeuvres with headlong charges like that of Porus's son Hages at Alexander's troops crossing the Jhelum. By this time chariots acquired specialised or ceremonial roles, and were mostly used as command and control platforms. This trend was not unique, but is observable in Neo-Assyria as well, as we shall see.

---

70 *JB*, 3.94.

71 *ṚV*, X: 103,4—*bṛhaspate pári dīyā ráthena rakṣohāmítrāṅ apabādhamānaḥ/ prabhañján sénāḥ pramṛṇó yudhā jáyann asmākam edhy avitā ráthānām.*

72 C. Aldred, *Akhenaten and Nefertiti*, New York, Brooklyn, 1973, p. 13.

73 Bagley, 'Shang Archaeology', p. 208.

Weapons and Equipment

Archery

Archery is the traditional weapon associated with the chariot, though it may not always have been so. Egyptian accounts of the battle of Kadesh claim that Hittite chariots did not use the bow but only lances, a claim that Dawson has refuted.[74] Further, the Linear B tablets have put paid to the theory that the Mycenaeans were averse to archery, though they might indeed have had chivalric regrets about its use. In the *Iliad*, archery was certainly used by the Trojans, and presumably by the Achaeans as well. The bow, among the bewildering range of weapons including magical and supernatural ones that is mentioned in the epic, is the most spectacular and esteemed of all weapons, in contrast to its position in the *Iliad*.[75] However, nowhere in the epic or other literature is the bow adequately described, nor have any specimen or sculptural representation of the Vedic or early IA bow been discovered anywhere in South Asia.

In his foreword to Bakshi's *Mahabharata: a Military Analysis*, Pant has ambiguously remarked that the spans of bows of great warriors were nine *vitastā*s (palm's widths), i.e. four and half cubits, those of others 96 *aṅgula*s or four cubits, the *Piṇāka* and *Śārnga*, along with inferior bows, were three and a half cubits, and that bows of the nobility were shorter.[76] All that can be made of this convoluted statement is that there were several types of bows between three and a half to four and a half cubits long. Now, the great warriors largely fought from chariots, and the four-and-a-half-cubit bow would be too unwieldy for them unless the length here was of the stave along the curve.

74 Dawson, *The First Armies*, p. 148.

75 *ṚV*, VI: 75.2 and 3.

With Bow let us win kine, with Bow in battle, with bow be victory in our hot encounters,

The Bow brings grief and sorrow to the foeman: armed with Bow may we subdue all regions.

Close to his ear, as fain to speak, she presses, holding her well-beloved friend in her embraces.

Strained on the Bow, she whispers like a woman – this bow-string that preserves us in ... combat.

76 Bakshi, *Mahabharata*, pp. xii-xiii.

We may assume that the bow used by the warriors was composite in construction. The composite bow, which had started appearing since the late 3rd millennium across the inter-zone between the steppes and South Asia,[77] had a *force–draw curve* above the flat curve of the simple bow.[78] They were constructed by layering the stave with extension-resistant material like mashed tendon on the back and compression-resistant material like horn, bone, or baleen in the belly. Obviously, such bows are difficult to discern from sculptures, unless they were given pronounced recurves, which was another technique to enhance their power by enhancing the length of the draw by using multiple fulcrums.[79]

The material and enhanced draw offsetting the loss of power resultant from shortening of stave, powerful bows small enough to be used on board the chariot could be constructed. Warriors are often mentioned as taking replacement bows when the one in use was shattered, implying multiple bows in the chariot; like steppe archers, they probably carried two types, one for close combat and another for long range work. In fact, bow-names in the epic do suggest composite designs. The *śārṅga*, i.e. *of horn*, could not but have been a composite bow, as not bows mentioned with *metal or bone tips*, tip here being ends of the staves and not arrowhead.[80] Arjuna's wooden bow was called *Gāṇḍīva*, which meant *knotted*, and probably had a stave composed of several types of wood pasted and knotted together so as to exploit their diverse characters, making it a *reinforced* rather than *composite* bow.

In addition to these bows were what must have been longbows, as suggested by the twelve spans long (*dvādaśaratni*) bow called

77 The earliest indication of any composite, reflex bow to appear anywhere was the Σ bow on the Stele of Naran Sim. Their designs kept evolving. The Hun bow, which was large but with unequal arms probably developed around 3–2nd centuries B.C. The contrasting Scythian bow has a smaller, Cupid's bow shape. Vadim V. Gorbunov and Aleksei A. Tishkin, 'Weapons of the Gorny Altai Nomads in the Hunnu Age', *Archaeology, Ethnology & Anthropology of Eurasia*, vol. 4, no. 28, 2006, pp. 79–85.

78 D. Miller, E. McEwen, and C. Bergman, 'Experimental Approaches to Near Eastern Archery', *World Archaeology*, vol. 18, 1986, pp. 182–84.

79 Not all self-bows were low-powered—the English longbow was a self–bow but the stave was cut in such a way that exploited the opposite properties of the heartwood and sapwood, making it functionally composite.

80 *ṚV*, I:282, and VI:75.

bhārasādhana,[81] obviously used by foot archers. Other bow types were the *vaṅśa-cāpa*, another longbow, and the *ajagava*.

It is also known that while improved bow designs had appeared earlier, the traditional material for arrowheads remained abundantly available bone. It was only in mid-2nd millennium that metal arrowheads appeared for the first time, leading to the ascendancy of the chariot which could carry vast numbers of the enhanced ammunition, and make the bow a mobile arm on the battlefield. In fact, bows were general purpose weapons that could use several types of arrows, and it was arrow quality—stability of flight and penetration—that determined its effectiveness.[82]

Quality of arrow was a function of shaft and arrowhead. As arrows were held against the *outside* of the stave while the plane of the bowstring passed through its centre, arrows were required to *curl around* the stave and regain a line on the plane of the bowstring in order to hit the target and not miss it by an increasing offset. This could be possible only if the shaft had just enough flexibility to curl around the stave without the feather touching it, which would throw the arrow off in the opposite direction. This curling also would create an oscillation, which had to be insignificant enough not to cause the arrow to wobble in flight. Later–day Turcoman archers would praise the *sarkaṇḍā* cane-brakes of North India as far superior to the willow that they used in Central Asia, which made for wobbly arrows; the *Mahabharata* chariots would certainly have carried volumes of such arrows.

While the composite bow gave a powerful launch and the shaft a steady flight, behaviour of the arrow at the end of its flight, i.e. its terminal dynamics, depended upon material and shape of the arrowhead. Penetrativeness is a technical question. Assyrian hunting scenes show lion shot through and through,[83] but military arrowheads need not have been as penetrative as pain threshold of man is lower than that of animals. Also, while hunting arrow needed to be extractable for reuse, military arrowheads had barbs to make extraction difficult. Thus, while the general

81 *Mbh*, Southern Recension, VI: 74.53, and VII: 144.21.

82 Richard H. Lane, 'Review: The Bow: Some Notes on its Origin and Development by Gad Rausing', *American Anthropologist*, N. S., 70/5, 1968, p. 978.

83 Michaela R. Reisinger, 'New Evidence about Composite Bows and Their Arrows in Inner Asia', in *The Silk Road*, vol. 8, 2010, pp. 42–62.

pattern of arrowheads worldwide was like the leaf- or cow's tail-shaped *gopuchha*, many arrowheads had clumsy to elegant barbs at their rears.

In addition to the above, numerous types of arrowheads were in use, like the ārāmukha (saw–mouthed), *kṣurapra* (razor like?), *ardhacandra* (crescent), *vaitastika* (palmate?),[84] *kṣudraka* (small?),[85] *vatsadanta* (calf's tooth),[86] *viśikha* (flame shaped?),[87] *vikarṇa*,[88] and *bastaka* (goat's horn or tortoise nail) in IA sources.[89] Without any definite descriptions, their meanings can at best be guessed, but most of these seem to be special purpose arrows. More evolved designs like cross-sectionals with fine points and chiselled edges for anti–armour work, or trilobites with three cutting edges that were stiffer than the *gopuchha*, are not known in South Asia.

The hymn of the *iśukāra*, a remarkably secular lyric that speaks of travelling fletchers making arrows for clients,[90] mentions copper arrowheads.[91] However, copper arrowheads could not have been too effective unless alloyed with a stiffening material, but no bronze arrowheads like the finished ones of 6th century Carchemish appear anywhere in South Asia. Terms like *śiladhauta*, *śilimukha*, or *śilāśita*, often taken as arsenic bronze, probably meant arrows smeared with arsenic poison.[92] Of iron arrowheads, a few with tangs have been found at Atranjikhera, while the megalithic site of Mahurjhari near Mysore has yielded a finely finished, cylindrical arrowhead of iron with a neat slot at its base to receive the shaft, exhibiting a good understanding of terminal and wound ballistics. Most other iron arrowheads discovered across South Asia have no tangs and possess barbs, which are entirely regressive designs. Other iron arrowheads may have been in use. Heavy iron arrowheads with metal shafts

84 *Mbh,* Southern Recension, VII: 107.55.

85 *Mbh,* Southern Recension, VII: (Jayadrathavadha) 96.4.

86 *Mbh,* Southern Recension, VI: 57.41.

87 *Mbh,* Southern Recension, IX: 15.72.

88 *Mbh,* Southern Recension, VIII: 84.8.

89 *Mbh,* Southern Recension, VII: 100.81.

90 *ṚV*, IX: 112.

91 *RV*, IX:12.2, Īśukāra or fletchers made shafts with canebrakes or *sarkaṇḍā* that was available aplenty along Punjab river banks.

92 *ṚV*, VI: 75.11,15. Poisoned arrowheads are called *lipta* in the *Ṛgveda*.

could have been used to collapse chariots by shooting them through their wheels, while the *nārāc*, which some scholars take as an iron arrowhead, was probably a whistling arrow used for signalling or startling the enemy.

Though metal being ambivalently associated with arrows, arrowheads were mostly of bone, tooth, or horn. Bone was not only cheap and inexhaustible, but when cut and ground into shape had sufficient elasticity to retain a tight hold on the shaft inserted in the slot. However, these were not penetrative and suited only unarmoured targets, as seen in the repeated exhortations to shoot though *chinks* in the armour. Specialised arrows have been known in history, like those for piercing armour, cutting bowstrings,[93] or setting fire.[94] However, magical arrows that extinguished fire, multiplied, spewed snakes, or spread somnolence, were probably products of poetic imagination, their predominance in battle-pieces in the form of vivid imageries causing the epicto lack the raw realism of the *Iliad*. The *isúkāra* lyric speaks of other equipment, for instance bowstrings made of cow-hide thongs stretched to the utmost and glossed with fat.[95] Accessories like arm-bracers are mentioned in the *Ṛgveda*.[96]

Now, while improved bows and arrows had made the chariot a powerful weapon system, the chariot itself was not the ideal shooting platform. Unlike the mounted archer who timed the release of shot at the apex of gallop, chariot archers had to shoot from spring-less, jerky platforms and consequently had poor accuracy. Though immense power was a mark of the great warrior, the descriptions of archers shooting one another's equipment off and cutting bowstrings appear too formalised. Combat archery in the epic was preoccupied with clouds of arrows darkening the skies and warriors and chariots getting porcupined with arrows and yet carrying on. In other words, emphasis was upon volume and rate of fire rather than accuracy. It is true that that Assyrian kings shot lions through and through and Amenhotep III boasted that he once shot three copper targets in sequence from a chariot at full gallop,[97] shooting under combat conditions is wholly different from sport shooting, which

93 Marco Polo, *The Travels*, repr., Harmondsworth, 1980, p. 314.

94 *ṚV*, I: 66.4

95 *ṚV*, IX: 112.

96 *ṚV*, I: 66.4

97 Drews, *Coming of the Greeks*, p. 89.

any modern sports–rifle shooter who is also a combat soldier will attest. At the same time, volume of fire for chariot–borne archers could never match what mounted archers would attain because there were far fewer chariots than there would be horses on the battlefield.

Other Weapons, and Presence of Metal on the Battlefield

Even in other weapons present on the battlefield, like maces, javelins, and swords, use of metal is detectable to varying degrees like it is in the case of arrows. The earliest metal to be used was copper, and the generic Vedic and Old Avestan terms for metal, *ayas* and *aiiah*, come from one of the PIE roots for copper, **ayos*.[98] It also appears that the early PIIr,who had colonised the Urals in search of copper, had learnt of its use from Mesopotamia, as the PIE word for copper, **roudhos*, comes from Sumerian *urud*, while the IE words for battle-axe, *paraśu/pelekuσ/*peleku*, come from the Assyrian *pilakku*[99] or copper.

Earliest use of metal in weaponry probably started with the mace, the venerated Stone Age weapon which remained in ceremonial use across the known world. Pharaohs are seen dispatching sacrificial victims with the mace on the Narmer Palette, and the ceremonial mace of the 'Scorpion king' has been found at Nekhen. The popular mace in the epic, or *gadā*, has been called *aśmagarbhān*[100] or stone-wombed, suggesting that it had a stone core sheathed in a different substance, which was obviously a metal, like the maces with metal sheaths in Egypt and Mesopotamia.

Waradpande, to whom the *Mahabharata* occurred in 3102 B.C. and is associated with the Copper Hoards, accepts only such rudimentary use of metal. He denies the existence of long swords, suggesting that the few blades mentioned in the epic were no more than copper knives and dirks. He cites Sātyaki's grabbing Bhūriśravas by the hair and *sawing* his head off with the *karpaṇa* or *raukṣeyaka* as proof that only short-bladed knives were in use,[101] and correctly equates the 15 centimetre 'antenna swords',

98 See H. Hirt, *Die Indogermanen, ihre Verbeitung, ihre Urheimat and ihre Kultur*, Strasbourg, Trübner, 1905, vol 1, pp. 358–59. Also see the entry under *aes* in A. Ernout and A. Meillet, *Dictionnaire étymologie de la langue latine*, Paris, Klinckseik, 1939.

99 Piggott, *Prehistoric India*, p. 249.

100 *Mbh*, VI: 80,26.

101 N.R. Waradpande, 'The Weaponry in the Bhārata War', in Shastri (ed.), *Mahābhārata*, pp. 99–111.

a common component of the Copper Hoards, with the *hūla* or caltrop, obviously fixed to logs and buried upright to stop horses.[102]

It is true that during the transition from Neolithic to early Chalcolithic, which corresponds with Waradpande's date, metal sheaths on maces had just been introduced and technology for long blades did not exist. However, his very date is questionable, and the epic mentions advanced copper alloys, weakening his position. During her *svayaṁvara*, Draupadī greets a victorious Arjuna with goblet and mirror of white bronze (*vīrakāṁsya*).[103] In another episode, she collects Yudhiṣṭhira's blood in *sauvarṇam pātraṁ kāṁsyaṁ*, i.e. 'gilded vessel of white bronze' when he is struck by Virāṭ.[104] Such alloys, which indicate use of zinc and other metal, suggest a more advanced metallurgy. In fact, placing the war so far back in antiquity destroys the structure of the narrative itself, as it does away with the ubiquitous chariot.

Waradpande also seems to have overlooked the part that just before he was killed, Bhūriśravas had towered over a prone Sātyaki and *raised* his sword to strike him when his arm was lopped off by Arjuna's arrow. If Bhūriśravas could strike a prone figure with a blade while standing, the blade must have been long enough to be called a sword. In fact, swords do appear at several places in the epic. Jayadratha's blade is called *mahānasiḥ* or full length, Dhṛṣṭaketu fights Paurava with what is called *nistṛṅśa*, i.e. thirty *aṅgula* (finger) long and thus long enough to be a sword, Dhṛṣṭadyumna beheads Droṇa with a sword, Karṇa and Bhīma fight with swords, and Nakula is especially called a swordsman.[105] The *maṇḍalāgra* (circle–fronted), which Waradpande thinks was a short copper blade, was probably the straight-sword ending in a saw–toothed disc common in later temple sculpture. The epic contradicts itself in its praise for the sword—the *Virāṭaparvan* calls the *Naiṣādhya* or Niṣāda sword as the best[106] while the *Sabhāparvan* gives this honour to the *Aparānta* or western sword.[107]

102 *Mbh*,Southern Recension, VII: 166.20. These antennae 'swords' could never be used as swords because the antennae or prongs would interfere with the wielder's wrist.

103 *Mbh*, I: 176.30.

104 *Mbh*, IV: 63, 47.

105 *Mbh*, III: 255.10

106 *Mbh*, IV: 142.14.

107 *Mbh*, II: 51.28.

There are some crucial pointers to the metal used in swords. In one episode, Jayadratha's sword catches in Abhimanyu's quiver and shatters when he tries to yank it out;[108] in another, Śikhaṇḍin's sword is shattered by Karṇa's arrow, and when he flings the bit left in his hand at Karṇa, the latter shatters that too. Shattering was a typical iron sword problem, the result of enthusiastic smiths making the blade too brittle by hammering it longer than required.[109] The terms *pīta* and *saikya/śaikya*, which appear several times in the epic in the context of weaponry, is interpreted by Fitzgerald as meaning *quenched* and *boiled* respectively, and seen by him as indicators of advanced iron working techniques like tempering and quenching to produce carburized, mild steel.[110] There are several other references to iron weapons, like the *nārāc* arrow, Karṇa's bow which is of metal, and the *gadā* which has been called *śaikyāyasi*.[111]

These evidences go well with our placing the epic at the turn of the first millennium, when iron was coming into use across the known world, rather than Waradpande's placing of the epic at the juncture between the Neolithic and early Calcholithic and his identification of the *Mahabharata* with the Copper Hoard.[112] However, that iron was present does not automatically imply that the Iron Age was in full flow—iron had been known in West Asia as early as in 2800 B.C., from when comes the iron sword found at Tell Asmar in Egypt, but at that early age it was too expensive for general use. Iron is estimated to have been at least eight times the price of gold in Assyria in the early 2nd millennium B.C. and used only for ornamental purposes, such expensiveness probably because the little iron available was of meteoric origin. This is hinted at in the curious remark of Bhīṣma in the epic, that swords were invented when *ulkā*s or meteors were studied.

108 *Mbh*, VII: 13.68.

109 While hammering added small amounts of carbon to create a mild steel, and also created microscopic serrations along the edgeby causing the steel to fold over itself, giving a superlative cutting edge, too much hammering increased the proportion of carbon beyond the optimal and made the blade brittle.

110 James Fitzgerald, 'Pīta and Śaikya/Saikya: Two Terms of Iron and Steel Technology in the Mahābhārata', *Journal of the American Oriental Society*, vol. 120, no.1, January–March 2000, pp. 44–61.

111 *Mbh*, VII: 59.11.

112 This identification is not convincing, and the hoards have been associated with Late Harappans and Munda by others.

Iron became more accessible in West Asia after 1600 B.C., after which it was used for utilitarian purposes in Anatolia and the Yaz I culture in the Kopet Dag Mountains.[113] This was also the time from which the first indicators of iron appear in South Asia—implements like double-edged daggers, socketed axe–heads, flat-axes with broad edge, and diverse spearheads and arrowheads have been found from Eran near Nagda and at other parts of Madhya Pradesh, the eastern Vindhyas, and the Central Gangetic plains.[114] Vibha Tripathi sees little evidence of import of iron from West Asia and Iran,[115] and traces diffusion of iron in South Asia from Central India—iron appears in Haryana in 1200 B.C. and at PGW and Swat cultures in the north and in Karnataka in the south around 1000 B.C. At the same time, it would be too simplistic to deny any movement of iron into South Asia, especially because of its contiguity with the Iranic world. Dani argues that folks who brought fractional burial into the Gandhara Grave culture also brought iron,[116] while many Deccan Megaliths sites, like Hallur, Mahurjhari, or Adichanallur, were created by iron-using immigrants. We have already encountered the advanced iron arrowhead at Mahurjhari; Adichanallur has a grave in a stone cavity that could not have been cut without iron tools.

In the epic, there is negligible mention of *kāṅsya* or bronze in the context of weapons, while iron is denoted with terms derived from copper with the qualifiers *red* or *black*, i.e. *lohāyas* and *kṛṣṇāyas*. It would however be too ambitious to conclude that iron was already used for utilitarian purposes—bronze was still superior to wrought iron while steel production was irregular, vaguely comprehended, and unreliable. One must agree with Vibha Tripathi that Griffith's translation of the Vedic

113 Jane C. Waldbaum, 'The First Archaeological Appearance of Iron', in Theodore A. Wertime and James D. Mulhy (eds.), *The Coming of the Age of Iron*, New Haven, Connecticut, Yale University Press, 1980, pp. 69–98, especially pp. 75–77. Hattusilis tried to appease Shalmaneser III with a gift of ornamental iron, Forbes, *Studies in Ancient Technology*, Leiden, E.J. Brill, 1964, vol. 9, pp. 253–255, also Waldbaum, 'Iron', p. 80. One reason why iron was so expensive is that its production could not be detected, predicted, or controlled. See Theodore A. Wertime, 'The Pyrotechnologic Background', in Wertime and Mulhy (eds.), *Coming of the Age of Iron*, pp. 1–24.

114 Rakesh Tewari, 'The origins of iron-working in India: New Evidence from the Central Ganga Plain and the Eastern Vindhyas', *Antiquity*, vol. 77, no. 297, 2003, pp. 536–544. The Ramayana enemies have iron; see V.K. Jain, *Prehistory*, pp. 124–27.

115 Tripathi, *Iron*, pp. 34–35, 208.

116 Dani, 'Pastoral–Agrarian', pp. 406–7.

terms *dhaṅdhamant* and *saṅdamanti* as *welding* was a bit far–fetched![117] At the same time, the continuance of a Bronze Age cannot be deduced from the mere mention of bronze objects, like in the context of Draupadī. These articles, of bronze and brass burnished white or gold by adding zinc, appear only in the elite and ceremonial context, just as even today meals on auspicious occasions in Indian households are served in brass utensils. The ceremonial position of bronze is highlighted in the lament that on the eve of the destruction of the world, dirt will lie on dishes of white bronze (*kāṅsyabhāṇḍa*), while sacrificial offerings will be made on dishes of the worst kind (*kupātraka*).[118] In fact, bronze was an elite material that seldom survived a non–elite context, as seen in the case of the Mughals.[119]

The above taken together suggests there is no reason to be as conservative as Waradpande about the use of metal, and that iron was present on the battlefield. There is however no ground to presume iron-heavy armies in the *Mahabharata* like those of mid-1st millennium. A wide range of weapons was in use, including those of bone, copper, bronze, and iron, like West Asia where iron and steel weapons and tools coexisted with those of bronze.[120] Weapons like the śakti, *ṛṣṭi*, and *tomara*[121] (javelins, spears, and clubs), which were of iron in the medieval period, may still have been of bronze at Kurukṣetra. Even foresters', hunters', and pastors' weapons of the Stone Age, like the *avaṣkanda* and *pāśa*, i.e. noose and lasso, *āstara* or throwing stick, and discus or quoit, were present. Also, whatever iron was present on the battlefield was of both indigenous and West Asian origin, seen best in the contradictory statements regarding the *Naiṣādhya* and *Aparānta* swords.

117 Vibha Tripathi, *History of Iron Technology in India (From Beginning to Pre–Modern Times)*, New Delhi, Rupa, 2008, p. 33; also *ṚV* X.31.3

118 *Mbh,* XII: 220.113.

119 Copper production centred around Agra, which was the core of the empire; K.K. Trivedi, *Agra: Economic and Political Profile of a Mughal Suba,* Ravish, Pune, 1988, pp. 137–8, 217. Most production of bronzes was for temple establishment and royalty, see M. Mukherjee, *Metalcraftsmen of India*, Anthropological Survey of India, Calcutta, 1978, pp.5–6. Production depended upon scrap metal in which there was a brisk trade, see D.K. Chakrabarti and N. Lahiri, *Copper and its Alloys in Ancient India*, Munshiram Manoharlal, Delhi, 1996, pp. 157 ff.

120 Waldbaum, 'The First Archaeological Appearance of Iron', pp. 84-85.

121 *Mbh,* Southern Recension, VI (*Bhīṣmavadhaparvan*): 52.22.

Closely associated with weapons was armour, which chariot warriors required for their protection above the waist. Impregnable *varma*s are mentioned, often of costly and fabulous material, chinks through which were to be targeted. The appeal of armour extended to the supernatural—Karṇa was born with an impregnable armour which he was tricked into parting with, while Duryodhana becomes naturally armoured by the pious glance of Gāndhāri (who removes her blindfold to behold him for a moment), except for the loins which he had kept covered out of modesty, in a theme reminiscent of Achilles' heel. Repeated references to magically impregnable *varma*s, and to warriors carrying on despite being porcupined with arrows, suggest that armour was effective, though in one comic episode Duryodhana, who turns up wearing a borrowed *varma* reputed to be impregnable, is riddled through its chinks by Arjuna and driven away.

It is unlikely that in the suffocating heat of South Asia, massive armours of the *Iliad* type, probably like the one found at Dendra, were used. Rather, concomitant mention of *carma* or leather suggests that armour was mainly of hide reinforced with metal bosses, like the Hittite (Hurrian) *sharyan* which was a leather tunic covered with bronze scales.[122] Shields were of similar material, bull-hide or ārṣabhacarma being most popular.

Armour protection was probably limited to the elite, the laity making do with cheaper material, and their agility. Hopkins has given a survey of the jewel and ornaments that nobles went to battle bedecked with,[123] but these references seem to be later interpolation made during more relaxed and lavish times when kings supervised and did not lead the fight, and were not in immediate danger.

At the end of this chapter we can conclude that the *Mahabharata* armies centred on fabulously rich warriors who fought in medium armour from superlative chariots, their primary weapon being the composite bow though they were comfortable enough wielding a variety of other weapons, of bronze as well as iron. These men were accompanied by the laity, armed in a more plebeian manner, which supposedly was organised in a strict hierarchy and was capable of forming itself into arrays, two aspects which

122 Drews, *Coming of the Greeks*, p.88; one helmet of the *sharyan* could have as many as 140 to 200 scales

123 Hopkins, 'Ruling Caste', pp. 317–18.

shall be inspected again in the next chapter. References to siege weapons like *śataghni* were probably later interpolations,[124] and we must not bother too much with the fabulous weapons associated with gods and potent sages that were often used on the battlefield, but like Waradpande, invite their champions to demonstrate how they worked.

124 *Mbh*, CE VIII: 7.8, though the *śataghni* has also been called a spike–studded ball.

CHAPTER 7

Reconstructing the Battle

The 'First Ten' Days' Action

The last chapter gave us a rundown of the eighteen days of battle, also discussing organizations, formations, and weapon and equipment, including the chariot. This chapter will inspect some of these aspects again to derive a reasonable reconstruction of the course of the war.

It is seen that the first major warrior to fall was Bhīṣma, shot down on the tenth day of battle, an event that was followed by the appointment of Droṇa as the next Kuru marshal. Bhīṣma's attitude is crucial—he had agreed to be the Kuru marshal only on conditions that he would do everything short of killing the Pandu who were dear to him, he had stated that he would not fight Śikhaṇḍin, a person of ambiguous gender, and he refused to fight alongside Karṇa. To Yardi, the conditions regarding the Pandu and Śikhaṇḍin, and the story of Bhīṣma's goof-up in abducting brides for his two half-brothers which led to the birth of Śikhaṇḍin (see later), had been introduced by Sūta, and that regarding Karṇa by Sautī. In the latter story, on being asked by Duryodhana to assess the warriors on either side, Bhīṣma had rated Karṇa only as *ardharatha* (half-a-warrior), because, first, he had given away his natural protection to Indra, and second, he bore a curse (of Bhārgava Rama) that would make him unable to recollect the use of his best weapons at the moment of crisis, this assessment leading to a fallout between them. Obviously, the *ardharatha* story conceals the later disapprobation directed at Karṇa for being of 'charioteer' origin, while the other two stories help make grounds for Bhīṣma's ineffectual fight, and strange conduct when it came to fighting Śikhaṇḍin.

An aspect noticeable through the first ten days' narrative is that suspense is repeatedly built up and relaxed, each spike, related to an earlier one by pathos or irony, coming closer to climax but at times finishing in anti-climax. Major chiefs clash repeatedly, coming closer to their ends, but while they lose their charioteers and have chariots dashed under them in a sequential network of engagements, only their *anugāḥ* or followers (see later), or junior warriors like the Mātsya and Kuru brothers, are killed while they themselves are extricated. All in all, the ten days of *Bhīṣmaparvan* seem to have been arranged for listening pleasure, as much the purpose of the epic as moral instruction; the above technique, which we shall call *brinkmanship* for lack of a better one, was one of the methods of ensuring such pleasure.

Brinkmanship is most evident in the contest between Arjuna and Bhīṣma. The two clash tremendously on the first day and Arjuna has to be extricated by Sātyaki. On the second day, Sātyaki kills Bhīṣma's charioteer but gets into trouble himself and has to be extricated. On the third, exasperated at Arjuna's reluctance to kill Bhīṣma, Krishna rushes to do so with his discus and is barely restrained by Arjuna. On the fifth day, Śikhaṇḍin attacks Bhīṣma, at which Bhīṣma turns away leaving Droṇa to drive him back. On the ninth day, Arjuna and Śikhaṇḍin come near to killing Bhīṣma but desist out of reverence, and Krishna again threatens to kill Bhīṣma, this time with his whip. On the tenth, Bhīṣma is felled by Arjuna and Śikhaṇḍin. It can be seen that, while Bhīṣma's prowess over Arjuna is initially underlined, Arjuna and Śikhaṇḍin each are individually brought close to killing him once, and then once together, all setting the stage for the finalé. Also, while the second instance of Krishna flying at Bhīṣma with his whip is more in flow of the narrative and suits its terse language, the first episode appears to be interpolated in order to build tension twice—the listener holds his breath lest Krishna break his vow and sighs in relief when he does not at last.[1] With suspense built up in this manner, Arjuna and Śikhaṇḍin jointly fell Bhīṣma on the tenth day, but only immobilizing and not killing him.

Similar narrative techniques are observed in other traditions—in the *Iliad*, what was a single Trojan charge forcing the palisades and reaching the beached ships was worked into *two* attacks, the first making a great start but petering out, and the second renewing the charge again. More

1 Karve, *Yugānta*, pp. 23, 27.

instances of brinkmanship are discernible in the *Mahabharata*. Arjuna extricates his son Abhimanyu from an ambush on the fourth day, an episode that will serve as a pathetic reminder when Abhimanyu is butchered on the thirteenth day, with no Arjuna to help him this time. On another occasion, Abhimanyu has three Kuru brothers in his power but spares them just as he was about to kill them so that Bhīma could fulfil his vow of killing all the hundred; this was obviously designed to make the listener wonder about the fate of Bhīma's vow.

Through the 'ten' days, Duryodhana endlessly remonstrates with Bhīṣma for not doing enough as marshal, to which Bhīṣma retaliates by needling him and Duḥśāsana on their past conduct, telling them that the war was futile, and advising them to make peace, in fact doing everything to break their morale. Dhṛtarāṣṭra is also berated by his friend and counsel Sañjaya for his obstinacy and blind affection towards his erring sons. Such moralization, and the precondition laid down by Bhīṣma of not slaying the Pandu, serve to explain the ineffectual fight under Bhīṣma's command.

A touching episode occurs in the evening of the ninth day when the Pandu *visit the Kuru camp* and learn from Bhīṣma that the secret of killing him was to place Śikhaṇḍin ahead of Arjuna, as he would not wield his weapons in the presence of the former. The story of Śikhaṇḍin is told here. It so happened that Bhīṣma abducted the three daughters of the Kāśī chief for his two half-brothers, but the eldest, Ambā, turned out to be already betrothed to Śālva. She was rejected by Śālva when Bhīṣma, on learning the truth, sent her honourably to him; afterwards, she was rebuffed by Bhīṣma who was under a vow of celibacy. Consequently, Ambā gave up her life by penance, vowing to take birth again to kill Bhīṣma. It was she who was born as a princess to Drupada of Pañcāla, who later converted to a male, Śikhaṇḍin.

There is a major difficulty with the plot here. A visit to the Kuru camp is of doubtful authenticity, and not only because it was a highly dangerous thing for the Pandu to do. Bhīṣma had been twice observed, on the fifth and ninth days, to break contact at the approach of Śikhaṇḍin and thus it was *not necessary* for the Pandu to be actually *told* to deploy Śikhaṇḍin in order to fell him. At the same time, as per the tenets of *karma* which was increasingly becoming popular in the 1st millennium, one's gender in the previous birth did not disqualify one from being fought in the current one. The difficulty was that Ambā *alias* Śikhaṇḍin was born a *girl* and *later turned* male; in other words, the 'sex–change' occurred in the *current life*, showing that Śikhaṇḍin was some sort of transgender or eunuch.[2] Now, eunuch generals have been part of Asian militaries since the Middle Ages and Śikhaṇḍin himself is seen as not only fighting valiantly but also commanding an entire *akṣauhiṇi*. None of the other warriors have any qualms in fighting him, and in fact he gives Droṇa an especially hard time. In the light of the above, Bhīṣma's reluctance to fight Śikhaṇḍin seems to be an over-reaction.

It will be further observed that Bhīṣma is *not actually killed but only immobilised* by the duo, and is left lying on the battlefield surrounded by a trench to keep the jackals out, his favourite Arjuna having arranged for headrest and water by driving arrows into the ground while Duryodhana, who offered him soft cushions and water in precious vessels, is rebuked. It is long after the battle, when he would be visited by grieving women and would give the Pandu much kingly advice, that he would pass away with the winter solstice. We will return to the question of Bhīṣma's demise again.

A Scheme Emerges

In contrast to the indeterminate slogging under Bhīṣma, a scheme emerges with Droṇa's elevation as marshal, which also coincides with Karṇa joining the battle. Fascination with vivid battle formations disappears and *vyuhas* become functional and practical. Duryodhana and Droṇa plan to capture Yudhiṣṭhira, with the intention of forcing the Pandu back to the negotiating table and into another 'exile'. They try to give shape to this plan over the next three days, during which the action, split in two spheres, is marked by overt brinkmanship. On the first of these, i.e. the eleventh day, the Pandu trounce many Kuru warriors though no major one is killed, but late in the day Droṇa drives Dhṛṣṭadyumna off and almost captures Yudhiṣṭhira who is just saved by the opportune appearance of Arjuna. Realising that it would be quite impossible to capture Yudhiṣṭhira as long as Arjuna was at large, Droṇa deploys the Trigarta to keep him away from Yudhiṣṭhira on the twelfth day.

2 Yardi, *The Mahabharata*, p. 18.

The Trigartas take the *saṁsaptaka* oath and launch what has been popularly called a *suicide mission*; with Arjuna engaged, the Kuru mount a determined attack on Yudhiṣṭhira killing many princes like Ketama, Vasudhāna, the Pañcāla princes Vṛka, Pāñcālya, and Satyajit, and the Matsya prince Śatānīka. The situation worsens towards the end of the day when Bhīma is attacked by the elephants of the *mleccha* king of Aṅga (not Karṇa, who is *Aṅgarāja* elsewhere) and Bhagadatta, the ancient king of Prāgjyotiṣ. In a part–comic sequence, Bhīma's horses are spooked by Supratīka, Bhagadatta's gigantic elephant, who violently sprays them with mucus; it then dashes his chariot to pieces. Bhīma attacks on foot and kills the elephant of the Aṅga king, but gets entangled with the legs of Supratīka—he hits him in the testicles, causing the beast, mad with pain and rage, to spin round and round trying to crush him. The hilarious suspense at the narrator's court at all this can be imagined.

Reinforcement for Bhīma appears in the shape of the king of Daśārṇa, an eastern ally of the Pandu, who attacks Supratīka with his own mighty elephant; though this beast is killed, Bhīma takes the opportunity to escape. In the meanwhile, hearing the roars of Supratīka and Bhīma and sensing trouble, Arjuna *disengages* from the Trigarta and rushes to Bhīma's aid. A picturesque pathos is added here—with an arrow Arjuna clips the bandana that keeps the wrinkles of old Bhagadatta from falling over his eyes, and when Bhagadatta, shorn of his weapons, hurls his elephant goad at Arjuna, it turns into a garland and settles on the neck of Krishna because it was charged with the charm of Vishnu. The venerable Supratīka, mortally wounded and no longer able to respond to command, stands swaying and is about to collapse when Bhagadatta is decapitated by a crescent arrow. Arjuna now carries the counteroffensive at Droṇa; Śakuni's sons are killed fighting heroically beside Droṇa while Śakuni just escapes, which is when the day's battle ends.

That evening, Duryodhana needles Droṇa, who also was loth to actually kill the Pandu, into deploying the notorious *circle-* or *cakravyūha* the next day, the secret of negotiating which was supposedly known only to Arjuna. But next morning Arjuna is again 'called away' by the Trigarta, and his young son Abhimanyu volunteers to lead the attack on the *cakravyūha*, insisting that he possessed the secret of breaking into it, having overheard that part when he was in his mother's womb as Arjuna explained to her its mechanics. He however confesses that he did not know how to get out of it again as his mother had fallen asleep halfway through the epic pillow-talk; despite misgivings, Yudhiṣṭhira lets Abhimanyu lead the attack, arranging to follow at his heels so that they could break out together. However, things go wrong at once, and the Pandu, unaware of the mechanics of the *vyūha*, fail to keep up with Abhimanyu and are cut off by Jayadratha. In an episode of extreme pathos, young Abhimanyu is surrounded and unhorsed, reduced to fighting with broken pieces of his chariots, and butchered. As per Yardi, much of this episode was added as late as Sautī.[3]

On both previous days, Arjuna had appeared in the end to save Yudhiṣṭhira and Bhīma; in fact, on the previous day he had *disengaged* from the Trigarta on *hearing* the roars of Supratīka and Bhīma. On this fateful day, however, though he supposedly knew that the Kuru had deployed the *cakravyūha*, he does nothing of the sort and returns to camp in the evening after demolishing the Trigarta. As he nears the camp, he is affected with a sense of foreboding and the silence and averted glances tell him that his son had been killed, the pathos heightened by the recollection of the fourth day when he had extricated his son from a Kuru ambuscade. He is consoled by Krishna who repeats some of the exhortations of the *Gītā*.

It can be seen that the action of these three days is divided into two scenes, one around Arjuna, and the other around the rest of the Pandu. The fourteenth day, action takes an entirely new tempo, becoming focused, relentless, and destructive. Before we examine the course of the battle, we will take a survey of chariot fighting across the world and try to comprehend its many traditions. This will be followed by a second look at the structure of the armies engaged.

Nature of Combat

Mahabharata combats apparently follow rules of chivalry, with warriors challenging one another to duels, fighting mounted with bow and arrow, driving and dodging, till one of them is killed or driven away. At the same time, chivalric precepts are easily violated—'inviolate' charioteers are targeted, heroes kill droves of infantry when not engaged with equals, and trickery is used. The above structure of fighting resembles somewhat

3 Yardi, *The Mahabharata*, p. 179.

the *Li* oriented chariot–archery of the *Spring and Autumn* period in China or that of the *Iliad*, though there is lesser presence of chariot archery in the latter and warriors fight dismounted at close quarters.

The *Iliad* style of fighting was resembled by European and Cyrenaican chariotry of the late 1st millennium B.C., in that warriors drove about posturing but fought dismounted, though the heroic element is subdued here. These traditions were different from West Asian chariotry which, shorn of the heroic element, revolves around sweeping manoeuvres of vast squadrons. Quite understandably, as chariots remained in military use in different geostrategic spheres for more than a millennium, during which their technology and sociology evolved at varying rates, several styles of chariot fighting emerged none of which should be generalized as *the* manner of chariot warfare.

Shaughnessy grouped these styles across time and space into three stages—an *incipient* or *rudimentary stage* when West Asia was taken over by early chariot powers, a *stage of maximum potential*, i.e. the five centuries of the Golden (actually Bronze) Age of chariotry which saw the emergence of the great chariot empires and flowering of chariot elites, and the *stage of obsolescence*, through which chariotry faded out as the main arm of decision.[4] In the *incipient stage*, which Anthony or Piggott placed in the Urals[5] and Littauer and Crouwel in West Asia,[6] armies deployed only a few vehicles in auxiliary roles like flanking, scouting, pursuit, or as command and control platforms.[7] With improving technology, horses, and means of control, larger and larger numbers of chariots came into use, leading to the stage of *maximum potential*; the walls of the Amon Temple in Karnak[8] record the 15th century battle of Megiddo (Armageddon) which is renowned for Pharaoh Thutmose III's strategic masterstroke of forced–marching for 19 days *via* rugged, little known routes to outflank the Mitanni and suddenly appear below the walls of Megiddo. Though there is not much action—taken by surprise, the garrison hastily withdrew

4 Shaughnessy, 'Historical Perspectives', pp. 210.

5 Piggott, 'Chinese Chariotry', pp. 32–51, and Piggott, *Earliest Wheeled Transport*, pp.103–04.

6 Littauer and Crouwel, 'Origin of the True Chariot', p. 51, note 26.

7 Drews, *Coming of the Greeks*, pp. 102–105.

8 For a fuller account of the Megiddo Battle, see James Henry Breasted, *Ancient Records of Egypt: Historical Documents*, Part 2, Chicago, University of Illinois, 1906, p. 407.

abandoning its chariots except those which it could hoist over the wall—,[9] it is evident that more chariots were used than ever before,[10] they were deployed independent of infantry, and also associated with the composite bow.

Further, chariots at Megiddo must have been light and agile—the Egyptians made an arduous approach march through rugged terrain while the Megiddans *hoisted* many over their walls. A couple of centuries later in 1274 B.C. was fought the well-documented battle of Kadesh which saw the use of even greater numbers of chariots. This mobile battle seems to have been precipitated when Pharaoh Rameses II, misled by Hittite spies into crossing the Orontes River, blundered into an ambush of hundreds of chariots swarming out from behind a low hill. Rameses extricated himself with great difficulty, charging six times. He then counterattacked the Hittite king Muwattalis's chariots which had pursued him across the Orontes but had stopped to plunder his camp, driving them back across the river. Both sides claimed victory in the battle that saw the use of an estimated 7000 chariots, including reinforcements, but all that can be concluded is that Egyptian losses were not as high as the Hittites claimed; the pharaoh claimed personal credit for rallying his army, berating his nobles for cowardice.

Egyptian records claim that while their chariots had archers, there were none with the Hittites who carried spears instead. Use of spears on board chariots is a contentious issue. While P.A.L. Greenhalgh, examining pictorial representations from the *Geometric Period*, argues that Achaean chariots did not fight in the Homeric style at all but fought dogfights with spears from chariots,[11] this thesis, supported by no more than one single instance in the *Iliad* where Diomedes hurls a javelin from his chariot at Hector, is difficult to accept. Littauer and Crouwel have shown that a moving chariot was not a suitable platform for either throwing or thrusting spears—the throw would lack power and accuracy, while the thrust could

9 The Egyptian victory was not complete because they started plundering the baggage.

10 894 chariots were captured by the Egyptians, while in two other contemporary battles the Egyptians capture 730 and 1092 chariots from their enemies; if so many were captured, presumably many more were in use. Shaughnessy, 'Historical Perspectives', p. 212.

11 See P.A.L. Greenhalgh, *Early Greek Warfare: Horsemen and Chariots in the Homeric and Archaic Ages*, New York, Cambridge University Press, 1973, pp. 14–15.

knock the wielder off or drag him away if the point got caught in the target.[12] Also, javelins were not effective as far fewer javelins could be carried than arrows, most of which would soon be irretrievably lost, while the need to carry them upright would make chariots unstable.

It is true that Caesar recorded British charioteers hurling spears, but though he has spoken very highly of the control and agility of the charioteers, he never said how effective the spears were[13]; on the whole the intention seems to have been to raise a scare. Even the Chinese halberd or *ge* used from chariots was a *slashing* and *not thrusting* weapon designed for use against infantry and not chariots. Robin Archer has argued that Egyptian records were propaganda misrepresentations, probably due to conventional reason,[14] and archery was associated with West Asian chariotry as much as with the Egyptians. It is unconvincing that the Hittites would attempt to fight the Egyptians, who were renowned archers, without archers of their own—in fact, most bas reliefs of Hittite chariots have three–man crews, a driver, a shield-bearer, and a third man who is seen variously wielding the bow or a spear.

Drews, to whom the chariot had relegated infantries to baggage and garrison duties,[15] gives archery a predominant role in West Asian chariot battles which he visualises as great lines of chariots sweeping across the battlefield shooting at each other, and passing through repeatedly till

12 Littauer and Crouwel, 'Chariots in Late Bronze Age Greece', in Littauer and Crouwel, *Selected Writings*, pp. 53–61. Also, M.A. Littauer, 'Review: P.A.L. Greenhalgh, *Early Greek Warfare*', *Classical Philology*, vol. 72, no. 4, October 1977, pp. 363–65.

13 Caius Julius Caesar, *De Bello Gallico" and Other Commentaries by Caius Julius Caesar*, trans. W. A. MacDevitt, 1915, Project Gutenberg EBook available at http://www.gutenberg.org/files/10657/10657.txt, accessed 21 Aug 2015.

> '*display ... the speed of horse,* [together with] *the firmness of infantry; and by daily practice and exercise attain to such expertness that they are accustomed, even on a declining and steep place, to check their horses at full speed, and manage and turn them in an instant and run along the pole, and stand on the yoke, and thence betake themselves with the greatest celerity to their chariots again*'.

14 Robin Archer, 'Developments in Near–Eastern Chariotry and Chariot Warfare in the Early First Millennium BCE and their Contribution to the Rise of Cavalry', in Garrett G. Fagan and Matthew Trundle (eds.), *New Perspectives on Ancient Warfare*, Leiden, Brill, 2010, pp. 57–79, especially pp. 61–62.

15 Robert Drews, *End of the Bronze Age: Changes in Warfare and the Catastrophe ca. 1200 BC*, Princeton, Princeton Univ. Press, 1993, pp. 137–141.

one side broke.[16] This idea, if borrowed from that of fighter squadrons sweeping through one another, ignores the fact that aircraft casualties usually *drop out* of the sky and do not drift as smoking ruins—sweeping lines of chariots passing through one another would only lead to endless collisions and pileups, causing more fatalities than enemy action, and the battlefield would look like a scrapyard after two passes. Further, it is doubtful if horses, loth to charge steady infantry, could be made to charge at a line of rushing chariots which would be overhung by a solid wall of dust.

Now, while Drews nowhere explicitly mentioned aerial battles, Otterbein advanced a model of chariot combats based on the aerial dogfight wherein hero–warriors drove around fighting one another, being extracted and replaced, and killed in case they fell.[17] Otterbein's model, which resembles *Mahabharata* chariotry, in associating the chariot with the hero–warrior at once reduces its numbers to manageable and practicable levels. We will return to Otterbein's model and its association with the hero–warrior after considering some other models of chariot warfare.

Returning to the *Iliad*, it is pertinent to note that this epic contains only one episode of a running chariot battle. Its Aegean warriors use chariots as transport but fight dismounted with hefty spears, heavy swords, maces, and massive stones, and finally grapple with bare hands. It is understandable that the Aegean never developed the sweeping manoeuvres of West Asia—paucity of space in its broken and intensively cultivated islands ruled out such tactics. Yet, the *Iliad*'s battle-pieces are often so exaggerated and fabulous that Homer, who otherwise displays remarkable familiarity with weaponry and human anatomy, has been castigated as ignorant of epic period warfare[18] and anachronistically juxtaposing horse-based chivalric combat from his own time, i.e. the mid-1st millennium.

16 Drews, *End of the Bronze Age*, pp. 127–129.

17 Keith F. Otterbein, *How War Began*, Texas A&M University Anthropology Series, no. 10, 2004, p. 170–71.

18 See, for instance, E. Delebecque, *Le cheval dans l'Iliade, suivi d'un lixique du cheval chez Homère et d'un essai sur le cheval pré-homérique*, Paris, C. Klincksieck, 1951, pp. 51, 86–109; G.S. Kirk, *Songs of Homer*, Cambridge, 2005, pp. 39, 124–5, 189–90; A. Snodgrass, *Early Greek Armour and Equipment,* Edinburgh, Edinburgh University Press, 1964, pp. 159–63.

J.K. Anderson cites the consistency in chariotry legends across the Aegean to argue in favour of authenticity of Homeric accounts, suggesting that castigation of Homer is equivalent of suggesting that the only manner of chariot combat was the massed manoeuvres of Kadesh, and those found in the *Old Testaments* and other Mediterranean documents.[19] While consistency in legends and accounts does not essentially imply actual prevalence of such warfare and may be attributed to one *widely perceived view* of warfare which all authors had depended upon, accounts from other periods and places do seem to uphold the 'battle-taxi' style of Homer. Diodorus Sicilus and Strabo attest that Gallic wars resembled Homeric warfare,[20] while the Greek nation of Cyrenaica, serving as mercenaries in the African wars of Thibron and Ophelas in the late 4th century, used chariots to arrive fresh in combat as reminiscent of Homer. In his *De Bello Gallico*, Caesar writes that the British

> '*drive about* … [their *essada*] … *in all directions and throw their weapons and generally break the ranks of the enemy with the very dread of their horses and the noise of their wheels; and when they have worked themselves in between the troops of horse, leap from their chariots and engage on foot. The charioteers in the meantime withdraw some little distance from the battle, and so place themselves with the chariots that, if their masters are overpowered by the number of the enemy, they may have a ready retreat to their own troops*'.[21]

The above shows that the 'battle–taxi' concept of transporting 'infantry' cannot be written off, and even Littauer and Crouwel have endorsed it to an extent.[22] While Snodgrass argues that men in super–heavy armour as in the *Iliad*, an example of which is the heavy, 15-pieced, articulated corselet found at Dendra in the Argolids from the 14th century,[23]

19 J.K. Anderson, 'Homeric, British and Cyrenaic Chariots', *American Journal of Archaeology*, vol. 69, no. 4, 1965, pp. 349–52.

20 Anderson, 'Homeric, British, and Cyrenaic Chariots', p. 350. Diodorus Sicilus (10.5.21.5) attested that this was '*just as the ancient heroes of Greece are related to have used them in the Trojan war*'

21 Caesar, *De Bello Gallico*, 4:33.

22 Littauer and Crouwel, 'Chariots in Late Bronze Age Greece', p. 61.

23 Drews, *Coming of the Greeks*, pp. 166.

could only fight aboard chariots,[24] Crouwel argues that men in such armour could only fight dismounted.[25]

Y. Yadin, a man of immense military experience in the Arab–Israeli wars, goes further and suggests that crews of Achaean and Hittite chariots were really *infantry* units delivered at the point of action,[26] like dragoons who moved on horse but fought on foot. Now, using an entire chariot to transport just *one* fighter would be sub-optimal unless that individual was far more effective than one infantryman—else, carts to transport entire squads would be preferable. The term infantry itself has plebeian connotations, and even though *Iliad* heroes fought on foot, they were not infantry, i.e. the kind of men who could be herded to fight as a body like a company of infantry. Except a few isolated instances when they fight together, they are seen ploughing their individual furrows. In other words, not any man who fought on foot was infantry, and the impact of the Greek hero–warrior, even when on foot, would have been sufficient to warrant dedication of an entire chariot to him.

Dismounted fighting is observed among Gallic charioteers too, who drew up facing the enemy, and stepped forward challenging, boasting, and cursing, all of which resembled acts of the Homeric hero–warriors. Though these and British chariot–warriors fight the Romans in gangs, they were elites in their own societies and, when fighting among themselves, may have followed the hero–warrior tradition of fighting on foot at close quarters.

To Pritchet, combat of the *Iliad* was loose order fight among 'knights' and *προμαχοι* (fore–fighters, akin to the Vedic *pramukha*—leader/foreman/spokesman) that took place *after* infantry formations had scattered in massed combat. Joachim Latacz, arguing in his 1977 monograph that Homeric descriptions were not entirely inaccurate,[27] puts it the other way round—combat of heroes and *προμαχοι* took place *before* massed combat broke out between infantry lines. In such engagements, unable to

24 Snodgrass, *Early Greek Armour*, p. 34.

25 J.H. Crouwel, *Chariot and Other Means of Land Transport in Bronze Age Greece*, Amsterdam, Allard Pierson Museum, 1981, p. 127.

26 Yadin, *War in Biblical Lands*, p. 109.

27 J. Latacz, *Kampfpäranese, Kampfdarstellung und Kampftwirklichkeit in der Ilias,bei Kallinos und Tyrtaios*, Perfect Paperback, Munich, 1977.

drive about at the head of their massed infantries, heroes would send their chariots to the rear and fight on foot at the head of their men.

Van Wees adjusted the above to create a realistic picture of Homeric combat.[28] He starts with positing that massed and loose order in the *Iliad* were one and the same thing, being differences in focus of the writer, and that there was no massed infantry in the *Iliad* as there would be in later times. To him, contingents of the various nations deployed in open order, where they stood posturing, throwing stones and discharging missiles, running up to contact and falling back. Chariots hung about in the rear, at times shooting arrows, at others, driving up through the gaps to deliver the warrior–hero, feudal or liege lord of the same men, at the head of their contingents to lead them on foot. In such situations, warriors would jump down and lead their men, especially the *προμαχοι* who to Van Wees were not a distinct class of fighters (as supposed by Latacz or Pritchard) but denoted anyone who moved up to fight at the front, test of courage being to remain *προμαχοι* the longest. It was only in explaining the origin of later–day phalanges with the help of the two (actually one) emergencies in the *Iliad* when Greeks pack up their lines quickly under divine inspiration (of Poseidon) to face Hector's assault on their ships that the first lines of their tight formations were called *προμαχοι*, a term that would be retained for the leading line of the phalanx.

Van Wees goes on to cite the observations of Margaret Mead on endemic warfare with heroic elements of primitive groups like the Papua New Guineans and the Dani. In this model, opponents assemble in loose order outside missile range, edging forward led by their leaders, taunting and cursing, dancing and shuttling all the while so as not to present targets, to clash briefly several times a day (between ten to twenty), in none of which more than a third of the troops would contact.[29] This would have resembled somewhat the combat of the *Iliad*, the upsurges and disengagements also explaining how warriors could come and go freely, even returning to camp in the middle of the day to deposit the wounded or store their spoils, and re-joining another part of the field.

28 Hans Van Wees, 'The Homeric Way of War: the 'Iliad' and the Hoplite Phalanx (I)', *Greece and Rome*, Second Series, vol. 41, no. 1, April, 1994, pp. 1–18, especially p. 6.

29 Van Wees, 'Homeric Way of War', p. 8.

Schulman has suggested that instead of infantry, chariots were used to reposition archers who would then engage on foot,[30] while Powell posited that chariot–archers operated in skirmish lines to cover deployment of infantry and then melt away.[31] We see that such use of chariots was suboptimal, the chariot being too expensive a contraption to be dedicated to one *foot* archer—chariots were so expensive that charioteers at times choose to save the chariot, abandoning a dismounted hero—while the secondary roles of skirmish lines were well within the ability of the elementary riding skills that had emerged by then. Even Littauer and Crouwel[32] were doubtful about dedicating an entire chariot to only one archer, whose accuracy would be extremely questionable in any case.

Robin Archer, on the other hand, gives the chariot a more central role as mounted archery platform, used to attack infantry in the flanks and rear, though never quite crashing into it which it could not. Watkins argues that chariots were held in reserve, committed only when victory was assured or to extricate infantry,[33] making it the arm of decision. Now, whatever role the chariot was used in, chariots would first have to win *freedom of movement* on the battlefield, something that would entail chariot–on–chariot engagement.

We have already seen that use of spears, either hurled or thrust, from moving chariots was impractical in chariot–on–chariot engagements. On the other hand, Drews' model of sweeping chariots would stand scrutiny if somewhat modified—chariots not actually passing through opposing lines but swinging away shooting arrows as they passed, and trying to outmanoeuvre the opponent and draw them into ambushes much like later-day mounted archers. And yet, this model would hold true only in West Asia where both space and resources to deploy vast numbers of chariots existed. In the Aegean, China, or South Asia, either space or resource

30 A. Schulman, 'Chariots, Chariotry and the Hyksos', *Journal of the Society for the Study of Egyptian Antiquities*, vol. 10, 1980, pp. 105–153.

31 T.G.E. Powell, 'Some Implications of Chariotry' in I. Foster and C. Adcock (eds.), *Culture and Environment: Essays in Honour of Sir Cyril Fox*, London, Routledge, 1963, pp. 165–66.

32 Littauer and Crouwel, 'Robert Drews and the Role of Chariotry in Bronze Age Greece', Selected Writings on Chariots, Other Early Vehicles, Riding and Harness, ed. P. Raulwing (Leiden: Brill, 2002), 66–74.

33 T. Watkins, 'The Beginnings of Warfare', in J. Hackett (ed.), *Warfare in the Ancient World*, New York, Facts on File, 1989, p. 31.

was at a premium, dictating far fewer chariots. This brings us back to Otterbein's model, which we see resembling battles of the *Mahabharata* where hero–warriors, of social status comparable with those of the *Iliad*, use chariots to fight with bows and arrows.

We can reconcile the different traditions of chariotry encountered thus far. While West Asian warfare, largely shorn of chivalric and heroic elements, revolved around sweeping manoeuvres of vast numbers of chariots, warfare elsewhere involved fewer chariots diffused among the nobility, associated with larger infantry formations, and marked by chivalric traditions. Hero–warriors who alone could afford chariots, like the Aegean *hippeis*, brought their contingents to battle, driving about through their loose order to supervise and exhort them, and shooting at opponents. At times, they could leap down to attack isolated groups of enemy infantry who possessed neither stamina nor skill to withstand them. At others, especially so in the case of the *Iliad*, they would lead assaults on foot at the heads of their contingents after sending their chariots to the rear, when they would be met by their opposite numbers on foot; though they would readily break contact if assaults floundered, this was probably the origin of the reputation of the Greek heroes fighting on foot and disdaining archery.

There would also be instances when they would 'brigade' all chariots together for other roles, like that of screens as postulated by Powell, or as reserve to deliver succour or *coup de grace* as proposed by Watkins. In such cases, they would attack enemy infantries with slashing weapons and arrows as they drove past, with the aim of making them edgy and nervous and ready for the charge of their own infantry. At other times, they would fight enemy chariots in small tactical groups, like Otterbein's dogfight, in order to win freedom of movement. Van Wees is not comfortable with the idea of such 'brigaded' use of the chariot, discarding the episode of Nestor's exhortation to all chariot–warriors to fight as a body, on the ground that these men being leaders of their contingents could not leave their men. His idea is hasty and not supported by the experience of medieval knights who, though also commanders of their 'companies' of yeomanry, 'brigaded' together to deliver lance charges or made small tactical units to fight others *in addition to* fighting dismounted at the heads of their companies.

This brings us back to the role of archery in such operations. Though the only pictorial depiction of a chariot–archer in Mycenaean art has been dismissed by Littauer and Crouwel as being from a hunting scene,[34] Achaean condemnation of archery as cowardly and fit only for Phrygians is contradicted by evidence of the *Linear B tablets* which mention Aegean kings with hundreds of chariots and thousands of bows.[35] Such condemnation of archery was obviously a chivalric overreaction, and use of bows and arrows, at least to some extent, by Aegean hero–warriors must not be ruled out.

We thus see several chariotry traditions existing together, from sweeping manoeuvres to attrition-oriented frontal combat, with increasing amounts of chivalry and ritualization. In fact, the same army or society could use chariots differently under different conditions, as for different operations in one battle. The Hyksos used chariots against the Egyptians in the deserts, but seldom in the marshy and riverine plains; later Egyptian armies used chariots for charges *outside* Egypt—in the Levant or in Libya—but used them only as command, control, and prestige vehicles within, the few representations of chariots in riverine battles being purely conventional.[36] At the same time, there were much interaction and influences between different traditions. While Anderson, who endorses the view that Mycenaeans had served the Egyptians as mercenaries,[37] sees evidence of Asiatic tactics in the shaft graves of Mycenae (though he never tells us what those tactics were), Yadin shows that the custom of duelling, common to the *Iliad* heroes, remarkable men representing their class the outcome of whose duels were acceptable to all, was introduced into West Asia from the Aegean by the Philistines.[38]

Most of the different chariotry options suited the *Mahabharata*, though with a somewhat larger role of archery, to understand which we must look again at the structure of its armies.

34 Littauer and Crouwel, 'Chariots in Late Bronze Age Greece', p.61, n. 3.

35 J. Chadwick, *The Mycenaean World*, Cambridge, Cambridge University Press, 1976, p. 167.Drews, *Coming of the Greeks*, p. 167; up to 10,000 arrowheads are mentioned.

36 See Archer, 'Near–Eastern Chariotry', pp. 74–75; also A. J. Spalinger, *War in Ancient Egypt*, Oxford, Blackwell, 2005, pp. 4–5.

37 As suggested by some, like S. Marinatos, *Crete and Mycenae*, London, 1962, pp. 81–82.

38 Yadin, *War in Biblical Lands*, p. 265–67.

Structure of *Mahabharata* Armies and their Style of Combat

The last chapter showed that the *akṣauhiṇi*s or divisions could be variously composed, and while chariots and infantry were their main arms,[39] they could also have 'proto-cavalries' of scouts, lookouts, and patrols, and possibly elephants. In addition to these, levies and mercenaries supplied by diverse chiefs could be appended to them. However, it is inconceivable that infantries of the period were numerous or disciplined and trained enough to be arranged into the great and complex *vyūha*s—perhaps not even the gigantic, elephant–headed *caturaṅga* quadrilaterals that would dominate the next thousand years—as Bronze Age organizational skills were simply not capable of mustering, equipping, maintaining, and commanding such vast bodies or men and animals. Nor is it possible to agree with S.D. Singh that there was a 'front' at Kurukṣetra which poetic imagination had failed to detect or reconstruct.[40] The vast plains of Kurukṣetra are likelier to have inter-digitated with encampments, bivouacs, and laagers of mobile contingents, which formed and re-formed smaller and dynamic formations or arrays as and when required.

This can be better understood if we inspect the organization of these armies, commencing from the chariot which was their *prima donna*. We encounter a curious form of organization of the chariot in the *Mahabharata*—we are told that such and such warrior was *protected by* such and such other warriors who were deployed to his *rear*. Obviously, the word 'protection'—*rakṣā*—is used in the sense of 'supported'. Also, the protectors or supporters are called *cakrarakṣau* or wheel–guards, the ending *au* implying a duo. To Hopkins, these were cadet knights of the champion's clan, placed as understudies by their parents for learning the family business of warfare and deriving incidental protection from the great warrior.[41] While such triangular organization is reasonable, the difficulty is that often it is not *junior* knights but renowned warriors who are *cakrarakṣau* of one another, like Arjuna and Bhīma of Śikhaṇḍin during the assault on Bhīṣma. This suggests that the threesome was not a permanent formation of warrior and fixed *cakrarakṣau*, but resembled

39 *sa grāmebhiḥ sanitā sa rathebhir*, *ṚV*, I:100.10.

40 S.D. Singh, *Ancient Indian Warfare*, p. 22. For descriptions of melee or *saṅkulayuddha*, see *Mbh,* CE VI: 53.10–13 and VI: 46.

41 Hopkins, 'Ruling Caste', pp. 260–61.

temporary '*vics*' of fighters wherein roles of flight commanders and wingmen could be rotated or rearranged between sorties.[42]

Behind the warriors and their *cakrarakṣau* were the *anugāḥ* and *anucarāḥ*, which Hopkins sees as remnants of the clannish corps of an older age enjoying a certain familiarity with the champion warrior—Karṇa would mourn the death of his *anuga* Durmukha. That the *anugāḥ* were small bodies is seen in their getting killed all at once along with the knight, or decamping together at his death. The *anugāḥ* were followed by the *padānugāḥ* or *foot-followers*, which Hopkins equates with the *bhṛta*, crowd of nameless hirelings which generated the later Hindustani word *bhīḍa* or crowd for the mass of factotums and followers. It is in these four organizational terms, the *cakrarakṣau, anuga* and *padānuga*, and the *bhṛta*, that lie the key to the organization of early chariot armies in South Asia.

The Mediterranean and China has yielded evidence of chariots being accompanied by squads of foot for close support. Men with swords and javelins are seen running alongside chariots in West Asian illustrations, Egyptian footmen are seen cutting off the heads of downed Hittites charioteers and warriors in the Kadesh reliefs, and ten men squads are indicated with Shang and Western Zhou chariots.[43] Such men as formed these squads needed to be really tough, if they were to keep up with chariots at a relentless trot; Dawson suggests that rather than soft local conscripts, the Mesopotamians hired mercenaries at great costs from the wild tribes of the mountains, which is substantiated by the Kadesh poem lamenting the Hittite king had no silver left after paying his mercenaries. There is evidence that the Mycenaeans had begun their military careers serving Egyptians as runners, and it was with tricks and weaknesses of chariot armies learnt here that the Aegean nations later turned the tables upon the chariot powers as the so-called *Sea Peoples*. Ratnagar has drawn our attention to the *Ingot God*, an iron figurine of a man with a spear and horned head-dress, which she identifies with the Sherden, one of these mercenary tribes.

42 *Cakra-rakṣau* and *anucaraḥ* or *anugaḥ*, Hopkins, 'Ruling Caste', pp. 57–376. This however is in no way designed to encourage visions of neat formations of chariots holding station.

43 Shaughnessy, 'Historical Perspectives', p. 198.

Now, another set of terms for chariot supporters—the *puraḥsara* and *pariṣkanda*—appear in Vedic literature. Of these, Hopkins interpreted *puraḥsara*[44] as 'leader', as against *anuga* which he calls 'follower'. In other words, he applied the term to the warrior or *rathī* himself. However, in the *Atharvaveda* the term often appears as a pair, i.e. *puraḥsarau*,[45] making its equation with a single warrior difficult. Also, the *puraḥsarau* are followed by *pariṣkandau*, also a duo. Appearing as they do in the archaic *Vājasaneyī Saṅhitā* of the *Yajurveda*[46], the terms may be taken as archaic, and it is more likely that they denoted a squad of runners—two forerunners (*puraḥsarau*) and two followers (*pariṣkandau*)—accompanying the chariot. At the same time, it may be remembered that the above may not denote a *foursome* at all, but four *detachments*.

Now, Hopkins is in error in calling the *anuga* as remnant of the clannish host, i.e. the *viś* militia, in an increasingly cosmopolitan context. In the *River Vision* episode after the war, perhaps the most poetic passage in the epic, the shade of each slain warrior appears to the mourners and friends across a river, accompanied by his horses, chariots, and importantly his *padānugāḥ*, the *anugāḥ* not being mentioned as a category at all. This means that the *anugāḥ* were counted among the warriors themselves—many of the warriors named in the episode, like many of the Kuru brothers or younger princes of other nations, have indeed been called *anugāḥ* of certain other warriors. At the same time, only the *padānugāḥ*, and not the *bhṛta*, are mentioned, indicating a close association between the former and the warriors. It is thus evident that not the *cakrarakṣau*, but the *anugaḥ* were the cadets and scions of the houses which could afford chariots, while the *padānugāḥ* was the remnant of the clannish corps or *viś* militia, standing entirely distinct from the *bhṛta*.[47]

Military authority and command in clannish or lineage societies were more diffused among the socially equal warriors than they were in feudal or industrial societies where societal protocol was more hierarchical. In the former, command was often by age, clan seniority, or reputation, as seems to have been the case in the epic. Graded by reputation as *adhiratha*,

44 *Mbh*, XII: 332.42.

45 *AV*, XV: 2.1, *et seq*.

46 *YV: Vājasaneyi Saṅhitā*, XXX.13.

47 I have elsewhere called the *anugāḥ* the remnants of the tribal hosts, but that was long ago. See Saikat Bose, *Boots, Hooves, and Wheels*, p. 102.

atiratha, *mahāratha*, and so on, the great warrior lords, heads of clans, came to battle with their sons, brothers, junior cousins, and nephews in tow. These latter fought on chariots as *anugāḥ* or *anucarāḥ* of the seniors, while their clannish hosts, which were possibly rudimentary in several cases, appeared as the *padānugāḥ*, quite like the companies of yeomanry accompanying medieval knights (though their pecuniary relations were entirely different). It was these *padānugāḥ* clan regiments that provided knights with close protection when static, scouted and skirmished for him, provided squads of runners, and possibly also formed proto–cavalries. Even mercenary groups, especially those from the *vrātya* fringes, would have been similarly organised because mercenary contingents usually retained their tribal structures.

In addition to runners, ambiguous groups like *sāra* and *prahārin* variously interpreted as flank and rear-guards, elite troops, or fore-fighters, would also have been drawn from the clannish *padānugāḥ*. The *padānugāḥ* were followed by the *bhṛta*, called mercenary by Hopkins[48] but better termed hirelings as the concept of mercenary in the pre-modern world had entirely different connotations with none of the negativity implicit in the word today. The *bhṛta* were common soldiers, initially employed as baggage guard and factotum but increasingly organized into functional companies. Terms like *senāgopāḥ* and *balamukhya* appear to indicate commanders and officers, who may have been commoners or men drawn out of *anugāḥ* or *padānugāḥ*. We can thus conclude that far from being organised in the strict hierarchy of the last chapter, which replicated later–to–come Iron Age organizational principles of the mid-1st millennium B.C., the *Mahabharata* contingents were amorphous groups of elite chariotries surrounded by clan regiments and hired infantries.

The opening sequences of the battle chapters stress that opponents were drawn up facing one another. This idea is immediately modified with descriptions of geometrically complex *vyūha*s in which the positions of the contingents and warriors were fixed. This in turn was contradicted by the sequence of combat, where warriors get at one another with no reference to their original locations. It is thus likely that contingents deployed in open or loose order, often inter-digitating on the plains. Here they would form local arrays to launch or ward off attacks, perhaps lashing together carts and wagons into pivots for chariots and proto–cavalries to

48 Hopkins, 'Ruling Caste', p. 260.

manoeuvre around, akin to the Vedic *saṅgrāma*.[49] Such engagements could take several forms. Chariots could raid and skirmish, 'brigade' together to attack infantry formations with arrows and try to stampede them, or lead clan contingents in assaults; when they could, runners would keep up at a trot, despatching casualties and gathering spoils.

Chariots could also thrust at enemy chariots, targeting selected warriors, often forming temporary tactical groups with warriors and *anugāḥ* acting as *cakrarakṣau* to one another. Combat of these temporary *vics* would resemble dogfights, with *padānugāḥ* and runners dropping out as they would get in the way; it was at such times that mounted duels might break out. At times chariots operating independently ahead of their infantry protection might get 'boxed in' by enemy foot and elephants,[50] when the *padānugāḥ*, if not the *bhṛta*, might try to receive them with a jungle of spears, hamstring the horses, pull the crew down and hack them to pieces.[51] When compelled to dismount in such or other cases, warriors would fight on with contact weapons but leap on another chariot at the first available opportunity.

At times, larger arrays would be adopted at higher levels, like crescents to envelop, wedges to channelize, circles to defend, and columns to break through. There being no logical reason other than aesthetics for commanders to lay out armies to resemble birds and animals from above, the zoonyms were obviously functional—the Roman *testudo* was named after the tortoise because of the box of shields, and not because it had eyes and legs. Possibly the *makara* was a formation that could close upon the enemy like the jaws of a crocodile, or the *krauñca* because it could quickly dart forward and withdraw, like a fishing bird, and so on. It can thus be seen that shorn of hyperbole and vivid imageries—whirling chariots crunching skulls of the fallen, skies blackening with arrows, severed heads with fair eyes and beautiful earrings lying in the blood—the type of fighting attested in the epic is not entirely improbable. However, the outer veneer of the narrative, often in the repetitive descriptions and stock phrases like '*with gauntlets and with clubs and bracelets in the fight*' that appear *ad*

49 Women were regularly involved in warfare in the steppes. Amongst the Sauromatian and some other tribes, a woman could not get married unless she had killed someone first. Christian, *Central Asia*, pp. 142–44.

50 *parivavruḥ samantataḥ enaṅ koṣṭhakīkṛtya sarvataḥ*, *Mbh*, VII: 171.2ff.

51 Dawson, *The First Armies*, pp. 156–7.

nauseum, represents poetic imagination of a later period when redactors knew little of warfare involving chariots and were only superimposing their notions.

Also, while the above derivation accounts for chariots, infantry, and cavalry, it does not for elephants, which appear not only as mounts for commanders but also as fighting animals in armies of eastern kings like those of Prāgjyotiṣ, Vaṅga, or Daśārṇa. We will soon see that the role of elephants was so peripheral to the narrative that its structure does not suffer if they are removed. Yet, baggage elephants may have been present, as were other services like engineers and surgeons whose existence should not be denied but who were probably not as organised as they would come to be later.[52]

The General Onset

Returning to the war, we see that after the debacle of the thirteenth day Krishna repeats several injunctions of the *Gītā* to Arjuna, shorn of its philosophical contents, at the end of which Arjuna swears that either he will kill Jayadratha, architect of the *cakravyūha*, by sundown or he would end his life on the next day. Such vows were not unusual in the chivalric world—the Samurai took them all the time—; what is remarkable is that it was proclaimed widely and the Kuru, on learning of it, took all measures to prevent Arjuna's reaching Jayadratha. They adopt a 'rare' *vyūha* in the shape of a wedge with a circle at the end, within which there was another *secret* array at the centre of which was deployed Jayadratha. The pace of the next day's contest, which takes the form of Arjuna's long and eventful drive to reach Jayadratha by sundown, is rapid and relentless, as is that on all subsequent days. The war has become more purposeful with the appointment of Droṇa, which brings us to role of the marshals and general-ship in early warfare.

General-ship and Command

We see that marshals on either side—Dhṛṣṭadyumna and Bhīṣma—were not the main aggrieved parties but men *selected* by general consent, like the Germanic war–chief selected by *rota*. Their rites of consecration, most vividly described in the case of Droṇa and which to Yardi were Sautī's

52 Surgeons mentioned in *Mbh*, V: 151; *Mbh*, VI: 120.55.

additions,[53] include ritual bathing seated on a throne of *uḍumbura* or fig wood, obeisance to the gods, and ritual driving of the chariot once in all directions. Interestingly, these were exactly the rites of consecration of the *rājan* or chief, which suggests that the office of the *rājan* had begun as a temporarily chosen war–chief but had since become more permanent, with more decision-making authority gathered in it than left to the marshal. Though the *rājan* is still not socially above the marshal in the epic, as seen in the constant bantering between the two, and though general-ship is a pre-requisite in a marshal,[54] none of the marshals have the authority of the ancient war–chief. Their roles are rudimentary, limited to selecting the day's *vyūha*, explaining its overall scheme, and then fighting exemplarily.

Even the *rathīs*, despite the overall *vyūha*, fight as best as they can but without heed to the overall scheme and at times at cross purposes, another factor militating against elaborate arrays being the patchy command and control apparatus available. All authority to modify the overall scheme, order advance or retreat, or move reserves, are seen to lie with the *rājan* alone—evidently, as a result of on-going sedentization, authority was increasingly gathered by hereditary chieftains rendering marshals as adjunct staff officer like the Mughal *bak̲shi*, whose position gradually fell from the marshal to the adjutant-general. The position of marshal was also highly politicised—Bhīṣma and Karṇa refused to serve with or under one another, Karṇa holding out of battle as long as Bhīṣma led, while Droṇa was appointed as a compromise candidate after Bhīṣma's invalidation.

We have also seen above that gradation of authority in these clannish armies was diffused, depending more on age, protocol, clan seniority, and reputation, with prowess of warriors promulgated in hero-lauds wherein they were made to behave superhumanly, an approach mirrored in pharaohs having themselves depicted larger than the others on paintings and represented as killing thousands of enemies.[55] The situation was curiously similar to the Mughal *mansabdāri*, which had no hierarchy, but among which he that held the highest *mansab* was commander; usually

53 Yardi, *The Mahabharata*, p. 179.

54 The marshal assures his king, '*I can make the mercenaries and those not mercenaries do their duty; in respect of marching, fighting, etc., I know as much as did Brihaspati; I know all the battle-orders of gods and of men*', *Mbh*, V: 165. 8.

55 Dawson, *The First Armies*, p. 145. At Kadesh, Rameses is given the credit for fighting on alone and restoring the situation after his nobles had decamped.

this was reserved for members of the ruling family (including co-opted members or *khanzadas*) who had been deliberately given astronomical *mansabs*, and the structure could collapse when such a real *khan* was not present, as happened at Daulambapur. The above will help understand the role of the series of Kuru marshals that would follow one another over the next few days.

Arjuna's Link-up and the Onset

When Arjuna rides out to reach Jayadratha on the fourteenth day, he is endlessly waylaid and intercepted by Kuru warriors. The first to attack him are the brothers Durmarṣaṇa and Duḥśāsana, the latter on an elephant, but Arjuna does not quite kill them as that was Bhīma's vow. Arjuna then runs into Droṇa who he is unable to overcome in the sharp battle that ensues; Droṇa 'seems to know no fatigue' and peppers his chariot and armour with arrows, and perforce Arjuna sneaks past with a greeting and heads for Jayadratha, still twelve miles away. Soon he runs into and defeats Kṛtavarman and Sudakṣiṇa, but then is dazed by Śrutāyu and Aśrutāyu and has to be resuscitated by Krishna. In an incident designed to underline the non-combatant status of Krishna, Śrutāyudha (distinct from Śrutāyu) hurls a mace at him, which, otherwise invincible, was charmed to backfire if used against a non-combatant; it recoils after striking Krishna and kills the thrower.

At this time, Krishna stops the chariot to give the horses a break, but just as he is about to unyoke them, Arjuna is attacked, of course unsuccessfully, by the brothers Vinda and Anuvinda, and then by Duryodhana who had appeared wearing Droṇa's armour. In a part–comic episode, Arjuna shoots Duryodhana through the chinks of the otherwise impenetrable metal, cuts his bowstring, breaks his bow, and harasses him in many ways till he flees. Finally, Krishna unyokes the horses, which roll in the mud to relieve their backs, a picturesque cameo that commemorates the efforts animals were forced to put in when man fought man.

The focus now shifts on another part of the battlefield where Dhṛṣtadyumna attacks Droṇa to prevent him from linking up with Jayadratha, who is seen panicking by this time. Dhṛṣṭadyumna comes off the worse and is extricated by the Pañcāla and Sātyaki. A little later Sātyaki himself is in trouble and is extricated by Dhṛṣṭadyumna. At this time, the blare of Krishna's conch–bugle, the *Pāñcajanya*, is heard, and Yudhiṣṭhira sends Sātyaki to link up with Arjuna, first yoking fresh horses to his chariot and placing a new box of arrows in it, another candid glimpse of chariot warfare. Sātyaki departs, but not without misgivings because Arjuna had 'charged' him with protecting Yudhiṣṭhira. A little later Droṇa renews his attacks on Arjuna and Yudhiṣṭhira sends Bhīma to reinforce Sātyaki and Arjuna.

Certain anachronisms become evident now. Though Arjuna bypassed Droṇa and headed for Jayadratha, Droṇa is already with Jayadratha organising his defence. Also, though Bhīma was dispatched later to Arjuna after Sātyaki, he arrives first and attacks Droṇa. One after the other Bhīma shatters eight chariots under Droṇa, hooting at his old teacher when challenged to stay and fight as he bypasses him to reach Arjuna. He then runs into Karṇa. In the meanwhile, Arjuna reaches Jayadratha. When Duryodhana complains that Droṇa had let Arjuna through, the latter only asks him to not cry over what is past and asks him to reinforce Jayadratha.

The narrative now loses all coherence. Droṇa, attacked by the Pañcāla, tries to stop Bhīma who was engaged with Karṇa. Also, Sātyaki, who had been despatched to aid Arjuna before Bhīma, is seen engaging Bhūriśravas, while Karṇa almost plays with Bhīma in a sequence exploding with adjectives, adverbs, and pejoratives. However, Bhīma gradually overwhelms Karṇa, shattering several of his chariots and killing another score of the Kuru brothers who had reinforced Karṇa. Desperate at the death of the brothers, especially of Durmukha who is his *anuga*, Karṇa bounces back with vengeance—the chariots of both are shattered and the duo fight on foot with mace and sword while the others (curiously, Arjuna too) pause to watch and applaud. Duryodhana's anguish at some Kuru warriors applauding Bhīma earns him a rebuke. Ultimately, an incensed Karṇa gets the better of Bhīma who must beat an ignominious retreat. As per Yardi, the ascendance of Bhīma and the killing of the Kuru brothers were added by Sautī, their purpose being to ameliorate Bhīma's humiliation and account for another score of the brothers.[56]

At this time Sātyaki is attacked by Bhūriśravas, grandson of Śāntanu's brother Bahīka Prātipeya who had gone off to the Punjab to rule, and whose family had a blood feud with the Vṛṣṇi over the hand of Krishna's mother

56 As per Yardi, these *adhyāyas*, i.e. 103–111 were added by Sautī and were not part of the original, their purpose being to give Bhīma a steadier face and kill off several of the Kuru brothers.

Devakī. Sātyaki is overpowered and falls in a swoon, taking the narrative a notch ahead in the game of brinkmanship; on the fifth day Sātyaki and his sons had been at the mercy of Bhūriśravas the expert swordsman and had been extricated by Bhīma. Just as Bhūriśravas towers over him preparing to strike him with his sword, Arjuna lops off his arm with a crescent arrow at Krishna's suggestion. Vehemently denouncing this dastardly conduct, Bhūriśravas lays out his arrows in the form of a mat and seats himself as though for meditation to give up his life; at that moment Sātyaki recovers, and before anyone realises what is happening, creeps up to the elderly man and beheads him. There is much disbelief and dissatisfaction at the conducts of Arjuna and Sātyaki.

Afterwards, Sātyaki attacks Karṇa on Krishna's personal chariot driven by Dāruka, shattering several of Karṇa's chariots and grounding him. Arjuna renews his charge through the cordon around Jayadratha and engages him; at this moment, the sun sets and the Kuru, who had been stealing anxious glances at the setting sun for a while, relax and let their guard down. However, Krishna tells Arjuna that the sun *was not set and it was he that had made it dark*, prompting him to decapitate Jayadratha with an arrow.[57] So incensed are the warriors at this act that the battle does not stop at all but continues everywhere with the help of torches; several of the major warriors are killed as Yudhiṣṭhira renews his attack, while the night-warfare expert Ghaṭotkac harries the Kuru so much that Duryodhana prevails upon Karṇa to use up his special weapon, Indra's spear which he had reserved for Arjuna, to kill him.

Droṇa is himself killed in a curious manner. Krishna recommends that it be proclaimed that Aśvatthāman, Droṇa's son, had been killed in order to break the sage–warrior's morale. While everyone is scandalised, Yudhiṣṭhira agrees to do the needful, likening his act to that of Śiva accepting poison for the good of all. Bhīma slays an elephant also called Aśvatthāman and yells that he had killed him; when Droṇa, certain that Yudhiṣṭhira would tell no lies, asks him for confirmation, Yudhiṣṭhira says that Aśvatthāmā had indeed been killed, though he mutters under his breath, '*Aśvatthāmā the elephant.*' This ignoble act causes the pious

57 Here occurs the quite incredible story which says that Arjuna actually shot arrow after arrow at the head of Jaydratha so that it was tossed towards the hermitage of his father Vṛddhakṣatra who had laid a curse on anyone who would cause his son's head to fall on the ground that his head too would shatter; the head fell on Vṛddhakṣatra's lap, and when the aged ex-king rose, it rolled on to the floor, causing his own head to shatter.

Yudhiṣṭhira's chariot, which so far had planed a few inches above ground, to slam down and always run jerkily on earth thereafter. Heartbroken, Droṇa casts his weapon away and sits down in his chariot in *yoga*, when his mortal enemy Dhṛṣṭadyumna creeps up with a sword and decapitates him, bringing to an end the four days of war under the command of Droṇa.

As night rolls into day, Karṇa is anointed the next marshal; curiously, Duryodhana asks Śalya to drive Karṇa's chariot, with which the latter is not happy and, as per his supposed promise to his nephew Yudhiṣṭhira, berates Karṇa continuously. Things precipitate—Bhīma attacks Duḥśāsana, shattering his chariot and pounding him to death after tearing off his arms and drinking his blood as he had vowed to Draupadī. Karṇa, shuddering at the sight, is talked around by Śalya who reminds him of his duties to Duryodhana; he now shoots a charmed arrow at Arjuna which Krishna evades by pressing his chariot into the mud, another of his alleged cheats. At this moment, Karṇa's chariot sticks in the mud and Krishna prevails upon a reluctant Arjuna to shoot him dead as he struggles to free the wheel; in response to Karṇa's appeal to honourable conduct, Krishna reminds him of his own misdeeds as regards to Draupadī and Abhimanyu.

With Karṇa dead, pressure for negotiation mounts on Duryodhana who appoints Śalya the new marshal. Interestingly, the *vyūha* under Śalya's command has a disproportionate number of nomadic tribes—Aśvatthāmā commands the Kamboja, Gautama stands with Śaka and Yavana, Kṛtavarman, the renegade Vṛṣni, commands the Trigarta. Soon the war draws to a cataclysmic finalé—Śalya is killed by Yudhiṣṭhira with a spear, Sahadeva shoots Śakuni dead, and the last surviving Kuru brothers are killed by Bhīma. Sore with wounds, Duryodhana retires to a 'watery place', possibly a marsh, where the Pandu follow, entering into philosophically charged arguments with him. To his entreaties that they should not attack him all at once but fight him one by one, Duryodhana is asked where this piece of *noblesse oblige* was when the Kuru had ganged up to butcher Abhimanyu.

Nevertheless, Bhīma attacks him alone with the mace. The two fight for a long time, watched by the others including Baladeva (Rāma) who had arrived just then at the end of his pilgrimage. And then, as though discussing Duryodhana's act of asking Draupadī to sit on his lap,[58] Krishna points to his own loins giving Bhīma a hint; at once Bhīma aims a blow below Duryodhana's belt, where he was vulnerable, breaking his thigh. In the recriminations that follow, including those by Baladeva who rushes at Bhīma with his plough but is held back by his brother, Krishna concedes that he hinted to Bhīma to hit below the belt because Duryodhana could not be trounced otherwise. While an unconvinced Baladeva leaves in a huff after berating Krishna and the Pandu on their immoral conduct, the gods applaud Duryodhana.

In the last episode of the war, Kṛpācārya, Aśvatthāman, and Kṛtavarman, the only three men left on the Kuru side, approach Duryodhana who appoints Aśvatthāman marshal. The three then raid the Pandu–Pañcāla camp at night, killing the Pāñcāla princes including Dhṛṣṭadyumna, which leaves only seven men—the Pandu, Krishna, and Sātyaki—alive on the other side. Duryodhana breathes his last after the trio report their success to him, and ascends to heaven applauded by the gods. Next day, the Pandu catch up with Aśvatthāman who attempts to discharges a charmed blade of grass at Abhimanyu's child in Uttarā's womb which Krishna diverts; the child is born in time, and was the Parīkṣit that succeeded Yudhiṣṭhira.

Review of the Course of Combat

Evidently, the indeterminate actions of the first ten days had given way to a meaningful schema from the eleventh to the thirteenth day, which then precipitated a general onset. The *brinkmanship* is seen continuing through the first three of these days—on the eleventh day Arjuna appears on the scene just in time to extricate Yudhiṣṭhira, on the twelfth, the Kuru had taken care to restrain him but he still disengages to aid Bhīma, but on the thirteenth day, even though he supposedly knew of the *cakravyūha*, he does not disengage from the Trigarta and fails to save his son. Now, Arjuna's battle with Droṇa on the eleventh evening is highly schematic and formal, and the battle with Bhagadatta on the next evening is rather curious. The *Prāgjyotiṣ* of Bhagadatta, i.e. *Light of the East* or *Lighted from the East,*[59] is traditionally associated with Assam, and yet Bhagadatta features

58 This was the second vow at the *Sabhā*, because Duryodhana had leeringly asked Draupadī to sit on his thigh—the first was to break Duḥśāsana's arm and drink his blood because he had pulled at her clothes.

59 *Mbh*, II: 49; 3.5.

not in Bhīma's eastern expedition but in Arjuna's northern expedition during the *rājasūya*.[60] Bhagadatta, who has been called *mleccha* and is seen commanding Yavana and Kirāta troops, i.e. Greeks and the *Cirrhidai* of Ptolemy associated with the western Himalayas, also pays tributes to Arjuna in the form of fine horses which is unlikely of an Assamese king.

Now, before Arjuna arrived, the king of Daśārṇa had already extricated Bhīma from Bhagadatta's attack, and yet we find Bhīma engaged with him. Evidently the elephant episode was inserted to provide exotica and comic relief[61] and comes from a time when eastern realms like Videha, Puṇḍra, Suhma, Tāmralipta, or Assam had become part of the Aryan world. It does not impact the storyline at all if it is removed. The two episodes of the eleventh and twelfth day, and the charged moment when, with the Kuru rejoicing at Bhīma's discomfiture at the hands of Bhagadatta, Karṇa warns them not to celebrate prematurely as Arjuna was still abroad, seem to be poetic arrangements to build suspense. Karṇa, always boastful and deprecatory of Arjuna, is unlikely to have actually made such statements; the reminder that Arjuna was still around, his timely arrival on the two days, and yet his failure to arrive on the thirteenth day, combined with the memory of the fourth day when he had arrived to extricate Abhimanyu, serve to highlight the pathos of Abhimanyu's felling, the general feeling evoked being '*if only dad was around*'.

This brings us to the movements of Arjuna himself. Arjuna is present through the first ten days of battle, but he kills no one important, extricates Abhimanyu once, and endlessly fights ever closer duels with Bhīṣma. He is present at the felling—not death—of the venerable warrior, but then only as a *partner* of Śikhaṇḍin. Bhīṣma's fall is an anomaly. In the epic, all warriors who have taken vows or made pledges are seen successfully fulfilling them. Dhṛṣṭadyumna kills Droṇa, Sātyaki kills Bhūriśravas, and Bhīma kills all Kuru brothers, drinks Duḥśāsana's blood, and breaks Duryodhana's thighs, to name a significant few. Śikhaṇḍin's is the only case where the vow is not fulfilled, as Bhīṣma is only *incapacitated* and hangs on to life thanks to a charm that enabled him to choose his moment of dying. After the battle, Bhīṣma is seen giving many forms of kingly advice to Yudhiṣṭhira and Bhīma who visit him at his deathbed. Much of the advice, as we shall see, is technically irrelevant, because they have to

60 *Mbh*, II: 26.9 for Arjuna's campaign, and II: 31.14–16 for Bhīma's expedition.

61 Yardi, *The Mahabharata*, p. 179.

do with a socio–political system that the Pandu do not belong to. Removal of the episode will not disturb the story structure at all.

Interestingly, what is *Bhīṣmaparvan* or the *Episode of Bhīṣma* in the Northern Recension is called *Bhīṣma–vadhaparvan* in the Southern Recension, where the term *vadha* is to slay. One gets the impression that Bhīṣma had actually been killed on the tenth day, but had been kept alive for didactic purposes. This impression can be taken a step forward—it was Śikhaṇḍin that had really killed Bhīṣma, but later chivalric difficulty came in the way of countenancing the fact that such a mighty warrior had been slain by a person of indeterminate gender, which led to the interpolation of the stories of Bhīṣma's youthful indiscretion (on his brothers' behalf), his strange conduct *vis-à-vis* Śikhaṇḍin, and the giving to Arjuna of a greater role in the felling of Bhīṣma. The special but unexplained hostility of Krishna for Bhīṣma, even though the latter was sympathetic if not partial to the Pandu and always respectful to Krishna, seems to shift the blame for the 'trick', where *Arjuna attacks* Bhīṣma under cover of Śikhaṇḍin, to divine intervention; in this respect, we see an admixture of poetic Krishnaism wherein Krishna's blood drawn by Bhīṣma's arrow flows scarlet against his dark skin like the *palash* tree in bloom against a sky lowing with dark clouds.

Further, Arjuna is engaged from the eleventh to the thirteenth day, on the eleventh with some other Kuru warriors, and on the twelfth and thirteenth specifically with the Trigarta *saṅsaptaka*s who challenge him (*āhvantyaḥ*) on both mornings at which Arjuna leaves the line and goes off to fight them. Yet, while on the eleventh and twelfth evenings he appears to aid Yudhiṣṭhira and Bhīma who are in distress, he fails to make an appearance on the thirteenth to rescue his ambushed son. Now, we have seen that his appearances on the eleventh and twelfth days are too formalised to be authentic, on the fatal thirteenth day he does not appear at all, and on the fourteenth day he has to undertake a long, arduous, and eventful approach to reach the main scene of action, eagerly awaited by his allies and vehemently resisted by his enemies. The journey is so long that it becomes necessary to give the horses a break.

The Kuru gambit of the thirteenth day was the *cakravyūha*, in which Abhimanyu is trapped and killed. The question that arises is, *why the Pandu, if they were not sure of how to get out of it, entered it in the first place at all*? We can simply restate the story of the *cakravyūha* as—Abhimanyu charged into an ambush, got separated from his companions, and was killed, the fate of many impetuous youngsters inveigled into ambush by nomad horse. In the light of the above, the act of the Trigartas and the *cakravyūha* can together be reinterpreted as a twin manoeuvre—using a force to separate and contain one major arm of the enemy, in this case Arjuna, and attacking the main body with typical nomad tactics, in this case targeting Yudhiṣṭhira but inveigling an important prince into an ambuscade and killing him. The architects of this twin manoeuvre deserve greater attention.

The Trigarta, longstanding Kuru allies who had aided them in the *gaviṣṭi* against the Mātsya, were the right kind of army to launch the containing manoeuvre against Arjuna. They were famed charioteers (*rathodārah*) and archers (*dhanurvedavida*), and hailed as invincible (*ajeyāḥ śatrubhiḥ*). The traditional explanation of their name—*Trigarta* or *three–holes* as the three valleys of Kangra in modern Himachal Pradesh—is not convincing, and the name may have been derived from pit dwellings or the body of the chariot, i.e. *garta*. Their coins from historical times depict a bird perched on a column, which Devendra Handa[62] interprets as the *kukkūṭa–dhvaja* or cockerel–standard of Karttikeya, the war–god of Scythia. Significantly, their elaborate *saṁsaptaka* oath includes the putting on of garments of *kuśa* grass with girdles of the *mūrv* to protect them, and taking the *raṇavrata* vow associated with the *vrātya*s.

The other actor Jayadratha, who sprung the *cakravyūha*, was chief of the Sindhu–Sauvīra, another of the tribal moieties associated with *vrātya* cavalry in later times. The Sindhu–Sauvīra, whom the Ā*pastambha Śrautasūtra* classes with outlying tribes like Magadha, Kalinga, Gandhāra, and Paraskaras or Karaskaras, were derided as men of mixed origin, and purifying rites like *Punaṣṭoma* and *Sarvapṛṣṭi* were prescribed for those who interacted with them[63] as they belonged to the marginal world of the *vrātya*.

The above shows that the architects of the twin manoeuvre were *vrātya* people of the Punjab and Indus plains, i.e. nomadic groups comfortable

62 Devendra Handa, 'Some Ancient *Janapadas* of *Uttarāpatha* vis-à-vis the *Mahābhārata*', in Ajay Mitra Shastri (ed.), *Mahabharata*, pp. 118–147, especially p. 135.

63 *Dharmasūtra*, I.1.32–33: ca. 4th century B.C., as per Bhandarkar.

with such tactics. That the Pandu were nomads themselves, or were so till recently, does not rule out their falling for the gambit—nomads have successfully used such tactics against one another, as at Ayn Jalut or Merv.

Much is made of Arjuna's killing Jayadratha after sundown, when technically the battle should have ceased for the day as per laws of chivalric combat. However, all other warriors and their contingents are seen to carry on with torches and *rehearsed* signals, which shows that night battles were not out of the ordinary, though the way the chariots, horses, and elephants are said to be festooned with lamps and torches is impractical.[64] A little reflection will show that all other Pandu 'misdemeanours', efforts to wash which away in the epic are evident, made perfect military sense. Krishna's counselling Arjuna, his diverting of Śrutayudha's mace, or pressing down the chariot to avoid Karṇa's missile, have all been considered 'foul-play' and 'unfair interference', but these are in reality the job of the charioteer, whose task it was to advise the warrior and keep him safe through aggressive and evasive driving. Also, as integral part of the weapon system, the charioteer was valid target, though not so while discharging his roles of herald or messenger. Lopping off Bhūriśravas' arm when he was about to kill Sātyaki was an act of mutual support between warriors, killing Karṇa when his chariot is immobilised is essentially good manoeuvre of dislocating and trapping the enemy on unsuitable ground, drinking Duḥśāsana's blood was magical rite common to many primitive people like Vikings and Danes, and was no more alarming than Achilles's brutalizing Hector's corpse, and ruses like that used to slay Droṇa were natural concomitants of *Real War*.

There are in fact many more violations of rules, but questions of morality and propriety are never raised except when they are associated with the Pandu. Evidently, the acts were perfectly normal and acceptable at that time, and only by mid-1st millennium, by when *Kṣatriya* chivalry had come to monopolise warfare, that 'proper and correct' conduct in what was *True War* was increasingly expected. These 'correct' laws, called *dharmayuddha*, or *vīrayuddha*,[65] lay down that knights must contend in

64 On each chariot the Kuru suspend five lights (*vidīpaka*), the Pandu ten, and so on; on each elephant, the Kuru three and the Pandu seven, and so on. Even footmen carry torches while the banners and standards are bedecked with lamps, till it was light as day. One king yells, 'throw away your weapons, seize your torches'. The descriptions, naturally, are schematic and fantastic.

65 *Mbh*, VI: 1. 27

an orderly manner with their equals, desist from attacking non-combatants or unarmed, disarmed, and disabled enemies, or those who are engaged with others or were retiring, never engage charioteers, heralds, weapon–carriers, trumpeters and drummers, and give notice before striking. These rules were the effort of the *Kṣatriya* chivalry, which had monopolised the privilege of warring and who now wanted to keep warfare more bearable in terms of hardship and number.

In contrast, fighting without heed to these rules was *kūṭayuddha*, *dasyudharma*, and so on, in other words the *Real War* of the extra–sedentary and pre-chivalric world to which the *Mahabharata* really belonged. It was only as the *Mahabharata* grew into the fount of public morality that its heroes needed to be cast as paragons of virtue and absolved of archaic acts lest they be cited as precedence. Thus, while Arjuna, when challenged for lopping off Bhūriśravas's arm, retorts that there is no rule in war, and if the rule of one man fighting only one was followed there would be no real combat,[66] later the act is put down to expediency, the doctrine of which is expounded in the *āpad-dharma* section by Bhīṣma. When logical justification was not possible, like in the killing of Karṇa or Duryodhana, these acts were attributed to the divine inspiration of Krishna and thereby taken beyond the realm of human reasoning.

Yardi has shown that most of the logical justifications appear in the *Bharata* redaction itself[67] and only the divine apologia appears in later times. Thus, one may conclude that chivalric attitudes had appeared at the time of the war, and were, as per Hopkins, followed at least in pretence by the sophisticated and 'worldly wise' Kuru but thoughtlessly violated by the Pandu and Vṛṣṇi, first generation nomads. At the same time, we see a certain chivalric attitude in Yudhiṣṭhira, who, mixing fatalism and honour, accepts the inevitability of the exile and refuses to do anything about it till its term was over, despite his Pañcāla and Vṛṣṇi allies offering to support him if he chose to resist. This of course may have been simply imputed at a later time, automatically supported by the fact that the Pandu were actually considered in exile for the 'full' term.

66 *Mbh*, VII: 143.28, *ekasyai' kena hi kathaṅ saṅgrāmaḥ sambhaviṣyati.*

67 Yardi, *The Mahabharata*, pp. 7–8.

Phasing and Situating the Course of Combat

The eighteen days of battle can now be divided into three phases—ten days of indeterminate combat, three days of manoeuvre that led to the separation of Arjuna and the killing of Abhimanyu, and five days of general onset in which all is destroyed. It will be seen that while the first thirteen days are neatly separated, the five days of the last phase run into one another; on the fourteenth day combat does not *stop* with sunset but goes on through the night, and continues after a brief pause to offer the *orison* on the next morning. Now, Baladeva (Rāma) is said to have reached the scene of the duel between Bhīma and Duryodhana on the seventeenth day,[68] which is followed by the night raid. It is the night raid, and not the encounter with Aśvatthāman the following morning, that is considered as the last act of the war. As per Indian reckoning, day is reckoned from sunrise to sunrise and not midnight to midnight, night being part of the previous day. This suggests that the battle really finished on the seventeenth day. The figure of eighteen is a complex idea.

Eighteen seems to have been a sort of special number with ritual significance as many concepts, things, and ideas appear in this number in the *Mahabharata.*[69] There are 18 volumes in the epic, 18 *akṣauhini*s fight the war, and 18 chapters in the *Gīta*; the elders pass away 18 years after the war, and the Andhaka–Vṛṣṇis (Vṛṣṇyandhaka) are destroyed after 36, i.e. twice 18, years of the battle. There are 18 *dvīpa*s or continents in early Indian geography, and a total of 18 *Purāṇa*s; as per the *Kaṭapayādi* numerology, *Jaya* is represented by the figure 18. King Hastin of Hastināpura is called ruler of Dabhala and 18 forest kingdoms, reminiscent of the modern *Aṭṭhārāhagarh* (Attharagarh) near Sambalpur.

Most significantly, eighteen people are required for Vedic sacrifices—16 priests of various classes, the *yajamāna,* and his wife.[70] The great impact of the war led to its equation with the sacrifice, which possibly led to popular lore that it was fought over 18 days, and the redactors, in

68 *Mbh*, CE, IX: 3.27

adya saptadaśāhani vartamānasya bhārata|

saṅgrāmasyā'tighorasya vadhayatāṁ ca bhito yudhi ||

69 Like the figure twelve in later times. Murthy has also demonstrated the ritual significance of five.

70 *Muṇḍaka Upaniṣad*, 1.2.7, *aṣṭādaśotkamavaraṅ yeṣu karmam.*

trying to construct the narrative from the massive, unconsolidated corpus of ballads, lays, and hero lauds, i.e. the *Jayaḥ*, as much for listening pleasure as moral, historical, and military instruction, recast the material in a common metre and wove it into eighteen days. Thus, while each of the contest and encounters in the epic may have indeed taken place, their sequence would have been different; several may have been enlarged, expanded, or split into several episodes in the *brinkmanship* style, building up and relaxing suspense to build the listener closer and closer to the climax.

Discerning the actual number of days being difficult, Holtzmann simply reduced the duration of the battle to three days, commanded by Bhīṣma, Karṇa, and Śalya apiece, writing off the command of Droṇa. Hopkins saw no reason to write off Droṇa, and settled for four days of battle.[71] It is argued here that rather than getting engrossed in the number of days, one should see the battle in terms of phases, of which we have already identified three. The first phase was the indeterminate days of skirmishing, when nothing major happened and the opponents lay raiding, probing, and posturing, or perhaps making the shallow and abortive onsets as observed by Mead among the Dani. This phase is represented by the ten days of uncoordinated, diurnal combat replete with repetitive and formulaic descriptions. In pre-modern warfare, armies often lay opposite one another for weeks, like Babur and Sanga at Khanua, at the end of which they at times retreated without a fight, like Maldeva against Sher Shah (a rear-guard fought valiantly). Perhaps Bhīṣma's chastisement of Duryodhana, his condition of not killing the Pandu, Duryodhana's remonstrations with him, all suggest that Bhīṣma had been putting off a decisive attack;[72] the supposed Pandu visit to Bhīṣma in the Kuru camp may preserve the memory of diplomatic efforts still going on in this phase, which lasted an indefinite number of days.

The second phase began after the felling of Bhīṣma, when Droṇa took over command of the Kuru, while the purposeful Karṇa, Arjuna's alter ego, also joined the fray. Droṇa launched the twin manoeuvre of containing

71 Hopkins 'Ruling Caste', p. 227.

72 Yardi, *The Mahabharata*, p. 34, says that the *adhyāya*s 61–70, added to the *Bhīṣmaparvan* by Sauti, add some more of the tedious and repetitive descriptions, and also some of the chastisement of Dhṛtarāṣṭra by Bhīṣma when the former remonstrates with him. Bhīṣma reminds Dhṛtarāṣṭra of the Kuru misconducts towards the Pandu. Obviously, we see the Pandu being justified and cleared.

Arjuna with the Trigarta and deploying the so-called *cakravyūha* against the rest of the Pandu. The redactors arranged this phase into three days of increasing suspense, but it is quite likely that this operation took no more than a day; we have seen that the narrative loses no structure if the relief of Yushiṣṭhira on the eleventh day and of Bhīma on the twelfth by Arjuna are removed. This operation led to the death of a prominent prince, proving a turning point of the war. Arjuna's containment by the Trigarta, and his long drive on the next day, suggests that he was at another end of the battlefield; his camp, on returning to which he heard of the debacle, must have been a different one from the main Pandu base, from which the news had been brought by runner or mounted post.

The killing of this prince made Arjuna charge through the cordons designed to contain him, link up with the Pandu, kill Jayadratha, and precipitate a general onslaught which barely stopped except for tactical pauses[73] till all major warriors—Droṇa, Karṇa, Duḥśāsana, Śalya, Śakuni, and even Duryodhana—were slain, bringing an end to the third phase. This phase would have lasted at least two days, as indicated by the night battle, and perhaps an extra day or two of pursuit and mopping up.

The above can be taken a little further. We have already noted the near-independent movement of Arjuna. In the first phase Arjuna did nothing significant, except for fighting with Bhīṣma and once extricating Abhimanyu; he fells Bhīṣma only jointly with Śikhaṇḍin. However, we have seen that Bhīṣma may really have been killed and not incapacitated—was Bhīṣma killed by Śikhaṇḍin alone, but when chivalric ideas made this difficult to countenance, it was given out that he was merely felled, that too by Arjuna? We have seen that Arjuna's role in these ten days were secondary, arranged according to the requirements of poetic suspense or *brinkmanship*. In the second phase, he is contained by the Trigarta, while the Kuru allies attack the Pandu, killing his son. Repetition of the exhortations of the *Gītā* on the thirteenth evening, and once more after the war, removes the sacrosanct position of the *Gītā* at its beginning. Can we say that Arjuna had held out through the first phase, and was persuaded to join by Krishna, only after the killing of Abhimanyu? The question as to why, if Arjuna had held off, his son had joined the Pandu has a simple answer—Abhimanyu, as son of Subhadrā, was really a Vṛṣṇi prince as per matrilineal rules of

73 On the fifteenth morning after the night's battle, soldiers stop at sunrise to offer the orison and continue. *Mbh*, VII: 186, 1–4.

succession that we have encountered so often in the *Mahabharata*. We will see that after the battle it is Yudhiṣṭhira and Bhīma who call on Bhīṣma at his bedside and obtain advice on kingship; can we say that Arjuna was leader of a distinct, and perhaps more volatile and independent, branch of the Pandu, whom Kuntī, like many a redoubtable nomad queen–mother, managed to keep united with the rest through the polyandrous marriage of Draupadī? We see only Draupadī accompanying the Pandu whereas all their other wives and sons, like Hiḍimbā and Ghaṭotkaca, Ulūpī and Irāvan, Citrāṅgadā and Babhruvāhana, or Subhadrā and Abhimanyu, had remained with their mother's people. The role of Krishna the Vṛṣṇi as the architect of the alliance and as persuader of Arjuna is significant here. It must be remembered here that it is he who is specifically called Pārtha, and is associated with exposure of the dead.

Situating the Combat

Many events of the *Mahabharata* are traditionally associated with spots within the quadrilateral Kaithal–Pehoa–Thanesar–Amin in and around the modern district of Kurukshetra in the state of Haryana, while most backdrop events lie within a radius of 100 miles (48 *kos*) of it (though needless to say that the circuit has been widened to include more and more places for obvious benefits).[74] There is however a wide archaeological hiatus between the regional layers older than the war, and settlements of the late 1st millennium B.C. when Greek and Scythian influence inter-digitated with local influence of Yajajita, Kuninda Amoghabhūti, the Agrodaka, or the Yaudheya. In other words, there is little that links the epic war archaeologically. However, some spots have very strong oral traditions linking them with events of the war; considering the possibility that some of these traditions could be authentic, the rest of this section will inspect these spots against the major events of the battle to see if they together form a picture.

On a mound near the modern township of Kurukshetra–Thanesar stands a fort that was used by late 1st millennium king Harshavardhana but reputed to have been founded by Dilīpa, an ancestor of the Kuru–Pandu. Probably this mound existed at the time of the *Mahabharata*, and

74 Limits of Nardak and its antiquities are elaborately discussed by General Cunningham in his *Archaeological Survey Reports*, vol. 2, pp. 212–226, and vol. 14, pp. 86–106, and *Ancient Geography*, pp. 329–336.

it was on this that the Āsaṅdivat or Kuru *throne–place* was located. At one place in the epic we are told that the Pandu deploy on the east, facing the Kuru on the west. In pre-modern wars, armies often marched and counter-marched before deploying, and their position on the battlefield may not be true to their relative directions. The spot of Josar or Jyotisar, five kilometres west of the modern township of Kurukshetra and through which passes one of the many relic channels of the Ghaggar, is associated with the promulgation of the *Gītā* in the opening scene of the war. Though Jyotisar is not acknowledged in the *Mahabharata* itself, we may take it as a working hypothesis that the Pandu had deployed astride Josar, facing the mound that was the pivot on which the Kuru based their deployment. The Pandu themselves may have reached the battlefield from Anyataplakṣa along the Sarasvatī–Ghaggar corridor *via* modern Hissar; Baladeva's also used the Sarasvatī–Ghaggar corridor from Dvārakā at the end of the battle and his pilgrimage.[75]

The epic however says that the Kuru were to the *west* of the Pandu, which indicates that Kuru mobile elements, and their allies from the Indus and the *Uttarāpatha*, had appeared on the west. Thus, the armies formed no front as such but occupied defended camps across the plains, with the Pandu roughly at the centre threatening the position of Āsandivat which the Kuru were keen to relieve. As the armies lay thus, with diplomatic negotiations in the background, their gaps and fronts were monitored with detachments, patrols, and scouts that raided, ambushed, and skirmished as opportunity presented itself. This was probably the actions of the first phase of the war.

Five kilometres south of the township lies Bāṇagaṅgā or Gaṅgahrada, the spot associated with the felling of Bhīṣma; this is compatible with Kuru deployment based on the mound, in an assault on which Bhīṣma may have been felled. The next major event of the battle is the felling of Abhimanyu, which is associated with the lofty mound of Amin or Abhimanyu Khera, seven kilometres south–southeast of Kurukshetra. This mound, 50 to 60 feet high and 800 feet wide and aligned north–south for 2,000 feet with tanks and a temple dedicated to Aditi, mother of the Sun, could have been used as a pivot by Kuru ambushing columns, which would mean that Abhimanyu was inveigled into believing that he was outflanking the Kuru

75 Yardi, *The Mahabharata*, p. 52. The *tīrtha*s important to the Bhargavas are described and their *mahimā*s recounted, obviously in a later interpolation.

position from the south. Little archaeological evidence has been yielded by this feature except two rectangular red-stone pillars with Kushan inscriptions and Śuṅga sculptures.

The mound of Bhor or Sarsa, 13 kilometres west of Thanesar, is considered as the place where Bhūriśravas was felled. As Arjuna had intervened in the fight between Bhūriśravas and Sātyaki while himself engaged with Jayadratha, felling the former, the spot where Jayadratha was felled may have also been nearby. Now the epic says[76] that Arjuna and Jayadratha were engaged three *yojana*s north of where Droṇa was engaged with Yudhiṣṭhira, i.e. the main scene of battle. This great distance of 27–30 miles is difficult to reconcile because the main scene of action appears in a triangle between Jyotisar, Kurukshetra, and Amin, with Bhor about six to eight kilometres from Jyotisar. Also, Arjuna when running hell for leather for Jayadratha, had bypassed Droṇa, who was already arranging Jayadratha's defences when he reached him, showing the fluidity of the narrative structure.

If, however, it is assumed that the distance of three *yojana*s mentioned was from Arjuna's *initial location*, which later was equated with Yudhiṣṭhira's location when Arjuna's distinct deployment was forgotten, the scheme makes sense. This is also compatible with the identification of Jyotisar with the *Gītā* which occurred long after the battle. A little west of Thanesar, and south of Aujas Ghat, is the 700 by 500 feet mound of *Asthipura* (place of bones) which is supposed to be the spot where the war dead were cremated; nearby is the spot of *Nar-kaṭāri*, which means where *men were cut down*. The 7th century Chinese pilgrim Hsuen Tsang claimed to have found this place strewn with bones, but Cunningham found only '*an extensive platform of unbaked bricks still 364 feet in length*', besides remains of walls and fragments of terracotta sculptures which to him were part of some funerary structure, like the Mughal *Ganj-i-Shahid* or *mound of the martyrs*, from Śaka or Hūṇa wars. It is unlikely that the bones Hsuen Tsang saw belonged to the *Mahabharata* war fought 1500 years before his time, but the spot may have been a cremation ground that went back to the *Mahabharata*.

76 *Mbh*,Southern Recension, VII: (*Jayadrathavadhaparvan*) 98.12.

CHAPTER 8

The Fallout

Family Drama

Concluding episodes of the war and in its immediate aftermath appear in four *parvans* after the *Śalyaparvan*. In the *Sauptikaparvan*, the last standing Kuru warriors launch a night raid on the Pandu–Pañcāla camp killing most of the somnolents, including the remaining sons of the Pandu. This is followed by the *Strīparvan* where all the widows visit the battlefield to lament the dead. Gāndhārī also lays a curse on Krishna: that the Vṛṣṇi will suffer a fate similar to that of the Kuru. The Śāntiparvan, which has only three *adhyāyas* but is one of the longest and most didactic of all *parvans*, starts with Yudhiṣṭhira's coronation and Draupadī's anointment as chief queen (*mahīṣī*) over the conjoint realm of Kuru–Pañcāla.It contains the many instructions on *rājadharma* (duties of the king), and *āpaddharma* (expediencies permitted under duress) that are delivered to Yudhiṣṭhira and Bhīma by Bhīṣma when they visit him on the battlefield. The instructions continue in the *Anuśāsanaparvan*, the next book, at the end of which, with the winter solstice, Bhīṣma passes away.

Several layers of additions are noticeable throughout these *parvans*. Yardi is of the opinion that the actions following the night raid—Pandu reprisals, retirement of Aśvatthāman, lament of Draupadī over the death of her sons—which appear in the *Aiśika*-sub-*parvan* (*adhyāyas* 10–18 of the *Sauptika*), were added by Sūta.[1] Also to Yardi, Sautī dramatized Yudhiṣṭhira's coronation scene with his tearful reluctance and elaborate rituals, and also added several eschatological passages to the *mokṣadharma*

1 Yardi, *TheMahabharata*, pp. 165–167.

section of Bhīṣma's injunction, summarising *sāṅkhya* philosophy. It is also evident that the *rājadharma* injunctions, clothed in parables like the story of the *śālmalī* (bombax) tree which in defying the wind suffered a fate like Duryodhana did in challenging Arjuna, were later accretions as they pertain to sedentary kingdoms rather than tribal *chiefdoms* of the time.

Though Yardi has suggested that all subsequent episodes had been added by Sūta, they cannot all be automatically disqualified as spurious. In the *Aśvamedhikaparvan*, which also has the *Anugītā* or a brief retelling of the *Gīta*, Vyāsa directs Yudhiṣṭhira to perform an *aśvamedha* in order to *overcome his grief* (!) In the next *Āśramavāsikaparvan*, the older generations, including Kuntī and Vidura, retire to the forests, where they are visited by Yudhiṣṭhira. The highly filial scene mentioned earlier—of Vidura symbolically transferring his organs to Yudhiṣṭhira—is acted out now, which has prompted suggestions that it was Vidura who had fathered Yudhiṣṭhira by *niyoga*. The *parvan* also has the beauteous *River Vision* episode, in which all the grievers have a temporary reunion with shades of their dead fathers, husbands, brothers and sons. The *parvan* ends with the older generation passing away in a forest conflagration 18 years after the war.

Fate of the Combatants

Gāndhārī's curse seems to come true in the *Mauṣalaparvan*, in which, after another 18 years, the young and old Yadu and Vṛṣṇi chiefs, while enjoying a picnic near Dvārāvatī, fall to fighting among themselves and are killed. The debacle is brought about when a sage they tease in jest curses them that they will fight to their death with *mūṣala*s or clubs. Baladeva is among those killed, and Krishna is just able to send a missive to Arjuna to come to their aid. However, by the time Arjuna arrives, even Krishna had been erroneously shot dead by a hunter who mistook his foot, exposed from where he hid in the brush, for a deer's face. Arjuna finds the island–city of Dvārāvatī barely holding out against a Śālva siege, having barricaded its gates and ceased all boat traffic. This part may be an exaggeration, as the nomadic Vṛṣṇyandhaka were unlikely to have had the opulent and fortified city that Dvāravati is said to be in this section.

After relieving the city and performing the last rites for his friends, Arjuna gathers the survivors, including the aged Vasudeva, the

Vṛṣṇyandhaka ruler, and starts for Hastināpura. However, the typically nomad migrant caravan is attacked by the Ābhīras, who carry away those women who do not commit the *satī*. Once back, Arjuna installs Vajra, the sole surviving grandson of Krishna, at Indraprastha; he however is never heard of again.

In the last two *parvan*s, the *Mahāprasthānika* and *Svargārohaṇa*, the Pandu decide to end their earthly careers and journey to heaven after appointing Parīkṣita as their successor, with Yuyutsu, the sole righteous Kuru brother who had survived the war, as his regent. After circumambulating the known world and making a series of pilgrimages, they make their way to heaven when first Draupadī, and then the brothers, drop dead one after the other, only Yudhiṣṭhira reaching intact. Many eschatological passages appear here, and many characters are seen enjoying themselves in heaven or suffering in hell according to their deeds. The most poignantly beautiful episode in these *parvan*s is that of the hound that follows Yudhiṣṭhira, to which the latter sticks till the end, and which turns out to be none other than *Sārameya* the hound of Yama.

Appraisal of the Outcome of the War

Several of the above episodes would have been historically authentic—the internecine war of the Yadu possibly precipitated by a potlatch that did not go well, the raid of the Śālva, kin to numberless invaders who infested the *Aparānta*, the intervention of Arjuna, and the taking away of the Yadu women by the Ābhīra who thereby adopted the Yadu name. However, it is doubtful that the two sets of events—the forest holocaust and the Yadu catastrophe followed by Pandu renunciation—really took place 18 and 36 years after the war; Parīkṣita would have been at least 35 years old at the time of his coronation if this were so, and *not needed* a regent.

Parīkṣit, a just and effective king, was killed by Takṣaka, king of the Naga who seem to have had a feud with the Pandu. In the lore, the Takṣaka infiltrates the chief's defences by hiding in an arrowhead. Parīkṣit is avenged by his son Janamejaya who conquers Takṣaśila, *Rock of Takṣaka*, and who in the *Mahabharata* performs a *sarpasattra* to exterminate the Nāga. This episode brings us back to the question of several Parīkṣit–Janamejaya pairs that we have met.

The *Atharvaveda* and some *Brāhmaṇa* texts mention a Parīkṣit who made the Kuru prosperous and their land 'flow with milk and honey',[2] while the *Purāṇa*s acclaim the *Pārīkṣita*s, i.e. the people of Parīkṣit, as thriving—*janaḥ sa bhadramedhati*—, and say that their king conquered the world and became *samrāṭ*.[3] To Witzel, this Parīkṣit was the old Parīkṣit whom the *Purāṇa*s call son of an early Kuru king, variously of Avīkṣit, Anāśva, or even Kuru himself, and grandfather of Pratiśravas and Pratīpa; in fact, Witzel opines that Parīkṣit son of Abhimanyu was not authentic.[4] However, Witzel has himself shown that the post-war Kuru–Pañcāla combine had stimulated the *Brāhmaṇa*s; it would thus be more reasonable to suppose that the *Brāhmaṇa*s would laud a post-war king, who as per the epic was Parīkṣit. In fact, interpreting the term '*Kauravya*' applied for Parīkṣit in the *Brāhmaṇa*s as not *son of Kuru* but as *of the Kuru*, Raychaudhuri takes both Parīkṣit–Janamejaya pairs as authentic, the older from a hoary period close to Kuru himself, and the later powerful monarchs of the *Brāhmaṇa*s.

Sarpidavī, the spot where Janamejaya performed his *sarpasattra*, is often identified with Safidon in Jind district of modern Haryana. Now, Janamejaya is also associated with Takṣaśilā which he conquered, where he often held court, and where he performed at least one *aśvamedha*. Now, while Takṣaśila and its neighbouring Puṣkalāvatī (Peshawar) are associated with Takṣa and Puṣkara, sons of Bharata of the *Ramayana*, Takṣaśilā is also associated with the Takṣaka who along with the Nāga were victims of Janamejaya's *sarpasattra*. No ethnic identity of Nāga or Takṣaka can be established. The Nāga is associated with the Neolithic Mother Goddess cults—numberless *Bhagsu–Nāga*s and *Khirsu–Nāga*s appear in the Śiva cult,[5] often as *Bhairava*s, the serpent is a primary element of this cult as Maṇikāla and appears as Śiva's *yajñopavīta* or 'sacred thread'. And yet, Nāga is associated with equestrian tribes— Takṣaka's brother is Aśvasena (literally horse–army), Arjuna's son Irāvan from Ulūpī the Nāga fights as cavalry, and the Nāga kings ousted by Samudragupta in later, historical times were associated with equestrian Śaka–Muruṇḍa groups. It appears

2 *AV*, XX: 127, 7–10.

3 *Bhagavata Purāṇa*, chapters 16 to 18.

4 M. Witzel, 'Early Sanskritization: Origins and Development of the Kuru State', *EJVS*, vol. 1, no. 4, 1995, pp. 1–26.

5 Which also indicates a series of Himalayan deities with names ending in 'Su' having been assimilated into the Śaiva religion as Nāgas and Bhairavas.

that the term Nāga was generic in import, like the word *Yavana* would be in time, sequentially indicating Ionian, Greek, Turcoman, generic foreigner, and finally Muslim.

Also of interest is that historically the environs of Takṣaśilā was occupied by the powerful Takka tribe, represented in the *Paraetacae* of the Greeks and in the Ṭāk Rajputs of the Pothwar plateau and Jammu. Ṭāk is a clan name in Kashmir while Jammu spoke a now extinct language called *Takri*. Probably the post-war Janamejaya's successful conquest of a group with similar affiliations was celebrated by an *aśvamedha*, which was confused with the *sarpasattra* of the *Sūtra* and *Brāhmaṇa* where one Janamejaya appeared as *adhvaryu* and Dhṛtrāṣṭra Airāvata as another officiant;[6] to Raychaudhuri, this appropriation, prompted by the similarity in names, aimed at accounting for Janamejaya's conquest of Takṣaśila.[7] Indeed a Kuru–Pūru line is found on the Indus by the Greeks—two Porus's contested Alexander, while Ptolemy found the *Pandooui* in Sākala or Sialkot. In the *Aitareya* and *Śatapatha Brāhmaṇa*s, one Janamejaya, patronymic Pārīkṣita,[8] is given an *Aindra Mahābhiṣekha* by his priest Tura Kāvaśeya. We shall return to this sacrifice later.

The Kuru–Pañcāla seem to have disintegrated shortly after Janamejaya, the Kuru realm getting divided into Kurukṣetra, Khāṇḍava (Indraprastha), Kuru (Hastināpura), and Kuru–Jaṅgala along the Sarasvatī. In the *Purāṇa*s, Janamejaya is succeeded by his son Śatānīka at Hastināpura while a nephew, Abhipratārin Kākṣasenī, son of a brother Kakṣasena (?), rules Indraprastha; Vajra, the grandson of Krishna, is nowhere mentioned. A later Kuru king is named Vṛddhadyumna Ābhipratāriṇa,[9] who may have been a son or descendant of Abhipratārin but where exactly he ruled is unclear. The *Jātaka*s state that *Indapattha*, i.e. Indraprastha, was ruled by a king of the *Yudhiṭṭhila Gotta*.

A few more rulers of the line appear, like Aśvamedhadatta, Adhisīma Kṛṣṇa, and Nicaksu, but despite their performing great sacrifices to avert the calamities predicted to befall them,[10] supposedly result of a curse of

6 *BŚS*, 17, 18, and *PB*, 25, 15.

7 Raychaudhuri, *Political History*, p. 31.

8 Raychaudhuri, *Political History*, pp. 11–17.

9 Raychaudhuri, *Political History*, p. 37.

10 Raychaudhuri, *Political History*, p. 36.

expulsion earned by Vṛddhadyumna due to a procedural error in a sacrifice, the line seems to peter out thereafter. The *Chandogya Upaniṣad* speaks of devastation and depopulation of the Kuru country by *maṭīci* or *maṭaci* (hailstone or locust); the Kuru are said to have emigrated to Kauśāmbi in the reign of Nicakṣu due to these calamities. Other texts mention floods as the reason behind the abandoning of Hastināpura. B.B. Lal dates traces of floods observed at Hastināpura to *c.* 800 B.C., which to him bears out the Kuru emigration, though Possehl gives these evidences a date *c.* 400 B.C.

After Nicakṣu there is only sporadic mention of the Kuru–Bharata. The *Bṛhadāraṇyaka Upaniṣad* calls the Pārīkṣita a *vanished dynasty*. A *Kururāṭṭha* (Kuru state), with its king Renu, is found in Uttara-Pañcāla, the king of Kauśambi is hailed as *Bhārata* in the *Svapna–Vāsavadattā*,[11] Kuyoya and the *Elder* Ratthapāla are Kuru chiefs mentioned in Buddhist *Ratthapāla Sutta* (*Sūtra*), and one Kṣemaka, a Kuru, is said to have been overthrown by the Nanda of Magadha.

The *Jaiminīya Brāhmaṇa* says that the Kuru were ousted by the Śalvas,[12] which Witzel unconvincingly interprets as a merger of the Kuru with the Śālva to become the Śūrasena. The Greeks, who never mention the Kuru, do attest to Pūru and Pandu presence on the Indus and Sialkot respectively, and call the Śūrasena cities of *Bridama*, *Malaita*, and *Tholoubana*—presumably Vṛndāvana, Mathura, and another undecipherable city—as *Porouaroi* cities.

Also, while the *Kāṭhaka Saṅhitā* says that two kings Keśin and Dalbhya divided the Pañcālas, a Pāñcāla ruler Keśin Dālbhya (son of Dalbhya, or Darbhya) appears elsewhere as successor to the Kuru *via* a maternal uncle who had no 'direct' successor. This shows the Pañcāla floundering as deeply as the Kuru. Evidently, Kuru lineages, which had really formed an oligarchy led by several *rājan*s under an overall tribal chief, had disintegrated into many cadet clans and septs among whom it would be fruitless to seek neat father–son successions. The situation was similar to that of Maurya and Gupta ruling houses which would spawn numberless cadet branches across South Asia that survived for centuries after their respective empire–states had passed. All that can be made out here is that a few generations after the war, the Kuru, probably compelled

11 Raychaudhuri, *Political History*, pp. 38–39.

12 *JB*, 2.206, *Sāṅkhāyana Śrautasūtra* (*SŚS*), 15.16.11–1.

by an ecological emergency, had dispersed eastwards, completing the process of sedentization that had been affecting many of their branches before the war. The above process, harbinger of the colonization of the Gangetic plains, is important to our enquiry because it would transform completely the type of warfare practiced by these early Kuru people and create the formats of warfare that would later, anachronistically, find their way into the epic's battle narratives.

Colonization of the Gangetic Plains

The early part of the 1st millennium saw a symbiotic agro–pastoral economy colonizing the Gangetic plains where rainfall was sufficient for dry farming.[13] This economy was accompanied by developments like use of draught cattle, ploughshare, and techniques like leaving land fallow, which shifted economic emphasis to agriculture and in time established a prosperous civilization as indicated by a rash of 200 NBPW sites on the plains.[14] However, Kosambi's view that iron lay dramatically at the root of this cultural efflorescence is not borne out by evidence; iron weapons are only hesitatingly mentioned, there is no references to iron implements that should have been essential to cutting down the great trees or turning the heavy alluvial, and most iron implements like sickles, chisels, hoes, or axes that have been found in the Gangetic plains are really no older than 600 B.C.[15] Even the many urban centres that appear from this time are not archaeologically associated with civic use of iron; only at Ujjain have some iron for weapons been found.[16]

This period also saw a new urbanization brought about by agrarian prosperity—Erdosy, among others, sees this *second* phase of urbanization of South Asia (the first being the Indus valley) as independent of the Harappan legacy.[17] Most urban centres of this phase seem to have started

13 See O.H.K. Spate, *India and Pakistan*, Methuen, London, 1954, p. 57 and fig 13 for dry farming in the Gangetic plains.

14 For reference to list of these sites, see Erdosy, 'Origin of Cities', p. 103 nn. 57.

15 Erdosy, 'Origin of Cities', p. 103, n. 58.

16 Erdosy, 'Origin of Cities', p. 95; also, for iron at Ujjain, see N. R. Banerjee, 'The Excavations at Ujjain', in E. Waldschmidt (ed.), *Indologen Tagung: 1959*, Vandenhoeck & Ruprecht, Gottingen, 1960, pp. 66–87.

17 Erdosy, 'Origin of Cities', p. 87. Also, A. Ghosh, *The City in Early Historic India*, Indian Institute of Advanced Study, Simla, 1973, pp. 73–88.

as walls enclosing vast spaces, which is what is left of the abandoned sites of Girivraja or Rājagṛha today. These were little more than fortified encampments of chiefs,[18] whose subjects were the new agrarian colonists of the country. The urban trend peaked *after* the Maurya period, from when do the cities finally yield archaeological evidence of the advanced civic features which anachronistically appear in the epics.[19]

The natural concomitant of such urban–agrarian prosperity was that land became the symbol of wealth, while pastoral opportunities grew restricted. Herds were limited to commons, corrals, and stalls, and disruptive procedures like *gaviṣṭi* and *vrātya* were gradually formalised or even discontinued—we see the Kuru and Pañcāla only formally inducting *vrātya*s in one another's' territory.[20] Society grew contemptuous of herders, just as the land–obsessed Peshawar Afghans are contemptuous of their *Powendah* brethren. Though cattle retained ritual importance and remained status symbols and markers of wealth—the *Arthaśāstra* talks of herders commissioned with holding 100 heads each of the state herd[21]—cattle–keeping was discouraged as it involved bloodshed. Beef–eating, not taboo earlier, was understandably banned[22] and agriculture whole–heartedly encouraged. The spate of clearance must have been acute, as while the Gangetic plains had been covered with dense forests at Buddha's time, Aśoka had to include injunctions against deforestation in his inscriptions; we find similar injunctions in Bhīṣma's dying injunction to the Pandu.[23]

18 See Erdosy, 'Origin of Cities', n. 4 for survey of other discussive works on 1st millennium urbanisation in South Asia. Especially see A. Ray, *Villages, Towns, and Secular Buildings in Ancient India*, Firma K. L. Mukhopadhyay, Calcutta, 1964.

19 See Sir John Marshall, 'The Excavations at Bhita', *Annual Report of the Archaeological Survey of India: 1911–12*, Calcutta, 1915, and G. R. Sharma, 'The Excavations at Kausambi, 1949–50', *Memoirs of the Archaeological Survey of India*, no. 74, 1969.

20 Witzel, 'Early Sanskritisation', pp. 17–18.

21 *Arthaśāstra*, II.46. It also suggests that states demand that these herds be grazed on the best land.

22 *ṚV*, II: 7.5; VI: 16.47; X: 91.14; *AV*, X: 10, *Vedic Index*, vol. 1, p. 10; *Ait.Br*, i.15; *TB*, II.17.11.1; ŚB, iii.41.2; *Āpastambha Gṛhyasūtra*, VIII.22.3-11. A guest was called *goghnya*. As against popular belief, nomads are not voracious eaters of meat but reserve it for special occasions. See *ṚV*, I: 162 on cooking meat.

23 *Mbh*,XII: 35.7 and 30.

Emergence of Varṇa

Sedentization, wherein older relic populations got assimilated in the process as postulated by Carneiro,[24] ethnically leavened the *Janapada*s making them cosmopolitan, the memory of their pioneering tribes surviving only in their names (like England or France named after Angles and Franks though they are composed of more Saxons, Jutes, Romans, Bretons, Danes, Vikings, Normans, Gauls, Basques, and Latins). Only upper classes stressed affiliation with the pioneering tribes, or tweaked descent patterns to do so like in the Greek city–states which tried to establish decent from one eponymous ancestor each. The laity, i.e. the *viś*, became deracinated.

The leavening resulted in permeation of 'caste'. In theory, Gangetic society was divided into four *varṇa*s, which were however not so much social class as definers of *ritual protocol.* Within each were networks of occupation-based breeding groups or *jāti*s, many of which had originated from tradesmen's guilds. While *jāti*s grew increasingly fastidious about socialising and commensality, often to the point of pseudo–speciation, the system remained extremely fluid and individuals and groups changed status all the time. In fact, one *jāti* could be member of different *varṇa*s in different regions.

In addition to the fastidiousness, society grew disturbingly contemptuous of manual labour, even IA groups that lived by the honest sweat of their brow dropped to the lowest rungs. In time, even agriculture would be discouraged—some *Brāhmaṇa* groups considered it sacrilege to *touch* a plough, while *Vaiśya*s were encouraged to take to the *once despised* occupations of money lending and trade. While endless *saṅkara-varṇa*s, i.e. 'half-castes', were defined as permutations of the *varṇa*s to account for the varied humanity of South Asia and fix their ritual protocol, the elitist and discriminatory institution was also marked by numerous peoples it left out, either *below* or *beyond* the *varṇa.*

One set it left out *beyond* were IA/IIr groups retaining their old occupation of running the caravan trade, i.e. the extra–Vedic *Banjara*s who survived till the pre-modern age, and probably also engendered the Gypsies of Europe. Also *beyond* were the mysterious *Amāvasu*, to account

24 Robert L. Carneiro, 'A Theory on the Origin of the State', *Science*, no. 169, 170, pp. 733–38.

for whose pastoral tendencies and bothersome cattle lifting habits the archaic term *vrātya* was re-appropriated now.

Evolution of Political and Societal Procedures

Agrarian sedentization also changed political formats of these proto–states, but in a direction quite *opposite* to that postulated by Witzel or Erdosy.[25] These esteemed scholars suppose that the Vedic people imposed their native format, monarchy, upon older populations, whose native format, the republic, resurfaced from time to time. However, we have seen that pastoral societies like those of the Vedic people were dispersive and unstable, their mobile members and perishable produce extremely difficult to tax. Taxes were more in the nature of voluntary offering or *bali*, reciprocated by the distributive *vidatha* ceremony;[26] equality of uncertainty permeating such societies made them essentially egalitarian with open decision making procedures by variously composed councils, which have been admirably discussed by Sharma.[27]

In other words, quite contrary to what Erdosy and Witzel believe, the republic, or rather the participative oligarchy, was the native Vedic political format, and far from *imposing* monarchy, the Vedic people gradually *lost* their native formats and were compelled by circumstances to adopt various stages of centralization and monarchy. The Vedic form persisted in *gaṇasaṅgha*s which had a range of decision-making processes. At one end of this range were the *āraṭṭa* or a-cephalous *vrātya* nations of the west which were governed by councils of excitable, volatile, and often uncouth elders, like the Afghan tribal *jirgah* which was empowered to call out the *lashkar* or tribal militia like the Vedic *samiti*,[28] and which came to decision by '*sense of the meeting*', agreeing in a mob-like manner,

25 Erdosy, 'Origin of Cities', p. 101, where he says that '*... many ... states, organised as tribal oligarchies, were probably of indigenous origin, and not the survivals of older Vedic institutions as has been claimed.*'

26 After capturing Delhi, Babur distributed all his gains making sure that even the junior-most soldiers received at least one *shahrukhi*.

27 J.P. Sharma, *Republics in Ancient India*, Brill, Leiden, 1968, sees tribal oligarchies as rooted firmly in Vedic institutions.

28 *AV*, XV: 9.2; also K.P. Jayaswal, *Hindu Polity*, p. 120. '*sabhā ca samitiśca senāca*. The *samiti* resembled the Roman *Comitia Centuriata*, Teutonic *Assemble*, or the Homeric *Assembly* in many functional ways.

jeering, punishing, and at times even lynching dissenters.[29] At the other were more formalised procedures of the evolved *gaṇasaṅgha*s, preserved today in the business of the Hīnayāna *saṅgha.* This change occurred as the *vrātya* nations drifted eastwards, seen in recent times by the Rohillas giving up their native *jirgah* for more organised procedures, even adopting the *panchayat.*

The changes, which would culminate in the great monarchies of the eastern Gangetic plains like Magadha, based on the highly ergonomic organization principles of the *Arthaśāstra,*[30] seem to have commenced before the end of Vedic period and the epic war. We have already seen how the *rājanya,* special families, often easily reshuffled, that once ran the oligarchies, had grown entrenched, re-emerging as the *kṣatra,* subverting distributive procedures, and *taking* rather than *giving* to the *sva.* Kaṅsa had tried to subvert the oligarchy among the Vṛṣṇi; Viḍūḍabha converted the Kosala, who in his father Prasenajit's time had been an oligarchy, into a monarchy. This centralization was possible because agrarian kingdoms could collect taxes, largely paid willingly in return for organised protection and agrarian infrastructure like canals and tanks, their kings able to adopt policies more sustainable than those that chiefs of inherently unstable tribal societies could. It was the wisdom of such kingship that appears in the *Śānti-* and *Anuśāsanaparvan*s, with an entire chapter devoted to kingly authority or *daṇḍa.*

The monarchical formats that Aryan settlers adopted belonged to the Neolithic substrate, many of whose cultural patterns they also assimilated. In the *Jātaka*s, Bimbisāra, Buddha's contemporary and king of Magadha, is anxious about his greying hair. Later, he is allegedly murdered by his son the anti-Buddhist Ajātaśatru, who is in turn followed by a string of parricide successors. We have encountered the theme of physical perfection as essential for kingship in the cases of Devāpi, Pāṇḍu, Dhṛtarāṣṭra, or Saubhūti; the killing of the Magadhan king is reminiscent of the Neolithic king–cult wherein the king was removed, violently and even fatally, when he was no longer physically perfect, unblemished, or even just young. The killing of the king Veṇa by the *Brāhmaṇa*s, ouster of Janamejaya by his priests (see later), and the legend noted by the Greeks of the Kathaian king

29 James W. Spain, *The Way of the Pathans*, Oxford University Press, Karachi, 1972, p. 50.

30 *Arthaśāstra*, II.1.

being poisoned by his wife who would then marry her lover and make him king, were instances of political changeover reminiscent of Neolithic religio–political procedures. Obviously, Bimbisāra's anxiety was not for mere loss of good looks, but because his end was nearing.

The *Mahabharata*, and more so the *Ramayana*,grew into its current form among such cultures, whose *Yajurvedin* or *Kṣatriya* classes, its main patrons, turned it into an elitist work that takes no notice of commoners, i.e. the *viś*.

Somewhat anticipating the Middle Age dichotomy between *Eastern* Rajputs and the so-called *High Tradition* Rajputs of the west was the variance between the 'elite' *Kṣatriya* lineages of the western *gaṇasaṅgha*s, which were more *tribe*, and the *Kṣatriya* families of the plains which were more *caste*. Even among the *gaṇasaṅgha*s, those on the Indus and beyond were 'homogenous' tribes (as far as tribes could be homogenous), while those which had descended on to the plains had two 'classes'—tribesmen, erstwhile *viś*, which used for themselves the term *Kṣatriya* (the plainsmen called them *vrātya*), and helots or *dāsa–karmakāra*. This situation, observed for western settlements in the Buddhist times—*Yona–Kambojeśu anneśu ca paccantimeśu janapadeśu dveva vanna–ayyo ceva dāso ca*, i.e. Greek, Kamboja and other western *janapada*s had two *varṇa*s, Ārya (*ayyo*) and Dāsa—, was also noted in the epic—*jātya cān sādṛśāḥ sarve kulena sadṛṣastathā*.[31]

Some such western *gaṇasaṅgha–janapada*s were the Prārjuna, Arjunāyana, and Yaudheya, *vrātya* versions of the Pandu who appeared in the aftermath of the war. The Yaudheya were initially found around Kurukṣetra, but from after the Greek hiatus their coins, hailing them as '*Yaudheya-gaṇasya-jayaḥ*' or *glory to the Yaudheya*,[32] have been found from a wide area astride the Divide. The tribe, probably the same as the *Johiya* Rajputs and *Yahya* Afghans[33] today, were celebrated in the *Prayāga Praśasti* of Samudragupta, and also by Somadeva Sūri, as a powerful and noble people. However, while they seem to have absorbed other tribes

31 *Mbh*, XII: 107.30.

32 V.N. Datta and H.A.Phadke, *History of Kurukshetra*, p. 49.

33 Henry Walter Bellew, *The Races of Afghanistan: being a Brief Account of the Principal Nations Inhabiting the Country*, Calcutta, Thacker, Spine, 1880, pp. 13–15.

like the Kuninda,[34] they never could absorb the Prarjuna and Arjunāyanas who remained politically independent for centuries, another pointer to the distinction between Yudhiṣṭhira and Arjuna.

Vrātya nations such as these were always looked upon ambivalently. They were revered for looks, purity of blood, and proper accent and speech. Onesikritos saw the Muśika (*Mousikanoi*) on the Indus as upright, correct, honest, healthy, and Spartan people who resisted the demoralizing forces of plenty in their plentiful land.[35] Both *Kṣatriya* and *Brāhmaṇa*s encouraged the *vrātya* to *Kṣatriya*-hood through the *vrātyaṣṭoma*, the ancient initiation ceremony in the rite of passage, in order to shore up their numbers and supporters. Entire groups were employed as mercenaries; though called *asibandhaku putta*, i.e. *son-of-a-sword-girdle*,[36] the purport of the phrase was quite different from that of *son-of-a-gun*, and there was no negative implication to it! They acted as professionally contracted soldiery. The *Nārāyaṇīya-senā*, i.e. the army of his that Krishna offers to Duryodhana, has been equated by Karve to military slaves who could be bought or sold,[37] but were more probably such mercenaries. Within their bands, *vrātya*s retained their tribal structures, forming corporations or *āyudhajīvi-saṅgha* which replicated, and at times *became*, *gaṇasaṅgha*s. In other words, these were precursors to the Rohilla horse–trader to *nawab* 'states'.

At the same time of being sought after and venerated, their political tendencies, disrespectful vivaciousness, love for cattle-lifting, and expertise with weapons, made *vrātya*s disliked by the plainsmen among whom a tight morality was then emerging. They were criticised for lack of fastidiousness regarding eating. While Karṇa castigates Śalya for eating beef, Onesikritos mentions common-messing among the Mousikanoi, like the Spartan *Syssitia* or the Yajurvedic *sagdhi* and *sapīti* messing

34 A.S.Altekar, *A New History of the Indian People*, vol. 6, 1946, pp. 21–29.

35 McCrindle, J.W., *The Invasion of India by Alexander the Great*, Westminster, Archibald and Constable, 1816, p. 26, n.4, and Arora, 'Onesikritos', p. 91. The *Mbh*, and *Markandeya Purāṇa* call the Mūśika a *people of the south*, which meant *their* south, *Mbh*, VI: 9.36, and *Mārk. Pur.*, LVIII, 16. Perhaps they are represented by the Moghsi of the Indus today.

36 *Saṅyutta Nikāya*, IV: 312, 314.

37 Karve, *Yugānta*, p. 185.

companies[38] which reappears in the Sikh *Guru–ka–langar*. Neither did *vrātya* heed caste rules. It was said that the Bahlīka could become a *Brāhmaṇa*, a *Kṣatriya*, a *Vaiśya*, and even a Śūdra; '*having been a twice-born (dvija), he becomes a Dāsa again ... in the same family, one may be a Brāhmaṇa, while the rest are common workmen.*'[39] The Gandhāra and Mādra were condemned because their *rājan* poured oblations themselves, as per the ancient practice, instead letting the *Brāhmaṇa*s do it for him.[40] The biting discourtesies exchanged between Karṇa and Śalya include references to promiscuity of Madra women (*godharma*), their fondness for the tipple,[41] their willingness to throw off their garments and dance, especially when intoxicated, and their penchant for public sex (*prakāśamaithuna,* or *nārīviṣaya*).[42] In fact, Megasthenes records that women of the Indus readily 'prostituted' themselves unless compelled to remain chaste by their husbands,[43] a situation resembling the nomad world where women were reputed to have sex with strangers and slaves. As late as the *Rājataraṅgiṇi*, *Brāhmaṇas* of the northwest are castigated for practicing incest.

In fact, so alarming were the customs of the north-westerners that the custom of *satī* was revived as a means of controlling society. In its original form, once common across the IE world from Sweden across Scythia to

38 D.D. Kosambi, *The Culture and Civilization of Ancient India in Historical Outline*, Delhi, 1972, p. 174. To him it also represented the *ekapātram* which the *Arthaśāstra* would use to subvert the freedom of the great Indian oligarchies.

39 *Mbh*, VIII: 30.

40 *Mbh*, VIII: 45.40; 40.29.

41 While the custom of women drinking had fallen out, in the *Vālmīki Ramayana*, Rama is seen handing a glass of *maireya*, a particularly strong wine, to Sītā when he notices her carrying

Sītāmādāya hastena madhu maireyakaṃ śuci|

pāyayāmāsa kākutsthaḥ Śacīmeva Purandaraḥ||

Sauvīra was considered poor—Sītā says that the difference between Rāma and Rāvaṇa was like the difference of the best of the wines from the poor *Suvīraka—Surāgrya-Sauvīrakayo yadantaraṃ*.

42 Herodotus, III.101; 1,203; Ktesias Jac. no. 688, f. 45 (33); Megasthenes no. 715, F. 204 (Athens, XII, 14, p. 517 D-518 B) … allegdly so given were Bahīka women to drinking that one of them declared '*yā māṅ suvīrakaṅ kaścidyācatāṅ dāyataṅ mama putraṅ dadyāma patiṅ dadyāṅ na tu dadyākaṅ suvīrakam*', in other words, *I shall give up my son, and my husband, but never, never my suvīraka. Mbh*, VIII: 40, 39–40.

43 Megasthenes, F. 32, cited in Strabo, *Geography*, XV, 1, 54.

South Asia,[44] wives, slaves, commanders, and soldiers competed to burn with the dead chief just like Mādrī had competed with Kuntī to burn with Pāṇḍu. The practice had fallen out of use with establishment of the Vedic order—in Book X, the widow lies on the pyre beside her dead husband and then is asked to rise and become wife of the latter's younger brother, the *didhīṣṇu*.[45] However, once the Scythian conquest refreshed it,[46] the practice was revived across the subcontinent as a means to *control* women, just as repression of Afghan women today is the result of Pakhtun society's felt need to suppress and extinguish their supposedly, and reputedly, *vigorous appetites*.

The above characteristics, though coloured by conservative vitriol, indicates that *vrātya* nations had not been everywhere equally affected by Brahminism and retained their old customs and *joie de vivre*. No wonder that the great 'renegade' movements like Buddhism and Jainism appeared and were most supported among *vrātya* nations, and patronised by the *Vaiśya*s who wanted to regain parity with the *Brāhmaṇa* and *Kṣatriya*. The *Mahabharata* itself is set among largely *vrātya* peoples, who on drifting eastwards, like the *vrātya* Śākya and the Malla, gradually adapted elaborate kingships and left behind pastoral brethren who retained older forms—*kecid deśa gaṇa-adhinaḥ, kecid raja adhinaḥ*. Thus we see monarchical and elaborate characteristics of the east entering the epic through the 1st millennium.

The Rāmāyaṇa

While the *Mahabharata* was situated among the Kuru–Pañcāla, two of the foursome along with the Kosala–Videha that enjoyed the highest position among the *janapada*s, the *Ramayana* or the *Journey of Rāma* has as its backdrop the other two. Kosala, intimately associated with Kāśī–Vārāṇasi (Benaras) tribes and further on the Gangetic plains,

44 In the *Iliad*, 23:166–67, '*Twelve sons of the great-souled Trojans were placed on the Pyre with Patrocles*'. There are instances of *suttee* in Sweden, in the 9th century A.D. *Flateyjabók* 1:63, *see* H.R.E. Davidson, *Gods and Myths of Northern Europe*, New York, Penguin, 1981 repr., *passim*; for female servants sacrificed in Sweden, *see* J. Skov K. Brønsted, *The Vikings*, Hammondsworth, Penguin, Middlesex, 1965, p. 293.

45 *ṚV*, X: 18.8—*rise up; come to the world of life, O woman; Thou liest here by one whose soul has left him. Come: thou hast now entered upon the wifehood of this thy lord who takes thy hand and woos thee*, trans., as per Macdonell, 1900, p. 126.

46 Arora, *Onesikritos*, p. 86.

remained a republic till the time of the Buddha, long after the events of the *Ramayana*, while Videha was associated with *vrātya* groups like the Licchavis till well into the 1st millennium A.D. However, the spectacular, urban–agrarian prosperous civilization, that was to flower in pre-modern Awadh–Lakhnau, had already started appearing in Kosala, making it the heartland of Gangetic Vedicism–Brahminism.

Also, while the Kuru chief was simply called *rājan* in the *Mahabharata*, the king of Videha was titled *samrāṭ*, a term originally meaning *equal–king* or *dual–king* but later appropriated to mean the great emperor of the *Aśvamedha*. This monarchical trend was commemorated in the story of Prasenajit and Viḍūḍabha. We thus see that the *Ramayana* is based, and had evolved, in a far more monarchical, centralised, and agrarian context than the *Mahabharata*. Understanding its structure thereby helps understand that of the *Mahabharata*.

In essence, the *Ramayana* is a twin story, with its parts quite independent of one another. Prince Rāma is denied the succession of the Ikṣvāku[47] by his stepmother's contrivance and banished by his father Daśaratha with his half-brother Lakṣmana and wife Sītā, daughter of the Videha monarch Janaka. In the forest, his wife is abducted by Rāvaṇa the *Rākṣa* king of Laṅkā, and is rescued by Rāma with the help of his Simian or *Vānara* allies.

Notwithstanding the focused narrative of the *Ramayana* which is occupied with current happenings and acts of its protagonists unlike the diffused and rambling *Mahabharata*, it has many symbolisms which must be taken note of. First, it displays a strong agrarian symbolism. In Valmīki's *Ramayana*, *Sītā*, a word which means furrow and is one of the few IA agrarian words in Vedic literature, was born at the tip of Janaka's plough; elsewhere, she is born of Daśaratha's plough. The *Adbhūta Ramayana* places her birth at Kurukṣetra, where it says Janaka came to plough. The epic ends with her disappearance into the earth, which is her mother, at once associating her with the Demeter–Persephone theme.

The *Adhyātma Ramayana* has the story of the princes' rescue from the dungeons of Ahi– and Mahi–Rāvaṇa, half-brothers of Rāvaṇa, by a bee or *bhrāmarī*, the bee being a very important theme in the goddess

47 In reality, the appointment was of *yuvarāja*, i.e. the junior king in the diarchy.

tradition. Also, Rāma is *Rāma–candra*, *Candra* being moon, night sun, *soma*, provider of coolth and cool virility, and 'lord of vegetation'. Two other Rāmas in Indian mythology also have strong agrarian symbolism. Bhārgava Rāma is associated with the *paraśu* double–axe (like the Cretan *labras*) and human sacrifice, while Baladeva (Rāma), who as *Saṅkarṣaṇa* always bears the plough, even in council, has many Bacchic features.

So strong are these agrarian symbolisms that Jacobi took the *Ramayana* as a retelling of the Indra–Vṛttra myth and story of vegetational fertility, and of doubtful historical value. This appears to be corroborated by the fact that no site associated with the *Ramayana* has yielded pottery evidence older than 700–600 B.C., though its story is set in the agrarian, prosperous, and urban Kosala abutting on the Sarayu or Sadānīra river, but many generations *before* the *Mahabharata*, in fact three generations before the BOTK.[48]

We have seen that in so early an age, Vedic peoples had barely ventured into the *mahāvana*s of the plains. The *Śatapatha Brāhmaṇa* story of Videgha Māthava crossing the Sadānīrā with Agni *Vaiśvānara*, i.e. the *world–fire*,[49] is not that of the clearing of forests by fire but of the spread of the Vedic sacrificial religion to the east,[50] which had started after the BOTK. Thus, only a few pioneering āśramas or hermitages practicing this religion were located in the forests, harried by foresters whose chastisement was almost a rite of passage for Aryan youth. It was long after the epic war, which may have triggered the population of the plains, that Kosala became the eastern limit of Aryandom. How is the *Ramayana* then placed before the *Mahabharata*?

The basic plot of the *Ramayana*, composed by the brigand–turned–poet Valmīki, was innovated independently by others like Kamba (Tamil), Tulasi (Gangetic plains), Ranganātha (Telegu), Kṛttivās (Bengal), or Divakar Bhatta (Kashmir). Some of them, like Kṛttivās and Tulasi, introduced the tighter morality of later ages, glossing over awkward episodes like that of Ṛṣyaśṛṅga, or meat eating and wine imbibing by the

48 As per Yāska; see F.E. Pargiter, *The Purāṇa Text of the Dynasties of the Kali Age*, Motilal Banarasidass, Delhi, 1972 (First Published 1913), pp. 147–8.

49 ŚB, i.4.1.14 ff.

50 Michael Witzel, 'Early Indian History: Linguistic and Textual Parameters', in G. Erdosy (ed.), *The Indo–Aryans*, p. 86.

protagonists. The touching episodes of Śabarī tasting fruits in order to select the best ones for her lord appears in Kamba, and to some extent in Ranganatha, showing that it was a Deccan innovation, while the stories of Sītā's banishment, dramatized only in Kalidasa's *Raghuvaṃśa* and Bhavabhūti's *Uttara-Rāma Carita*, appear only in the *Uttara-Ramayana*, which is a later addition.

In addition, a series of other *Ramayana*s, including the *Adhyātma–*, *Adbhūta–*, *Mahā–*, or *Duranta–*, are so different that they have been denounced as heretical. In the *Adbhūta Ramayana*, Sītā is daughter of Rāvaṇa, or at least of his wife Mandodarī, and in the *Adhyātma*, she is sister to Rāma, the latter also reflected in the *Daśaratha Jātaka* and the *Dīgha Nikāya*. Now, in the *Daśaratha Jātaka*, which is older than the text of the *Ramayana*, there is no abduction of Sītā or war with Rāvaṇa but only the succession intrigue. Daśaratha himself suggests to Rama that he should escape with his loyal brother Lakṣmaṇa, and return and claim his patrimony after his death. When Bharata (there is no Śatrughna in this *Jataka*) asks Rama to return, he is given his grass shoes to take back; Rama returns after another *three* years and is anointed king. In other words, this *Jātaka* only has the first part of the twin story.

The succession intrigue has complex undertones. Rāma's step–mother bears the name *Kaikeyī*, obviously an eponym indicating that she was princess of Kekaya, an Ānava people of the Pothwar plateau. Rāma's mother bears the name *Kauśalyā*, i.e. of Kośala, signifying that Rāma was full blooded Kosalan. The son whom *Kaikeyī* conspires to put on the throne is *Bharata*, named after the famous *Candravaṅśa* king of the Lunar line of the Kekaya; Bharata was attending the Kekaya court when the plot was hatched, a typical matrilineal arrangement. In other words, the plot seems to have been a Kekaya attempt to install their candidate on the Ikṣvāku throne, though either Bharata was not complicit, or he found public opinion too hostile, and chose to rule as regent of Rāma. Not once did he harry Rāma during the exile, rather trying to respectfully recall him, and sending him aid in his campaign against Rāvaṇa (in the later story).

Some important geographical pointers are important here. The Ikṣvāku have regular matrimonial relations with the Kekaya, and Gandhāra, while the early Ikṣvāku chief Mandhatṛ fought the Druhyu Aṅgāra, ancestor of the Gandhāra. All these, and other neighboring people, are invited to an

Ikṣvāku ceremony, but not the Kuru, Pañcāla, or Yadu, who are closer to the Ikṣvāku capital of Ayodhya. It is obvious that the Ikṣvāku resided closer to the Gandhāra and Kekaya than the Kuru and Pañcāla, which is borne out by the Kekaya taking direct interest in them—traditionally the western towns of Lahore and Kasur are associated with Rāma's sons Lava and Kuśa, while Takṣaśilā and Puṣkarāvati with Bharata's sons Takṣa and Puṣkara. Curiously, when rushing back from the Kekaya court at Girivraja, possibly Girjak near Rajouri, Bharata arrived at Ayodhya *from the east*, showing that the Ayodhyā referred to here was *west* of the Kekaya. Can we equate the Sarayu of the *Ramayana* was a western river, like the Horayu or Herat of Afghanistan?

Now, Valmīki the author of the *Ramayana*, claims only to have completed a story left *half complete* by Cyavana, which is also mentioned in Aśvaghosha's *Buddhacarita*. In fact, the story of the termite hill which features Valmīki in the *Ramayana* is related in the context of Cyavana in the *Mahabharata*.[51] So closely are both the sages affiliated with the *Ramayana* that, centuries later, Kṛttivās erroneously called Cyavana Valmīki's father. The resolutions that can be drawn from the above are tantalizing, and have been vehemently denounced by some scholars like Bhargava.[52]

Can we say that the palace intrigue was an ancient episode in the career of the Ikṣvāku and the subject of Cyavana's work, which was built upon (by Valmīki) generations later with the story of an Ikṣvāku–Kosala war with Rāvaṇa *after* the Ikṣvāku had *relocated to the regions they are traditionally associated with*? Indeed, while both stories have been demonstrated to be older than 500 B.C., the epic was given its final form only between 300 B.C. and 200 A.D., leaving enough time to weave together an ancient story of a favourite pair of Ikṣvāku king and queen with that of another pair of popular royals, and giving it a veneer of agrarian mythology. This would explain the archaeological dilemma[53] as also the confusion regarding the dates. That such confusions in references were common in early cultures is seen in the walls constructed by Sikandar Lodi at Mandi being attributed

51 *Mbh*, III: 122–5.

52 P.L. Bhargava, 'A Fresh Appraisal of the Historicity of Indian Epics', 1982, p. 21–23.

53 Nṛsiṃhaprasāda Bhāduḍi, *Vālmīkir Rāma o Rāmāyaṇa* (in Bengali), Ananda, Calcutta, 1998.

to *Sikandar* or Alexander.[54] Also, Rāvaṇa's Laṅkā, traditionally identified with Sri Lanka, probably lay in the Chhotanagpur–Chhattisgarh region[55] which is also called *Mahā–Kośala* or *Dakṣiṇa–Kośala*, i.e. Greater or Southern Kosala implying some form of Kosalan conquest and had a strong and early iron industry.

Thus, the *Ramayana* provides a clearer example of how any epic, in the hands of its users from a string of subsequent, sociologically evolving, ages, itself evolves, gathering new material but at the same time preserving much ancient and archaic material, all providing important insights into its career.

Evolution of Warfare through the 1st Millennium B.C.

Warfare among Vedic tribes had been evolving alongside the socioeconomic changes outlined above. We have seen that war in the *Mahabharata* had really belonged to a much older, pre-chivalric age, squarely in the realm of *Real War* with only an incipient element of chivalry, though it was later made out to be strongly chivalric to the point of impracticality. With colonization of the plains, kings of agrarian–urban civilization sponsored cities to tap into the burgeoning trade opportunities. The śreṣṭhin, originally *powerful man*, later *burgher* like the later word *seṭh*, were the commercial elite of the cities, hobnobbed with royalty, married into their families, and supported them with finances and guild troops, like the *ashraf* burghers of Rohilkhand would do later. At the same time, kings and nobles, largely the feudal chariot–elite of the countryside, were preoccupied with *ahaṅśreṣṭha* or one-upmanship and endlessly competed among themselves to advance in protocol primacy through warfare and sacrifices, setting the stage for the mid-1st millennium warfare.

The chariot elite, ubiquitous in the *Mahabharata*, hardly had a role in the *Ramayana*. Even in the *Mahabharata*, their portrayed role was correctly from the period when chariotry was past its prime and obsolescent.

54 William Moorcroft and Georg Trebeck, *Travels in the Himalayan Provinces of Hindustan and the Punjab; in Ladakh and Kashmir; in Peshawar, Kabul, Kunduz, and Bokhara; from 1819 to 1825*, 2 vols, L.P.P., Delhi, 2010, (First Published 1841), pp. 62–67.

55 In fact, there is a strong Rāvaṇa tradition in the modern Indian state of Madhya Pradesh adjoining Chhattisgarh and Chhotanagpur, where there are several temples dedicated to him. Veneration of Rāvaṇa extends across Central India into Rajasthan.

Though chariotry had remained in use in South Asia till late—the *Old Tamil* poet Maamulnaar mentions Maurya chariots in the Podiyil Hills in Tinnevelly, the *Param Kor.r.anaar* mentions *vamba Moriyar*, i.e. Maurya upstarts, '*cutting down of hill to make road for the chariot*',[56] chariots are mentioned in the early 1st millennium with kings like Rudradaman (151–2 A.D.)[57] and Kharavela—their nature had changed.

In fact, long before Hsuen Tsang, writing centuries later, mentioned chariots as command and control vehicles, chariots had grown elaborate, heavy, and clumsy, with multiple horses and large crews, even multiple drivers (as often mentioned in the *Mahabharata*), and had acquired large establishments of ground crew and support staff. This large establishment, like the *lance fournice* of medieval Europe, would have engendered the idea of the all–arms *paṭṭi*. Obsolescent as they were, they also operated in accordance to chivalric code developed by the class that monopolised them, abhorring *Kūṭa-yuddha* based on manoeuvre, surprise, and expediency, 'propounded' by Bṛhaspati and Śukra, Machiavellian preceptors of the gods and demons, and practiced by Krishna and Aśvatthāman in the *Mahabharata*. It was the formalized battles of this class of chariotry that had been projected backwards in the epics, its code of *darma-yuddha* expounded in the *Śāntiparvan* or the *Śiva–Dhanurveda*. The situation was not dissimilar to that in Greece, where the frontal, direct manner of fighting of later days, anticipating the so-called '*European way of war*', was projected back into the *Iliad*.

Such flowering of chivalry occurred elsewhere too, and it would be a good idea to compare the efflorescence and demise of chariotry across the known world, as we had earlier done its emergence. In China, Shang chariotry, an imitation from the northern nomads, had been used less militarily and more ceremonially.[58] The Western Zhou however had used

56 *Proceedings of the Transactions of the Second Oriental Conference*, pp. 319–322. P.C. Chakravarti (note 3 page 25) says that these may be the Mauryas of Konkan, the More.

57 *Epigraphica India*, VIII, 48.

58 Magdalene von Dewall, *Pferd und Wagen im Friihen China*, Bonn, Rudolf Habelt Verlag, 1964, pp. 91, 203–05. Shaughnessy has shown that the two late inscriptions associating the Shang with war-chariotry actually refer to chariots with their enemies like the Guifang. In a scapular inscription celebrating Shang victory the Shang confiscated a mere two chariots from the enemy. Shaughnessy, 'Historical Perspectives', pp. 217–220.

chariotry more effectively, winning the battle of Muye,[59] and raiding the Guifang nomads on the Ordos,[60] and rendering M. von Dewall or H.G. Creel's[61] writing its off as useless too hasty. Chariotry however underwent a flowering of chivalry in the *Spring and Autumn Period*, growing numerous, with diffused ownership, and its doctrine ritualised into the code of *Li*.[62] Chinese chariotry was finally marginalised by the *Warring States* period. It can be said that the wars of the epic *Zuozhuan* are really those of the *Spring and Autumn Period* projected backwards.[63]

In fact, we see that everywhere had chariotry peaked since its appearance in Armenian petroglyphs,[64] and then had grown formalised. In West Asia, the *Maryanni* had been defeated and dispersed as an international mercenary nobility, and finally blinded and butchered in Assyria. After the late 2nd millennium B.C. incursions of the *Sea Peoples*, Egypt had collapsed, the Hittites dispersed, and the Kassites left as horse-breeders in the Zagros Mountains. Through the 1st millennium, chariotry grew obsolescent everywhere.

The question that arises is, what form of warfare or weapon system was responsible for such obsolescence. To Xenophon, it was the scythed chariot introduced by his patron Cyrus the Mede.[65] However, though scythed chariots had proved effective on several occasions, like Cunaxa (395 B.C.) and Dascylium (where Pharnabazus routed a Greek army double his size with merely two such chariots[66]), they had not proved too effective at Gaugamela. Nefiodkin, to whom scythed chariots were introduced

59 Shaughnessy, 'The Date of the "Duo You Ding" and its Significance', *Early China*, vol. 9–10, 1983–85, pp. 55–69, and Di Cosma, 'Northern Frontiers', p. 920.

60 Barbieri–Low, p. 73. Though Barbieri–Low calls these raids petty, they were really nomad manoeuvres.

61 Herrlee G. Creel, *Origins of Statecraft in China: The Western Chou Empire*, Chicago, University of Chicago Press, 1970, p. 270, has called the Zhou chariots 'worse than useless'.

62 Shaughnessy, 'Historical Perspectives', p. 226.

63 See Hsaio–yun Wu, *Chariots in Early China: Origins, cultural interaction, and identity*, BAR International Series 2457, Oxford, Archaeopress, 2013 for the aspect of projection.

64 Littauer and Crouwel, *Wheeled Vehicles and Ridden Animals*, pp. 13–14.

65 Xenophon, *Cyropaedia*, 6.2.8.

66 Xenophon, *Hell.* IV.1.17–19 and Xenophon, *Anabasis*, 1.8.20.

during Artaxerxes I, i.e. *c.* 467 B.C.,[67] was never very convinced about their efficacy, just like Cawkwell.[68] Also, to Nefiodkin the scythed chariot was introduced as a counter to the Greek phalanx and not to chariotry. Jeffery Rop disagrees with Nefiodkin's view that scythed chariots were a response to phalanx warfare, and argues that they had been in use since the Neo–Assyrian period.[69]

There are only hazy references to the scythed chariot in the Roman wars against the British, and Anderson suggests that despite popularity of the scythe in British and Irish tradition, British chariots did not really use it.[70] Taken together, it appears that the scythed chariots had a lot of popular appeal due to their fiendish ingenuity but were really experimental vehicles with inconsistent results. There is no reference to scythed chariots in Indian sources, but the *rathamūṣala* or club–chariot of Ajātaśatru may have been a variant of this principle.

It is more reasonable to suppose that the chariot was rendered obsolescent by large infantry formations and effective cavalries, the actual effect of these two varying from region to region. While chariots could successfully stampede, and cut down poor infantries, of the Bronze Age, they were less effective against the large, iron armed infantries of the 1st millennium, like the gigantic *caturaṅga*s of South Asia, which were disciplined enough to hold their ground and receive chariot. In other regions, obsolescence of chariotry stemmed from mounted archery, which for a variety of reasons was more effective—there could be far greater numbers of horses, each animal carrying an archer unlike the huge establishment of the chariot thus making many more archers, and each unit, i.e. archer and horse, being far less vulnerable and far more manoeuvrable than the chariot.

67 Alexander K. Nefiodkin, 'On the Origin of the Scythed Chariots', *Historia: Zeitschrift für Alte Geschichte*, vol 53, no 3, 2004, pp. 369–378; for doubtful efficacy see pp. 376–8.

68 G. Cawkwell, *The Greek Wars: The Failure of Persia*, Oxford, 2005, p. 252.

69 Jeffrey Rop, 'Reconsidering the Origin of the Scythed Chariot', *Historia*, Franz Steiner Verlag, vol 62, no 2, April 2013, pp. 167–181. Rop's contention that scythed chariots are difficult to detect in vase paintings is doubtful—they would have been seen in frontal elevations.

70 Anderson, 'Homeric, British, and Cyrenaic Chariots', p. 350.

While the general consensus regarding emergence of mounted archery is that it began in the steppes where the bronze bit was taken from Mesopotamia,[71] Robin Archer contests this view and argues, based on his study of chariots and cavalry in West Asian wall art, that it did so in Assyria when charioteers started unyoking their chariots and riding the horses.[72] Archer has correctly shown an inverse relation between chariotry and mounted archery in West Asian wall-art. During 1200–1000 B.C., from the time of Ninurta–Tukulti–Assur and Ashurnasirpal I, chariots on Assyrian wall art are light vehicles with open bodywork; they grow in weight and size of body and crew through the ninth century (Ashurnasirpal II and Shalmaneser III), and finally, by the middle of the 7th century (Ashurbanipal), become immense, with huge wheels often as high as a man, best suited for observation (and lion–hunting as they made the lion leap upwards exposing its vulnerable lower parts).

Archer has also shown a corresponding increase in efficacy of cavalry, which first appears in the context of the battle of Qarqar fought during Shalmaneser III. Qarqar was still a primarily chariot battle wherein an Israeli corps of 2000 chariots, using larger Nubian horses, were absorbed into the Assyrian army where it was allowed to maintain an identity as a distinct, *elite*, corps. 'Mounted archer cavalry' appear in contemporary bas-reliefs like the Balawat Gates where archers are depicted timorously perched on the 'donkey seat' on the croupé of stationary horses, knees bunched up in fright, while a similarly mounted companion holds the reins. The uncomfortable postures and heavy halters with snaffle bits indicate that chariot horses had been unyoked, and were being used by the charioteer and archer as mounts. In later reliefs, riders are increasingly comfortable, and are confidently mounted by the time of Ashurbanipal.

Yet, Archer's contention that the homeland of mounted archery was Assyria itself, from where the skill percolated to the steppes, is unacceptable. So shaky, even comical, do the initial Assyrian efforts seem that they could never have inspired the idea of the *Centaur*, rider fused with mount, in Greek mythology. Littauer and Crouwel have already suggested that the horse was being ridden in the steppes for a long time already, while Anderson has given evidence of development in riding technology and equipment by this time.[73] It was evidently raids by Scythian, Cimmerian,

71 Drews, *Riders*, p. 99 n. 25.

72 Archer, 'Developments in Near–Eastern Chariotry', pp. 70–71.

73 J.K. Anderson, *Ancient Greek Horsemanship*, Berkeley and Los Angeles, 1961, p. 12.

or Median horse–archers from the steppes that had forced Assyrians charioteers to consider the immense psychological change of unyoking horses and riding them in pursuit, indicating a high willingness to change and innovate. Mounted archers appeared *independently* in China towards the end of the *Spring and Autumn Period*, throwing a serious challenge to chariotry, which was finally finished off by the large infantries organised by the *Shi* elite in the *Warring States* period.[74]

Probably the tactics used by these infantries, which were appearing everywhere at that time, had been innovated by mercenary runners with West Asian chariots who first rendered chariots obsolete in Greece.[75] Even in South Asia, iron-armed infantries of the Gangetic plains would have used similar tactics—mere absence of archaeological specimens of iron weapons does not rule out use of iron in the early 1st millennium armies, as the metal was probably recycled.[76] It was only in Western Europe, out of the orbit of mounted archery, that chariots persisted. Gallic chariots, whose warriors launched spears and then fought on foot, broke Roman cavalry as late as at Sentinum at 295 B.C.,[77] though chariots seem not to have played a major role at Telamon in 225 B.C.[78] In South Asia, sedentization, improvement in breeding and riding technology, and obsolescence of the chariot brought about a fascination with stallion and cavalry,[79] which reinforced the ritual importance of the horse.[80]

---

74 Kwang–Chih Chang, *Shang Civilization*, Yale, New Haven, 1980, p.6. Shang kings sent out armies of as many as 13,000 men, and are associated with the taking of vaster numbers of prisoners, often 30,000.

75 Drews, *End of the Bronze Age*.

76 Dhavlikar and Possehl take a different view, and deny to of the Gangetic plains. See M. K. Dhavalikar and G. L. Possehl, 'Subsistence Pattern of an Early Farming Community in Western India', *Puratattva*, vol 7, pp. 39–46.

77 Livy, 10.28–30.

78 Polybius, *The Histories of Polybius*, trans. E.S. Shuckburgh and Otto Hultsch, first published, 1889, reprint 1962, 2.28–29.

79 The archaic term *aśva* gradually fell out and the horse was now better known as *ghoṭaka* or *ghoḍā*, a term which first appears in the *Āp.ŚS.* Interestingly, another archaic word for the horse, *sāta*, which formed part of the *Sātvat*s, reappears as *Sātavahana*, *Sātakarṇi*. At the same time the horse never quite came into its own in South Asia, where pathogen loads increased by the high humidity made animals vulnerable to humidity related disease, need more effective nutrition, and get dwarfed.

80 *ṚV*, I: 83.1; IV: 32.17; V: 4.11.

Social and Religious Evolution

Transforming socio-political and economic structures of the IA tribes in the aftermath of the *Mahabharata* war had brought about a deracinated, urban civilization, marked militarily by populous infantries, obsolescent chariot, and chivalric mores, all of which had found their way back into the narrative of the epic and its battle-pieces, giving it an anachronistic veneer. Part of this veneer was an intensely religio–didactic colour, the nature and origin of which shall be seen in the remainder of this chapter to finish *framing* the epic.

The last episode of the epic is crucial—even though Krishna had already promulgated the *Vaikuṇṭha* of Vishnu as the ideal heaven, the Pandu still go to the archaic *svarga* of Indra, guided thither by the hound *Sārameya*, hounds being guides to the underworld in PIE mythology. Thus, the foundation of the epic which would have included the final outcome of the heroes was certainly older than the Vishnuism that permeated it later. In fact, religious evolution from late 2nd millennium till the establishment of the *laukika* or popular religions of mid-1st millennium are easily traceable through the epic.

We have seen earlier how the simple sacrificial religion had been complicating into the great *śrauta* sacrifices, which Witzel argued were developed deliberately to channelize and defang the violent *Kṣatriya*s preoccupied with *ahaṅśreṣṭha* or protocol ascendency. This situation was similar to *Spring and Autumn Period* China where the dukes were encouraged to adjust their protocols through noisy and expensive rites and sacrifices, known to us through the complex bronzes of little utilitarian but great status value, rather than warfare. The evolution is noticeable in the epics, in whose older redactions many a character is seen performing simpler versions of the sacrifices, but whose later redactions contain the great śrauta rituals. Women, too, are seen independently performing sacrifices, something that was to become taboo in later times—Kauśalya offers oblations into the fire, and in one place, Hanumant expects Sītā to be engaged in the evening rite of *Sandhyāhnik*, both male preserves. In other words, the core of the epic is older than not only the *laukika* cults but also the śrauta religion. This will help understand the Janamejaya dichotomy.

The Role of the Bhṛgu

Janamejaya, who is ambiguously associated with the *sarpasattra*, is also seen performing two *aśvamedhas*,[81] conducted by rival priests Indrota Daivāpa Śaunaka and Tura Kāvaśeya. In the *Purāṇas*, the priests led by Indrota Daivāpa Śaunaka, with whom the Bhūtavīra and Kāśyapa are also associated, quarrelled with the king over *sharing or grabbing the proceeds* of the sacrifice, forcing him to retire to the forests. Raychaudhuri interprets this as Janamejaya's position weakening as a result of quarrel with Indrota Daivāpi Śaunaka during the first sacrifice,[82] which led to him being given a second consecration or *punarābhiṣeka*, followed by an *Aindra Mahābhiṣeka*, by Tura Kāvaṣeya. To him, the second anointment, and its mandatory *aśvamedha*, occurred at Takṣaśilā, and was confused with the *sarpasattra* due to similarity of names. This idea is confirmed by the silence of the *Bharata*, which was commissioned and first recited at Takṣaśilā, on any *sarpasattra*.[83]

It is uncertain if '*grabbing the proceeds*' by priests resembled the Middle Age *Sanyāsi Akhāḍās* fighting over precedence, religious policing, and alms gathering rights at pilgrimage and fairs like Haridwar, Kurukshetra, or Kumbha, but it is known that the priests did encourage chiefs and performers of sacrifices to give more and more by the *dānastuti* hymns. The strengthening position of the priests, who had suppressed the unstable *shamans* and consolidated themselves into four, and then sixteen groups of priest–officiants of the sacrifice, is evident. They even outgrew the king, who had to descend from his throne and make obeisance to the *Brahmaṇas* after the *Aindra-mahābhiṣeka*;[84] the ascendance of the priest over the king is reflected in the decaying position of Veṇa (discussed above), who was killed by the priests who also consecrated his son Pṛthīn Vainya.

In fact, the *Brāhmaṇas* are seen to be strong enough to migrate independently, attracted by employment opportunities at courts which

81 *Ait.Br.*, viii.21.3; ŚB, xiii, 5.4.2; *SŚS*, 16.9.1; *Mātsya Purāṇa*, 50, 63–4 calls him *dvir aśvanmedham āhṛtya.* Also see Raychaudhuri, *Political History*, pp. 14–15.

82 Raychaudhuri, *Political History*, p. 32.

83 The *sarpasattra* is mentioned in the parts of the epic which have been identified as later redactions by Yardi, where it is said that the *Bharata* was recited there by Vaiśampāyana; those parts of the epic distilled as the Bharata are silent on the *sarpasattra*.

84 *Ait.Br*, viii. 9.

invited 'foreign' *Brāhmaṇa*s to counterbalance local ones.[85] The *Jātaka*s mention *Brāhmaṇa* youth training in archery,[86] showing that their migrations could also be violent, as also supposed by Renou.[87] One of the more military *Brāhmaṇa* groups was the Bhṛgu, probably an umbrella term of several lineages, and among whose numbers were many renowned sages like Aurva, Dadhīca, Rucika, Cyavana, Mārkaṇḍeya, Vipula, or Uttaṅka, in addition to those already mentioned.

While we have already encountered the Iranic affiliations of the Bhṛgu Vaśiṣṭha, we also know that the Bhṛgu are associated with the mythical *Daitya*, *Dānava*, and *Asura*, concepts with Iranic affiliations. Their name, which may be cognitive with *Phrygian*, itself comes from the root **bharj* which gives *phloks*, *flash*, and *effulgence*—the Bhṛgu have been explicitly associated with the fire-drill (*which after invention, or Prometheus-like theft, was given to them*). Indeed, the Bhṛgu, whose legendary hero was the Paraśu–Rāma of the anti-Kṣatriya wars, had started as a tribe associated with chariot–building and charioteering.[88] The above immediately associates the Bhṛgu with the Iranic/Parthian, charioteering, and sacrifice-sponsoring Bharata, who we have seen earlier as belonging to the tradition that had upset the ordered IIr world, defeated the older tribes like the Pañcajana, and assimilated the quiet, archaic cult of the celestial twins of the Yadu–Turvaśa into the cult of the warlike Indra. No wonder that the Bhṛgu, who were behind the compilation of the independent clan *ṛk*s into the *Ṛgveda saṁhitā* and also of the *Mahabharata*, made sure that the epic was proliferated with material pertaining to them.

85 M. Witzel, 'Toward a History of the Brahmins', *Journal of the American Oriental Society*, vol. 113, no. 2, 1993, pp. 264–268. Also see M. Witzel, 'Review: Swati Datta (nee Sen Gupta), Migrant Brahmanas in Northern India, their Settlement and General Impact c. A.D. 475–1030',*Journal of the Economy of the Near East*, vol. 35, pp. 364–366.

86 Śarabhaṅga Jātaka, Cowell (ed.), *The Jataka*, no. 522.

87 Renou, L., *Religions of Ancient India*, pp. 20. '*The background of the hymns is a troubled one, a scene of passionate rivalries and internal struggles, where great dangers have been faced and surmounted; the abandonment of the* surā, *the establishment of universal allegiance to Indra by gods and men alike, the eclipse of Varuṇa, the acceptance of the Aśvins, the advent of Rudra: none of these events could have been accomplished without great upheavals*'.

88 *ṚV*, IV: 16.20; X: 39.14. The carpenters or *sutāra*, which emerged from the chariot-building *Sūta*, call themselves *Bhārgava Brāhmaṇa* today.

Diffusion of the Vedic Religion and Emergence of Laukika Religions

The growing complexity of the sacrificial religion in South Asia is also mirrored by appearance of evidence of complex, sacrificial cults from across Central Asia, like in the Ural burials, which were undoubtedly independent developments. It is incorrect of Anthony and Vinogradov's equation of Ural burials with Vedic sacrifices like *aśvamedha* and *vājapeya*, as neither human sacrifice nor interment of the horse, integral part of the burials, are associated with the latter. In *ṚV*, VI: 163 which describes the Vedic *aśvamedha*, the horse is only briefly yoked to the chariot before being immolated,[89] ritually carved and eaten, and *not buried*. Even Anthony and Vinogradov's racing–chariot theory is not convincing—the Vedas make no distinction between race and raid,[90] and words like *arvan, vāji, turanga*, or *aśvo* were synonymous and there is no compelling reason to take them as racehorses.

Kelekna quite correctly associates Ural burials with Western Steppes tradition than with the IA customs.[91] The latter, which developed into the great śrauta rituals, had grown out of archaic procedures to claim pastures (*aśvamedha*) or distribute a slain warrior's legacy (the chariot race part of the *vājapeya*), along with accumulating several elements of Neolithic fertility cults. We also see that as the sacrificial religion grew complex, it also grew diffused, at first due to extreme elitism and expense, then by the emerging religious consciousness of the *Axial Age* which was satisfied neither with the *quid pro quo* gods of yore nor the mechanical universe of the *yajña*, and finally by the popular or *laukika* cults that gave vent to the religious aspirations of the laity through simple means of devotion.

The first step in the diffusion included emergence of regional śākhās of the sacrificial lore based on regional dialects, and the cosmopolitization of the religion[92] as seen in names like Bṛbu, Balbūtha, Varo Suśāman among IA chiefs, Kavaśa Ailūṣa and Tura Kāvaśeya among Vedic priests—Tura

89 *BŚS*, 15,24; Āp. ŚS, 20.16,1ff.

90 M. Sparreboom, *Chariots in the Vedas*, Memoirs of the Kern Institute, Leiden, 3, E.J. Brill, 1985, p.14.

91 Pita Kelekna, 'Impact of the Horse', p. 10.

92 Witzel, 'Early Sanskritisation', pp. 9–10.

Kāvaṣeya developed the *agnicayana* ritual[93]—, and men with Dāsa names offering sacrifices.[94] The acculturation is reflected in

> *indraṅ vardhanto apturaḥ kṛṇvanto viśvam āryam|*
>
> *apaghnanto arāvnaḥ||*[95]

The next step was the replacement of Indra with other gods. Though still characterised positively, Indra's position decayed to secondary roles while the esoteric idea of *Brahman* grew ascendant. However, even though personified as *Brahmā* the creator, the original Indian phallic god who also had a major role in the *Ramayana*,[96] the religion of *Brahman* proved too remote and rarefied and ultimately faded away. In contrast, the *Pāśupata* and *Bhāgavata* religions based on worship of Śiva–Paśupati and Viṣṇu grew far more popular. The former, which had started from the *shamanic*–ascetic cult of Rudra, absorbed Neolithic agrarian mythology of the Great Mother and her ithyphallic son–husband–father consort (Ishtar–Damuzzi, Isis–Osiris, or Venus–Adonis), and the cult of the bull.[97]

Independently but alongside the Śaiva religion grew the Śākta religion of the *Devī* or Mother Goddess, attaining fruition in Tantric cults one of whose integral components is the entwined pair of *nāḍī*–serpents, Īḍā–Piṅgaḷā, which is nothing but the *cadecaus* or *axis mundi*. The Goddess, associated with regeneration, mountains, underground caves, and lions, reminiscent of the Mediterranean mother goddesses Isis, Ishtar, Hera, or Cybele, is strongly associated with *Asura* themes—she kills *Asura*s, while

93 See Th. Proferes, 'The Formation of Vedic Liturgies', Harvard Ph.D. thesis 1999.

94 *ṚV*, VI: 63.9.

95 *ṚV*, IX: 63.5.

96 Pargiter, 1997; Brahmā provided the *pāyas* or rice cooked in cream which led to the birth of Rama and his brothers, his mind-born son Pulastya was Rāvaṇa's father, he created Rāvaṇa's flying Puṣpaka chariot and had made Rāvaṇa and Indrajit powerful, Rāvaṇa had ten heads like him, and it was his Brahmāstra alone that could kill Rāvaṇa. Crucially, the Bhṛgu, as both Cyavana and Valmiki were, have been called Brahma Rakṣas.

97 These old consciousness is encountered as Tārā at the shrine of Tārāpīṭha being depicted as the mother of Śiva who is depicted suckling in the little viewed original image. The popular cult goddess Manasā is daughter of Śiva, but blinded by his consort who thinks she is a rival, thus casting her both as daughter and consort. This story is reminiscent of the blinding of Hera by Juno out of jealousy for her husband Zeus.

Tantric fire–pits reflect the sacred geometry of BMAC city plans which also permeated post–Vedic fire altars.

The *Asura* tradition is crucial here. Not all *Asura*s are malevolent, and some like Bāṇa and Bali are especially revered. Many royal clans—legendary Bārhadratha, historical Kharavela, or pre-modern Rampur Bushehr, among others—claim descent from them, and the festival of *Oṇam* in Kerala is dedicated to Bali. *Asura*s are also associated with the Śiva lore, viz., Bāṇeśvara Śhiva, and legends of iron smelting in eastern India.[98] It may be surmised that as a result of contact with the Vedic folk, *Asura* worshippers dispersed from Balkh to the west and south. Those who went west developed the *Ahura* tradition of Iran in the heritage of Zarathustra, preoccupied with good, evil, categorization of sin, and lot of sinners, and tending towards monotheism. In contrast, those who moved into South Asia established as venerated communities and associated with Neolithic cults, but later were subverted and vilified in the religion of the Goddess. That these transitions were not shorn of violence is seen in the luridly gory tales which are part of the *Asura* tradition.

At the same time, it must not be imagined that there were neat dichotomies or divergences—many non-*Ahura* traditions persisted among the comity of *Ahura* worshipping nations, like the joyous *Miθraism* till ruthlessly stamped out by Xerxes. Also, the construct of IA groups encountering an *Asura* tradition in eastern South Asia is not fanciful—we remember that Mughals encountered Afghans once in the Hindukush, and then again in the swamps of lower Bengal and coastal Gujarat.

Now, though the *Pāśupata* religion was far more accessible than the rarefied cults of Brahmā or *Ahura*, a strong ascetic tradition permeated it, mirrored in the dual traditions of Brahmanhood—one of asceticism and another of the house-householder—observed by the Greeks.[99] On the other hand, though the *Gaurī* and *Lakṣmī* traditions of the Śākta religion grew popular, overall Śākta was considered remote, risky, and even malevolent—*Kālī*, the third form of the Mother Goddess, was given a wide berth till as late as the 18th century when the Bengali poet–seer Ramprasad Sen

98 Edward Tuite Dalton, *Descriptive Ethnology of Bengal*, 1872, pp. 96–97, cited in Tarundeb Bhattacharya, *Purulia* (in Bengali), Pharma KLM Pvt Ltd, Kolkata, 2009.

99 Arora, 'Onesikritios', 79; Megasthenes F. 33 (Strabo, XV, 1, 59).

stressed upon her peaceability, benevolence, and compassion and ensured her entry into common households.[100]

Another feature of the evolving religious consciousness was fascination with *tīrtha*s, at one time crossing places on rivers and in later times, bathing places on water bodies. Visits to these, some new but most of great antiquity even for that early period, were expected to bring merit equal to and often more than the expensive sacrifices.[101] It was against the backdrop of efflorescence of popular religious consciousness in the 1st millennium B.C. that the *Bhāgavata* or *Vaiṣṇava* religion, associated with the cults of the sun and the divine king, and thus primarily a *Kṣatriya* religion, evolved into the most accessible Krishnaism. Though Śaivism marked the initial stages of the *Mahabharata* as per Yardi, and Parpola, who equated the Pandu with the Deccan Megalithic folk, called them Śiva worshippers, it was Viṣṇu–Kṛṣṇaism that had the most significant impact upon the epic, which became the perceived agent of this religion.

The Religion of Viṣṇu–Kṛṣṇa

As the Vedas ascended beyond the reach of the laity which could neither understand their language nor afford their expensive sacrifices, the *Mahabharata* became the main vehicle of popular morality and instruction, so much so that it was proclaimed the *fifth Veda*. In tenor, it was essentially critical of the asceticism—not only Śaiva but also Buddhist and Jain—then permeating society, labeling it escapist and anti-social. Arjuna berates Yudhiṣṭhira for displaying ascetic intents on learning of his relation to Karṇa,[102] and the epic states elsewhere that only the wealthy householder was the real man (*pumān*) and learned (*paṇḍita*), and had friends and relatives,[103] a sentiment echoing the Greek social system wherein only the wealthy was considered the suitable citizen. The anti-asceticism, which reflects (or predicts) the statement of the *Milidapañha* that many hangers-

100 Before that, Kāli remained the preserves of ascetics, Tantrics, and brigands, and considered to reside in forests and cremation places.

101 J.A.B. van Buitenen, *Mahābhārata*: vol 2 and 3, p. 186–87.

102 *Mbh*, XII: 8.9–12.

103 *Mbh*, XII: 8.9–12.

on in Buddhist ascetic orders were only trying to escape the law and get a free livelihood,[104] is most persuasively propounded in the *Gītā*.

This is not to say that the *Mahabharata* or the *Gītā* propagate the doctrine of conspicuous consumption, greed, and avarice—the epic extols the Kuru as being prosperous without being avaricious, and the *Gītā* teaches that even a householder can be an ascetic, simply by remaining un-obsessed with his gains and surroundings while continuing his service to society by creating wealth. The *Gītā* uses Krishna's harangue to Arjuna to teach its anti-ascetic *sāṅkhya*-based doctrine, which also appears in the *mokṣadharma* section of the epic and in the Ayoda–Dhaumya episode in which the *ṛṣi* puts his three pupils through ordeals.

In fact, the *Gītā*, inimical to asceticism and mortifying *yoga* that did not contribute to society, was a proponent of social stability. It preached the upholding of the emergent *varṇāśrama* by integrating *yoga* alongside *sāṅkhya* into the *karmayoga*, the *asceticism of action*, which it says has a long tradition among kings.[105] At the same time, it elevates *dharma*, an ambiguous term with meanings ranging from *piety* through *righteousness* to *established order* (a thief's *dharma* it is to steal),[106] above *karmayoga*, equating it to *jñānayajña* or the ultimate knowledge of god (which it calls *rājavidyā*). Unfortunately, the peculiar attitudes of South Asia never let *jñānayoga* convert into a rational search to make sense of the world, and instead caused it to tend towards various brands of esoterism.

The Identity of Kṛṣṇa–Viṣṇu–Nārāyaṇa

Possibly the *Gītā*, which expounded an anti-ascetic, *sāṅkhya*-based philosophy, had at one point of time existed as an independent text, perhaps an *upaniṣad* propounded by a historical Krishna. This Krishna may well have been *Devakīputra* Krishna of the *Chandogya Upaniṣad*, who to Raychaudhri was the Krishna of the *Mahabharata*.[107] If so, the *Gītā* can

104 *Milindapañha*, II. 1.5, English trans., T.A. Rhys Davids, *The Questions of King Milinda*, Sacred Books of the East, pp. 49–50.

105 *Bhagavad Gītā*, IV.1-3.

106 Vivekananda Jha, 'Dharma and the Nature of Caste in the *Bhagavadgītā*', *Indian Historical review*, vol 29, nos. 1– 2, January and July 2002, New Delhi, 2004, pp. 1–28.

107 Raychaudhuri, *Political History*, pp. 119–20, note 3.

be said to have been added at a poignant moment in the epic,[108] whereafter it underwent its own redactions.[109] The epic portrays its author or teacher, Krishna, as the comprehensible, approachable, and even lovable face of Vishnu of the *Bhāgavata* religion, a religion which refutes costly and bloody sacrifices beyond the means of the householder and offers them easier access to Vishnu's *Vaikuṇṭha* heaven (*vi–kuṇṭhā*, without sorrow), as against Indra's archaic *svarga,* through the simple means of adoration of Vishnu–Nārāyaṇa[110] with mere offerings of flowers and leaves—*vilva–puṣpa–patra*—, or even water.

This brings us back to Krishna's complex identity. We have seen enough reason to identify the fugitive Krishna of Mathura with Krishna the chieftain of Dvārakā. The character of the fugitive cowherd *Gopāla*–Krishna was possibly based on a pastoral deity of Vṛndāvana—Krishna holds aloft the mountain *Govardhana* (cow-enhancer) on his little finger to shelter herdsmen against a deluge sent down by the by-now '*agrarian*' *rain-god* Indra. His worship as god, hills, cattle, and other motifs fashioned from cow-pat balls mixed with hay survives in the *Govardhan Pūja* performed on the morning after Dīpāvalī by many pastoralist groups like Jats, Ahirs, and Gujars. Even earlier episodes in his life, i.e. his antics as the child or *bāla* Krishna, are in continuation of other child-god cults of South Asia—Gaṇeśa child of Śiva–Pārvatī, or Kārttikeya child of the six *Kṛttikā*s or Pleiades who was later recast as another child of Śiva–Pārvatī. The child god, whose worship today centres on the loving adoration and care of its image on a cradle, also inspired the *Ramayana* where the pranks and antics of little Rāma in the *Bāla-Kāṇḍa* were modelled on those of *Bāla-Gopāla.*

The most vibrant and colourful aspect of the divinity of *Krishna of Mathura* is his relation with the *gopī*s or cowgirls. The love–lore, which ranges from playful, through mildly erotic, to disconcertingly lurid (as in the *Brahmavaivarta Purāṇa*), especially with Rādhā, a figure that

108 M. Winternitz, *History of Indian Literature*, vol. 1, p 457. While Hopkins regarded only the *Bhagavad Gītā* as a late addition, Winternitz goes so far as to believe that even Krishna did not appear in the original epic.

109 As per Yardi, these were added by Sautī. See Yardi, *Mahabharata*, p. 34.

110 *Mbh*, VI: 21.13.14—*yato dharmastato jayaḥ* to *yataḥ kṛṣṇastato jayaḥ*.

emerged not before the ninth century[111] and who in some systems is related to Krishna (though not by blood), is in reality part of the long regional tradition of worship *via* adoration of the opposite sex. This tradition, which is a continuation of mythic themes like those of Hara–Pārvatī and *Ardhanārīśvara,* co-option of the feminine principle or Śakti with Vedic gods—Śacī with Indra, Rudrāṇī with Rudra, and so on—, and associating female Vedic deities with male gods like Śri/Uṣas with Viṣṇu as Lakṣmī, survives in the human level in some *Sahajiya* and *Tantric* Buddhist schools, medieval *Vaishnava* cults, and *Tantric* branches of Śāktism and Śaivism, wherein adoration of couples, to varying degrees of explicitness, is integral. Perhaps the oldest form of this tradition survives in the secretive *Baul* cult of eastern India where attainment (not worship—divinity plays almost no role in this system) is sought through association with a partner of the opposite gender.

Rādhā's adoration of Krishna is really *bhakti* or devotion of worshipper for a personal god, at times so ambivalently represented that it appears erotic. Such representation of devotion as personal, often carnal, love is an old Asian system, encountered also in Sūfī methods, which had at one time led to the works of Omar Khayyam being discarded as erotica. The Rādhā–Krishna cult made Vishnuism most accessible, socially comfortable, and joyous, emphasizing on 'Platonic' relation with an otherwise unattainable woman.[112] The most uplifting manifestation of this system of worship is the Rāma–Sītā pair, which in the hands of a conservative population remained free of uncomfortable innuendos[113]—*Rama-ite bhakti is pure, it is that of a wife, whereas Krishnaite bhakti is more playful, it is the bhakti of lovers.*

A fourth aspect of the worship of Krishna, after pastor-god, child-god, and lover-god, is his ambivalent relation with the agrarian cults of Nāga and Madhu. The 'demon' king Madhu and his henchman Kaiṭabha are killed by Vishnu, Krishna's divine alter ego, giving him the epithet *Madhusūdana.* And yet, Krishna is *Mādhava,* i.e. descended from Madhu,

111 Rādhā is nowhere mentioned in either the *Harivaṅśa* or the *Bhāgavata Purāṇa.* See Yardi, *The Mahabharata,* p. 100.

112 Though certain schools have earned the notoriety of taking permissive directions that others were uncomfortable with.

113 See Raychaudhuri, *History of the Vaishnava Sect,* for discussion on the historicity and early life of Krishna.

the snake god wielding the plough and fond of his favourite tipple, i.e. *madhu* or mead. While this god is closely resembled by Krishna's brother Baladeva (Rāma), Krishna himself subjugates the Nāga Kāliya who becomes worshipful thereafter. That the cowherd god should get associated with agrarian cults, in this case both through himself and his more Bacchic brother, is natural in a pastoral society coming to terms with agriculture. But there is more to it which we shall see.

Karve sees political colour in the idea of Krishna's deification. To her, Krishna was a remarkable man who wanted to become *Vasudeva*, a ruler with character approaching divinity, which she believes was a sort of institution among the Vṛṣṇi. In trying to do so, as per Karve, he won the enmity of Kaṅsa and Baladeva, who in the Jain system are called *prati-vasudeva*, i.e. *anti–Vasudeva*, a similar position *vis-à-vis* Rama–Lakṣmaṇa being given to Rāvaṇa also.[114] Yardi, also taking this position, quotes from the *Vaiśampāyana* text which appears to say that of all *Vasudeva*s, Krishna best demonstrated the traits of divinity[115]: *Sarveṣāṁ vāsudevānām kṛṣṇe lakṣmiḥ pratiṣṭhita.*[116]

The difficulty in these references[117] is that the word used is not *vasudeva*, but *vāsudeva*, i.e. (*son*) *of Vasudeva*. In fact, if anyone was Vasudeva, it was Krishna's father who survived till the end of the *Mauṣalaparvan*. Also, we hear nothing of any other Vasudeva in other generations. In this light, we should interpret the above line as not 'of all *Vasudeva*s Krishna was the best', but as '*of all the children of Vasudeva* (i.e. Vāsudevas)*, Krishna showed the most divine traits*'. Possibly, he was a historical, political figure who taught *sāṅkhya* philosophy, perhaps propagating it as an *Upaniṣad* before it was co-opted in the *Mahabarata*, a work based on events which he may have helped precipitate.

As the success of his protégés made the *Mahabharata* and the *Gītā* popular, a religion averse to sacrificial elitism was also encouraged. In the *Govardhana* episode in Krishna's life, Krishna protects pastoral folk from the *sacrificial demands* of the rain-making Indra, while in the *Gītā* he calls

114 Karve, *Yugānta*, pp. 167–69.

115 Yardi, *The Mahabharata*, pp. 81–82.

116 *Mbh*, CE, VIII: 27.62.

117 A logical and not etymological argument, apparent to the author who is not a Sanskrit scholar.

upon one and all to submit to Viṣṇu–Nārāyaṇa–Krishna—*sarva-dharma parityajya māmekaṁ śaraṇaṁ vraja*—and worship him through simple *puja.* In other words, this religion anticipated eschatological schools like Buddhism or Jainism, similar to the *sāṅkhya* system in their own ways, which also challenged Vedic orthopraxy. At the same time, the joyous *bhakti* of Krishna stood apart from the fatalistic *bhakti* of the Buddha and Jaina, as seen in contemptuous references to *eḍūka*s in the *Mahabharata.*[118]

The *Gīta* also propounds the doctrine of death and rebirth, a concern of all in a world when life was still unsure, especially those of the battle-obsessed *Kṣatriya.* Also, in a world where *Death* was not *scientific absence of life* but a *negative force*, contact with which was inauspicious, disturbing, and polluting,[119] man wanted to die and go to heaven with unblemished body, and *remain* 'dead' as long as possible before descending again to earth.[120] The idea of the *second death of the soul*, or *punarmṛtyu* in the Indian system, permeates Central Asia. Most Tibeto–Mongol head lamas of monasteries are reincarnations of ancient gods whose shrines these monasteries once were, and who have since been continually reincarnated. In fact, the *Bardo Thodol* or *Book of the Dead* of the Red Hat sects describe how the soul should train in life, through masked dances *et al*, to elongate the surrealist experience of *staying dead* by not getting scared of the furies met then, and dreaming the right dreams, till it eventually fell prey to sexual dreams and got caught in a human womb. It was this idea of a second death was developed in Brahminical thought as the doctrine of *karma.*[121]

The inevitability of death and rebirth was present in the *Upaniṣad*, while several *Brāhmaṇa*s and *Āraṇyaka*s show an intense aspiration to escape the cycle of *punarmṛtyu* and attain *mokṣa.* The *Mahabharata*, and the *Gītā*, make the idea of death less worrisome to the *Kṣatriya* or *Yajurvedin*, their main sponsors, by highlighting its inevitability, extolling honourable death, and assuring continuity of the soul till *mokṣa.* The inevitability of death appears not only in the *Gītā* but in the epic—Vyāsa consoles Yudhiṣṭhira by narrating the story of Nārada consoling a grieving

118 *Mbh*, III: 190.65, 67

119 Warriors performed expiation ceremonies even after killing their enemies in battle.

120 *YV: Maitrāyani Saṅhitā*, 1.8.6.

121 S.W. Jamison and M. Witzel, 'Vedic Hinduism', 1992, p. 74, www.people.fas.harvard.edu/~witzel/vedica.pdf, seen 17 April, 15.

Akampana, whose son had just been killed in battle, by telling him another story of how Brahmā creates the female deity of Death to help Yama, Lord of Death—frame-in-tale at its best. The difference between these systems and that of the Tibetans is that it was not conduct *after* death, a surreal idea, but that *during* life, something real and comprehensible enough, that determined the next birth.

To Suvira Jaiswal, the *Gītā* is a mass of ideas that the Krishna saga conglomerated into a harmonious whole.[122] All in all, the Krishnaism it preached took religion to the masses, encouraging it to renounce expensive sacrifices and meaningless asceticism alike, offering it a comforting idea of death, easier access to heaven, and possibility of attaining *mokṣa* (the highest of the four *puruṣārtha*s), all through the self-forgetting *bhakti* akin of the lovelorn *gopī*. Alongside this went the gradual deification of Krishna, who was equated with Vishnu by the early Middle Ages.[123] He soon grew to be the supreme god, his epiphany being the *Viśvarūpa* which was revealed not once in the epic—to Arjuna on the battlefield—but twice more, once at the Kuru court and again when Uddālaka attacked him for not having prevented the war. Krishna also assimilated the worship of Nārāyaṇa, which had developed from the non-Vedic *Pañcarātra* cult of the Sātvatas[124] propounded in the *Nārāyaṇīya* section of the *Harivaṅśa*. The cult, once associated with Brahmā,[125] later apotheosized the Vṛṣṇi heroes whom it identified with Vishnu;[126] in the *Harivaṅśa*, Nārāyaṇa himself is its first performer, Nārada its enunciator, and the Kāṇva *ṛṣi*s its priests.

Krishnaism also systematised itself by assimilating other cults and deities as the *Daśāvatāra* or ten–avataras. Rama was deified, most

122 Suvira Jaiswal, *The Origin and Development of Vaiṣṇavism*, p. 65, who has quoted Kosambi in support of this view.

123 In the beginning, Vaishnavism was a religion of Vishnu, sun, and ruler, with none of the features of modern Vaishnavism like obsessive vegetarianism.

124 See Susmita Pande, 'The Pañcarātra Cult in the Śāntiparvan of the *Mahābhārata*', in Shastri (ed.), *Mahābhārata*, pp. 228–242, for an overview of the cult and the evolution of its pantheon. The Sātvats were *Ekāntins* who worshipped only Vasudeva, whereas others were the Śikhins who worshipped other forms—the Mūlas worshipped Nārāyaṇa, Nṛsiṃha, Varāha and Kapila, while the Vaikhānasa worshipped Vishnu, Puruṣa, Satya, Acyuta, and Aniruddha, and so on.

125 Tarapada Bhattacharya, *The Cult of Brahmā,* Varanasi, 1969, p. 65.

126 *Bhagavad Gītā*, VII.24.

evidently in the *Bāla* and *Uttara Kāṇḍas*,[127] while in the *Adhyātma Ramayana* Kauśalyā recite the same *Vishnu Vandanā*, i.e. adoration of Vishnu, which was recited by Devakī at the moment of Krishna's birth. Tulasidas made little Rāma commit all the mischiefs of the little Krishna in the *Bhāgavata Purāṇa*.

The Archaic Associations of Kṛṣṇa

While the deification of Krishna is evident, his archaic associations are not so at once, like his associations with the *glance of the waking god* in Teutonic mythology, encountered in an earlier chapter. Hiltebeitel has drawn our attention to the curious story of the mythical battle of Brávellir, wherein Odinn disguised himself as Bruno (brown/swarthy), herald and charioteer of the blind king Haraldus Hyldetan who led an army against his nephews, and killed him (Haraldus) after *revealing* himself at an opportune moment. The parallels are obvious, though inverted. In the *Mahabharata*, the uncle, who does not lead the army himself, is blind; Krishna (sable/swarthy) is charioteer, though he drives the chariot of the nephew. He *reveals his real form* in an epiphany during the battle and helps defeat the uncle. Interestingly, in this Norse battle, another uncle was porcupined with arrows like Bhīṣma was.[128]

It is argued here that such parallels do not necessarily mean that human actors were artificial constructs and mere shadows of divine characters, but that as some men were deified, their lives, and those of others around them, were rearranged in tales and legends according to extant mythic themes and theological dramas, creating the parallels. Hiltebeitel has presented several examples of such parallels.[129] It may thus be hypothesised that, as Krishna, a historical, and historically effective, hero, increasingly became the visible face of the hazy *Bhāgavata* tradition of the post-Vedic age, or that of Nārāyaṇa who is personification of *śāśvata* or *goptā*, i.e. esoteric wisdom, he was increasingly associated with many mythic themes that were current then.

127 These *kāṇḍas* have been dropped from eth C.E., which to Nṛsiṁhaprasāda Bhāduḍi are not justified. See, Bhāduḍi, *Ramayana*, p. 83. It is better to say that not the entire *kāṇḍas* had been *added*, but large parts of other *Kāṇḍas* were, which is also the view of the *Ramayana* scholar N.J. Shende. 'The Authorship of the Ramayana', *Journal of the American Oriental Society*, vol. 45, 1925, pp. 202–219.

128 Hiltebeitel, *Ritual of Battle*, p. 58.

129 Hiltebeitel, *Ritual of Battle*, pp. 37–38, 56–57, 82–85.

Closely associated with this stage of Krishna's deific career is his relation with Madhu, the Bacchus-like god of agrarian folk who had been demonised, 'killed', and then co-opted as Saṅkarṣaṇa in the *Nārāyaṇa–Saṅkarṣaṇa* cult. Now, as per the Greeks,[130] it was Dionysus that had taught the Indians how to yoke oxen to the plough, grow vines, and use long hair and turbans. Dionysus, who was worshipped with Bacchic rites, closely matches the character of Krishna's brother Baladeva (Rāma), who is fair, is immensely strong, bears the plough (even in council) which he uses as weapon, flies the Palmyra standard, and is a great wine bibber. In effect, as *Hala–Saṅkarṣaṇa* or Plougher, he is kin to Dionysus–Bacchus–Tammuz–Śiva. In contrast, Nārāyaṇa has more Poseidonic features—*nāra-ayaṇa*, i.e. *one who goes by way of water*, associated with conch shell, lotus, and darkness.

Thus, Krishna–Balarama was the more human face of the Nārāyaṇa–Saṅkarṣaṇa cult, which continued into historical times from when coins with two figures on their opposite sides, one with a cow and the other a plough. In fact, in the highly popular Hindu name *Ramakrishna*, Rāma is not the *Dāśarathī* Rāma of Ayodhya but Baladeva (Rāma) of Mathura. The implications are deeper. Krishna, as Vishnu whose mount is *Garuḍa* the eagle, is Sun and thus *Mitra/Miθra*. At the same time, as dark *Nārāyaṇa* of nautical symbolisms, he is *Varuṇa*, lord of the night sun and cosmic ocean. In other words, while Krishna–Baladeva (Rāma), deified as *Nārāyaṇa–Saṅkarṣaṇa*, are brother–gods, Krishna himself, as Vishnu–Nārāyaṇa, is *Mitra–Varuṇau*. Both themes—of brother gods, and of a dark and a fair god—bring us back to the celestial twins, the *Aśvinau*.

While the cult of the twins had been subsumed by that of Indra, the politico–military principles they represented, that of diarchy, had persisted in amended forms.[131] Brothers were often *purohita* and king, like Devāpī and Śāntanu,[132] where the *purohita* offered prayers for the king

130 Periplus, in Majumdar, *Classical Accounts*, pp. 222-3.

131 Asko Parpola, 'Gandhāra Graves and the Gharma pot, the Nāsatyas and the nose: In pursuit of the chariot twins', in M. F. Kosarev, P. M. Kozhin & N. A. Dubova (ed.), *U istokov tsivilizatsii: Sbornik statej k 75-letiyu Viktora Ivanovicha Sarianidi*, Moskva: Staryj sad, 2004, pp. 102–128, republished in: *Ancient Pakistan*, 16, Peshawar: Department of Archaeology, University of Peshawar.

132 *ṚV*, X: 6.

and *handed him the bow*.[133] The trend extended to the divine sphere also. Of the *Mitrāvaruṇau*, sombre Varuṇa, the senior, was shrewd chaplain or *purohita* to vivacious Mitra the chariot-riding sun–king. Even Indra, once *Brahmaṇaspati* himself, acquired *Brahmaṇaspati* or *Bṛhaspati* as charioteer–chaplain. Now, Bṛhaspati is also Agni, priest of the gods, and is referred together with Indra as *Indrāgni*. Indra's charioteer in popular lore, Mātali, is actually *Mātariśvan* in Vedic lore. Mātariśvan is none other than *fire* or *agni*, associated with Prometheus-like theft of fire;[134] he 'stole' the fire, *charioteer of the sacrifice*, and brought it to the Bhṛgu, whose association with chariots and the fire cult we have encountered and discussed already. These references show that though subsumed by the sacrificial religion of Indra, the celestial twins had lived on in religious consciousness.

The twins were not as indistinguishable as is often supposed. In most mythologies, one was white and the other sable. Further, of the Dioskouroi, one is fighter and the other takes care of horses; Kastor is good at taming horses (*hippódamos*), while Peleudykos at fist-fighting (*pùks agathós*).[135] In the *Ṛgveda*, one of the *Aśvin*s is 'victorious lord of *sumakha*' (*makha* being to fight, like the Greek *maχesasθai*, 'to fight'), and the other 'fortunate son of heaven'.

The twins, as seen, reappear in more identifiable godheads, like Rāma–Lakṣmaṇa in the *Ramayana*, or as Baladeva (Rāma) and Krishna in the *Mahabharata*.

The twins also have sisters—the *Aśvin*s have *Uṣas* or *Suryā Sāvitṛ*, child of the sun, *Kastor* and *Peleudykos* have *Helen Tyrche*, and the Latvian and Lithuanian twins have *Saules Meita* (Maiden or Daughter of the Sun) and *Saules Dukryte* (Daughter of the Sun). The relation between the trio is complicated by the sister, because in most systems, she is *married* to one of the brothers (there is no consistency as to whether the fair or the dark one). The sister appears in the case of the epic godheads too. In the 'renegade' *Adhyātma Ramayana* and the *Daśaratha Jātaka*, Sītā is also Rāma's sister. The *Dīgha Nikāya* tells the story of how king Okkāka (Ikṣvāku) banished

133 *Āśvalāyana Gṛhyasūtra*, 111.12.

134 *ṚV*, I: 190, 2. Isler has shown this to have come from Ātariśvan, where Ātar as fire is preserved in the Avestan. Mātali is associated with the medicinal roles of Aśvins.

135 *Iliad* 3,237.

his son and daughter to the forests where, fearful that they might lose one another, they marry, giving rise to the Śākyas. The story, probably introduced by the Śākya to explain their legendary origin from a brother–sister marriage like that of the Licchavi,[136] acknowledges a tradition of Rāma and Sītā being siblings, offspring of Okkāka of Daśaratha. It is little known that Subhadra, sister of Baladeva (Rāma) and Krishna, is also married to the former.[137]

Now, while the brother–sister marriage was common practice in a very hoary age,[138] even in historical times it had been used as an expedient to replace the *mother's husband–daughter's husband* succession with the *father–son* succession. However, later sensibilities, shocked at such incest, wanted to explain the quirk away as eagerly as emerging patrilineal society wanted to explain away matrilineal succession. In Hellenic mythology, succession to Sparta by Helen's husbands Menelaus and *not her brothers*, was *explained away* by identifying her with *Helen Tyrche*, and then giving it out that her brothers were killed and deified as *Kastor* and *Peleudykos*, at once doing away with the marriage of *Helen Tyrche* with one of her brothers. In the *Mahabharata*, Subhadra is married to Arjuna in a comic episode of elopement encouraged by Krishna but resented by Baladeva; the story looks like the easing out of Baladeva and substituting him with Arjuna, who is really a cousin, thus brother again, to Subhadra.

Deification of Krishna and Arjuna is attested in Paṇini;[139] each had his specific set of worshippers, the *Arjunaka*s and *Vāsudevaka*s, but were also worshipped together as *Nara–Nārāyaṇa*, god associating with man, aboard the chariot. Probably, rather than the *Nārāyaṇa–Sankarṣaṇa*, it was

136 In this important stage in transition from matrilineal to patrilineal inheritance, the son marries the sister and inherits the title, thus setting precedence for a father–son succession.

137 Subhadra is co-deity Mahālakṣmī or Śrī with the brothers, often with Jagannātha and at time Baladeva (Rāma), as in the 14th century *Skanda Purāṇa*, but in popular tradition she appears as their sister. She is also equated with Rādhā.

138 Irawati Karve, 'Kinship Usages and the Family Organisation in Ṛgveda and Atharvaveda', in *Annals of the BORI*, vol. 20, April–June 1939, pp. 213–234. In *ṚV*, X: 10 Yama refuses to marry his twin sister Yamī, which established the brother–sister taboo. Yama is associated with the *Bhrātṛdvitīya* or *Bhai-dūj*, the ceremony that establishes the sacred relation between the brother and sister. Also, Irawati Karve, 'Kinship Terminology and Kinship Usages in Ṛgveda and Atharvaveda', in *Annals of the BORI*, vol. 20, 1938–39, pp. 69–96 and 109–144.

139 Paṇini, *Aṣṭādhyayi*, IV.3. 98: *vāsudevārjunābhyām vun.*

the *dvandva* of *Kṛṣṇārjuna* (*Kṛṣṇau*, i.e. the *two Krishnas*[140]), that was more popular among the Vṛṣṇi nomads. It is obvious that the duo harks back to the *Aśvinau*—Krishna the 'senior' charioteer, advisor, and protector of the Arjuna the junior and warrior. Interestingly, Draupadī also is associated with the duo as Kṛṣṇā, i.e. swarthy, making a triad of *Krishnas*.[141]

We remember that the *Aśvins* had been special gods of the Yadu–Turvaśa and their Kāṇva priests before their cult was subsumed by Indra-worshipping newcomers like the Pūru–Bharata. Now, as the *aśvinau* resurface in the *Kṛṣṇārjuna*, we notice that its senior member, Krishna, is associated with the Yadu and has the more important role of charioteer–advisor. Further, milk and milk products are especially important in the veneration of Krishna, just as they were in the veneration of the celestial twins in the *gharmya* rite described earlier. Perhaps it is significant that the *junior* member of the duo, Arjuna, is associated with Indra as his son. Indra's position was at that time being increasingly challenged by Krishna (the *Govardhana* episode), and other *laukika* godheads. In fact, Arjuna had not superseded Baladeva (Rāma) everywhere—in the Jagannātha cult of Odisha, which was patronised by the Cedī, clan, a branch of the old Yadu, Krishna reigns as *Jagannātha* with brother *Balarāma* and sister *Subhadra*. The world-renowned importance of the chariot to the worship of the triad reflects the importance of the chariot to the cult of the *Aśvins*—interestingly, in both cases the chariot is essentially non-military in nature.

140 Alf Hiltebeitel, *Ritual of Battle*, p. 61. In the *Karṇaparvan*, when Śalya is driving the chariot of Karṇa, the former drives haphazardly, endlessly needling Karṇa with comparisons with Arjuna, and extolling the invincibility of the *Kṛṣṇau*. To Hiltebeitel, the passages are designed to highlight the lack of harmony between the two, in the process highlighting the harmony between the *Kṛṣṇau*.

141 To Hiltebeitel, while the triad of Krishna–Arjuna–Draupadī represented the *Bhakti* triad of Viṣṇu, Śiva, and Devī respectively, the other triad of Krishnas, Krishna–Arjuna–Kṛṣṇadvīpāyana Vyāsa, represents the *trimūrti* of that of Viṣṇu, Śiva, and Brahmā. See Alf Hiltebeitel, 'The Two Kṛṣṇas on One Chariot: Upaniṣadic Imagery and Epic Mythology', *History of Religions*, vol. 24, no. 1, 1984, pp. 1–26.

Epilogue

"History records the name of royal bastards, but cannot tell us the origin of wheat"

—Jean Henri Fabre.

Robert Antoine states concisely on evolution of epic poetry that:

> ... [E]*pic poetry is usually retrospective. It develops at a time when tribal society enters into contact with a higher civilization and tends to project in the past certain elements of modern culture which give to the old capitals an anachronistic aspect of modernity. It is this marginal character of epic poetry which explains how tribal heroes can gradually be transformed into national heroes.*[1]

The above statement not only explains the anachronism in material culture evident in the epic and repeatedly underlined in this book, but also underlines the major anachronism in moral culture and outlook. Though failing to make a proper distinction between tribal and feudal society, Antoine identifies the various *casus belli* for the warriors not only of the *Mahabharata* but also of the other Indian and Greek epics, showing that these reasons for conflict and vendetta, common in the days of endemic warfare, again become prominent in the age of feudal chivalry. In contrast, tribal societies fought for more 'tribal' reasons which, due to anachronistic projections backward of the mores of later ages, have become camouflaged by warfare of urbanising feudal societies, just as the case of their material culture.

1 Robert Antoine, 'Indian and Greek Epic', in Abu Sayeed Ayyub and Amlan Datta (eds.), *Ten Years of Quest*, Bombay, Manaktalas, 1966, pp. 22–38.

Scratching the surface and the feudal–chivalric veneer of the *Mahabharata*, this book has shown that the Kuru, Yadu, Pañcāla, Mātsya, or Śūrasena impetuses to war, or those of the various *vrātya* nations, were much more 'tribal', and in that sense 'national', than is evident from the heroic narratives of the epic which are the foundation of later-day moral culture of South Asia. At the same time, it has shown why, where the *Iliad* did not indiscriminately gather material and turn into a *Magna–Iliad*, the *Bharata* did. While the *Iliad* was meant to be a war-book whose characters were never meant to be deified, the purpose of the *Mahabharata* was different—not to glorify war, but to underline its futility. Thus, while the *Iliad* is focussed on its present, dealing with the current conduct of heroes except for a few asides and reminiscences, the *Mahabharata* wanders widely, its purpose being not to document war but highlight the '*calmed state arising from the renunciation of destructive worldly ambition*', as stated succinctly by Warder.

Obviously, such difference had to do with inherent differences in outlooks of the peoples in whose realms the respective epics developed. With the concepts of impermanence of man and insignificance of his work coming to colour South Asian *weltanschauung*, the characters were readily superhuman-ised and gradually deified, Krishna, the historically effective character *par excellance*, most readily so.

Bibliography

Early South Asian Sources

Hymns of the Atharva Veda, trans. R.T.H. Griffith, Banaras, Lazarus, 1895.

Atharva Veda Saṅhitā, trans. W.D. Whitney, ed. Ch R. Lanman, I–II, Massachusetts, Harvard University Press, 1905.

Aitereya Brāhmaṇa, (*Ait. Br*).

Āpastambha Śrautasūtra, (*Āp.ŚS*).

Aśvalāyana Gṛhyasutra, (*Aś.Gṛ*).

Baudhāyana Śrautasūtra, (*BŚS*), trans., Sparreboom, 1983.

Baudhāyana Śulbasūtra

Beal, Samuel, trans., *Buddhist Records of the Western World.*

Bhagavata Purāṇa

Bṛhadāraṇyaka Upaniṣad.

Chandogya Upaniṣad, (*Ch.U*).

Gautama Dharmasūtra.

Hemacandra, *Triśaṣṭiśalākāpuruṣacarita*

Jaiminīya Brāhmaṇa of the Sāma Veda, ed. Raghu Vira, Lahore, International Academy of Indian Culture, 1937.

Jaiminīya Upaniṣad Brāhmaṇa

Kauśītaki Upaniṣad

Kautilya, *Arthaśāstra*, http://www.sanskritdocuments.org/all_pdf/artha.pdf (accessed 10 May 2014).

Kātyāyani Śulbasūtra

Lāṭyāyana Śrautasūtra, (*LŚS*)

Mahābhārata, Gita Press, (*Mbh*).

The Mahabharata, 12 vols., trans., Kisari Mohan Ganguli, New Delhi, Munshiram Manoharlal, [1884-96], 1970, [*Mbh* (KMG)].

Mahābhārata: Text as Constituted in its Critical Edition, eds., Sukthankar, Vishnu S., and S.K. Belvalkar, 24 vols. with *Harivaṃśa*, Pune, BORI, 1933–70, (*Mbh*, CE).

Mahābhārata, Southern Recension, Kumbakonam Edn.

Mānava Dharmaśāstra,in Patrick Olivelle (ed. and trans.), *Manu's Code of Law*, Oxford, 2005, (*Manu*).

Mātsya Purāṇa

Milindapanha,trans. T.W. Rhys Davids asthe *Questions of King Milinda* in 2 parts, in *Sacred Books of the East,* vols. 35 and 36, Oxford, Clarendon, 1890.

Muṇḍaka Upaniṣad.

Pañcaviṅśati Brāhmaṇa, (*PB*).

Paṇini, *Aṣṭādhyāyi*.

Patañjali, *Mahābhāṣya*.

Hymns of the Sāma Veda, trans. R.T.H. Griffith, Kotagiri, Nilgiri, 1896.

Rāmāyaṇa, (*Rmn*).

Rai Bahadur Lala Baijnath trans*., The Adhyatama Ramayana,* Allahabad, the Panini Office 1913, repr. as extra vol. 1 in the *Sacred Books of the Hindus*, New York, AMS Press, 1974.

Rig Veda, Hymns from the, 2 vols., trans. R.T.H. Griffith, Kotagiri, Nilgiri, 1896, 2nd edn.

Śarabhaṅga Jātaka, Cowell (ed.), *The Jātaka*s, no. 522.

Śatapatha Brāhmaṇa, trans. Julius Eggeling, Netlancers (first published 1882), 2014, (ŚB).

Saṅyutta Nikāya.

Sāṅkhāyana Śrautasūtra, (SŚS).

Saṅyutta Nikāya.

Śrīharṣa, *Naiśadhīya Carita.*

Taittirīya Āraṇyaka.

Taittirīya Brāhmaṇa.

Vāmana Purāṇa.

Viṣṇu Purāṇa.

Text of the White Yajurveda, trans. R.T.H. Griffith, Munshiram, New Delhi, 1897 repr.

Yajurveda, The Vedas of the Black Yajus School: Taittiriya Sanhita, trans. Arthur Barriedale Keith, Delhi, Motilal Banarasidass, 1967.

Period Sources; European Writing

Caesar, Caius Julius, *"De Bello Gallico" and Other Commentaries by Caius Julius Caesar*, trans. W. A. MacDevitt, 1915, Project Gutenberg EBook available at http://www.gutenberg.org/files/10657/10657.txt, accessed 21 Aug 2015.

Diogene Laërtius, *Lives of Eminent Philosophers*, 2 vols., trans. R.D. Hicks, Harvard University Press, Loeb Classical Library, 1925.

Homer, *The Iliad of Homer*, trans. Alexander Pope, Cassell, London, 1909.

Jordannes, *Gothic History.*

Majumdar, R.C., *The Classical Accounts of India*, Calcutta, Firma K.L. Mukopadhyaya, 1960.

McCrindle, J.W., *The Invasion of India by Alexander the Great*, Westminster, Archibald and Constable, 1816.

Megasthenes, *Fragm*: *LVI.* in Pliny, Hist. Nat. VI. 21. 8–23. 11.

Pliny, *Naturalia Historia.*

Polybius, *The Histories of Polybius*, trans. E.S. Shuckburgh and Otto Hultsch, first published, 1889, reprint 1962.

Strabo, *Geography*, 3 vols., trans. H.C. Hamilton, ed. H.G. Bonn, 1854–57.

Tacitus, *Complete Works of Tacitus: Germania*, ed. Alfred John Church, William Jackson Brodribb, Lisa Cerrato, New York, Random House, repr., 1942.

Xenophon, *Anabasis*.

Xenophon, *Cyropaedia*.

Secondary Sources and Works

Agarwal, D.P. and A. Ghosh (eds.), *Radiocarbon and Archaeology*, Bombay, Tata Institute of Fundamental Research, 1973.

Agarwal, Vishal, 'On Perceiving Aryan Migrations in Vedic Ritual Texts', New Delhi, *Puratattva* (Bulletin of the Indian Archaeological Society), no. 36, 2005–06, pp. 155–165.

Agrawal, A., (ed.), *Vedic-Harappan Relationship*, Delhi, Voice of India, 2005.

Ahmed, Mukhtar, *Ancient Pakistan: An Archaeological History*, vol. 3: Harappan Civilization—the Material Culture, Reidsville, Foursome Group, 2014.

Aldred, C., *Akhenaten and Nefertiti*, New York, Brooklyn, 1973.

Allchin, Bridgit and Raymond Allchin, *The Birth of Indian Civilization: India and Pakistan before 500 B.C.*, Baltimore, Penguin Books, 1968.

———, *The Rise of Civilization in India and Pakistan*, New Delhi, 2007.

Altekar, A.S., *A New History of the Indian People*, vol. 6, 1946.

Anderson, J.K., *Ancient Greek Horsemanship*, Berkeley and Los Angeles, 1961.

———, 'Homeric, British and Cyrenaic Chariots', *American Journal of Archaeology*, vol. 69, no. 4, 1965, pp. 349–52.

Anthony D.W. and N.B. Vinogradov, 'Birth of the Chariot', *Archaeology*, no. 48, 1995, pp. 36–41.

Anthony D. W. and Dorcas R. Brown, 'Eneolithic Horse Exploitation in the Eurasian Steppes: Diet, Ritual, and Riding', *Antiquity*, vol. 74, 2000, pp. 75–86.

Anthony, D.W., 'The "Kurgan Culture", Indo–European Origin and the Domestication of the Horse: A Reconsideration', *Current Anthropology*, no. 27, 1986, pp. 291–304.

———, 'The Domestication of the Horse', in R. Meadow and H.P. Uerpmann (eds.), *Equids in the Ancient World*, vol. 2, Weisbaden, Dr. Ludwig Reichart Verlag, 1991, pp. 256–57.

———, 'The Opening of the Eurasian Steppe at 2000 BCE', in *The Bronze Age and Early Iron Age Peoples of Eastern Central Asia*', vol. 1, 1998.

———, *The Horse, the Wheel, and Language—How Bronze-Age Riders from the Eurasian Steppes Shaped the Modern World*, New Jersey, Princeton University Press, Princeton, 2007.

Antoine, Robert, 'Indian and Greek Epic', in Abu Sayeed Ayyub and Amlan Datta (eds.) *Ten Years of Quest*, Bombay, Manaktalas, 1966, pp. 22–38.

Archer, Robin, 'Developments in Near–Eastern Chariotry and Chariot Warfare in the Early First Millennium BCE and their Contribution to the Rise of Cavalry', in Garrett G. Fagan and Matthew Trundle (eds.), *New Perspectives on Ancient Warfare*, Leiden, Brill, 2010, pp. 57–79.

Arnold, E.V., *Vedic Metre in its Historical Development*, Cambridge, Cambridge Univ. Press, 1905.

Arora, U.P., 'Fragments of Onesikritos on India—An Appraisal,' *The Indian Historical Review*, vol. 32, no. 1, January 2005, pp, 35–102.

Athavale, V.B.,'The Movements of the Pandavas', *Annals of the BORI*, vol. 29, 1948, pp. 85–95.

Baden-Powell, B. H., 'Notes on the Origin of the 'Lunar' and 'Solar' Aryan Tribes, and on the 'Rājput' Clans', *Journal of the Royal Asiatic Society*, n.v., 1899, pp. 295–328, 519–63.

Bagley, Robert, 'Shang Archaeology', in Loewe and Shaughnessy (eds.), *The Cambridge History of Ancient China*, pp. 124–231.

Bakshi, G.D., *Mahabharata: A Military Analysis*, NewDelhi, Lancer, 1990.

Bandyopadhyay, Haricharan, 'Akṣakrīḍā o Prāṇidyūta' (Bengali), in *Desh*, vol. 11, no. 1, Nov 1943, pp. 77–79.

Banerjee, N.R., 'The Excavations at Ujjain', in E. Waldschmidt (ed.), *Indologen Tagung: 1959*, Gottingen, Vandenhoeck & Ruprecht, 1960, pp. 66–87.

———, *The Iron Age in India*, Delhi, Munshiram Manoharlal, 1965.

Banerjee, N.R., 'The Iron Age in India',in V.N. Mishra and M.S. Mate (ed.), *Indian Prehistory*, Poona, 65, 1964, pp. 177–218.

Barbieri–Low, Anthony J., 'Wheeled Vehicles in the Chinese Bronze Age (c. 2000–741 B.C.)', *Sino–Platonic Papers*, no. 99, Feb 2000, pp. 1–98.

Bart D. Ehrman, *Misquoting Jesus: The Story Behind Who Changed the Bible and Why*, HarperSanFrancisco, 2005.

Basham A.L. (ed.), *A Cultural History of India*, Oxford University Press, 1975.

Bauer, Robert S., 'Sino–Tibetan *Kolo "Wheel"', *Sino–Platonic Papers*, no. 47, August, 1994.

Bellew, Henry Walter, *The Races of Afghanistan: being a Brief Account of the Principal Nations Inhabiting the Country*, Calcutta, Thacker, Spine, 1880.

Belloc, H., *Creçy*, series: British Battles, London, Stephen Swift, 1912.

Bergaigne, Abel, *La Religion Védique d'après les hymnes du Rig-Veda*, 3 vols., Paris, 1878–83.

Bhāduḍi, Nṛsiṃhaprasāda, *Vālmīkir Rāma o Rāmāyaṇa*, Calcutta, Ananda, 1998.

Bhandarkar, D.R., 'Aryan Immigration into Eastern India',*Annals of the BORI*, vol.12, pp. 103–116.

Bhargava, M.L., *The Geography of Ṛgvedic India*, Lucknow, Upper India Publishing House, 1964.

Bhargava, P.L., 'Fresh Appraisal of the Historicity of the Indian Epics', *Annals of the BORI*, vol. 63, no.1/4, 1982, pp. 15–28.

Bhattacharya, Tarapada, *The Cult of Brahmā*, Varanasi, 1969.

Bhattacharya, Tarundeb, *Purulia* (in Bengali), Calcutta, Firma K.L.Mukhopadhyaya, 2009.

Bivar, A.D.H., 'The Bactrian Treasures of Qunduz', *Journal of the Numismatic Society of India*, XVII, 1955, pp.37–52.

Blench, Roger and Matthew Spriggs (eds.), *One World Archaeology and Languages*, London, Routledge, 1999.

Bose, A.B., 'Pastoral Nomadism in India: Nature, Problems and Prospects', in *Pastoralists and Nomads in South Asia*, 1975, pp. 1–15.

Bose, Saikat K., *Boots, Hooves, and Wheels, and the Social Dynamics behind South Asian Warfare*, Delhi, Vij Books, 2015.

Boyce, M., 'Priests, Cattle and Men', *Bulletin of the School of Oriental and African Studies*, University of London, vol. 50, no. 3, 1987, pp. 508–526.

———, 'The Bipartite Society of the Ancient Iranians', in M. A. Dandamayev *et al* (eds.), *Societies and Languages of the Ancient Near East: Studies in Honour of I. M. Diakonoff*, Warminster, 1982, pp. 33–34.

Boyle, J.A.,*The Mongol World Empire, 1206–1370*, London, Variorum revised edns, 1977.

Breasted, James Henry, *Ancient Records of Egypt: Historical Documents*, Part 2, Chicago, University of Illinois, 1906.

Brockington, J.L., *The Sanskrit Epics*, part 2, vol. 12,Leiden, Brill, 1998.

Brønsted, J. Skov K., *The Vikings*, Hammondsworth, Middlesex, Penguin, 1965.

Brown, D.R. and D.W. Anthony, 'Bitwear, Horseback Riding and the Botai Sites of Kazakhstan', *Journal of Archaeological Sciences*, vol. 25, 1998, pp. 331–347.

Brownrigg, Gail, 'Horse Control and the Bit', in Sandra L. Olsen, Susan Grant, Alice M. Choyke, and László Bartosiwicz (eds.), *Horse and Humans: The Evolution of Human–Equine Relationships*, BAR International Series 1560, 2006, pp. 165–171.

Bryant, E., *The Quest of the Origins of Vedic Culture: The Indo–Aryan Invasion Debate*, Oxford, 2001.

———, "''Somewhere in Asia' and No More", Response to 'Indigenous Indo–Aryans and the Ṛgveda by N. Kazanas', *Journal of Indo–European Studies*, vol. 30, 2002, pp. 136–48.

Burrows, T., 'The Early Āryans', in A.L. Basham (ed.), *A Cultural History of India*, pp. 20–29.

Cambrensis, Giraldus, 'Topographic Hybernia', in J. Puhvel, *Comparative Mythology*, pp. 269–276.

Campbell, Joseph,*Myths and Symbols in Indian Arts and Religion*, New York, Harper Torchbooks, 1965.

———, *The Masks of God*, vol.1: Primitive Mythology, London, Condor, 2000 (first published 1959).

Carneiro, Robert L., 'A Theory on the Origin of the State', *Science*, no. 169, 170, pp. 733–38.

Cawkwell, G., *The Greek Wars: The Failure of Persia*, Oxford, 2005.

Chadwick, J., *The Mycenaean World*, Cambridge, Cambridge University Press, 1976.

Chakrabarti, D.K. and N. Lahiri, *Copper and its Alloys in Ancient India*, Delhi, Munshiram Manoharlal, 1996.

Chakravarti, P.C., *The Art of War in Ancient India*, New Delhi, LPP, 2010, First Published 1941.

Chattopadhyaya, B.D., *Aspects of Rural Settlements and Rural Society in Early Medieval India*, Calcutta, 1990.

Chaudhuri, Nanimadhab, 'Some Aspects of the Worship of Nārayāṇa',*The Indian Historical Quarterly*, vol 22, 1946, pp. 191–199.

Christian, David, *Inner Eurasia from Prehistory to the Mongol Empire*, vol. 1 of series: A History of Central Asia and Mongolia, Massachusetts, Blackwell, 1998.

———, 'State Formation in the Steppes',in Perkins and Tample, *Europe: Prospects and Retrospects*, pp. 243–58.

Clutton–Brock, Juliet (ed.), *The Walking Larder: Patterns of Domestication, Pastoralism, and Predation*, London, Unwyn Hyman, 1989.

Creel, Herrlee G., 'The Role of the Horse in Chinese History', *American Historical Review*, 70, 1965, pp. 647–72.

———, *Origins of Statecraft in China: The Western Chou Empire*, Chicago, University of Chicago Press, 1970.

Crouwel, J.H., *Chariot and Other Means of Land Transport in Bronze Age Greece*, Amsterdam, Allard Pierson Museum, 1981.

Cunningham, A., *Ancient Geography of India*, 2 vols., London, Trübner, 1871.

———, *Archaeological Survey Report: Report for the year 1878–79*, CASR, vol. 14, 1882.

Dalrymple, W., *Return of the King: The Battle for Afghanistan*, Bloomsbury, 2013.

Dandamayev, M. A. et al (eds.), *Societies and Languages of the Ancient Near East: Studies in Honour of I. M. Diakonoff*, Warminster, 1982, pp. 33–34.

Dandekar, R.N. (ed.), *Ramkrishna Gopal Bhandarkar as an Indologist: a Symposium*, BORI, Poona, 1976.

———, 'Vaiṣṇavism and Saivism', in R.N. Dandekar (ed.), *Ramkrishna Gopal Bhandarkar as an Indologist: A Symposium*, Poona, BORI, 1976.

Dange, S.S., *Vedic Beliefs and Practices through Atharva Veda*, Aryan Books International, Delhi, 2004.

Dani, A.H. and V.M. Masson (eds.), *History of Civilizations of Central Asia*, vol. 1, Paris, UNESCO, 1992.

Dani, A.H., 'Gandhara Grave Complex in West Pakistan', *Asian Perspective*, vol. 9, 1968, pp. 99–110.

———, 'Origins of Bronze Age Cultures in the Indus Basin: A Geographical Perspective', *Expedition*, Winter, 1975, pp. 12–18.

———, 'Pastoral–Agricultural Tribes of Pakistan in the Post-Indus Period', in A.H. Dani and V.M. Masson (eds.), *History of Civilizations of Central Asia*, vol. 1, Paris, UNESCO, 1992, pp. 395–420.

Dasgupta, Shashi Bhushan, *Bhārater Śakti Sādhanā o Śākta Sāhitya*, Calcutta, Sahitya San, 1392 Baisakh.

Datta, Swati, *Migrant Brāhmanas in Northern India: Their Settlement and General Impact c. A.D. 475–1030*, Delhi, Motilal Banarasidass, 1989.

Datta. V.N. and H.A.Phadke, *History of Kurukshetra*, 1984.

Datta, B.N., 'Vedic Funeral Customs and Indus Valley Culture', *Man in India*, vol. 16, pp. 223–307.

Davidson, H.R.E., *Gods and Myths of Northern Europe*, New York, Penguin, 1981.

Davis–Kimball, J., V.A. Bashilov, and L.T. Yablonsky (eds.), *Nomads of the Eurasian Steppes in the Early Iron Age*, Berkeley, Zinat Press, 1995.

Davis–Kimball, Jeanine, Eileen M. Murphy, Ludmila Koryakova, and Leonid T. Yablonsky (eds.), *Kurgans, Ritual Sites and Settlements: Eurasian Bronze and Iron Age*, BAR International Series, 890, Oxford, Archeopress, 2000.

Dawson, Doyne, *The First Armies*, London, Cassell, 2001.

Delebecque, E., *Le cheval dans l'Iliade, suivi d'un lixique du cheval chez Homère et d'un essai sur le cheval pré-homérique,* Paris, C. Klincksieck, 1951 (ÉTUDES ET COMMENTAIRES, IX).

Denwood P. (ed.), 'The Arts of the Steppelands', *Colloquies on the Art and Archaeology of Asia*, no. 7, London, 1978.

Dey, N.L., *Geographical Dictionary of Ancient and Medieval India*, London, Cassell, 1927.

Dhavalikar, M. K. and G. L. Possehl, 'Subsistence Pattern of an Early Farming Community in Western India', *Puratattva*, vol. 7, pp. 39–46.

Di Cosma, Nicolo, 'Northern Frontiers of Imperial China', in Loewe and Shaughnessy (eds.), *The Cambridge History of Ancient China*, pp. 885–966.

———, 'Introduction: Inner Asian Ways of Warfare', in N. Di Cosmo (ed.), *Warfare in Inner Asian History (500-1800)*, Leiden, Brill, 2002, pp. 3–12.

Dillon, Matthew and Linda Garland, *Ancient Greece: Social and Historical Documents from the Archaic Times till the Death of Alexander the Great*, Routledge Sourcebooks for the Ancient World, 2000.

Drews, Robert, *End of the Bronze Age: Changes in Warfare and the Catastrophe ca. 1200 BC*, Princeton, Princeton Univ. Press, 1993.

———, *The Coming of the Greeks: Indo–European Conquests in the Aegean and the Near East*, Princeton, Princeton Univ.Press, 1998.

———, *Early Riders: The Beginnings of Mounted Warfare in Asia and Europe*, New York, Routledge, 2004.

Dubuisson, Daniel, 'La Préhistoire des Pāṇḍava', *Revue de l'histoire des religions*, vol. 202, no. 3, July–September, 1985, pp. 227–241.

Dumézil, Georges, *The Destiny of the Warrior*, trans. Alf Hiltebeitel, Chicago, University of Chicago Press, 1970.

———, *Naissance d'archanges (Jupiter, Mars, Quirinus III): Essai sur la formation de la théologie zoroastrienne*, Paris, 1945.

Dumont, P.-E., *L'Aśvamedha: Description du sacrifice solonnel du cheval dans le culte védique d'après les textes du Yajurveda blanc*, Paris, Paul Guethner, 1927.

Eliade, Mircea (ed.), *The Encyclopaedia of Religion*, New York, Macmillan, 1987.

——— (trans.), W.R. Trask, *Yoga: Immortality and Freedom*, New Jersey, Princeton University Press, 1990.

———, *Essential Sacred Writings From Around the World*, New York, HarperSanFrancisco, 1992.

Ellis Davidson, H.R., *Gods and Myths of Northern Europe*, Middlesex, Penguin Books, 1964.

Elst, Koenrad, *Update on the Aryan Invasion Debate*, Delhi, Aditya Prakashan, 1999.

Erdosy, George, *Ethnicity in the Rigveda and its Bearing on the Question of Indo-European Origins*, Cambridge, South Asian Studies, vol. 5, 1977.

———, 'The Origin of Cities in the Ganges Valley', *Journal of the Economic and Social History of the Orient*, vol. 28, no. 1, 1985, pp. 81–109.

——— (ed.), *The Indo-Aryans of Ancient South Asia: Language, Material Culture and Ethnicity Indian Philology and South Asian Studies*, vol. 1, series ed. A. Wezler and M. Witzel, Berlin, 1995.

Ernout A. and A. Meillet, *Dictionnaire étymologie de la langue latine*, Paris, Klinckseik, 1939.

Fagan, Garrett G. and Matthew Trundle (eds.), *New Perspectives on Ancient Warfare*, Leiden, Brill, 2010.

Falk, Harry, 'Das Reitpferd im vedischen Indien', in B. Hänsel, Stefan Zimmer *et al* (eds.), *Die Indogermanen und das Pferd*, Akten des Internationalen interdisziplinaren Kolloquiums, Freie Universitat Berlin, 1992, Bernfried Schlerath zum, 70, Geburtstag gewidmet, Budapest 1995, pp. 91–101.

Fitzgerald, James, 'Pīta and Śaikya/Saikya: Two Terms of Iron and Steel Technology in the Mahābhārata', *Journal of the American Oriental Society*, vol. 120, no.1, January–March 2000, pp. 44–61.

Fleet, John F., *Corpus Inscriptionum Indicarum: Inscriptions of the Early Guptas*, vol. 3, Calcutta, Government of India, Central Publications Branch, 1988.

Fleisher, Michael L., *Kuria Cattle Raiders: Violence and Vigilantism on the Tanzania/Kenya Frontier*, Michigan, University of Michigan, 2000.

Foster, I. and C. Adcock (eds.), *Culture and Environment: Essays in Honour of Sir Cyril Fox*, London, Routledge, 1963.

Fox R. (ed.), *Realm and Region in Traditional India*, Delhi, Vikas, 1979.

Francfort, H–P., 'La Civilization de l'Oxus et les Indo–Iraniens et Indo–Aryens en Asie Centrale', in G. Fussman, J. Kellens, H–P. Francfort, and X Temblay (ed.), *Âryas, Aryens et Iraniens en Asie Centrale*, Paris, 2005, pp. 253–328.

Fussman, G., J. Kellens, H–P. Francfort, and X Temblay (ed.), *Âryas, Aryens et Iraniens en Asie Centrale*, Paris, 2005.

Geiger, W., *Civilization of the Eastern Iranians in Ancient Times*, vol. 2, trans. D. P. Sanjana, London, 1886.

Gening, V. F., G.B. Zdanovich, and V. V. Gening, *Sintashta: Arkheologicheskie pamyatniki arijskikh plemen Uralo-Kazakhstanskikh stepej* (in Russian), vol. 1: Chelyabinsk: Yuzhno-Ural'skoe knizhnoe izdatel'stvo, 1992.

Gening, V.F., 'The Cemetery at Sintashta and Early Indo–Iranian Peoples', *Journal of Indo–European Studies*, vol. 7, 1979, pp. 1–30.

Genz, Hermann, 'Chariot and the Role of Archery in the Near East at the Transition from the Middle to the Late Bronze Ages: is there a Connection?', in André J. Veldmeijer and Salima Ikram (eds.), *Chasing Chariots, Proceedings of the First International Chariot Conference (Cairo 2012)*, Leiden, Sidestone, 2013, pp. 95–106.

Gervers, M., and W. Schlepp, (eds.), *Nomadic Diplomacy, Destruction and Religion from the Pacific to the Atlantic*, Toronto, Toronto Studies in Central and Inner Asia, 1994.

Ghirshman, R., *Iran: From the Earliest Times to the Islamic Conquests*, London, Penguin, 1954.

Ghosh, Amalkar and Hassan, 'The Lost Course of the Sarasvati River in the Great Indian Desert: New Evidence of LANDSAT Imagery', *The Geographical Journal*, vol. 145, pt. 3, 1979, pp. 446–51.

Gilman, Benedicte, (ed.), *Masterpieces of the J. Paul Getty Museum: Antiquities*, the J. Paul Getty Museum, Los Angeles, 1997.

Gimbutas, Marija, *Bronze Age Cultures in Central and Eastern Europe*, The Hague/London, Mouton, 1965.

Goldman, R.P., *Gods, Priests and Warriors: the Bhrgus in the Mahabharata*, New York, Columbia Univ. Press, 1977.

Gonda, Jan, *Ancient Indian Kingship from the Religious Point of View*, Leiden, Brill, 1969.

Gorbunov, Vadim V., and Aleksei A. Tishkin, 'Weapons of the Gorny Altai Nomads in the Hunnu Age', *Archaeology, Ethnology & Anthropology of Eurasia*, vol. 4, no. 28, 2006, pp. 79–85.

Greenhalgh, P.A.L., *Early Greek Warfare: Horsemen and Chariots in the Homeric and Archaic Ages*, New York, Cambridge University Press, 1973.

Grigoriev, S.A., 'The Sintashta Culture and Some Questions of Indo-Europeans Origins', *Proceedings of the Chelyabinsk Scientific Center*, vol. 2, 1998, pp. 82–85.

Gubaev, A., G. Koshelenko, and M. Tosi, 'The Archaeological Map of the Murghab Delta: Preliminary Reports 1990–95', *Istituto Italiano per l'Africa e l'Oriente* (*IsIAO*), and also Francfort 2005, pp. 295–304.

Gupta, Chandrashekhar, 'Yaksha Cult in the Mahābhārata', in Ajay Mitra Sastri (ed.), *Mahābhārata*, pp. 243–53.

Gupta, S.P. and S.K. Ramachandran (eds.), *Mahabharata: Myth and Reality, Differing Views*, Delhi, Agam Prakashan, 1976.

Gurney, O.R., *The Hittites*, Penguin, 1952.

Habib, Irfan, *Atlas of the Mughal Empire*, Delhi, Oxford University Press, 1982.

Hackett, J. (ed.), *Warfare in the Ancient World*, New York, Facts on File, 1989.

Hagalia, Wenche, 'Changing Rangeland Use by the Nomads of Samad in the Highlands of Eastern Ladakh, India', M.Sc. Thesis, Noragric, Agricultural University of Norway, 2004.

Handa, Devendra, 'Some Ancient Janapadas of Uttarāpatha vis-à-vis the Mahābhārata', in Ajay Mitra Shastri (ed.), *Mahābhārata*, pp. 118–147.

Harmatta, J., 'The Emergence of the Indo–Iranians: the Indo–Iranian Languages', in A.H. Dani and V.M. Masson (eds.), *History of Civilization of Central Asia*, vol. 1, pp. 357–78.

Heather, Peter, *The Goths*, series The Peoples of Europe, Wiley–Blackwell, 1998.

Heesterman, Jan, 'Vrātya and Sacrifice', *Indo–Iranian Journal*, vol. 6, 1963, pp. 1–37.

———, *The Ancient Indian Royal Consecration*, S'Gravenhage, Mouton and Co., 1957.

Henning, W.B., *Zoroaster, Politician or Witch Doctor*, Oxford, 1951.

Hiebert F.T. and C.C. Lamberg–Karlovsky, 'Central Asia and the Indo-Iranian Borderlands', *Iran*, vol. 30, 1992, pp. 1–15.

Hillebrandt, A.,*Vedsiche Mythologie*, Breslau, 1891–1902.

Hiltebeitel, Alf, *The Ritual of Battle: Krishna in the Mahābhārata*, Ithaca, Cornell University Press, 1976.

———, 'The Two Kṛṣṇas on One Chariot: Upaniṣadic Imagery and Epic Mythology', *History of Religions*, vol. 24, 1984, pp. 1–26.

———, *Rethinking the Mahabharata: A Reader's Guide to the Education of the Dharma King*, Chicago, Univ. of Chicago Press, 2001.

Hirt, H., *Die Indogermanen, ihre Verbeitung, ihre Urheimat and ihre Kultur*, vol. 1., Strasbourg, Trübner, 1905.

Holay. P.V., 'The Year of the Kaurava–Pāṇḍava War', in Ajay Mitra Shastri (ed.), *Mahābhārata*, pp. 58–89.

Holtzman, Adolf, *Das Mahabharata und seine Theile*, 4 vols., Kiel, Osnabrück Biblio, 1892.

Hopkins, E. Washburn, *The Great Epic of India: Character and Origin of the Mahabharata*, Delhi, Motilal, first published 1901, repr. 1993.

———, 'Bharata and the Great Bharata', *American Journal of Philosophy*, vol., 19, 1898, pp. 1–24.

———, 'The Social and Military Position of the Ruling Caste in Ancient India as Represented by the Sanskrit Epic', *Journal of American Oriental Society*, vol. 13, 1889, pp. 57–376.

Hsaio–yun Wu, *Chariots in Early China: Origins, cultural interaction, and identity*, BAR International Series 2457, Oxford, Archaeopress, 2013.

Hutton, James,*Central Asia: From the Aryan to the Cossack*, New Delhi, Manas, first published 1871, repr.2005.

Hyland, Anne, *The Horse in the Ancient World*, Sutton, Gloucestershire, 2003.

Jacobsen–Tepfer, Esther, 'The Image of Wheeled Vehicle in the Mongolian Altai: Instability and Ambiguity', *The Silk Road*, vol. 10, 2012, pp. 1–28.

Jain, Ram Chandra, *Jaya: The Original Nucleus of the Mahabharata*, Delhi, Agam Kala Prakashan, 1979.

Jain, V.K., *Prehistory and Protohistory of India: An Appraisal*, Perspective in Indian Art and Archaeology, no. 7, D.K. Printworld, New Delhi, 2006.

Jaiswal, Suvira, *The Origin and Development of Vaiṣṇavism*, Delhi, Munshiram Manoharlal, 1967.

Jamison S. W. and M. Witzel, *Vedic Hinduism*, 1992, available at www. people.fas.harvard.edu/~witzel/vedica.pdf, seen 17 April, 15.

Jarrige, J–F., 'Excavation at Nausharo', *Pakistan Archaeology*, vol. 23, 1987–8, pp. 149–213.

Jayaswal, K.P., *Hindu Polity: A Constitutional History of India in Hindu Times*, 2 vols., Butterworth, 1924.

Jettmar, K., 'The Altai Before the Turks', *The Museum of Far Eastern Antiquities*, Stockholm, Bulletin, vol. 22, 1951.

———, 'The Origin of Chinese Civilization: Soviet Views', in David Kingsley (ed.), *The Origins of Chinese Civilization*, Berkeley, Univ. of Calif. Press, 1983.

———, 'Non-Buddhist Traditions in the Petroglyphs of the Indus Valley', in J. Schottsman–Wolfers and M. Taddei (eds.), *Asian Archaeology 1985: Proceedings of the Seventh International Conference of the Association of South Asian Archaeologists in Western Europe (Bruxelles)*, Naples, Instituto Universitario Orientale, pp. 751–77.

Jha, Vivekananda, 'Dharma and the Nature of Caste in the Bhagavadgītā', *Indian Historical Review*, vol. 29, nos. 1– 2, January and July 2002, New Delhi, 2004, pp. 1–28.

Jones–Bley, Karlene, 'The Sintashta "Chariots"', in Jeannine Davis–Kimballet *et al* (eds.), *Kurgans, Ritual Sites and Settlements: Eurasian Bronze and Iron Age*, pp. 135–140.

Kapoor, Subodh (ed.), *An Introduction to Epic Philosophy*, 6 vols., New Delhi, Cosmo Publications, 2004.

Karnal District Gazetteer, 1892.

Karve, I., 'Kinship Terminology and Kinship Usages in Ṛgveda and Atharvaveda', *Annals of the BORI*, vol.20,1938, pp. 69–96 and 109–144.

———, 'The Kinship Usages and the Family Organisation in Ṛgveda and Atharvaveda', *Annals of the BORI*, vol.20, 1938, pp. 213-234.

———, *Yugānta: The end of an Epoch*, Disha Books, 2007, first published 1967.

Kazanas, N., 'The Ṛgveda and Indoeuropeans', *Annals of the BORI*, vol. 80, 1999, pp. 15–42.

———, 'The Ṛgveda and Harappa', in A. Agrawal (ed.), *In Search of Vedic-Harappan Relationship*, Delhi, Voice of India, 2005.

Keith, A. Berriedale, 'The Age of the Rigveda', in E.J. Rapson (ed.), *The Cambridge History of India*, vol. 1: Ancient India, Cambridge, Cambridge University Press, 1922, pp. 77–113.

Kelekna, Pita, 'The Politico–Economic Impact of the Horse on Old World Cultures: An Overview', *Sino–Platonic Papers*, no. 190, June 2009, pp. 1–31.

Kenoyer, J.M., 'Cultures and Societies of the Indus Tradition', in R. Thapar (ed.), *India: Historical Beginnings and the Concept of the Aryan*, Delhi, NBT, 2006, pp. 41–97.

Khazanov, A.M., 'The Spread of World Religion in Medieval Nomadic Societies of the European Steppes', in Gervers and Schlepp, *Nomadic Diplomacy, Destruction and Religion from the Pacific to the Atlantic*, 1994, pp. 11–33.

Kierman, Frank A. and John K. Fairbank (eds.), *Chinese Ways in Warfare*, Cambridge, MA, Harvard University Press, 1974.

Kierman, Frank A, 'Phases and Modes of Combat in Early China', in Kierman andFairbank (eds.), *Chinese Ways in Warfare*, pp. 52–53.

Kingsley, David (ed.), *The Origins of Chinese Civilization*, Berkeley, Univ. of Calif. Press, 1983.

Kirk, G.S., *Songs of Homer*, Cambridge, 2005.

Kochhar, Rajesh, *The Vedic People: their History and Geography*, Delhi, Orient Blackswan 2009.

Kosambi, D.D., 'The Autochthonous Element in the Mahabharata', *Journal of the American Oriental Society*, vol. 84, Baltimore,1964, pp. 31–44.

———, *The Culture and Civilization of Ancient India in Historical Outline*, Routledge and K. Paul, 1964.

———, *The Culture and Civilization of Ancient India in Historical Outline*, Delhi, 1972.

Kuiper, F.B.J., 'An Austro-Asiatic Myth in the Rigveda', *Medeleengen der Koninklijke Nederlandse Akademie van Wetenschappen*, Afd. Letterkunde, Niewe Reeks, Deel 13, no. 7, Amsterdam, Noord-Hollandsche Uitg. Maatschappij, 1950.

Kulke, H. and D. Ruthermunde, *A History of India*, New York, 1986.

Kuzmina, Elena, *The Prehistory of the Silk Road*, Victor H. Mair ed., Philadelphia, University of Pennsylvania Press, 2008.

Kuzmina, Elena., 'The Eurasian Steppes: The Transition from Early Urbanism to Nomadism', in Jeannine Davis-Kimball *et al* (eds.),

Kurgans, Ritual Sites, and Settlements: Eurasian Bronze and Iron Age, pp. 118–123.

Kwang–Chih Chang, *Shang Civilization*, Yale, New Haven, 1980.

Lal, B.B. and S.P. Gupta (eds.), *Frontiers of Indus Civilization*, Delhi, Books and Books, 1984.

Lal, B.B., 'Excavations at Hastināpura and Other Explorations in the Upper Gaṅgā and Sutlej Basins: Excavations of B.B. Lal', *Ancient India*, nos. 10 and 11, 1950, 1950–52.

———, 'Archaeology and the Two Indian Epics', *Annals of the BORI*, vol. 54, parts 1/4, 1973, pp. 1–8.

———, 'This is How and Archaeologist looks at the Historicity of the Mahābharata', in Shastri (ed.), *Mahābhārata*, pp.1–25.

Lamberg–Karlovsky, C.C., 'Language and Archaeology: The Indo–Iranians', *Current Anthropology*, vol. 43, 2002, pp. 63–88.

Lambrick, H.T., 'The Indus Flood Plain and the 'Indus Civilization'', in G.L. Possehl (ed.), *Ancient Cities of India*, pp. 313–322.

Lane, Richard H., 'Review: The Bow: Some Notes on its Origin and Development by Gad Rausing', *American Anthropologist*, N. S., 70/5, 1968, p. 978.

Lassen, Chr., *Indische Alterthumskunde*, 4 vols., Leipzig, 1858, 1858-74

Latacz, J., *Kampfparanese, Kampfdarstellung und Kampftwirklichkeit in der Ilias*, bei Kallinos und Tyrtaios, Munich, Perfect Paperback, 1977

Lattimore, Owen, *Mongol Journeys*, Varanasi, Pilgrim, 2006.

———, *Inner Asian Frontiers of China*, Oxford University Press, 1940.

Lawergren, Bo, "Oxus Trumpets, CA, 2200–1800 BCE: Material, Overview, Usage, Societal Role, and Catalog", *Iranica Antiqua*, vol. 38, 2003, pp. 41–118.

Leshnik, L.S. and G–D. Sontheimer (eds.), *Pastoralists and Nomads in South Asia*, Wiesbaden, Otto Harassowitz, 1975.

Levine, Marsha, C. Renfrew, and K. Boyles, (eds.), *Prehistoric Steppe Adaptation and the Horse*, Cambridge, Macdonald Institute of Archaeological Research, University of Cambridge, 2003.

Levine, Marsha, 'The Origin of Horse Husbandry on the Eurasian Steppes', in Levine *et al* (eds.), *Late Prehistoric Exploitation of the Eurasian Steppe*, pp. 5–58.

Levine, Marsha, Yuri Rassamakov, Y. Y. Rassamakin, A. M. Kislenko, and N. S. Tatarintseva (eds.), *Late Prehistoric Exploitation of the Eurasian Steppe*, Cambridge, McDonald Institute, 1999.

Levy, Gertrude, *The Sword from the Rock: An Investigation into the Origins of Epic Literature and the Development of the Hero*, London, Faber and Faber, 1953.

Lidchi-Grassi, Maggi, *The Great Golden Sacrifice of the Mahabharata*, 2 vols., vol. 1: The Battle of Kurukshetra, New Delhi, Roli Books, 1986.

Lincoln, Bruce, *Priests, Warriors and Cattle*, University of California Press, 1981.

Lines, Kevin P., 'Is Turkana Cattle Raiding a part of Turkana Ethnicity? An Anti Anti-Essentialist View of both Internal and External Factors for Ngingoroko', *Intercultural Studies*, Wilmore, KY, Asbury Theological Seminary, December 2009, pp. 1–14.

Littauer, M.A. and J.H. Crouwel, *Wheeled Vehicles and Ridden Animals in the Ancient Near East*, Leiden, Brill, 1979.

———, *Chariots and Related Equipment from the Tomb of Tutankhamun*, London, Oxford, Griffith, 1985.

———, 'The origin of the true chariot', in M.A. Littauer and J. Crouwel, *Selected Writings on Chariots, Other Early Vehicles, Riding and Harness*, ed. Peter Raulwig, Leiden, Brill, 2002, pp. 45–53, originally published in *Antiquity*, no. 70, 1996, pp. 934–939.

———, 'Chariots in Late Bronze Age Greece', in Littauer and Crouwel, *Selected Writings*, ed. Peter Raulwig, pp. 53–61.

———, 'Robert Drews and the Role of Chariotry in Bronze Age Greece', in Littauer and Crouwel, *Selected Writings*, ed. Peter Raulwig, 2002, pp. 66–74.

———, *Selected Writings on Chariots, Other Early Vehicles, Riding and Harness*, ed. Peter Raulwig, Leiden, Brill, 2002.

Littauer, M.A., 'The Function of the Yoke Saddle in Ancient Harnessing', *Antiquity*, vol. 42, 1968, pp. 27–31.

———, 'Review: P.A.L. Greenhalgh, *Early Greek Warfare*', *Classical Philology*, vol. 72, no. 4, October 1977, pp. 363–65.

Loewe, Michael and Edward Shaughnessy (eds.), *The Cambridge History of Ancient China from the Origins of Civilization to 221 BC*, Cambridge, Cambridge University Press, 1999.

Lüders, Heinrich, 'Das Würfelspiel im alten Indien, Abhandlungen der königlich Gessellschaft der Wissenschaftlissen zu Göttingen', *Philologische–historischen Klasse*, n.s. 9, no. 2, Berlin, 1907.

Ludwig, Alfred, *Der Rigveda oder die Heiligen Hymnen der Brâhmana*, verlag von F. Tempsky, Prag, 1881, vol. 3.

Lymner, Kenneth, 'Petroglyphs and Sacred Spaces at Terektye Aulie, Central Kazakhstan', in Jeanine Davis–Kimball *et al* (eds), *Kurgans, Ritual Sites, and Settlements: Eurasian Bronze and Iron Age*, pp. 311–321.

Macdonell, A.A., *History of Sanskrit Literature*, Delhi, Motilal Banarasidass, 1990.

Macdonell, A.A. and A.B. Keith, *Vedic Index*, 2 vols., Delhi, 1958.

Mair, Victor H., 'Mummies of the Tarim Basin', *Archaeology*, March/April 1995, pp. 28–35.

Majumdar, A.K., *Concise History of India*, vol. 2, New Delhi, 1980.

Majumdar, D.N., 'The Culture Patterns of Polyandrous Society', in *Man in India*, vol. 20, nos. 1–2, 1940, pp.82–83.

Majumdar, R.C., *The Classical Accounts of India*, Calcutta, Firma K.L. Mukhopadhyaya, 1981.

Majumdar, R.C., H.C. Raychaudhuri, and Kalikinkar Dutta, *An Advanced History of India*, London, MacMillan, 1963.

Mallory J.P. and D.Q. Adams, *Encyclopaedia of Indo–European Culture*, London, Fitzroy Dearborn, 1997.

Mallory J.P. and Victor H. Mair, *The Tarim Mummies*, Thames and Hudson, 2008.

Mallory, J.P., *In Search of the Indo-Europeans: Language, Archaeology and Myth*, London, Thames and Hudson, 1989.

Margabandhu, C., 'Technology of Transport Vehicles in Early India', in D.P. Agarwal and A. Ghosh (eds.), *Radiocarbon and Archaeology*, Bombay, Tata Institute of Fundamental research, 1973, pp. 182–88.

Marinatos, S., *Crete and Mycenae*, London, 1962.

Marshall, Sir John, 'The Excavations at Bhita', *Annual Report of the Archaeological Survey of India: 1911–12*, Calcutta, 1915.

Masson, V.M., 'The Decline of the Bronze Age Civilization and Movements of the Tribes', in Dani and Masson, *History of Civilization*, vol. 1, pp. 337–356.

McEwer, Edward, Robert L. Miller, and Christopher A. Bergman, 'Early Bow Design and Construction', *Scientific American*, 264 (6), June, 1991, pp. 50–56.

Meadow, R. and H.P. Uerpmann (eds.), *Equids in the Ancient World*, vol. 2, Weisbaden, Dr. Ludwig Reichart Verlag, 1991.

Mehendale, M.A., 'Review: Yardi's The Mahābhārata, its Genesis and Growth—A Statistical Study', *Annals of the BORI*, vol. 69, no. 1/4, 1988, pp. 349–355.

———, 'Has the Vedic rājasūya any relevance for the epic game of dice?', in V. N. Jha (ed.), *Vidyā-vratin: Professor A. M. Ghatage Felicitation Volume*, Sri Garib Dass Oriental Series, No. 160, Delhi, Sri Satguru, 1992, pp. 61–67.

———, 'Is there only one version of the game of dice in the Mahābhārata?', in S.P. Narang (ed.), *Modem evaluation of the Mahābhārata*, (Prof P. K. Sharma felicitation volume), Delhi, Nag Publishers, 1995, pp. 33–39.

Middleton J. and D. Tait, *Tribes Without Rulers*, London, 1964.

Miller, D., E. McEwen, and C. Bergman, 'Experimental Approaches to Near Eastern Archery', *World Archaeology*, vol. 18, 1986, pp. 182–84.

Misra, V.N., 'Climate, a Factor in the Rise and Fall of the Indus Civilization', in Lal and Gupta, *Frontiers of Indus Civilization*, pp. 461–89.

Moorcroft, William, and Georg Trebeck, *Travels in the Himalayan Provinces of Hindustan and the Punjab; in Ladkah and Kashmir; in Peshawar, Kabul, Kunduz, and Bokhara; from 1819 to 1825*, 2 vols., L.P.P., Delhi, 2010, (First Published 1841).

Moorey, P.R.S., 'The Emergence of the Light, Horse-Drawn Chariot in the Near East c. 2000-1500 B.C.', *World Archaeology*, vol. 18, no. 2, 1986, pp. 196–215.

Moorti, U.S., *The Megalithic Culture of South India: Socio-Economic Perspectives*, Varanasi, 1994.

Morgenstierne, G., 'Orthography and Sound System of the Avesta', in G. Morgenstierne (ed.), *Irano–Dardica*, Wiesbaden, 1975, pp. 31–83.

Mughal, M. R., 'New archaeological evidence from Bahawalpur', in A. H. Dani (ed.), *Indus Civilization: New Perspective*, Islamabad, Centre for the Study of the Civilizations of Central Asia, Quaid-e Azam University, 1981, pp. 33–41.

Mughal, M.R., 'The Post-Harappan Phase in Bahawalpur District', in B.B. Lal and S.P. Gupta (eds.), *Frontiers of Indus Civilization*, 1984.

———, 'The Consequences of River Changes for Harappan Settlement in Cholistan', *The Eastern Anthropologist*, vol. 45, 1992, pp. 105–16.

Muir, John, *Original Sanskrit Text on the origin and history of the people of India, their religion and Institutions*, 2 vols., London, Trübner, 1868.

Mukherjee, B.N., *Central Asian and South Asian Documents on the Old Śaka Era*, Varanasi, Bharat Bharati, 1973.

Mukherjee, M., *Metalcraftsmen of India*, Anthropological Survey of India, Calcutta, 1978.

Murthy, S.S.N., 'The Questionable Historicity of the Mahabharata', *Electronic Journal of Vedic Studies*, vol. 10, no. 5, 2003, pp. 1–15.

Muztar, Bal Krishna, *Kurukshetra: Political and Cultural History*, Delhi, 1978.

Nath, Vijay, 'King Vena, Niṣāda and Pṛthu', *Indian Historical Review*, vol. 29, nos. 1 and 2, January–July 2002.

Nefiodkin, Alexander K., 'On the Origin of the Scythed Chariots', *Historia: Zeitschrift für Alte Geschichte*, vol. 53, no. 3, 2004, pp. 369–378.

Novgorodova, Eleanora A., *Drvniaia Mongolia [Ancient Mongolia]*, Moscow, Nauka, 1989.

Novozhenov, Victor, *Chudo Kommunikatsii I drevneishii Kolesnyi Transport Evrazii [The Miracle of Communcation and the Earliest Wheeled Transport in Eurasia]*, Moscow, Taus, 2012.

O'Brien, S., 'Dioscuric Elements in Celtic and Germanic Mythology', *Journal of Indo–European Studies*, vol. 10, 1982, pp. 117–36.

O'Flaherty, W.D., *The Rig Veda: An Anthology 108 Hymns, translated from the Sanskrit*, Harmondsworth, Penguin Classics, 1981.

Oates, J., 'A Note on the Early Evidence of Riding of Equids in Western Asia', in Levine*et al* (eds.), *Prehistoric Steppe Adaptation and the Horse*, 2003, pp. 115–25.

Oldenberg, 'Uber die Liedverfasser des Rigveda', *Zeitschrift der Deutschen Morgenländischen Gesellschaft* (*Journal of the German Oriental Society*), vol. 42, p. 207.

Olivieri, Luca Maria, 'The Rock-Carvings of Gogdara I (Swat) Documentation and Preliminary Analysis', *East and West*, vol. nos. 1–2, Rome, 1998, pp. 57–91.

———, 'Painted Rock Shelters of the Swat-Malakand Area from Bronze Age to Buddhism—Materials for a Tentative Reconstruction of the Religious and Cultural Stratigraphy of Ancient Swat', *Zur Erlangung des Doktorgrades eingereicht am Fachbereich Geschichts- und Kulturwissenschaften der Freien Universität Berlin*, Rome, November 2010.

Olsen, Sandra L., 'The Exploitation of Horses at Botai, Kazakhstan', in Levine*et al* (eds.), *Prehistoric Steppe Adaptation and the Horse*, 2003, pp. 83–103.

Olsen, Sandra L., Susan Grant, Alice M. Choyke, and László Bartosiwicz (eds.), *Horse and Humans: The Evolution of Human–Equine Relationships*, BAR International Series 1560, 2006.

Otterbein, Keith F., *How War Began*, Texas A&M University Anthropology Series, no. 10, 2004.

Pande, Susmita, 'The Pañcarātra Cult in the Śāntiparvan of the Mahābhārata', in Shastri (ed.), *Mahābhārata*, pp. 228–242.

Paniker, K. Ayyappa, *Indian Narratology*,Kalasamalochana Series, Delhi, IGNCA, 2003.

Pargiter, F.E., 'Nations of India in the Battle between the Pandavas and the Kauravas', *Journal of the Royal Asiatic Society*, 1908, pp. 309–336.

———, *The Purāṇa Text of the Dynasties of the Kali Age*, Delhi, Motilal Banarasidass, 1972 (First Published 1913).

———, *The Purāṇa text of the Dynasties of the Kali Age*, London, Oxford University Press, 1913.

———, 'Earliest Indian Traditional 'History'',*Journal of the Royal Asiatic Society*, vol. 46., no. 2, 1914, pp.267–96.

———, 'The North Pañcāla Dynasty', *Journal of the Royal Asiatic Society*, 1918, pp. 229–248.

———, 'Ancient Indian Genealogies and Chronology', *Journal of the Royal Asiatic Society*, 1919, pp. 1919–20.

Parpola, A., 'Gandhāra Graves and the Gharma pot, the Nāsatyas and the nose: In pursuit of the chariot twins', in M. F. Kosarev, P. M. Kozhin and N. A. Dubova (eds.), *U istokov tsivilizatsii: Sbornik statej k 75-letiyu Viktora Ivanovicha Sarianidi*, Moskva: Staryj sad, 2004, pp. 102–128; republished in: *Ancient Pakistan*, vol. 16, Peshawar: Department of Archaeology, University of Peshawar.

———, 'The Coming of the Aryans to Iran and India and the Cultural and Ethnic Identity of the Dasas', *International Journal of Dravidian Linguistics*, vol. 17, no. 2, June 1988, pp. 85–229.

———, 'The Face Urns of Gandhara and the Nasatya Cult', in Michael Willis (ed.), *Migration, Trade and Peoples, Proceedings of the*

Eighteenth Congress of the European Association of South Asian Archaeologists, London, 2005, the British Association for South Asian Studies, London, British Academy, 2009, pp. 149–162.

———, 'Pandaiŋ and Sītā: On the Historical Background of the Sanskrit Epics, *Journal of the American Oriental Society*, vol. 122, no. 2, Indic and Iranian Studies in Honor of Stanley Insler on His Sixty-Fifth Birthday, April–June 2002, pp. 361–373.

———, 'Pre-Proto–Iranians of Afghanistan as initiators of Śâkta Tantrism: On the Scythian/Saka affiliations of the Dâsas, Nuristanis and Magadhans', *Iranica Antiqua*, vol. 37, pp. 233–324.

———, 'Problem of the Aryan and Soma: Textual–Linguistic and Archaeological Evidence', in George Erdosy (ed.), *The Indo–Aryans*, pp. 353–381.

———, 'The Formation of the Aryan Branch of the Indo–Europeans', in Blench and Spriggs (eds.), *One World Archaeology and Languages*, 1999, pp. 188–207.

———, 'The Nāsatyas, the Chariot and Proto–Aryan Religion', *Journal of Indological Studies*, nos. 16 & 17, 2004–2005, pp. 1–63.

Patil, Sharad, 'Myth and Reality of Ramayana and Mahabharata', *Social Scientist*, vol. 4, no. 8, 1976, pp. 68–72.

Penner, Sylvia, *Schliemanns Schachtgräberrund und der europäische Nordosten: Studien zur Herkunft der frühmykenischen Streitwagenausstattung*, Saarbrücker Beiträge zur Altertumskunde, v. 60, Bonn: Rudolf Habelt Verlag GMBH, 2004.

Perkins, J. and J. Tample (eds.), *Europe: Prospects and Retrospects*, Sydney, South Highland Press, 1996.

Perry, Edward Delavan, 'Indra in the Rig-Veda', *Journal of Oriental and African Studies*, vol. 11, 1881, 1885, pp. 117–208.

Phadke, H.A., 'Kurukshetra: A Historical Reconstruction', *Quarterly Review of Historical Studies*, Calcutta, vol. 23, no. 1, 1983–84.

Phadke, H.A., 'Date of Bharata War', in Gupta and Ramachanadra, *Mahabharata: Myth and Reality*, 1976.

Piggott, Stuart, *Ancient Europe*, Chicago, Aldine, 1965.

———, *Prehistoric India to 1000 B.C.*, Harmondsworth, Penguin, 1950.

———, 'Chariot Burials in the Urals', *Antiquity*, vol. 49, 1975, pp. 189–90.

———, 'Chariots in the Caucasus and China', *Antiquity*, vol. 49, 1975, pp. 289–90.

———, 'Chinese Chariotry: An Outsider's View', in P. Denwood (ed.), *The Arts of the Eurasian Steppelands*, London, Percival David Foundation of Chinese Art, 1978, pp. 32–51.

———, *The Earliest Wheeled Transport: from the Atlantic Coast to the Caspian Sea*, Ithaca, Cornell University Press, 1983.

———, *The Earliest Wheeled Transport: From the Atlantic Coast to the Caspian Sea*,Ithaca, Cornell University Press, 1983.

———, *Wagon, Chariot and Carriage: Symbol and Status in the History of Transport*, London, Thames and Hudson, 1992.

Pollett, G.(ed.), *India and the Ancient world: history, trade and culture before A.D. 650*, P.H.L. Eggermont Jubilee Volume, Leuven, 1987.

Possehl, G.L. (ed.), *Ancient Cities of the Indus*, Vikas, Delhi, 1979 (first published 1971), pp. 234–42.

———, 'The End of a State and the Continuity of a Tradition', in R. Fox (ed.), *Realm and Region in Traditional India*, 1979, pp. 234–54.

———, 'The Transformation of the Indus Civilization', *Journal of World Prehistory*, vol. 11, 1997, pp. 425–72.

———, *The Indus Civilization: A Contemporary Perspective*, Walnut Creek, CA, AltaMira Press, 2002.

Powell, T.G.E., 'Some Implications of Chariotry' in I. Foster and C. Adcock (eds.), *Culture and Environment: Essays in Honour of Sir Cyril Fox*, 1963, pp. 165–66.

Proferes, Theodore Nicholas, 'The Formation of Vedic Liturgies', Harvard Ph.D. thesis, 1999.

Puhvel, J., *Comparative Mythology*, London, John Hopkins University Press, 1987.

Pusalkar, A. D, 'Social world in the Mahābhārata', *Journal of the Ganganatha Jha Research Institute*, vol. 26, nos. 1–3, 1970, pp. 575–80.

———, *Studies in Epics and Purāṇas*, Bombay, Bharatiya Vidya Bhavan, 1965.

Rapson, E.J.,*Ancient India*, Cambridge, 1914.

Ratnagar, Shereen, *Encounter: The Westerly Trade of the Harappan CivilizationDelhi*, OUP, 1981.

———, *The Other Indians: Essays on Pastoralists and Prehistoric Tribal People*, Gurgaon, Three Essays Collection, 2004.

———, *The End of the Great Harappan Tradition*, New Delhi, Manohar, 2002.

Rau, Wilhelm, *The Meaning of Pur in Vedic Literature*, Abhandlungen der Marburger Gelehrten Gesellschaft, Munich, Munich Willhelm Fink Veerlag, 1976.

Ray, A., *Villages, Towns, and Secular Buildings in Ancient India*, Firma K. L. Mukhopadhyay, Calcutta, 1964.

Raychaudhuri, H.C., *Political History of Ancient India: from the accession of Parikshita to the extinction of the dynasty*, Calcutta, University of Calcutta, 1938.

———, *Materials for the Study of the Early History of the Vaishṇava Sect*, Calcutta, 1936.

Reisinger, Michaela R., 'New Evidence about Composite Bows and Their Arrows in Inner Asia', *The Silk Road*, vol. 8, 2010, pp. 42–62.

Renou, Louis, *Religions of Ancient India*, [Jordan Lectures, 1951], Athlone, University of London, 1953.

———, 'L'hymne aux Aśvin de l'Ādiparvan', in S.M. Katre and P.K. Gode (eds.), *A volume of eastern and Indian studies presented to F.W. Thomas*, Bombay, Karnatak Publishing House, 1939, pp. 177–87.

Rommelaere, C., *Les chevaux du Nouvel Empire Ègyptian: Origines, races, harnechement*, Brusssels, 1991.

Rop, Jeffrey, 'Reconsidering the Origin of the Scythed Chariot', *Historia*, Franz Steiner Verlag, vol. 62, no. 2, April 2013, pp. 167–181.

Roy, Kumkum, *The Emergence of Monarchy in North India: Eighth to Forth Centuries B.C.*, Delhi, Oxford, 1994.

Ruben, Walter, *Krishna: Konkordanz und Kommentar der Motive Seines Heldenlebens*, Istanbul, IstanbulYazilari, 1944.

Runciman, W.G., 'Origins of States: The Case of Archaic Greece', *Comparative Studies in Society and History*, vol. 24, no. 3, 1982, pp. 351–77.

Sachau, Edward C., *Albiruni's India*, London, 1888.

Sarianidi, V., 'Temples of Bronze Age Margiana', *Antiquity*, vol. 68, 1994, pp. 388–97.

Scharfe, Hartmut, *The State in Indian tradition*, Handbuch der Orientalistik. Zweite Abt, Indien, Dritter Band, Geschichte. Zweiter Abschn, Leiden, Brill, 1989.

Schlingloff, Dieter, 'The Oldest Extant Parvan–List of the Mahābhārata', *Journal of the American Oriental Society*, vol. 89, no. 2, April–Jun 1969, pp. 334–338.

Schmidt, H–P. 'Notes on the Rigveda, 7.18.5–10', *Indica*, Organ of the Heras Institute of History and Culture, Bombay, 1980, pp. 17, 41–47.

Schottsman–Wolfers, J. and M. Taddei (eds.), *Asian Archaeology 1985: Proceedings of the Seventh International Conference of the Association of South Asian Archaeologists in Western Europe (Bruxelles)*, Naples, Instituto Universitario Orientale.

Schulman, A., 'Chariots, Chariotry and the Hyksos', *Journal of the Society for the Study of Egyptian Antiquities*, vol. 10, 1980, pp. 105–153.

Sensharma, P., *Kurukshetra War: A Military Study*, Ganganagar and Calcutta, 1975.

Shaffer J.G. and Diane A. Lichtenstein, 'The concepts of "cultural tradition" and "paleoethnicity" in South Asian archaeology,' in G. Erdosy (ed.), *The Indo-Aryans*, p. 126–154.

Shaikh, Khurshid Hasan, and Syed M.Ashfaque, *Mohenjodaro—a 5000 Years Old Legacy*, Geneva, UNESCO, 1981.

Sharma, G. R., 'The Excavations at Kausambi, 1949–50', *Memoirs of the Archaeological Survey of India*, no. 74, 1969.

Sharma, J.P., *Republics in Ancient India*, Leiden, Brill, 1968.

Shastri, Ajay Mitra, (ed.), *Mahābhārata: The End of an Era (Yugānta)*, New Delhi, Aryan, 2004.

Shaughnessy, Edward L., 'The Date of the "Duo You Ding" and its Significance', *Early China*, vol. 9–10, 1983–85, pp. 55–69.

———, 'Historical Perspectives on the Introduction of the Chariot into China', *Harvard Journal of Asiatic Studies*, vol. 48, no. 1, June 1988, pp. 189–237.

———, *Sources of Western Zhou History*, Berkeley, University of California Press, 1991.

Shejwalkar, T.S., 'The Mahābhārata Data for Aryan Expansion in India I', *Bulletin of the Deccan College Research Institute*, vol. 5, Sukthankar Memorial Volume, 1943–44, pp. 201–219.

Shende. N.J., 'The Authorship of the Ramayana', *Journal of the American Oriental Society*, vol. 45, 1925, pp. 202–219.

Shilov, 'The Origin of Migration and Animal Husbandry in the Steppe of Eastern Europe', in Juliet Clutton–Brock (ed.), *The Walking Larder*, 1989, pp. 119–126.

Singh, Gurdip, 'The Indus Valley Culture,' in G.L. Possehl (ed.), *Ancient Cities of the Indus*, 1979, pp. 234–42.

Singh, S.D., *Ancient Indian Warfare, with Special Reference to the Vedic Period*, New Delhi, Motilal Banarasidass, 1989.

Singh, Vijaya Lakshmi Singh, *Mathura: The Settlement Pattern and Cultural Profile of an Early Historical City*, New Delhi, Sundeep Prakashan, 2005.

Sircar, D.C., *Studies in the Religious Life of Ancient and Medieval India*, Delhi, Motilal Banarasidass, 1971.

Skoggard, Ian and Teferi Abate Adem, 'From Raiders to Rustlers: The Filial Disaffection of a Turkana Age-Set', *Ethnology*, vol. 49, no. 4, Fall 2010, pp. 249–62.

Smith, M.C., *The Warrior Code and India's Sacred Song*, New York, 1992.

Snodgrass, A., *Early Greek Armour and Equipment*, Edinburgh, Edinburgh University Press, 1964.

Sörensen, S., *An index to the names in the Mahabharata*, Delhi, Motilal Banarasidass, [1904], 1963.

Spain, James W., *The Way of the Pathans*, Karachi, Oxford University Press, 1972 (1st published 1962).

Spalinger, A. J., *War in Ancient Egypt*, Oxford, Blackwell, 2005.

Sparreboom, M., *Chariots in the Vedas*, (Memoirs of the Kern Institute, Leiden, 3), Leiden, Brill, 1985.

Spate, O.H.K., *India and Pakistan*, Methuen, London, 1954.

Srimali, K.M., *The Historicity of the Pa*ñcāla, vol. 1, Delhi, 1983.

Srinivasan, D.M., *Mathura: A Cultural Heritage*

Srivastava, K.M., 'Possible Location of Kāmpilya in the Mahābhārata,' in Ajay Mitra Shastri (ed.), *Mahabharata*, pp. 112–17.

Sukthankar, V.S., *On the Meaning of the Mahābhārata*, Bombay, Asiatic Society, 1957.

Suryavanshi, Bhagwan Singh, *Geography of the Mahabharata*, Ramanand Vidya Bhavan, 1986.

Telegin,Dmitry Y. and J.P. Mallory (eds), *Derievka: A Settlement and Cemetery of Copper Age Horse Keepers in the Middle Dniepr*, (trans.) V.K. Pyatkovskiy, BAR International Series 287, 1986.

Tewari, Rakesh, 'The origins of iron-working in India: New Evidence from the Central Ganga Plain and the Eastern Vindhyas', *Antiquity*, vol. 77, no. 297, 2003, pp. 536–544.

Thakran, R.C., *Dynamics of Settlement Archaeology*, Delhi, Gyan Publication, 2000.

Thapar, R., *From Lineage to State: Social Formations in the Mid-First Millennium B.C. in the Ganga Valley*, Oxford University Press, 1984.

——— (ed.), *India: Historical Beginnings and Concept of the Aryan*, New Delhi, National Book Trust, 2006.

Thapliyal, Uma Prasad, *Warfare in Ancient India: Organizational and Operational Dimensions*, Delhi, Manohar, 2010.

Tripathi, Vibha, *History of Iron Technology in India (From Beginning to Pre–Modern Times)*, New Delhi, Rupa, 2008.

Triveda, D.S., 'The Original Home of the Aryans', *Annals of the BORI*, vol. 20, 1938–39, pp. 49–68.

Trivedi, K.K., *Agra: Economic and Political Profile of a Mughal Suba*, Ravish, Pune, 1988.

Tucci, Giuseppe, 'Preliminary Report on an Archaeological Survey in Swat', *East and West*, vol. 9, no. 4, 1958, pp. 279–328.

———, 'The Tombs of the Asvakayana-Assakenoi', *East and West*, nos. 14, 1963.

Turney–High, H.H., *Primitive war: Its Practice and Concepts*, Columbia, SC: University of South Carolina Press, 1949.

Tusa, Sebastiano, 'The Swat Valley in the 2nd and 1st Millennia B.C.: A Question of Marginality', *South Asian Archaeology*, vol. 6, 1977, pp. 675–695.

Van Buitenen, J.A.B., *Mahābhārata*, vol. 2: Book 2: The Book of Assembly; Book 3: The Book of the Forest, Chicago, 1975.

Van Wees, Hans, 'The Homeric Way of War: the 'Iliad' and the Hoplite Phalanx (I)', *Greece and Rome*, Second Series, vol. 41, no. 1, April, 1994, pp. 1–18.

Veldmeijer, André J. and Salima Ikram (eds.), *Chasing Chariots, Proceedings of the First International Chariot Conference (Cairo 2012)*, Leiden, Sidestone, 2013.

Vidale, Massimo and Luca M. Olivieri, 'Painted Rock Shelters of the Swat Valley Further Discoveries and New Hypotheses', *East and West*, vol. 52, nos. 1–4, December, 2002, pp. 173–224.

Von Dewall, Magdalene, *Pferd und Wagen im Friihen China*, Bonn, Rudolf Habelt Verlag, 1964.

Von Schroeder, Leopold, *Indiens Literatur und Cultur*, Leipzig, 1887.

Waldbaum, Jane C., 'The First Archaeological Appearance of Iron', in Wertime and Mulhy (eds.), *The Coming of the Age of Iron*, 1980, pp. 69–98.

Waldschmidt, E. (ed.), *Indologen Tagung: 1959*, Gottingen, Vandenhoeck & Ruprecht, 1960.

Waradpande, N.R., 'Weaponry in the Bharata War', in A.M. Shastri (ed.), *Mahabharata*, pp. 99–111.

Warder, A.K., 'Classical Literature', in A.L. Basham (ed.), *A Cultural History of India*, 1975.

Watkins, T., 'The Beginnings of Warfare', in J. Hackett (ed.), *Warfare in the Ancient World*, 1989, pp. 15–35.

Watson, William, *Cultural Frontiers in Ancient East Asia*, Edinburgh, Edinburgh University Press, 1971.

Watters, T., *On Yuan Chwang's Travels in India*, London, 1905.

Weber, Georg, *Outlines of Universal History, from the Creation of the World to the Present Time*, Revised and Corrected with the Addition of A History of the United States of America by Francis Bowen, (trans. M. Behr), Brewer and Tilestone, 1853.

Wertime, Theodore A. and James D. Mulhy (eds.), *The Coming of the Age of Iron*, New Haven, Connecticut, Yale University Press, 1980, pp. 69–98.

Wertime, Theodore A., 'The Pyrotechnologic Background', in Wertime and Mulhy (eds.), *Coming of the Age of Iron*, pp. 1–24.

White, D.G., *Myths of the Dog-Man*, Chicago, University of Chicago Press, 1991.

Whitehouse, D., 'Excavations at Kandahar, 1974: First Interim Report', *Afghan Studies*, 1, pp. 9–39.

Wikander,S., *Der arische Männerbund*, Lund, 1938.

Winckler, H., *Orientalistische Literaturzeitung*, vol. 13, 1910.

Winternitz, M., *A history of Indian Literature*, trans. S. Ketkar, 2 vols., Calcutta, University of Calcutta, 1962 (first published as *Geschichte der indischen Literatur*, 3 vols., Leipzig, C.F. Amelangs Verlag, 1908–22).

Witzel, M., 'Toward a History of the Brahmins', *Journal of the American Oriental* Society, vol. 113, no. 2, April–June 1993, pp. 264–68.

———, 'Review: Swati Datta (née Sen Gupta), migrant Brahmanas in Northern India, their Settlement and General Impact, c. A.D. 475–1030', *Journal of the Economy of the Near East*, vol. 35, pp. 364–366.

———, *Sur le Chemin du Ciel*, *BEI*, 2, Leiden, Institut Kern, 1984, pp. 213–279.

———, 'On the localisation of Vedic texts and schools', in G. Pollet (d.), *In India and the Ancient World: history, trade and culture before A.D. 650*, P.H.L. Eggermont Jubilee Volume, Leuven, 1987, pp. 173–213.

———, 'Rigvedic History: poets, chieftains and polities', in Erdosy (ed.), *The Indo-Aryans of Ancient South Asia*, 1995.

———, 'Substrate Languages in Old Indo-Aryan (Ṛgvedic, Middle and Late Vedic)', *Electronic Journal of Vedic Studies*, 5–1, 1999, pp. 1–67.

———, 'Early Sanskritization: Origins and Development of the Kuru State', *Electronic Journal of Vedic Studies*, 1–4, 1995, pp. 1–26; available at www.ejvs.laurasianacademy.com/ejvs0104/ejvs0104article.pdf, accessed 04 May 2014.

———, 'Autochthonous Aryans? The Evidence from Old Indian and Iranian Texts', *Electronic Journal of Vedic Studies*, 7–3, 2001, pp.1–115.

———, 'The Realm of the Kurus: Origin and Development of the First State in India', *Nihon Minami Aija Gakkai Zenkoku Taikai, Hōkoku*

Yōshi (Summaries of the Congress of the Japanese Association for South Asian Studies), vol. 1, part 4, Kyoto, 1989.

———, 'Linguistic Evidence of Cultural Exchange in Prehistoric Western Central Asia', *Sino–Platonic Papers*, no. 129, Philadelphia, December 2003.

———, 'Early Indian History: Linguistic and Textual Parameters', in G. Erdosy (ed.), *The Indo–Aryans of Ancient South Asia*, 1985, pp. 85–125.

Xinru Liu, 'Introduction', in Xinru Liu (ed.), *India and Central Asia; A Reader*, New Delhi, Permanent Black, 2012.

Yadin, Y., *The Art of Warfare in Biblical Lands in the Light of Archaeological Studies*, 2 vols., New York, McGraw–Hill, vol. 1.

Yardi, M.R., *The Mahabharata: Its Genesis and Growth*, Poona, BORI, 1986.

———, 'My Studies on the Mahābhārata: A Clarification', *Annals of the BORI*, vol. 70, no. 1/4, 1989, pp. 235–241.

Zimmer, Heinrich F., *Altindischen Leben*, Berlin, 1879.

———, *Myths and symbols in Indian Artand Civilization*, New York, Harper, 1962.

Index

A

Abhyāvartin Cāyamāna, 35, 58, 69, 73

Abhimanyu, 136, 154, 158, 192–93, 195, 258, 265; attack of the *cakravyūha* by, 234–35; killing of, 225, 232, 235, 256–59, 263, 265, 267; wife and son of, 184, 257, 271; mother of, 183, 265–266

Ābhīra, 168, 169, 170, 271

Achilles, 29, 228, 261

Aesir, 65; *see also* Asura, Vaenir, Pani

Ahicchatra, 118, 143; *see also* Kāmpilya, Pañcāla

Airiiyanam Vaejo, 33, 64

Ahura, 65, 299; Ahura Mazda 65, 110. *See also* Asura

Aja, 71. *See also* Śigru and Yakṣu

Alexander, 6, 55, 76, 182, 197, 217, 273, 288

Amāvasu, 40–41, 47, 48, 67, 70, 77, 154, 277

Amenhotep, 222

Andronovo Cultural Horizon, 61–63, 64, 66

Anu, 3, 47, 49, 65, 18738, 49, 50, 68, 70, 75

Anyang, 104–05, 161; chariot, 203, 205, 214; metal object, 211

Anyataplakṣaḥ, 42, 267

Aparānta, 77, 147, 152, 168–72, 180, 183, 186, 224, 271; sword, 227

Āraṭṭa, 41, 47, 67, 77, 125, 278

Arghandab, 40; see also Helmand

armour, 228; chinks, 222; arm-bracer, 222; *varma*, 204n., 228; sharyan, 228

Āsandivat,132, 186, 189, 267. *See also* Hastināpura

asceticism, 10, 117, 299, 300, 306; and the *Gītā*, 301, 306; ascetic cult, 298–99

askesis, 42

āśrama, 44, 45n., 46, 139–140, 143, 285; *varṇāśrama*, 301

ass, 93, 200, 209–210

Assyria, 65, 97n., 99, 103, 109, 220, 222, 223, 225, 290, 162; neo-, 217, 291–93

Asura, 47, 48, 64–65, 110, 125, 157, 159, 298–99; Maya 147, 151; battle-formation, 193; association with Bhṛgu, 296. *See also* Ahura, Aesir

aśvattha (tree), 42

Aśvattha (chieftain), 69

Aśvatthāmā, 139–140, 193, 255, 256–57, 263, 269, 289

Aśvaka, 46, 55, 140

Aśvakāyana, *see* Aśvaka

Aśvin, 3, 65, 78, 90, 108–09; *gharmya* ritual, 56, 81, 108, 118, 135; *adhvaryu*, 81; *madhumantha* and *madhuparka*, 17; horse-lore, 90; affiliation with Yadu– Turvaśa, of, 110, 311; sister of, 79, 309; celestial twins, 92, 308–10; diarchy, 135, 217, 308; chariot, and, 209, 216; Nāsatya, 40, 65n., 100, 216, 308n.,

Atharvaveda, 19n., 42, 78, 82–84, 110,114, 115, 199, 211, 248, 272, 310n. *See also Pṛthvi–sūkta*

Aθravan, 84, 96, 110; Atharvan 110

Atithīgva, 49–50, 69

axe, *see* battle-axe

Axial Age, 78, 297

Āyu, 5, 40–41, 47–49, 69, 77, 115

B

Bactria–Margiana Archaeological Complex (BMAC), 54–56, 61, 62–66, 94n., 100, 107, 158–59, 299. *See also* Bahlīka

Bahīka, 136, 140; Prātipeya, 115, 130, 136, 140–41, 254; women, 282

Bahlīka, 141, 187, 254; Bactra, 115; Balkh, 51, 54, 61–63, 141, 155, 299. *See also* BMAC

battle-axe, 62, 101–02, 223, 226

Battle of Ten Kings (BOTK), *see* *Dāśarājña*

Baladeva, 121n., 166, 168; Bacchic, 119, 171–72, 285, 304; with Krishna and Subhadra 308–11, 147–48; in battle 21, 186, 256–57, 263, 267; death of, 270

Beas, 113; Jamlu, 76; crossing the swollen, 38

Berserkr, 43–44. *See also* werewolf, männerbund

Bhagadatta, 140, 149, 194, 234, 257; of Assam or *Uttarāpatha*, 140, 149, 257–58

Bhalāna, 3, 70; see Bolan

Bhargava see Bhṛgu

Bhāṭa *see* Sūta

Bhīma, 157, 159, 265; youth and adventures, 146, 182, 183; tunnel, 147, 148 ; expeditions, 147, 149; killing of Jarāsandha, 150, 158, 258; in diarchy, 158, 266, 269; *incognito*, 183–84; in battle, 190, 192, 194, 224, 232, 234, 235, 246, 253–55, 257, 259; killing of Aśvatthāmān, 255; killing Duḥśāsana, 155, 178, 256; mace-duel, 17, 21, 256–57, 263; other Bhīmas, 150; and Hiḍimbā, 157

Bhīṣma, 13, 18, 138–40, 165, 170, 225, 261, 258; vow 133; half-brother of Vyāsa, 164; as commander, 190–93, 232–33, 264; derision of Karṇa, 215, 230, 252; reluctance to fight Śikhaṇḍin, 233; felling of, 193, 230–31, 246, 258, 259; dying injunction, 262, 265–76 *passim*

Bhīṣmaparvan, 16, 17, 227, 231, 259, 264

Bhīṣmavadhaparvan, see Bhīṣmaparvan

Bhūriśravas, 140, 192; as swordsman, 254–255; death of, 223–24, 255, 258, 261–62, 268

Bisvaṭi, Lake, 41

bit, *see* equipment

Bolan, 51, 55, 56, 59, 66, 78, 186; rivers, 69. *See also* Bhalāna

Bow 83,109, 163, 214, 218–19, 224, 235, 244–45, 253; *Gāṇḍīva*, 2, 147; ceremonial position, 80 n., 218, 309; composite, 102–03, 105–06, 212, 219–20, 228, 237–38; longbow, 220; construction, 220, 222

Brahma, 125, 298

Brāhmaṇa (text), 9, 25, 72, 81, 83, 112, 119, 124, 272, 305; *Jaiminīya Brāhmaṇa*, 36, 71, 142, 144, 200; Śatapatha, 9, 41, 115, 120, 127, 130, 142, 206, 216, 285; *Taittirīya*, 120, 199; *Pañcaviṅśati* 134; *Aitereya* 125, 167

Brāhmaṇa (Class), 84, 109, 117, 127, 129, 134, 185, 281–83, 295–96; regicide 116–117, 279; warriors 214, 296; rathakāra as Brāhmaṇa 215; touching the plough by, 277

bronze, 45, 51, 54–56, 102–103, 105–06, 137, 221, 204, 226–27; technology 103, 226; arsenic bronze 221; elite material 227, 294; chariot technology 204–07, 213–14, 227, 292; armour 228

Bronze Age, 7, 38, 123, 197, 200, 214, 236, 246, 291

C

cakrarakṣau see wheel guard

cāraṇa, *see* sūta

cart, ox-drawn 61, 95; on the Rhine 61, 95; in the steppes 95; absence from Mesoamerica 105; in Harappa 52, 107; in the Vedas 34, 200; in battle 241, 249

caravan, trade 33, 131, 182, 277; migration 39, 170, 186n., 271

caste, 277–80, 282

Castor and Pollux, *see* Aśvin

cattle raid, 86; *gaviṣṭi*, 86–89, 260, 276; in Africa 86–88. *See also* Masai, ngingoroko, morani

caturaṅga, 195, 246, 291

Cayamāna, 35, 69, 73. *See also* Abhyāvartin

Cemetery H culture, 57, 67, 74, 122–23

chariot, 11, 15, 101, 136–38, 141, 149–50, 182, 197–99; construction and maintenance, 100, 200–01, 204, 207–11, 213, 215; illustration, 91, 100, 102, 106–08, 205–07, 211, 212, 290, 292; fabulous, 117, 147, 200, 298n.; proto-chariot, 92; Sintashta, 89, 92, 95–96, 202–03, 207; Steppe chariot 99, 210; Mediterranean, 104, 201, 204, 240, 244; Egyptian, 204–05, 209, 247; West Asian, 98–99, 207, 209; Lchaschen, 105, 207; Chinese, 100, 105–07, 203–08, 210, 214, 247, 293; South Asian, 107–10, 204–06, 209; Śuṅga, 111, 201, 207; Sanchi, 209; West European, 206, 241, 291, 293; scythed, 290–

91; ideal terrain, 205; horse, 14, 90, 209–210, 212, 253–54, 297; ceremonial position of, 126, 213; in sub-military tactics, 89, 96, 206, 297; in battle, 11, 72, 98–99, 101, 111, 141, 163, 183, 191–93, 196, 230–31, 234–34, 240–46, 250–51, 253–58, 261–62, 291; dogfight, 239, 243–44; battle-taxi, 240; elaboration and obsolescence of, 217, 289–90, 292–94; *see also vipatha*, horse, bow, Śulbasūtra, Kikkuli, wagon

chariot, adoption of 105

chariot crew, 238; charioteer, 190, 210–11, 214–17, 262; bard, 30; chariot maker, 24, 136, 181, 211, 296; chaplain, 309, 311; exalted position of, 216–17; lowering position of, 230; warrior, 26, 127, 210, 214–15, 260; *anugāḥ*, 231, 247–50, 254; chariot runner, 247, 248; bow, 102, 106, 218–20, 222–23, 243; battle-axe, 102, spear and javelin on board, 237–238; elite and chivalry, 97, 98, 103–104, 236, 288; *raθaestar* 96, 104, 109; diarchy, 217

Cheek-piece, *see* Riding Equipment

Chitral, 57, 75

chivalry 10, 163, 187, 213, 244–45, 251, 259, 262, 288; laws of combat 12, 188, 191, 218, 235, 239, 241, 261, 312–13; *dharma-yuddha*, 261; and ritualization 11, 215, 245, 262, 265, 288–89, 290, 294. *See also Kṣatriya*, Hippeis, Samurai

club, 18, 45, 101, 227, 250, 270; club-chariot 291

Copper Hoard, 121–23, 223–24, 225

D

dadhi, *see* Horse

Dadhikravān, 50, 212,

Dakṣiṇāpatha, 140, 167–68, 171, 186,

Daiamabad, 51, 54

Dānava, 58, 296; Danu 60, 66

Darada, 3, 48, 75

Dāśarājña, 3, 4, 5, 7, 9, 13–15, 39, 50, 70–73, 77, 80–85, 110–111, 112, 116, 132, 142, 143, 183, 186, 285

Dasikomgcun chariot, 105

Dasyu, 40, 49, 50, 58–59, 67, 110; *dasyudharma*, 262

Dendra corslet, 228, 240. *See also* armour

Devayānī, 47, 159

Dharmacchala, 21

dharmayuddha, *see* chivalry

Dhṛṣṭadyumna, 144, 190; in battle, 190,193, 233, 251, 253; killer of Drona, 224, 256, 258; death of, 257

Dhṛtrāṣṭra, 2, 28, 69, 115, 133–36, 145–46, 156, 164–65, 184–85, 216, 232, 264, 279; discarding of, 134, 165, 177; other Dhṛtrāṣṭra, 134

Diarchy, 128, 135, 158, 217, 284

dicing, 15, 17, 147–48, 151, 173–74; technique, 174–75; loaded 173; officials in, 126, 175, 184; ritual-ised, 128, 176–77

didacticism, 1, 7, 11–12, 14, 18, 20, 21, 26, 31, 149, 172, 182, 259,

269, 294

digvijaya, 10, 179; of the Pandu, 23, 147–49, 151, 172, 176; in *rājasūya* 128; of Karṇa,137

dīkṣā, 44–45

Dio Chrysostom, 20

Diomedes, 237

Diouskouroi, *see* Aśvin

discus *see* quoit

Divodasa, 58, 67–69, 70; see *Atithīgva*

Draupadī, 13, 16, 31, 146–47, 148, 157, 165, 180, 183, 227, 266, 269, 271, 311; polyandrous marriage, 138, 146–47, 158, 160, 185, 224; humiliation of, 22, 172, 177–78, 256–57; as *Sairindhṛ*, 184

Droṇa, 13, 17, 139, 192–94, 224, 230–31, 233–34, 251–52, 253–255, 257, 264–65, 268; preceptor 46, 146; poor Brahmana, 139, 143; *Uttarāpatha* affiliations, 140; vendetta with the Pañcāla, 144, 155; death of Droṇa, 255–56, 258, 261

Dṛṣadvatī, 68, 113

Druhyu, 3, 47, 136, 286; Anu, 38, 49, 50, 68, 70, 75

Duḥṣanta, 72, 73; father of Bharata, 73, 115, 116

Duḥśāsana, 22, 135, 155, 158, 232, 253, 256, 265; as diarch, 135, 154; blood drinking, 155, 178, 257–258, 261

Duryodhana, 12, 134,136, 139, 141, 146, 148, 154, 180, 270; as Kuru chief, 135, 137, 165, 177; diarchy, 135, 158; *and* Karṇa, 136–37, 141, 256; and Krishna, 166, 185, 281; humiliation of Draupadī, 172, 257; in battle, 193, 200, 230, 232–34, 253–56, 264–65; mythical armour, 228; mace-duel 11, 17, 21, 178, 257–58, 262–63

Dvārakā, 30–31, 147, 166, 169–71, 267, 270, 302; Krishna of, 168–69, 172, 302

E

equipment: bit 55, 98n., 99, 211, 214, 292; bit-wear 94; bridle, 57, 214; cheek-piece, 56–57, 94, 104; nose-ring, 98–99; harness, 152, 206–209; whip, 212; yoke-saddle, 209; chariot: rein-holder, 212

Erymanthus, 38; *see also* Helmand

F

face-urns, 57, 63, 68, 108; *gharmya ritual*, 56

forts, iron, 67, 69; *pakhsa*, 67–68

fractional burial, 51, 146, 153, 226

frame-in-tale, 1, 20, 183, 306

G

gaṇarājya, see republic

gaṇasaṅgha, see republic

Gandhāra, 6, 41, 47, 73, 136, 140, 164, 177, 187, 260, 282, 286–87; Horse, 199, 208; Gandhara Grave culture, 55, 68, 73, 75, 108, 171, 208, 226

Gandharva, 42, 47, 67, 75, 77, 139, 179

gāṇḍīva, 2, 147, 219. *See also* bow.

Gaṅgā, 10, 38, 40, 72, 143; interfluve, 9, 75, 114, 118, 124; goddess, 138, 154; paleo-channel, 143

Gāthā, 73, 83–84, 110

Genghis (Khan), 74, 80, 160, 162; cattle-raid, 96; women in family of, 160; genealogy of, 162

Ghaggar–Hakra, 32, 39, 51, 53, 112–14, 116, 121–24, 186, 188, 267

gharmya, *see* face-urn, milk

Ghaṭotkaca, 136, 146, 154, 192–94, 255, 266

Gītā, 10, 16, 17, 31, 46, 187, 190, 235, 251, 263, 265, 267–68, 270, 301–06; *Anugītā* 18, 270. *See also sāṅkhya*

Gomal, 6, 55, 59, 74, 76, 186; Gomal grave culture, 55–56

Gothic genealogy, 48, 86, 142

Grāma, 85, 124; *grāmiṇi*, 85

gṛhapati, 78, 80

H

Hades, 175; *see also* Yama

Hamun, 36, 40, 75, 159; margara, 159; dasht-e-margow, 36, 64, 75, 159

Haihaya, 199

Harappa *see* Indus Valley Civilization

Hari-rud, 68, 75; *see also* Sarayu

Harivaṃśa, 16, 18, 22, 167–68, 303, 306; Harivaṃśakāra, 31

Hariyūpiyā, 59, 69

Hastināpura, 6, 114–16, 188, 123, 132, 134, 145–47, 149, 164, 186, 188–89, 263, 271, 273–74; *see also* Āsandivat

Hector, 29, 163, 237, 242, 261

Helen, 162–64, 187, 310; Helen Tyrche, 164, 309–10

Heljarann, House of, 56

Helmand, 38, 40, 68, 73, 75

Hengist and Horsa, *see* Aśvin

Herat, 38, 40, 68, 75, 287; *see also* Hari-rud, Horayu and Sarayu

Hiḍimbā, 146, 149, 157, 266; goddess, 82, 157

Hippeis, 214, 244

Hittite, 52, 97–100, 103, 163, 290; battle of Kadesh 99, 102, 217–18, 237–38, 240, 247, 252; archery 102; armour 228; chariots 238, 241, 247, Hattushas, capital of, 100. *See also* Paris

Homer, 29, 237, 278; Homeric Warfare, 239–242, 291

Horax$_v$aiti, 38, 68, 75; *see also* Sarasvatī *and* Arghandab

Horayu, 38, 68, 287. *See also* Sarayu

horse, as food, 89, 94–95; horse economy, 34, 84, 90; pasturage and domestication, 54, 60–61, 89; religious status, 55–57, 89, 90, 92, 107, 199, 212, 248; horse-lore, 90, 217; funerary rites, 56, 66, 90, 97, 99, 129, 248, 297; representation in art, 91, 107; supplies and breeding, 36, 39, 99, 103, 186, 258; horse peoples, 60, 136, 140, 149, 199, 272, 281, 290–93; nomad horse: gelding or mare, 199,

218; stallion, 213; in Gandhara grave, 208; Arjuna's, 1; riding, 54, 91, 93, 94, 107, 199; traction, 95, 97–98, 101, 103–04, 200–02, 206, 207; training, 100–101; in cattle-raid, 86–87; in battle, 14–15, 89, 98, 163, 191, 196–200, 224, 234, 239, 241, 250, 253–54, 259, 260, 261, 292; *see also aśvamedha*, horse equipment, chariot, Dadhikra, Aśvin, Kikkuli

Hsuen Tsang, 118, 268, 289,

Hunza–Nagar, 75, 77

Hurrian, 97, 100, 228; *see also* Hittite and Mitanni

Hyksos, 97, 98–99; chariots, 245

I

Ikṣvāku 47, 48, 75, 167, 199, 284, 286–87; Pūru sub-tribe, 71; in the *Dīgha Nikāya*, 309

Iliad, 11–13, 25, 29, 92, 101, 231, 236, 289, 309, 313; *'Indian Iliad'*, 20; duel of Paris and Menelaus, 162; succession in, 162–63, 187, 283; archery in, 181, 218, 222; armour, 228, 240; chariotry, 236–37, 239, 244; fighting, 241–242, 245; Epic-cycle Poems, 29; *see also* Homer

Indraprastha, 6, 17, 118–19, 132 147–49, 151, 170, 185, 186, 271, 273

Indus, 14, 36, 40, 50–52, 57, 60–61, 64–65, 77, 95, 112–13, 116, 120–23 *passim*, 137, 140–41, 152, 159, 170–71, 186, 275; confluence with Ghaggar, 122; Cultures on, 32, 34, 54, 67, 75; peoples on the Indus, 41, 46, 48, 180, 187, 260, 267, 273–74, 280, 281–82. *See also* Sindhu

Indus-Valley Civilization, 32, 34, 39, 56, 59–60, 78, 107, 113–14, 120, 122, 131, 275; Cotton Rush 51; regionalization era, 51; localization, 54; copper supplier, 51–52; Mature, 8, 51, 59; trade with Mesopotamia, 51–52, 61; Post-mature, 52–55, 57, 121; collapse of, 55, 56, 66, 120–23. *See also* Cemetery H culture

iron, 5, 6, 8, 10, 14, 55, 57, 120, 143, 152, 225, 227–28, 275, 291, 293; arrowhead, 221–22, 225; sword, 225; technology and industry, 225, 288, 299; agriculture, 6, 8, 275

Iron Age, 5–7, 10, 14–15, 20, 92, 122–23, 132, 202, 206, 221, 225–26, 249, 275

Megalithic sites *see* Iron Age

J

Jamlu *see* Beas

janapada, 9, 123, 126, 132, 135, 189, 260, 277, 280; *mahājanapada*, 9; cadet lineage, 10; colonization, 5–6, 9, 95, 123–24, 275–76, 288; urbanization, 131, 275; Kamboja, 280; Kosala–Videha, 283; *see also* republic, *gaṇasaṅgha*

Jarāsandha, 150–51, 157, 177; attacker of Krishna, 169–70, 176,

Jātaka, 273, 279, 296; *Vessantara*, 202, 204–07; *Daśaratha*, 178, 286, 309

Jayaḥ, 19, 20, 22, 23, 28, 30, 264

K

Kadesh, battle of, *see* Hittite

Kali Age, 7, 15, 20, 132, 174; *see also* Iron Age

Kalpasūtra, 9

Kampilya, 143, 189

Kaṅsa, 163, 169, 279, 304

Kāṇva, 37–38, 49, 306; Yadu associate, 73, 311

Karṇa, 17, 136, 138, 141, 159–60, 182, 184, 215, 224–25, 230, 233, 247, 252, 254–56, 258, 261, 264–65, 281–82; miraculous birth of, 136, 180–81, 228; with the Pandu, 160, 164, 185, 300; places associated with, 137, 188; as *Aṅgarāja* 140, 234; death of, 261–62,

Kāśī, 42, 69, 134, 232; –Videha, 41, 49; –Kosala, 77; Vārāṇasi, 283

Kassite, 97, 102, 217; takeover of Babylon, 52, 98; horse-breeders, 103, 290

Kastor and Peleudykos, *see* Asvin

Kekaya, 6, 46, 159, 187, 193, 199; *Kaikeyī*, 286; *Aśvapati*, 131, 136, 199; Lunar line, 286–87;

Khāṇḍava, 16, 116, 147, 273; forest clearance, 147–48

Khittim, 100; *see also* Hittite

Khyber, 6, 59, 67, 74, 75

Kīcaka, 117, 183–84

Kīkata, 71, 86, 113–14

Kikkuli, 100–101. *See also* Horse training

Kingship: grades of, 128, *samrāṭ*, 128, 150, 151, 176, 272; consecration, 128, 130, 295

Kinnara, 47, 75, 77

Kopet Dag, 61, 226

Krishna, 12, 15, 18, 21, 22, 138, 150, 166, 178, 181, 188, 190, 192, 193, 202, 215, 231, 234, 253, 269, 270, 281, 301; Krishna of Dvārakā or Krishna of Mathura, 30–31, 168–169; as youth, 168, 169; *Arghyābhiharaṇa* and Śiśupāla*vadha*, 170; killing of Jarāsandha, 170; rescue of Draupadī, 172, 178; as counsel, 3, 188, 192, 235, 251, 255, 257, 261, 265, 266, 289; *dharmacchala*, 21; hostility towards Bhīṣma, 170, 259; deification of, 262, 294, 300, 301–311; as *Nārayāna*, 3, 306–308; Vishnu, 10, 294, 302; relation with Bacchanal cults (Nāga, Madhu), 119, 171, 308; pastoral god, 169, 172, 302; brother of Subhadra, 147–148; Norse legends, 166, 185, 307; death of, 270; Krishna–Balarama and Krishna–Arjuna, *see Twin Gods*

kṣatra, 8, 109, 125, 127, 279; see also *Kṣatriya*.

Kṣatriya, 6, 25, 109, 117, 161, 216, 280, 282–83, 300; feudal 6, 176; chivalry, 31, 261–262, 294, 305; Viśvāmitra, 84; progenitor of *sūta*, 215; enmity with Paraśurama, 296

bhraṣṭa Kṣatriya, see vrātya

Kṣudraka–Mālava, 20, 49; as *vrātya*,149

Kunti, 145–46, 154–55, 156, 158, 160, 182, 185, 266, 270, 283; matrimo-

nial relation,164–65; Kunti–Bhoja, 167–68; mother of the Pandu, 181; Karṇa, 136, 138, 182,

Kurgan, 66, 92n., 153n.

Kutsa, 49, 50, 69

L

lākṣāgṛha,16, 146, 148

Lchaschen chariot, 105, 207

Licchavi, 46, 163, 165n., 284, 310; *see also* Śākya

Linear B, 104, 218, 245

M

mace, 45, 101, 193, 214, 223, 239, 253, 254, 256, 261; duel, 11, 17, 21, 225, ceremonial, 223; metal, 223–24; *see also* club

Madhu, *Madhuparka*, *Madhumantha* see horse

Madra, 6, 46, 141, 145, 159, 164, 184, 187, 199, 282; Kuru allies, 165; Uttara Madra, 6; *aśvapati*, 199. *See also* Kīcaka

māgadha, *see sūta*

Mahabharata Recensions, 16, 30; Kashmir, 21; Southern, 21, 220–221, 224, 227, 259, 268; Northern, 259

Mahāsammata, 133

Mahurjhari copperplates, 221, 226

Malla, 46, 283

männerbund, 43–45, 88, 103, 214

mānava, see Manu

mantra, formula, 9–10, 81, 83, 109; Age, 10, 123, 176

Mānuṣa, *see* Manu

Manu, 47, 48, 73, 159; *Manusmṛtiḥ*, 117, 167

Marya, 43, 45, 84, 96, 97, 103–04, 109–110, 214

Maryannu, 97, 104, 290

Masai, 44,86, 114

Mathura, 149, 151, 168, 171, 186–87, 274, 308; Krishna of, 30–31, 168–70, 172, 302

Mātsya, 17, 175, 183, 187, 231, 234, 313; Sudeṣṇā, 184, 216; Kīcaka 117, 183, 184; Trigarta raid, 260; Uttara, 183, 191, 215; Uttarā, 183, 257. *See also virāṭ*

Megalith, 152–53, 155, 181, 221, 226, 300

Megiddo, 99, 236–37

Mehrgarh, 34, 51, 61; South Cemetery, 54; rice in, 114n.

Meluhha, 52. *See also* Harappa

messing, common, 281–82

Military Horizon, 13, 88–89, 97,

milk, 93, 108, 139, 272; distributor of, 126, 176; products, 60, 90, 216; in ritual, 76, 88, 108, 311

Mitanni, 63, 97–99; migration from Central Asia, 100; language, religion and customs, 100; brides to Egyptians, 103; Battle of Megiddo, 99, 236–37. *See also* Maryannu

Mitra: day-light, 64; chariot, 109; Sun,

308–09

Miθra, 64, 83, 101, 299, 308

Mitra–Varuṇau, 64, 65, 73, 100, 109, 308–09

Mongol, 61, 161, 183; nomad 35, 85; descent, 48; alliance, 48, 142; Tibet, 305; *khoomei*, 79; religion, 80; cattle-raiding, 86, 96; chariot petroglyph, 91, 106–07; *see* Genghis

Morani, 44, 88

Mycenae, 98, 104, 126, 162, 163, 214–15, 218, 245, 247

N

Nāga, 62n., 118–19, 134, 143, 147–49, 171, 271–73; Kāliya 119, 304; cults, 119,157, 272, 303; Ulūpi, 148, 158, 272; Karkoṭaka-167; *see also* Takṣaka, *Sarpasattra*, Hastināpura, *and* Ahicchatra

Nāŋhaiθya, 64. *See also* Aśvin

Naimiṣāraṇya, 16, 19, 26, 28, 119, 144

naojot, 45. *See also dīkṣā, upanayana*

Nārayāna, 3, 301–02, 305–07, 310; *Nārāyaṇīya*, 166, 281; *Saṅkarṣaṇa* 308, 310

Nāsatya, *see* Aśvin

Nestor, 92, 244.*See also* Aśvin

niyoga or levirate, 133, 145, 155–56, 164; Yudhiṣṭhira, 270

Niṣāda, 117, 159, 206, 224

Ngingoroko, 44, 87–88

Nomad: pasture usage, 34, 49, 84–85, 89, 124, 129, 131, 169, 179; *aśvamedha*, 297; taboo against place-names, 35; *see also* sedentization

O

Oṅkāra, 79

Out-of-India Theory, 32–33, 62, 63, 65, 70

P

padapāṭha, 20, 37, 83

Pañcajana, 3, 47, 48, 50, 67–70, 71, 75, 77, 110, 116, 123, 159, 187, 296; Asura affiliations, 48

Pāṇḍu, 3, 16, 133–134, 139, 145, 156, 279, 283; *Pandu-Rajar-Dhibi*, 51, 146; *see also* fractional burial

Paṇi, 58, 62, 66; *parṇa*, 62; *see also* Vaenir

Paraitakai, 140. *See also* Tak Rajput

paraśu, *see* battle-axe

Paris, 162–63, 182; lost and found,163

Parjanya, 79. *See also* Perkunos

Parthian, 35, 73, 153; affiliations, 158–59, 163, 296; Pārtha, 159, 266

pāśaka, *see* dicing

Paśupati, 78, 298

Perkunos, 79. *See also* Parjanya

petroglyph, 91, 92, 96, 106, 107, 108, 111, 200, 290; *see also* Sky Burial

phalanx, 195, 242, 291; *see also vyūha*

Pharaoh, 102–03, 212, 214, 217, 223,

252; Rameses II, 205, 217, 237, 252; Thutmose III, 99, 212, 236; *see also* Megiddo

Pit Grave culture, *see* Yamnaya culture

plough, 8, 114, 275; mythic kings with plough, 117, 284; Sītā at the tip of, 117; Saṅkarṣaṇa, or Baladeva, 171, 257, 285, 304, 308; Dionysus, 308; taboo, 277

polyandry, 16, 147, 153–154, 160, 179, 266

Porus, 116, 136, 217, 273

pottery: Lustrous Red Ware, 51; Ochre Coloured Pottery, 121–22; Black on Red, 57; Black and Red Ware, 121–23; Painted Grey Ware (PGW), 67, 74,113, 120, 121–23, 137n., 143, 174, 189, 226; Northern Black Polished Ware, 122–23, 275; *also see* Cemetery H

Pṛthu, 116–17

Pṛthvi–sūkta, 78

puṅścalī, 43, 45

Pura: Vedic 61; Dasic, 50, 58–59, 67, 69, 99

Purukutsa, 50, 58, 72. *See also* Kutsa

Purūravas, 41, 42, 47, 115, 138–39, 154, 181

Q

Qandahar, 6, 67–68,

Qarqar, 292

quoit, 117, 192, 227,

R

Raja Karan ka Tilla, 121, 137

rājan, 85, 125–27, 131, 132–33, 143, 252, 274, 282, 284; by Rota, 125

rājanya, 8, 279; tribe, 149.

rājasūya, see yajña

Rākṣa, 47, 192–93, 196, 284, 298; see Rāvaṇa

Ramayana, 1, 11, 24, 36, 41, 46, 165, 178, 189, 272, 280, 282–288; renegade versions of, 117, 136, 178, 284, 286, 307, 309, *Uttara-Ramayana*, 20, 31, 286; Horse and chariot in, 210, 298; iron in, 226; Twin Gods, 309; Child God in, 302; Vishnu *Vandanā*, 307, women in, 165

Rāmopākhyāna, 31

Rāvaṇa, 117, 210, 282n., 284, 286–87, 288, 298n., 304

Ravi, 4, 50, 70–71, 112, 121,

real war, 262, 289

republic, 131, 133, 140, 159, 187–88, 278–81; oligarchy 125, 131, 161, 274

river-crossing, 39; bridge-keeper, 85; ford 185–86

Rudra, 43, 45, 78, 181, 296 n., 298, 303; hounds of, 43

S

Śaka, 20, 47–48, 135, 141, 149, 194, 199, 256, 268, 272

Śakuni, 136, 147, 154, 177; and dicing, 173; in battle, 192, 234, 256,

265

Śākya, 46, 163, 283, 310. *See also* Licchavi

Śālva, 120, 187, 232, 270–71, 274

Śalya, 17, 193, 194, 256, 264–65; Kuru ally, 141, 165; indignation of, 215, 256, 282, 311

Śambara, 58, 60, 69

Samurai, 251

Śamī, 41, 42, 153, 183

saṅgha, 169–70; Buddhist, 279; āyudhajīvi-, 281

saṅgrāma, 89, 250, 262–263n.

Sañjaya, 28, 30, 184, 216, 232

sāṅkhya, 10, 42, 46, 270, 301, 304–305; *see also Gītā*

saṁsaptaka, 234, 259, 260. *See also* Trigarta

Sarasvatī, 17, 32–33, 38, 40, 68; *Nadītamā*, 39–40; *Vināśanā*, 32, 39, 40, 112–13, 120, 124, 186, 267, 273. *See also* Horax$_v$aiti, Arghandab

Sarayu, 38, 58, 68, 75; in Kosala, 9, 285, 287. *See also* Hari-rud, Horayu *and* Herat

Sarmiṣṭhā, 47, 159

Sarvadeva, 127

Satluj, 39, 76, 113; crossing of, 39

sattra, 9, 43, 81; as original form of *yajña*, 43; *sarpasattra*, 2, 16, 19, 28, 134, 271–273, 295

Sātvata (also Sātvat) 72, 167–68, 199, 293, 306; *see also* Yadu

Sātyaki, 166, 171, 190; in battle, 191–92, 231, 253–55, 257–58, 261, 268; killing Bhūriśravas, 223–24

Scythian, 8, 63n., 67n., 106n., 135, 138, 156n., 163, 167, 197, 199, 200, 219, 266, 282–83, 292; war-god, 260. *See also* Śaka

Sea Peoples, 53, 247, 290; Ingot God, 247

Sedentization, 124, 127, 155, 177, 275; sedentary culture, 6, 8, 15, 81, 213, 216, 252, 262, 270, 277–78, 293; iron 14. *See also* Nomad

shamanism, 8–9, 66, 78–79; animism 8, 76; in the Vedas, 8, 34, 78; shamanism in the IVC, 78; self-praise, 34; departure from, 34, 81–84, 85, 92, 110, 295; shape-shifters, 43; trance, 79; political importance, 80; Kirāta, 181; Śiva 298

Shang, 102, 104, 105–07, 161, 165–66, 203–05, 208, 211, 217, 247, 289

Sharyan, *see* armour

Śigru, 71; *see also* Aja and Yakṣu

Śikhaṇḍin, 13, 190, 192–93, 225, 230, 246; birth of 230, 232–33; killing of Bhīṣma, 231–33, 258–59, 265;

Sindhu, 36, 39, 49, 71. *See also* Indus

Sindhu–Sauvīra, 32, 49, 141, 180, 187, 260; wine of Sauvīra, 282

Sintashta–Arkhaim–Petrovka culture, 56, 61, 63–64, 107,158; burial practices, 84, 153; and the Avestan world, 84; proto-chariot, 89–92, 95–96, 97, 99, 105,

202–03, 207; horse, 208

*Śi*va, 117, 119, 255, 298–99, 300; Neolithic 157, 181, 272, 302, 308; shaman 82, 181; *Kirāta*, 180–81; *See also* Paśupati, Rudra

Sky Burial, 92, 108

Soma, 8, 43, 45, 78–81; hymns, 37, 110; cult 37, 43, 80, 108; hallucinogen, 79; offering to Indra, 108; *haoma*, 109; ephedra, 79

Spring and Autumn Period, 101, 161, 236, 290, 293–94

Śrautasūtra, *see Sūtra*

Sṛñjaya, 4, 41, 72, 82, 116, 130, 141–144; Daivavāta, 68–69, 72; Iranic affiliations, 159

Standard of Ur, 93

Subhadra, 147–48, 154, 158; as deity, 310–11; mother of Abhimanyu, 183, 265–66

sub-military warfare; among the Dani, 242, 264; *see also* cattle-raid and military horizon

Sudās, 3, 69, 70–71, 82, 83, 142; *also see Dāśarājña*

Śulbasūtra, 80, 200–202; chariot dimensions, 207

sūta, as class 183, 216; as bard 19, 24, 28, 215; Vaiśampāyana, 16, 19; Bharata, 16, 22, 28, 30, 166, 295, 304; Lomaharṣaṇa, 19, 28, 146, 147, 166, 172, 178, 181–185 *passim*, 269–70; Ugraśravas, 16, 19, 28, 185

sūta as chariot-maker, 136–37, 181, 184, 215, 296

sutar, *see sūtradhāra*

sūtradhāra, 215, 296; *see Sūta* as chariot-maker

Sūtra, 10, 83, Śrautasūtra, 9, 81, 119, 260, 273; *Baudhāyana*, 40–42, 47, 134; *Lāṭyāyana*, 43; *Sāṅkhāyana*, 82, 274; Āpastambha, 119; *Gṛhyasūtra*, 24, 81, 276, 309; Āśvalāyana *Gṛhyasūtra*, 19, 20; *Dharmasūtra*, 81, 213, 260

sword: antenna sword,121, 223; in battle, 192, 193, 196, 214, 223–224, 254, 255–56; of bronze, 54; of iron, 8, 224–25, 227; shattering of, 225; in the Aegean, 239; in West Asia, 247

T

Tak Rajput, 140, 273. *See also* Takṣaka

Takṣaka, 118, 140, 147, 271–72; Takṣaśila, 271–73, 287, 295

Tāṭakā, 46

temple, 81, 224, 227; in BMAC, 62; Joshimath and Manali, 82, 157; *devāyatana*, 80; Karnak, 102, 236; Lakhamandal, 179; Kurukṣetra, 267; to Rāvaṇa, 288,

Tepe Hissar, 100

Testudo, 196, 250. *See also Vyūha*

Theyyam, 79. *See also* shamanism

Trasadasyu, 39, 50, 68, 70, 115, 212n.

Trigarta, 141, cattle-raid, 183–84, 187, 260; *saṅsaptaka*, 194, 233–35, 256, 257, 259–60, 265

Tṛtsu, *see* Sṛñjaya

Turvaśa, 3, 47–49, 141–42, 167, 187, 199; Yadu- 36, 38, 50, 68, 69, 73,

75, 108, 110, 171, 296, 311;

U

Upaniṣad, 2, 19, 37, 119, 156, 305; *Chandogya*, 2, 31, 172, 199, 274, 301; *Bṛhadāraṇyaka*, 131, 274; *Kauśītaki*, 200; *Muṇḍaka*, 263; *Gītā* as an *Upaniṣad*, 301, 304; death and rebirth in, 305

upanayana, 45. *See also dīkṣā, naojot*

Ural, 36, 56, 61, 104; proto-chariot, 91, 236; Ural burials, 297; copper in, 223

Urvaśi, 41, 42, 73, 75, 139, 154, 181

Usig, 35, 36, 73, 109

Uśij, 73, 109–10

Uttara-Kuru, *see* Kuru

Uttarāpatha, 7, 14, 15, 26, 77, 114, 137, 177, 186, 188, 193; people and migration along, 140, 143, 182, 267;

Uzarli-Tepe, 64

V

Vaenir, 65

Vaiśampāyana *see s*ūta

Vajra, 79, 101, 121, 191, 193

Vāraṇāvata, 146, 148, 179, 186

Vārāśikha, 58, 69

varṇa, 277–80; *varṇāśrama*, 301; *see also* caste

Vaśiṣṭha, 3, 4, 38–39, 46, 71, 72–73, 80, 83, 186; as priest, 70, 71, 73; Iranic affiliations, 73, 110, 296

Vara, 62, 66

Varuṇa: Night Light 3, 64, 65; helping Sudās 72; chariot, 109; Vṛttra, 125n.; Nārāyaṇa, 308; *see also Mitra–Varuṇau.*

Vayya and Turvīti, 36, 49, 50, 69; *see* Yadu– Turvaśa

Verethragna, 83

Veṇa, 117, 184, 279, 295. *See also Pṛthu*

Vessantara Jātaka, see Jātaka,

Vidatha, 126, 278

Videha, 77, 140, 258, 284; Kāśī, 41; Kosala, 47–49, 139, 283

Vidura, 133, 146, 164–65, 185, 216, 270; father of Yudhiṣṭhira, 156, 270

vipatha (chariot), 200–203, 206–09, 211, 217. *See also* chariot

Virāṭ, 17, 175, 183–184, 190–91, 224; Nagara 183. *See also* Mātsya

Virāṭ (regnal title), 128, 183

Vishnu, 10, 76, 117, 234, 294, 302–06, 308; *Vaikuṇṭha*, 294, 302; Vishnu *Vandanā*, 307

Viśvāmitra, 38–39, 80, 82, 186; as shaman 83–84, 110

vrata, 42, 46, 260

vrātya, 40, 42, 43, 77, 136, 167, 168, 170, 183, 188, 279–80, 281–83, 284, 313; initiation, 8, 43–44, 46, 281; männerbund 44; warband and mercenaries, 13, 45, 140, 184, 249, 260; *puṅścalī*, 43; wolves, 43; cattle-raiding, 45, 88, 132, 276, 278; *gaṇarājya*, 131, 159;

vipatha, 211, 217; promiscuity, 282–83; *see also marya, puṅścalī*

vrātyaṣṭoma, 43, 44, 46, 281

Vṛṣṇi, 13, 15, 49, 147, 151–52, 158, 166–69, 170–71, 186, 187, 190, 254, 256, 262–63, 265–66, 270–71, 304, 306, 311; destruction of 18, 172, 269, 270, 304. *See also* Kaṅsa

Vṛttra, 66, 91, 118, 125, 285

Volga, 36, 66, 74, 90, 104

vyūha, 12, 190–96, 233, 246, 249, 252, 256; zoomorphic names 196; *cakravyūha*, 194, 234–35, 251, 257, 259–60, 265; *see also* phalanx

Vyāsa, 4, 19, 22, 28, 133, 156, 164, 270, 305, 311n.; eponymous, 30; *see also* Bhrgu

W

wagon, 61, 95, 200, 249; laagered, 89; battle, 93, 95, 98–99; turning-radius, 98

Waking God, 166–67, 307

welding, 50, 227

werewolf, 43–45

wheel, 100, 104, 105, 107, 111, 222, 240; wheeled toys, 105; in Harappa, 107; in ritual, 129; technology, 60, 95, 200, 203–05, 210–11; of chariot, 93, 97–08, 200–02, 203, 206–09, 213, 292; preservation, 213; Piggott's reconstruction, 202; representation 91, 137; array 194–95; Karṇa, 256; *also see* wheel guard

wheel guard, 246–48, 250;

wine, 45, 282, 285, 304, 308; drinking-songs, 30; funerary drink, 90

X

Xia 105, 161, 166

Y

Yadu, 3, 47, 49, 72, 73, 77, 119, 140, 164, 166–72, 186–87, 287; Turvaśa, 36, 38, 49, 50, 68–9, 75, 108,110, 296, 311, 313; fall of, 18, 172, 270–71

yajña, 9, 43, 81, 109, 297; *aśvamedha*, 18, 50, 88–89, 128, 130; *govitāta*, 130; *puruṣamedha*, 129; *rājasūya*, 10, 17, 23, 81, 126–129, 150–51, 155, 170–71; original form, 126, 176–77; dicing in, 128, 148, 173, 176; *digvijaya*,148, 158, 172, 258; *Arghyābhiharaṇa*, 170; *vājapeya*, 91, 127n., 129, 297 ; races, 129; funerary, 91–92, 129, 297; *gavāmayaṇa*, 129. *See also sattra*

Yajurvedin, *see Kṣatriya*

Yakṣa, 47, 75, 77, 135, 146, 182

Yakṣu, 49, 71, 73, 168. *See also* Aja *and* Śigru

Yama: God of death, 3, 117, 182, 306; House of Yama, 56; Yama– Yamī, 64, 108, 310n.; hound of, 271. *See also* Yima, Hades, Heljarann

Yamnaya culture, 61, 95

Yamuna, 38–40, 71, 72, 113, 120, 143, 169, 179, 185–86, 188; interfluve, 9, 75, 114, 118, 119, 124, 143

Yayāti, 47, 115

Yima, 62, 73, 83; *vara*, 62

Yudhiṣṭhira, 3, 11–12, 18, 21, 26, 31, 134, 141, 147–49, 154, 159, 160, 178, 182–83, 233–35, 253–60, 262, 268–69, 271, 281, 300, 305; *aśvamedha*, 270; son of Vidura, 156, 270; dicing, 156, 172–77, 184, 224; diarchy, 158, 266

yuvarāja, 135, 154, 284n. *See also* diarchy

Z

Zhou, 101, 105–07, 161; Western, 106, 165, 203–05, 208, 213–14, 247, 289

www.ingramcontent.com/pod-product-compliance
Lightning Source LLC
Chambersburg PA
CBHW021148230426
43667CB00006B/305
* 9 7 8 9 3 8 6 4 5 7 5 6 1 *